THE SCHOMBURG LIBRARY OF
NINETEENTH-CENTURY BLACK WOMEN WRITERS

General Editor, Henry Louis Gates, Jr.

Titles are listed chronologically; collections that include works published over a span of years are listed according to the publication date of their initial work.

A Voice From the South

A Voice
From the South

ANNA JULIA COOPER

With an Introduction by
MARY HELEN WASHINGTON

New York   *Oxford*
OXFORD UNIVERSITY PRESS
1988

Oxford University Press

Oxford   New York   Toronto
Delhi   Bombay   Calcutta   Madras   Karachi
Petaling Jaya   Singapore   Hong Kong   Tokyo
Nairobi   Dar es Salaam   Cape Town
Melbourne   Auckland

and associated companies in
Beirut   Berlin   Ibadan   Nicosia

Library of Congress Cataloging-in-Publication Data

Cooper, Anna Julia Haywood, 1858–1964.
A voice from the south/by Anna Julia Cooper; introduction by
Mary Helen Washington.
p. cm.—(The Schomburg library of nineteenth-century black
women writers)
Reprint. Originally published: Xenia, Ohio: Aldine Printing
House, 1892.
1. Afro-American women—Southern States—History—19th century.
2. Southern States—Race relations.   I. Title.   II. Series.
E185.86.C587 1988   975′.00496073—dc19   87-26364
ISBN 0-19-505246-3
ISBN 0-19-505267-6 (set)

2 4 6 8 10 9 7 5 3

Printed in the United States of America
on acid-free paper

The
Schomburg Library
of
Nineteenth-Century
Black Women Writers
is
Dedicated
in Memory
of
PAULINE AUGUSTA COLEMAN GATES

1916–1987

PUBLISHER'S NOTE

FOREWORD
In Her Own Write

Henry Louis Gates, Jr.

One muffled strain in the Silent South, a jarring chord and a
vague and uncomprehended cadenza has been and still is the
Negro. And of that muffled chord, the one mute and voiceless note has been the sadly expectant Black Woman, ...

The "other side" has not been represented by one who "lives
there." And not many can more sensibly realize and more
accurately tell the weight and the fret of the "long dull pain"
than the open-eyed but hitherto voiceless Black Woman of
America.

. . . as our Caucasian barristers are not to blame if they
cannot *quite* put themselves in the dark man's place, neither
should the dark man be wholly expected fully and adequately
to reproduce the exact Voice of the Black Woman.

—ANNA JULIA COOPER, *A Voice From the South* (1892)

The birth of the Afro-American literary tradition occurred
in 1773, when Phillis Wheatley published a book of poetry.
Despite the fact that her book garnered for her a remarkable
amount of attention, Wheatley's journey to the printer had
been a most arduous one. Sometime in 1772, a young African girl walked demurely into a room in Boston to undergo
an oral examination, the results of which would determine
the direction of her life and work. Perhaps she was shocked
upon entering the appointed room. For there, perhaps gath-

ered in a semicircle, sat eighteen of Boston's most notable
citizens. Among them were John Erving, a prominent Boston merchant; the Reverend Charles Chauncy, pastor of the
Tenth Congregational Church; and John Hancock, who would
later gain fame for his signature on the Declaration of Independence. At the center of this group was His Excellency,
Thomas Hutchinson, governor of Massachusetts, with An-
drew Oliver, his lieutenant governor, close by his side.

Why had this august group been assembled? Why had it
seen fit to summon this young African girl, scarcely eighteen
years old, before it? This group of "the most respectable
Characters in *Boston*," as it would later define itself, had assembled to question closely the African adolescent on the
slender sheaf of poems that she claimed to have "written by
herself." We can only speculate on the nature of the questions
posed to the fledgling poet. Perhaps they asked her to identify and explain—for all to hear—exactly who were the Greek
and Latin gods and poets alluded to so frequently in her
work. Perhaps they asked her to conjugate a verb in Latin
or even to translate randomly selected passages from the Latin,
which she and her master, John Wheatley, claimed that she
"had made some Progress in." Or perhaps they asked her to
recite from memory key passages from the texts of John Milton and Alexander Pope, the two poets by whom the African
claimed to be most directly influenced. We do not know.

We do know, however, that the African poet's responses
were more than sufficient to prompt the eighteen august
gentlemen to compose, sign, and publish a two-paragraph
"Attestation," an open letter "To the Publick" that prefaces
Phillis Wheatley's book and that reads in part:

> We whose Names are under-written, do assure the World,
> that the Poems specified in the following Page, were (as we

verily believe) written by Phillis, a young Negro Girl, who
was but a few Years since, brought an uncultivated Barbarian
from *Africa,* and has ever since been, and now is, under the
Disadvantage of serving as a Slave in a Family in this Town.
She has been examined by some of the best Judges, and is
thought qualified to write them.

So important was this document in securing a publisher for
Wheatley's poems that it forms the signal element in the
prefatory matter preceding her *Poems on Various Subjects, Religious and Moral,* published in London in 1773.

Without the published "Attestation," Wheatley's publisher
claimed, few would believe that an African could possibly
have written poetry all by herself. As the eighteen put the
matter clearly in their letter, "Numbers would be ready to
suspect they were not really the Writings of Phillis." Wheatley and her master, John Wheatley, had attempted to publish
a similar volume in 1772 in Boston, but Boston publishers
had been incredulous. One year later, "Attestation" in hand,
Phillis Wheatley and her master's son, Nathaniel Wheatley,
sailed for England, where they completed arrangements for
the publication of a volume of her poems with the aid of the
Countess of Huntington and the Earl of Dartmouth.

This curious anecdote, surely one of the oddest oral ex-
aminations on record, is only a tiny part of a larger, and
even more curious, episode in the Enlightenment. Since the
beginning of the sixteenth century, Europeans had won-
dered aloud whether or not the African "species of men," as
they were most commonly called, *could* ever create formal
literature, could ever master "the arts and sciences." If they
could, the argument ran, then the African variety of humanity was fundamentally related to the European variety. If not,
then it seemed clear that the African was destined by nature

to be a slave. This was the burden shouldered by Phillis Wheatley when she successfully defended herself and the authorship of her book against counterclaims and doubts.

Indeed, with her successful defense, Wheatley launched two traditions at once—the black American literary tradition *and* the black woman's literary tradition. If it is extraordinary that not just one but both of these traditions were founded simultaneously by a black woman—certainly an event unique in the history of literature—it is also ironic that this important fact of common, coterminous literary origins seems to have escaped most scholars.

That the progenitor of the black literary tradition was a woman means, in the most strictly literal sense, that all subsequent black writers have evolved in a matrilinear line of descent, and that each, consciously or unconsciously, has extended and revised a canon whose foundation was the poetry of a black woman. Early black writers seem to have been keenly aware of Wheatley's founding role, even if most of her white reviewers were more concerned with the implications of her race than her gender. Jupiter Hammon, for example, whose 1760 broadside "An Evening Thought. Salvation by Christ, With Penitential Cries" was the first individual poem published by a black American, acknowledged Wheatley's influence by selecting her as the subject of his second broadside, "An Address to Miss Phillis Wheatly [*sic*], Ethiopian Poetess, in Boston," which was published at Hartford in 1778. And George Moses Horton, the second Afro-American to publish a book of poetry in English (1829), brought out in 1838 an edition of his *Poems By A Slave* bound together with Wheatley's work. Indeed, for fifty-six years, between 1773 and 1829, when Horton published *The Hope of Liberty*, Wheatley was the *only* black person to have published a book of imaginative literature in English. So central was this black woman's role in the shaping of the Afro-American literary tradition that, as one historian has maintained, the history of the reception of Phillis Wheatley's poetry *is* the history of Afro-American literary criticism. Well into the nineteenth century, Wheatley and the black literary tradition were the same entity.

But Wheatley is not the only black woman writer who stands as a pioneering figure in Afro-American literature. Just as Wheatley gave birth to the genre of black poetry, Ann Plato was the first Afro-American to publish a book of essays (1841) and Harriet E. Wilson was the first black person to publish a novel in the United States (1859).

Despite this pioneering role of black women in the tradition, however, many of their contributions before this century have been all but lost or unrecognized. As Hortense Spillers observed as recently as 1983,

> With the exception of a handful of autobiographical narratives from the nineteenth century, the black woman's realities are virtually suppressed until the period of the Harlem Renaissance and later. Essentially the black woman as artist, as intellectual spokesperson for her own cultural apprenticeship, has not existed before, for anyone. At the source of [their] own symbol-making task, [the community of black women writers] confronts, therefore, a tradition of work that is quite recent, its continuities, broken and sporadic.

Until now, it has been extraordinarily difficult to establish the formal connections between early black women's writing and that of the present, precisely because our knowledge of their work has been broken and sporadic. Phillis Wheatley, for example, while certainly the most reprinted and discussed poet in the tradition, is also one of the least understood. Ann Plato's seminal work, *Essays* (which includes biographies and poems), has not been reprinted since it was published a cen-

tury and a half ago. And Harriet Wilson's *Our Nig,* her
compelling novel of a black woman's expanding consciousness in a racist Northern antebellum environment, never received even *one* review or comment at a time when virtually
all works written by black people were heralded by abolition-
ists as salient arguments against the existence of human slavery. Many of the books reprinted in this set experienced a
similar fate, the most dreadful fate for an author: that of
being ignored then relegated to the obscurity of the rare book
section of a university library. We can only wonder how
many other texts in the black woman's tradition have been
lost to this generation of readers or remain unclassified or
uncatalogued and, hence, unread.

This was not always so, however. Black women writers
dominated the final decade of the nineteenth century, perhaps
spurred to publish by an 1886 essay entitled "The Coming
American Novelist," which was published in *Lippincott's
Monthly Magazine* and written by "A Lady From Philadelphia." This pseudonymous essay argued that the "Great
American Novel" would be written by a black person. Her
argument is so curious that it deserves to be repeated:

> When we come to formulate our demands of the Coming
> American Novelist, we will agree that he must be native-
> born. His ancestors may come from where they will, but we
> must give him a birthplace and have the raising of him. Still,
> the longer his family has been here the better he will represent
> us. Suppose he should have no country but ours, no traditions
> but those he has learned here, no longings apart from us, no
> future except in our future—the orphan of the world, he
> finds with us his home. And with all this, suppose he refuses
> to be fused into that grand conglomerate we call the "Amer-
> ican type." With us, he is not of us. He is original, he has
> humor, he is tender, he is passive and fiery, he has been

taught what we call justice, and he has his own opinion about it. He has suffered everything a poet, a dramatist, a novelist need suffer before he comes to have his lips anointed. And with it all he is in one sense a spectator, a little out of the race. How would these conditions go towards forming an original development? In a word, suppose the coming novelist is of African origin? When one comes to consider the subject, there is no improbability in it. One thing is certain,—our great novel will not be written by the typical American.

An atypical American, indeed. Not only would the great American novel be written by an African-American, it would be written by an African-American *woman:*

Yet farther: I have used the generic masculine pronoun because it is convenient; but Fate keeps revenge in store. It was a woman who, taking the wrongs of the African as her theme, wrote the novel that awakened the world to their reality, and why should not the coming novelist be a woman as well as an African? She—the woman of that race—has some claims on Fate which are not yet paid up.

It is these claims on fate that we seek to pay by publishing The Schomburg Library of Nineteenth-Century Black Women Writers.

This theme would be repeated by several black women authors, most notably by Anna Julia Cooper, a prototypical black feminist whose 1892 *A Voice From the South* can be considered to be one of the original texts of the black feminist movement. It was Cooper who first analyzed the fallacy of referring to "the Black man" when speaking of black people and who argued that just as white men cannot speak through the consciousness of black men, neither can black *men* "fully and adequately . . . reproduce the exact Voice of the Black Woman." Gender and race, she argues, cannot be conflated, except in the instance of a black woman's voice, and it is this voice which must be uttered and to which we must listen. As Cooper puts the matter so compellingly:

> It is not the intelligent woman vs. the ignorant woman; nor the white woman vs. the black, the brown, and the red,—it is not even the cause of woman vs. man. Nay, 'tis woman's strongest vindication for speaking that *the world needs to hear her voice*. It would be subversive of every human interest that the cry of one-half the human family be stifled. Woman in stepping from the pedestal of statue-like inactivity in the domestic shrine, and daring to think and move and speak,— to undertake to help shape, mold, and direct the thought of her age, is merely completing the circle of the world's vision. Hers is every interest that has lacked an interpreter and a defender. Her cause is linked with that of every agony that has been dumb—every wrong that needs a voice.
>
> It is no fault of man's that he has not been able to see truth from her standpoint. It does credit both to his head and heart that no greater mistakes have been committed or even wrongs perpetrated while she sat making tatting and snipping paper flowers. Man's own innate chivalry and the mutual interdependence of their interests have insured his treating her cause, in the main at least, as his own. And he is pardonably surprised and even a little chagrined, perhaps, to find his legislation not considered "perfectly lovely" in every respect. But in any case his work is only impoverished by her remaining dumb. The world has had to limp along with the wobbling gait and one-sided hesitancy of a man with one eye. Suddenly the bandage is removed from the other eye and the whole body is filled with light. It sees a circle where before it saw a segment. The darkened eye restored, every member rejoices with it.

The myopic sight of the darkened eye can only be restored when the full range of the black woman's voice, with its own special timbres and shadings, remains mute no longer.

Similarly, Victoria Earle Matthews, an author of short stories and essays, and a cofounder in 1896 of the National Association of Colored Women, wrote in her stunning essay, "The Value of Race Literature" (1895), that "when the literature of our race is developed, it will of necessity be different in all essential points of greatness, true heroism and real Christianity from what we may at the present time, for convenience, call American literature." Matthews argued that this great tradition of Afro-American literature would be the textual outlet "for the unnaturally suppressed inner lives which our people have been compelled to lead." Once these "unnaturally suppressed inner lives" of black people are unveiled, no "grander diffusion of mental light" will shine more brightly, she concludes, than that of the articulate Afro-American woman:

> And now comes the question, What part shall we women play in the Race Literature of the future? . . . within the compass of one small journal ["Woman's Era"] we have struck out a new line of departure—a journal, a record of Race interests gathered from all parts of the United States, carefully selected, moistened, winnowed and garnered by the ablest intellects of educated colored women, shrinking at no lofty theme, shirking no serious duty, aiming at every possible excellence, and determined to do their part in the future uplifting of the race.
> If twenty women, by their concentrated efforts in one literary movement, can meet with such success as has engendered, planned out, and so successfully consummated this convention, what much more glorious results, what wider spread success, what grander diffusion of mental light will not come forth at the bidding of the enlarged hosts of women writers, already called into being by the stimulus of your efforts?
> And here let me speak one word for my journalistic sisters

who have already entered the broad arena of journalism. Before the "Woman's Era" had come into existence, no one except themselves can appreciate the bitter experience and sore disappointments under which they have at all times been compelled to pursue their chosen vocations.

If their brothers of the press have had their difficulties to contend with, I am here as a sister journalist to state, from the fullness of knowledge, that their task has been an easy one compared with that of the colored woman in journalism.

Woman's part in Race Literature, as in Race building, is the most important part and has been so in all ages. . . . All through the most remote epochs she has done her share in literature. . . .

One of the most important aspects of this set is the republication of the salient texts from 1890 to 1910, which literary historians could well call "The Black Woman's Era." In addition to Mary Helen Washington's definitive edition of Cooper's *A Voice From the South*, we have reprinted two novels by Amelia Johnson, Frances Harper's *Iola Leroy*, two novels by Emma Dunham Kelley, Alice Dunbar-Nelson's two impressive collections of short stories, and Pauline Hopkins's three serialized novels as well as her monumental novel, *Contending Forces*—all published between 1890 and 1910. Indeed, black women published more works of fiction in these two decades than black men had published in the previous half century. Nevertheless, this great achievement has been ignored.

Moreover, the writings of nineteenth-century Afro-American women in general have remained buried in obscurity, accessible only in research libraries or in overpriced and poorly edited reprints. Many of these books have never been reprinted at all; in some instances only one or two copies are extant. In these works of fiction, poetry, autobiography, biography, essays, and journalism resides the mind of the nineteenth-century Afro-American woman. Until these works are made readily available to teachers and their students, a significant segment of the black tradition will remain silent.

Oxford University Press, in collaboration with the Schomburg Center for Research in Black Culture, is publishing thirty volumes of these compelling works, each of which contains an introduction by an expert in the field. The set includes such rare texts as Johnson's *The Hazeley Family* and *Clarence and Corinne*, Plato's *Essays*, the most complete edition of Phillis Wheatley's poems and letters, Emma Dunham Kelley's pioneering novel *Megda*, several previously unpublished stories and a novel by Alice Dunbar-Nelson, and the first collected volumes of Pauline Hopkins's three serialized novels and Frances Harper's poetry. We also present four volumes of poetry by such women as Mary Eliza Tucker Lambert, Adah Menken, Josephine Heard, and Maggie Johnson. Numerous slave and spiritual narratives, a newly discovered novel—*Four Girls at Cottage City*—by Emma Dunham Kelley (-Hawkins), and the first American edition of *Wonderful Adventures of Mrs. Seacole in Many Lands* are also among the texts included.

In addition to resurrecting the works of black women authors, it is our hope that this set will facilitate the resurrection of the Afro-American woman's literary tradition itself by unearthing its nineteenth-century roots. In the works of Nella Larsen and Jessie Fauset, Zora Neale Hurston and Ann Petry, Lorraine Hansberry and Gwendolyn Brooks, Paule Marshall and Toni Cade Bambara, Audre Lorde and Rita Dove, Toni Morrison and Alice Walker, Gloria Naylor and Jamaica Kincaid, these roots have branched luxuriantly. The eighteenth- and nineteenth-century authors whose works are presented in this set founded and nurtured the black women's literary tradition, which must be revived, explicated, analyzed, and debated before we can understand more completely the formal shaping of this tradition within a tradition, a coded literary universe through which, regrettably, we are only just beginning to navigate our way. As Anna Cooper said nearly one hundred years ago, we have been blinded by the loss of sight in one eye and have therefore been unable to detect the full *shape* of the Afro-American literary tradition.

Literary works configure into a tradition not because of some mystical collective unconscious determined by the biology of race or gender, but because writers read other writers and *ground* their representations of experience in models of language provided largely by other writers to whom they feel akin. It is through this mode of literary revision, amply evident in the *texts* themselves—in formal echoes, recast metaphors, even in parody—that a "tradition" emerges and defines itself.

This is formal bonding, and it is only through formal bonding that we can know a literary tradition. The collective publication of these works by black women now, for the first time, makes it possible for scholars and critics, male and female, black and white, to *demonstrate* that black women writers read, and revised, other black women writers. To demonstrate this set of formal literary relations is to demonstrate that sexuality, race, and gender are both the condition and the basis of *tradition*—but tradition as found in discrete acts of language use.

A word is in order about the history of this set. For the past decade, I have taught a course, first at Yale and then at Cornell, entitled "Black Women and Their Fictions," a course that I inherited from Toni Morrison, who developed it in the mid-1970s for Yale's Program in Afro-American Studies. Although the course was inspired by the remarkable accomplishments of black women novelists since 1970, I gradually extended its beginning date to the late nineteenth century, studying Frances Harper's *Iola Leroy* and Anna Julia Cooper's *A Voice From the South*, both published in 1892. With the discovery of Harriet E. Wilson's seminal novel, *Our Nig* (1859), and Jean Yellin's authentication of Harriet Jacobs's brilliant slave narrative, *Incidents in the Life of a Slave Girl* (1861), a survey course spanning over a century and a quarter emerged.

But the discovery of *Our Nig*, as well as the interest in nineteenth-century black women's writing that this discovery generated, convinced me that even the most curious and diligent scholars knew very little of the extensive history of the creative writings of Afro-American women before 1900. Indeed, most scholars of Afro-American literature had never even read most of the books published by black women, simply because these books—of poetry, novels, short stories, essays, and autobiography—were mostly accessible only in rare book sections of university libraries. For reasons unclear to me even today, few of these marvelous renderings of the Afro-American woman's consciousness were reprinted in the late 1960s and early 1970s, when so many other texts of the Afro-American literary tradition were resurrected from the dark and silent graveyard of the out-of-print and were reissued in facsimile editions aimed at the hungry readership for canonical texts in the nascent field of black studies.

So, with the help of several superb research assistants—including David Curtis, Nicola Shilliam, Wendy Jones, Sam Otter, Janadas Devan, Suvir Kaul, Cynthia Bond, Elizabeth Alexander, and Adele Alexander—and with the expert advice of scholars such as William Robinson, William Andrews, Mary Helen Washington, Maryemma Graham, Jean Yellin, Houston A. Baker, Jr., Richard Yarborough, Hazel Carby, Joan R. Sherman, Frances Foster, and William French, dozens of bibliographies were used to compile a list of books written or narrated by black women mostly before 1910. Without the assistance provided through this shared experience of scholarship, the scholar's true legacy, this project could not have been conceived. As the list grew, I was struck by how very many of these titles that I, for example, had never even heard of, let alone read, such as Ann Plato's *Essays,* Louisa Picquet's slave narrative, or Amelia Johnson's two novels, *Clarence and Corinne* and *The Hazeley Family.* Through our research with the Black Periodical Fiction and Poetry Project (funded by NEH and the Ford Foundation), I also realized that several novels by black women, including three works of fiction by Pauline Hopkins, had been serialized in black periodicals, but had never been collected and published as books. Nor had the several books of poetry published by black women, such as the prolific Frances E. W. Harper, been collected and edited. When I discovered still another "lost" novel by an Afro-American woman (*Four Girls at Cottage City,* published in 1898 by Emma Dunham Kelley-Hawkins), I decided to attempt to edit a collection of reprints of these works and to publish them as a "library" of black women's writings, in part so that I could read them myself.

Convincing university and trade publishers to undertake this project proved to be a difficult task. Despite the commercial success of *Our Nig* and of the several reprint series of women's works (such as Virago, the Beacon Black Women Writers Series, and Rutgers' American Women Writers Series), several presses rejected the project as "too large," "too limited," or as "commercially unviable." Only two publishers recognized the viability and the import of the project and, of these, Oxford's commitment to publish the titles simultaneously as a set made the press's offer irresistible.

While attempting to locate original copies of these exceedingly rare books, I discovered that most of the texts were housed at the Schomburg Center for Research in Black Culture, a branch of The New York Public Library, under the direction of Howard Dodson. Dodson's infectious enthusiasm for the project and his generous collaboration, as well as that of his stellar staff (especially Diana Lachatanere, Sharon Howard, Ellis Haizip, Richard Newman, and Betty Gubert), led to a joint publishing initiative that produced this set as part of the Schomburg's major fund-raising campaign. Without Dodson's foresight and generosity of spirit, the set would not have materialized. Without William P. Sisler's masterful editorship at Oxford and his staff's careful attention to detail, the set would have remained just another grand idea that tends to languish in a scholar's file cabinet.

I would also like to thank Dr. Michael Winston and Dr. Thomas C. Battle, Vice-President of Academic Affairs and the Director of the Moorland-Spingarn Research Center (respectively) at Howard University, for their unending encouragement, support, and collaboration in this project, and Esme E. Bhan at Howard for her meticulous research and bibliographical skills. In addition, I would like to acknowledge the aid of the staff at the libraries of Duke University, Cornell University (especially Tom Weissinger and Donald Eddy), the Boston Public Library, the Western Reserve Historical Society, the Library of Congress, and Yale University. Linda Robbins, Marion Osmun, Sarah Flanagan, and Gerard Case, all members of the staff at Oxford, were

extraordinarily effective at coordinating, editing, and producing the various segments of each text in the set. Candy
Ruck, Nina de Tar, and Phillis Molock expertly typed reams
of correspondence and manuscripts connected to the project.

I would also like to express my gratitude to my colleagues
who edited and introduced the individual titles in the set.
Without their attention to detail, their willingness to meet
strict deadlines, and their sheer enthusiasm for this project,
the set could not have been published. But finally and ultimately, I would hope that the publication of the set would
help to generate even more scholarly interest in the black
women authors whose work is presented here. Struggling
against the seemingly insurmountable barriers of racism *and*
sexism, while often raising families and fulfilling full-time
professional obligations, these women managed nevertheless
to record their thoughts and feelings and to *testify* to all who
dare read them that the will to harness the power of collective
endurance and survival is the will to write.

The Schomburg Library of Nineteenth-Century Black
Women Writers is dedicated in memory of Pauline Augusta
Coleman Gates, who died in the spring of 1987. It was she
who inspired in me the love of learning and the love of literature. I have encountered in the books of this set no will
more determined, no courage more noble, no mind more
sublime, no self more celebratory of the achievements of all
Afro-American women, and indeed of life itself, than her
own.

A NOTE FROM
THE SCHOMBURG CENTER

Howard Dodson

The Schomburg Center for Research in Black Culture, The New York Public Library, is pleased to join with Dr. Henry Louis Gates and Oxford University Press in presenting The Schomburg Library of Nineteenth-Century Black Women Writers. This thirty-volume set includes the work of a generation of black women whose writing has only been available previously in rare book collections. The materials reprinted in twenty-four of the thirty volumes are drawn from the unique holdings of the Schomburg Center.

A research unit of The New York Public Library, the Schomburg Center has been in the forefront of those institutions dedicated to collecting, preserving, and providing access to the records of the black past. In the course of its two generations of acquisition and conservation activity, the Center has amassed collections totaling more than 5 million items. They include over 100,000 bound volumes, 85,000 reels and sets of microforms, 300 manuscript collections containing some 3.5 million items, 300,000 photographs and extensive holdings of prints, sound recordings, film and videotape, newspapers, artworks, artifacts, and other book and nonbook materials. Together they vividly document the history and cultural heritages of people of African descent worldwide.

Though established some sixty-two years ago, the Center's book collections date from the sixteenth century. Its oldest item, an Ethiopian Coptic Tunic, dates from the eighth or ninth century. Rare materials, however, are most available for the nineteenth-century African-American experience. It is from these holdings that the majority of the titles selected for inclusion in this set are drawn.

The nineteenth century was a formative period in African-American literary and cultural history. Prior to the Civil War, the majority of black Americans living in the United States were held in bondage. Law and practice forbade teaching them to read or write. Even after the war, many of the impediments to learning and literary productivity remained. Nevertheless, black men and women of the nineteenth century persevered in both areas. Moreover, more African-Americans than we yet realize turned their observations, feelings, social viewpoints, and creative impulses into published works. In time, this nineteenth-century printed record included poetry, short stories, histories, novels, autobiographies, social criticism, and theology, as well as economic and philosophical treatises. Unfortunately, much of this body of literature remained, until very recently, relatively inaccessible to twentieth-century scholars, teachers, creative artists, and others interested in black life. Prior to the late 1960s, most Americans (black as well as white) had never heard of these nineteenth-century authors, much less read their works.

The civil rights and black power movements created unprecedented interest in the thought, behavior, and achievements of black people. Publishers responded by revising traditional texts, introducing the American public to a new generation of African-American writers, publishing a variety of thematic anthologies, and reprinting a plethora of "classic texts" in African-American history, literature, and art. The reprints usually appeared as individual titles or in a series of bound volumes or microform formats.

The Schomburg Center, which has a long history of supporting publishing that deals with the history and culture of Africans in diaspora, became an active participant in many of the reprint revivals of the 1960s. Since hard copies of original printed works are the preferred formats for producing facsimile reproductions, publishers frequently turned to the Schomburg Center for copies of these original titles. In addition to providing such material, Schomburg Center staff members offered advice and consultation, wrote introductions, and occasionally entered into formal copublishing arrangements in some projects.

Most of the nineteenth-century titles reprinted during the 1960s, however, were by and about black men. A few black women were included in the longer series, but works by lesser known black women were generally overlooked. The Schomburg Library of Nineteenth-Century Black Women Writers is both a corrective to these previous omissions and an important contribution to Afro-American literary history in its own right. Through this collection of volumes, the thoughts, perspectives, and creative abilities of nineteenth-century African-American women, as captured in books and pamphlets published in large part before 1910, are again being made available to the general public. The Schomburg Center is pleased to be a part of this historic endeavor.

I would like to thank Professor Gates for initiating this project. Thanks are due both to him and Mr. William P. Sisler of Oxford University Press for giving the Schomburg Center an opportunity to play such a prominent role in the set. Thanks are also due to my colleagues at The New York Public Library and the Schomburg Center, especially Dr. Vartan Gregorian, Richard De Gennaro, Paul Fasana, Betsy

Pinover, Richard Newman, Diana Lachatanere, Glenderlyn Johnson, and Harold Anderson for their assistance and support. I can think of no better way of demonstrating than in this set the role the Schomburg Center plays in assuring that the black heritage will be available for future generations.

INTRODUCTION

Mary Helen Washington

Given Anna Julia Cooper's unparalleled articulation of black feminist thought in her major work, *A Voice From the South by a Black Woman of the South*, published in 1892; given her role as a leading black spokeswoman of her time (she was one of three black women invited to address the World's Congress of Representative Women in 1893 and one of the few women to speak at the 1900 Pan-African Congress Conference in London); given her leadership in women's organizations (she helped start the Colored Women's YWCA in 1905 because of the Jim Crow policies of the white YWCA and in 1912 founded the first chapter of the Y's Camp Fire Girls); and given the fact that her work in educating black students spanned nearly half a century, why is Anna Cooper a neglected figure, far less well known than such distinguished contemporaries as Frances Harper, Ida B. Wells, and Mary Church Terrell? One of her biographers, Dr. Paul Cooke, suggests that Cooper's role as a scholar limited her public profile: "Cooper was continually the scholar. She was in the library when Mary Church Terrell was picketing the drugstores and cafeterias in downtown Washington D.C. She chose the lesser limelight, while Terrell chose the Civil Rights route and carried the media." [1] In her personal and professional life Cooper made similar choices for the "lesser limelight." In middle age, in the prime of her intellectual and professional life, she adopted five small children. She was a principal and teacher at the renowned Dunbar High School in Washington, D.C., for years, and in her retirement, she continued her life's dedication to the "education of neglected people" by starting a night school for working people who could not attend college during the day. In 1982, when Louise Hutchinson, staff historian at the Smithsonian Institution, completed her biography of Cooper, she called for an official Smithsonian car and hand delivered the first copy of the biography to Mrs. Regia Haywood Bronson, the eldest of the five children Anna Cooper had adopted in 1915. Then in her late seventies, Mrs. Bronson took the book from Hutchinson, and holding it to her breast, she rocked back and forth with tears streaming down her face, but not saying a word. When Hutchinson asked her why she was crying, Bronson said, "Nobody ever told me Sis Annie was important."[2]

In her first and only full-length book, *A Voice From the South by a Black Woman of the South*, Cooper wrote prophetically about the dismissal of the intellectual: The thinker who enriches his country by a "thought inestimable and precious is given neither bread nor a stone. He is too often left to die in obscurity and neglect. . . ."[3] But the exclusion of Cooper from black intellectual history is more than simply disdain for the intellectual. The intellectual discourse of black women of the 1890s, and particularly Cooper's embryonic black feminist analysis, was ignored because it was by and about women and therefore thought not to be as significantly about the race as writings by and about men. (As a black Catholic priest said to me when I asked about the position of women in the church, "We're here to talk about black Catholics, not about feminism.") Cooper thought differently, maintaining, in fact, that men could not even represent the race. At the heart of Cooper's analysis is her belief that the status of black women is the only true measure of collective racial progress. Because the black woman is the least likely to be among the eminent and the most likely to be responsible for the nurturing of families, it is she, according to Cooper, who represents the entire race:

> Only the BLACK WOMAN can say "when and where I enter, in the quiet, undisputed dignity of my womanhood, without violence and without suing or special patronage, then and there the whole *Negro race enters with me.*"[4]

A Voice From the South begins with this dramatic challenge to the prevailing ideas about black women, and Cooper never softens that uncompromising tone. She criticizes black men for securing higher education for themselves through the avenue of the ministry and for erecting roadblocks to deny women access to those same opportunities.

> while our men seem thoroughly abreast of the times on almost every other subject, when they strike the woman question they drop back into sixteenth century logic. . . . I fear the majority of colored men do not yet think it worth while that women aspire to higher education.[5]

If black men are a "muffled chord," then black women, writes Cooper, are the "mute and voiceless note" of the race, with " *'no language—but a cry.'* "

Cooper is equally critical of the white women's movement for its elitism and provinciality, and she challenges white women to link their cause with that of all the "undefended." Always she measures the ideals and integrity of any group by its treatment of those who suffer the greatest oppression.

The feminist essays that comprise the first half of *A Voice From the South* are extremely compelling for contemporary readers. And yet I must confess to a certain uneasiness about Cooper's tone in these essays, a feeling that while she speaks *for* ordinary black women, she rarely, if ever, speaks *to* them. I find myself wondering how Cooper imagined the relationship between herself, an articulate, powerful speaker and writer—an intellectual—and the woman she describes as a "mute and voiceless note," "the sadly expectant Black Woman." Clearly, she sees herself as the *voice* for these women, but nothing in her essays suggests that they existed in her imagination as audience or as peer.

We must remember that the emphasis on social uplift by educated nineteenth-century women was the direct result of their own perilous social position. As Mary Church Terrell explains, the motto of the National Association of Colored Women—"Lifting As We Climb"—grew out of the recognition by elite black women that they were tethered to the destinies of the masses of disadvantaged black women:

> Colored women of education and culture know that . . . the call of duty, . . . policy and preservation demand that they go down among the lowly, the illiterate and even the vicious, to whom they are bound by the ties of race and sex . . . to reclaim them.[6]

We "have determined to come into the closest possible touch with the masses of our women," Terrell continues, because the womanhood of the race will always be judged by these groups. While Terrell's open condescension seems offensive, the discreet distance Cooper maintains between herself and those "mute and voiceless" black women is probably the result of the same vulnerability Terrell felt. To counteract the prevailing assumptions about black women as immoral and ignorant, Cooper had to construct a narrator who was aware of the plight of uneducated women but was clearly set apart from them in refinement, intelligence, and training.[7] And there were other vulnerabilities. As a woman, Cooper had to fight against both black and white men who posed tremendous obstacles to her own education. As a single woman for nearly all of her adult life (she was widowed after only two years of marriage), she was considered, like all women, to be a sexual being whose personal and professional activities had to be circumscribed. And as a passionate and committed feminist, she had to struggle against the masculinist bias in black intellectual circles and against the racism among white feminists. These circumstances help us to understand the limitations of Cooper's writings. Her voice is not radical, and she writes with little sense of community with a black and female past. But in the light of her special vulnerabilities—and that is how we must examine Cooper's life and work—it is all the more remarkable that she develops in *A Voice From the South*, with her critique of dominant groups, an analysis that asserts black womanhood as the vital agency for social and political change in America.

Born Annie Julia Haywood in 1858 in Raleigh, North Carolina, Cooper was the child of a slave woman, Hannah Stanley Haywood, and her white master, George Washington Haywood. In a brief autobiographical statement of her early years, Cooper wrote, "My mother was a slave and the finest woman I have ever known. . . . Presumably my father was her master, if so I owe him not a sou & she was always too modest & shamefaced ever to mention him."[8] Cooper knew very well that Haywood was her father, because in 1934, when she requested information about her family tree from Haywood's nephew, he wrote back that "Wash" Haywood, who was a prominent and successful lawyer in Raleigh until the Civil War, had "one child by his slave Hannah without benefit of Clergy."[9] When the Episcopal Church opened St.

Augustine's Normal School and Collegiate Institute for the newly freed slaves in 1868, Annie Haywood, then about nine and a half years old, was among the first to enter, her admission perhaps reflecting the social and cultural standing of the Haywood family.

As a teenager, Cooper began protesting against sexism when she realized that men, as candidates for the ministry at St. Augustine's, were given preferential treatment, while women were steered away from studying theology and the classics. She complained to the principal that "the only mission open before a girl . . . was to marry one of those candidates." Writing of that experience in *A Voice,* she remembered the difficulties a black girl faced in her struggle for education and how easy the way was made for males:

> A boy, however meager his equipment and shallow his pretentions, had only to declare a floating intention to study theology and he could get all the support, encouragement and stimulus he needed, be absolved from work and invested beforehand with all the dignity of his far away office. While a self-supporting girl had to struggle on by teaching in the summer and working after school hours to keep up with her board bills, and actually to fight her way against positive discouragements to the higher education.[10]

In 1877, at the age of nineteen, Cooper did in fact marry one of those candidates for the ministry, George Cooper. His death two years later left her a widow, which ironically allowed her to pursue a career as a teacher, whereas no married woman—black or white—could continue to teach. She began writing letters to Oberlin in 1881 to request free tuition and to apply for employment so that she could earn her room and board. As at St. Augustine's, Cooper rejected the distinctly inferior "Ladies Course" at Oberlin and, like many of the women, chose the "Gentleman's Course," which she says sarcastically caused no collapse at the college, though the school administrators thought it was a dangerous experiment:

> [It] was adopted with fear and trembling by the good fathers, who looked as if they had been caught secretly mixing explosive compounds and were guiltily expecting every moment to see the foundations under them shaken. . . .[11]

Cooper attained a B.A. and later an M.A. at Oberlin, and in 1887, as one of the few blacks with a graduate degree, she was recruited by the Superintendent for Colored Schools to teach at Washington's only black high school—first known as the Washington Colored High School, then as M Street High School, and finally as the famous Dunbar High School.[12] For several decades the school educated the children of the aspiring black middle class and gained a reputation for having both high academic standards and a deep-seated snobbery based on class and color. During her initial tenure at M Street, where she was first a math and science teacher (she later taught Latin) and then the school principal, Cooper was in the midst of a male and racist stronghold that would eventually bring about her humiliating expulsion from the school. According to a former student at the school, Annette Eaton, Cooper might have expected male hostility:

> You must also remember that as far as the Negro population of Washington was concerned, we were still a small southern community where a woman's place was in the home. The idea of a woman principal of a high school must account in some part for any reaction Dr. Cooper felt against her.[13]

Cooper became the principal of M Street in January 1902, when she was forty-four years old. At the time Booker T.

Washington's program of vocational and industrial training was emerging as *the* model for black education and consequently was playing into the prejudices of whites who believed in black intellectual inferiority. By contrast, Cooper staunchly maintained M Street's orientation toward preparing black youth for college. In defiance of her white supervisor—Percy Hughes, who told her that colored children should be taught trades—Cooper sent several of her students to prestigious universities, including Harvard, Brown, Oberlin, Yale, Amherst, Dartmouth, and Radcliffe. During her tenure as principal, M Street was accredited for the first time by Harvard. For her intransigence, Cooper became the central figure in the "M Street School Controversy" and was eventually forced to resign. A letter by Annette Eaton testifies to the role of white racism in Cooper's dismissal.

> If you could smell or feel or in any way sense the aura of D.C. in those days, you would know that it only took her daring in having her students accepted and given scholarship at Ivy League schools to know that the white power structure would be out to get her for any reason or for no reason. It was pure heresy to think that a colored child could do what a white child could. I well remember a year when I was in the fourth grade and Bill Hastie in the eighth, when the Board of Education decided to check the reading competency of D.C. students. All schools were told to select their best fourth grade and eighth grade readers, and send them to a special Board meeting. Bill and I were sent, were told to read until we were stopped, and naively did so. I was told later that I didn't miss a word until I got to the twelfth grade level. Heaven only knows how far Bill went. But the Board never held that test again. My great-grandfather was on the Board at the time, so the story became a family legend. I cite it only to show you what resentment existed in the city

whenever the Negro children succeeded in any way, or surpassed the whites. So I must fix Dr. Cooper's removal on the ill-feeling created among the power structure in education because of the way her students stood up. And then, you must remember that she was out in front, highly visible, and therefore caught the brunt of the hatred that really belonged to her faculty.[14]

Cooper was brought before the D.C. Board of Education in 1905 and, according to the minutes of the Board meeting, she was charged with the following: (1) refusing to use a textbook authorized by the Board; (2) being too sympathetic to weak and unqualified students; (3) not being able to maintain discipline (two students had been caught drinking); and (4) not maintaining a "proper spirit of unity and loyalty."

The Cooper case was reported extensively in two prominent Washington newspapers, the black *Washington Bee* and the white *Washington Post*. There was considerable support for her side. A delegation that included former Congressman George H. White of North Carolina sat in on the Board's deliberations and waited until after 10 P.M. to speak on Cooper's behalf. The Board claimed to have "damaging testimony" that "cast some aspersion upon Mrs. Cooper's record in North Carolina," but such evidence never materialized. The dispute dragged on for almost a year until 1906 when the Board voted to dismiss her.[15]

Racism aside, the sexism behind this decision was apparent to all who understood the male-dominated D.C. school system of spoils that did not include black women in its inner circles. As Annette Eaton points out, among the factors in Cooper's dismissal, three were the result of sexual politics:

First, AJK [*sic*] was a woman, a "condition" very much frowned upon in Washington school circles, especially at the

secondary or administrative level. It was O.K. for women to
be elementary school teachers and principals, but they were
not supposed to aspire to any higher rank. Second, she had
been married, and married women were not wanted, or even
for a time allowed, to teach. She got away with it because she
was a widow, but I remember even as early as my elementary
school days, my mother could not get a teaching position until
she divorced my father. The third factor is that she rented
out a room in her house to a man (teacher, I think) named
John Love, and the whole city of Washington was rife with
the gossip that she was having an affair with him. I suspect
that it was this, and not the quality of her teaching, that
caused my mother to refuse to let me study Latin under her.[16]

The rumor of Cooper's alleged affair with John Love was
another example of the Victorian double standard: Since
women's behavior, no matter how innocent, could be sexu-
alized, it had to be contained and repressed. Single women
especially were victimized. When Fannie Jackson taught at the
Philadelphia Institute for Colored Youth in the 1880s, she
had to hire the janitor to escort her home in order to avoid
the appearance of impropriety. In 1883 Lucy Ellen Moten
was refused the position of principal of Washington's Minor
Normal School because the all-male Board of Trustees felt
that the tall, elegant mulatta "cut too fine a face and figure"
for the job. Moten appealed to one of the trustees, the eminent
Frederick Douglass, who told her he would intercede for her
if she agreed to give up dancing, playing cards, going to the
theater, entertaining gentlemen callers—and her fine clothes.
She agreed to all conditions and got the job.[17]

John Love and his sister Emma, orphaned as teenagers,
had been taken in by Cooper as her foster children. They
were still living with Cooper several years later, along with

four women teachers, who, according to the 1902 census data, were "boarders" in her home, of which she was listed as owner and "head of household." Indeed John Love, who by this time was a teacher of English and history at M Street, did eventually fall in love with Cooper. There was a thirteen-year difference in their ages; by 1906 Love would have been thirty-five years old and Anna Cooper an attractive forty-eight-year old woman.

Students at M Street were very much aware of their closeness; as Annette Eaton indicated, some parents went so far as to refuse to let their children study Latin under Cooper because of the suspected affair. A former student said that John Love supported Cooper by maintaining discipline at M Street, and another student, ninety-five years old at the time of her recollection, crossed her index and second fingers to indicate the closeness between Love and Cooper. Both of them were dismissed from M Street at the same time, and each took teaching jobs in the Midwest, Cooper in Jefferson City, Missouri at the all-black Lincoln University. Apparently during their exile, John Love wrote to Cooper with a proposal of marriage, which she refused. The love letters from Love to Cooper appear to be lost. Her grandniece, Regia Bronson, who was the eldest of the children Cooper adopted and who died shortly after I began my research, apparently threw the letters out in a wave of housekeeping, but not before she told one of Cooper's biographers, Dr. Paul Cooke, about their existence. Perhaps the age difference deterred Cooper from returning Love's affection, or perhaps she simply felt the romance was improper since she had formerly been his guardian. For many years they worked and taught together as professional and intellectual comrades, but in her writings the only reference that I could find to John Love is in her account of the weekly soirees with the Grimké family: "Mr. Love, especially, had a fine baritone voice, and a favorite from him was 'O Rest in the Lord, Wait Patiently for Him' from Mendelssohn's Elijah."

In 1910 a new superintendent of M Street summoned Cooper back to resume her position as a Latin teacher. She was fifty-two years old, and the next fifty years of her life (she died at the age of 105 in 1964) were as active as the first. Perhaps to assuage the humiliation of her exile, Cooper began to study for her doctorate at Columbia. Before she could complete Columbia's one-year residency requirement, she adopted, in 1915, five orphaned children, who ranged in age from six months to twelve years and were the grandchildren of her half-brother. She brought all five children from Raleigh to Washington where she had bought a new home "to house their Southern exuberance." As difficult as it was to become the mother of five at age fifty-seven, Cooper tackled it with characteristic resolution and defiance:

> With butter at 75 cents per lb. still soaring, sugar severely rationed at any price and fuel oil obtainable only on affadavit in person at regional centers, the Judge at Children's Court . . . said to me: "My, but you are a brave woman!" Not as brave as you may imagine, was my mental rejoinder—only stubborn, or foolhardy. . . .[18]

In spite of a newly acquired mortgage, a family of five small children, and a full schedule of teaching, Cooper continued—"for 'Home Work,' " as she called it—to work on her doctorate, this time with the Sorbonne. Once she enrolled the children in boarding schools, she began to study summers in Paris, and in 1924, having requested a sick leave from her teaching job, she went to Paris to fulfill the residency requirements. Apparently the leave had not been granted, and after fifty days in Paris she received this cable from a friend: "Rumored dropped if not returned within 60 days."[19] Not willing to risk the loss of her retirement benefits or income, Cooper returned to her classroom "5 minutes before 9 on the morning of the 60th day of my absence," greeted by the applause of her students. Despite these obstacles from her supervisors at M Street (now Dunbar High), Cooper defended her dissertation in the spring of 1925 and was awarded a doctorate from the University of Paris. At the age of sixty-seven, she was the fourth American black woman to receive a Ph.D.*

Cooper continued to write well into the 1940s, but she never again singled out black women as her major subject, nor did she ever again take the explicitly feminist stance that she did in *A Voice*. The critical questions to ask about Anna Cooper's career are these: What happened to her early feminist voice in the years after *A Voice* was published? What stymied the development of a fully mature feminism? What happened to the critical position she took against male privilege in *A Voice?* What of her steadfast resolve that "there be the same flourish of trumpets and clapping of hands" for the achievement of women as for men?[20]

We can speculate that a life of professional uncertainty and of financial insecurity made it difficult for her to continue her writing. Cooper came of age during a conservative wave in the black community, a period in which Afro-American intellectual and political ideas were dominated by men. In the

---

*The other three were also associated with M Street School. Georgiana Rose Simpson and Eva B. Dykes taught there, and Sadie Tanner Alexander was a former student.

very year that Cooper published *A Voice From the South,*
Frederick Douglass, when asked by historian M. A. Majors
to name some black women for inclusion in Majors' biographical work on black women, responded: "I have thus far seen
no book of importance written by a negro woman and I know
of no one among us who can appropriately be called famous."[21] Five years later in 1897, when leading black
intellectuals such as Francis Grimké, W. E. B. Du Bois, and
Alexander Crummell formed the prestigious American Negro
Academy "for the promotion of Literature, Science, and Art,"
they limited their membership to "men of African descent."[22]
Deeply committed to the intellectual and moral goals of the
ANA, Cooper reviewed the opening meeting for the February
1898 issue of *Southern Workman,* in which she noted the
exclusion of women with the simple comment, "Its membership is confined to men." She did not comment further, even
though she knew that outstanding black women intellectuals
were being denied membership. Nor did she comment on the
obvious exclusion of women from the masculine imagery of
the ANA, which was determined to rescue and elevate "black
manhood."

In spite of the reverential way she referred to her male
colleagues—Douglass, Du Bois, Grimké, and Crummell in
particular—her distinguished counterparts rarely returned the
compliment in print. Cooper's relationship with Du Bois
underscored how women got left out of black political life.
She obviously knew and respected the eminent Dr. Du Bois.
She was one of the few black women to address the 1900
Pan-African Congress, which Du Bois helped to organize.
She wrote to him at least three times, once in 1936 to ask if
he would publish her biographical sketch of her friend
Charlotte Grimké. Du Bois said it was too long, although he

praised the idea. When she suggested he run it in three serials (probably in the *Crisis*), he neither answered nor returned her notes for the sketch. She wrote to him in 1929, urging him to write a response to *The Tragic Era*, a racist book on Reconstruction by Claude Bowers:

> It seems to me the Tragic Era should be answered—adequately, fully, ably, finally, and again it seems to me *Thou are the man!* Take it up seriously thro the Crisis and let us buy up 10,000 copies to be distributed broadcast thro the land.
> Will you do it?
> Answer
>
> Faithfully,
> Anna J. Cooper

Du Bois' famous book, *Black Reconstruction*, was the result of his response to Cooper's urgings.[23]

In another poignant letter, written on October 27, 1929, she wrote Du Bois about her regrets at not being able to attend the Pan-African Congress that year: "But why oh why don't you have your Congresses in summer time when working people might go with out having their heads thrown to the crows."[24]

I cannot imagine Du Bois being similarly faithful to Anna Cooper, offering to publicize her work, or being willing to hawk 10,000 copies of one of her speeches on women's equality, nor can I imagine that any of the male intelligentsia would have been distraught at not being able to attend the annual meetings of the colored women's clubs. In a compassionate and generally progressive essay called "On the Damnation of Women," Du Bois sympathetically analyzes the oppression of black women, but he makes no effort to draw on the writings of black women intellectuals for their insights

into the problems facing black women. In fact, in a remarkable oversight in this essay, Du Bois quotes Cooper's brilliant
observation that "only the black woman can say 'when and
where I enter' " and attributes the statement *not* to her but
anonymously to "one of our women." [25]

Though the embryonic black feminist viewpoint suggested
in *A Voice* was never fully developed in any of her subsequent
writings, Cooper maintained a natural feminist sensibility that
made her—at least occasionally—an outspoken critic of patriarchal politics. Once asked by a white friend why the men
of her race seemed to outstrip the women in mental attainment, Cooper said that men's intellectual superiority was
merely an illusion created by their posturing: " '. . . the
women are more quiet. They don't feel called to mount a
barrel and harangue by the hour every time they imagine
they have produced an idea.' " [26] She instinctively rebelled
against the power males exerted over female life, even when
that male was a trusted friend. In 1936 the Reverend Francis
Grimké, one of the most respected men in Washington and
a good friend of Cooper's, sent her a copy of a sermon called
"Suicide or Self-Murder," which he had preached after the
death of feminist writer, Charlotte Perkins Gilman. The
sermon was a judgmental and condemnatory pronouncement
of Grimké's deep regret that Gilman had failed to bear her
afflictions with Christian courage and patience. Cooper's reply
to Grimké's moralism, dated April 9, 1936, shows her
unwillingness to have a female life subjugated by a male text.
She strongly objected to Grimké's depreciation of Gilman's
achievements by focusing only on her death:

> I wish in the leaflet on Frances [*sic*] Perkins Gilman you had
> given your readers more of the life history of your subject.
> . . . I am sure the facts in that life, leaving out its tragic
> end, would have been full of inspiring interest and stimulating

encouragement. But you are always *the preacher* you know
and *must* draw your moral for the benefit or the confusion of
the rest of us poor sinners. I forgive you. . . .[27]

If Cooper was unwilling to have women's lives subordi-
nated to male texts, she was equally unwilling to have black
lives dominated by white texts. It is important to understand
that Cooper's criticism was mainly directed at a system of
white male power. As a literary critic, she was uncompromising in her denunciation of white control over the black
image, and she took on such nineteenth-century establishment
figures as William Dean Howells, Joel Chandler Harris, and
George Washington Cable. She blasts Howells and Harris
in *A Voice* for attempting to portray black people and black
culture in their work, even though they were arrogantly
ignorant about that life:

> [They] have performed a few psychological experiments on
> their cooks and coachmen, and with astounding egotism, and
> powers of generalization positively bewildering, forthwith
> aspire to enlighten the world with dissertations on racial traits
> of the Negro.[28]

Cooper made this same complaint against white critics of
the 1940s whose power and position made them the arbiters
of what was "authentic" black life. Black critics were afraid
to criticize Richard Wright's *Native Son* once it was selected
for the Book-of-the-Month Club because, in Cooper's words,
it was so "richly upholstered by cash and comment." She was
also angered that praise from the white poet Vachel Lindsay
had made criticizing Langston Hughes nearly impossible:

> It is the curse of minorities in this power-worshipping world
> that either from fear or from an uncertain policy of expedience
> they distrust their own standards and hesitate to give voice to
> their deeper convictions, submitting supinely to estimates and

characterizations of themselves as handed down by a not
unprejudiced dominant majority.[29]

Everywhere in *A Voice From the South*, Cooper is concerned
about the unrestrained power of a dominant majority to crush
the lives of the weak and powerless. As Hazel Carby points
out in her essay on black women intellectuals at the turn of
the century,[30] Cooper's position was never narrowly confined
to the women's issue because she saw this dominance of the
strong over the weak as the critical issue, and she saw that
tendency to abuse power in the labor and women's movements,
both of which were deeply entrenched in "caste prejudice"
and hostile to the needs and interests of black women. The
sympathy of the labor movement for "working girls" never
included black working women who were confined to the
most menial and strenuous physical labor:

> One often hears in the North an earnest plea from some
> lecturer for "our working girls" (of course this means white
> working girls). . . . how many have ever given a thought
> to the pinched and down-trodden colored women bending
> over wash-tubs and ironing boards—with children to feed
> and house rent to pay, wood to buy, soap and starch to
> furnish—lugging home weekly great baskets of clothes for
> families who pay them for a month's laundrying barely
> enough to purchase a substantial pair of shoes![31]

While Cooper believed strongly in the power of the wom-
en's movement to challenge patriarchal power, she was not
naive about the capacity of white women to condone and
perpetrate race prejudice. Knowing how deeply the South had
influenced the women's movement, she devotes an entire
chapter in *A Voice* to attacking the white supremacist ideas
that had crept into the movement. Women emancipators must

first be released from the "paralyzing grip of caste prejudice,"[32] Cooper asserts, and she takes on movement leaders
Susan B. Anthony and Anna B. Shaw for their failure to take
a strong stand against racism. What precipitated this censure
was the refusal of a women's culture club, of which Shaw
and Anthony were members, to admit a "cream-colored"
applicant to what Cooper called "its immaculate assembly."
Cooper felt that as leaders Shaw and Anthony had the power,
which they failed to use, to telegraph down the lines of their
networks clear disapproval of such attitudes and behavior.
She was further troubled by a speech entitled "Woman Versus
the Indian," in which Shaw complained that white women
were humiliated at being treated less courteously than "Indians
in blankets and moccasins." Cooper responded:

> Is not woman's cause broader, and deeper, and grander, than
> a blue stocking debate or an aristocratic pink tea? Why should
> woman become plaintiff in a suit versus the Indian, or the
> Negro or any other race or class who have been crushed
> under the iron heel of Anglo-Saxon power and selfishness?[33]

For Cooper, the greatest potential of the women's movement lay not with white women but with the women who
were "confronted by both a woman question and a race
problem." And it is precisely at this juncture of racial and
sexual politics that we would expect Cooper to make her
strongest statements in *A Voice*. Her language, when she
speaks of the special mission of black women, is beautiful
and stirring, almost evangelical: "But to be a woman of the
Negro race in America, and to be able to grasp the deep
significance of the possibilities of the crisis, is to have a
heritage, it seems to me, unique in the ages."[34] The rhetoric
is compelling, but the ideas in this section of *A Voice*, where

Cooper tries to connect race and gender issues and to place black women at a pivotal point in that discussion, are disappointing. She is never able to discard totally the ethics of true womanhood, and except for the one passage about black laundry women, she does not imagine ordinary black working women as the basis of her feminist politics. While she admits that black women are an "unacknowledged factor" in both race and gender issues, she insists that their quiet and unobserved presence as they stand "aloof from the heated scramble [of politics]" will eventually make itself felt. Here Cooper is falling back on the true womanhood premise that women need not possess any actual political power in order to effect political change; in true womanly fashion, black women could pressure their husbands to vote the right way by whispering "just the needed suggestion or the almost forgotten truth."[35] The dictates of true womanhood confined women's authority to the domestic realm where they could supposedly derive power from their ability to influence their husbands.[36] Such drawing-room scenarios were hardly relevant to the lives of most black women. Even the examples Cooper gives of black women leaders (Sojourner Truth, Amanda Smith, Charlotte Forten Grimké, Frances Harper) are undermined by the genteel language of true womanhood: They are "pleasing," or "sweet," or "gentle," or "charming," or with a "matchless and irresistible personality."[37]

How did Cooper, a woman who in some ways is so clear-eyed about the need to resist the subordination of women in all its forms, get trapped in the ideological underbrush of true womanhood? As some historians of women's history would claim, many of the tenets of true womanhood did lay the groundwork for a more radical form of feminism, and Cooper obviously expected black women to be at the forefront, if not the helm, of social change. As a middle-class black woman, Cooper, like all of her contemporaries—Fannie Jackson Coppin, Frances Harper, Mary Church Terrell, Ida B. Wells, Josephine St. Pierre Ruffin—had a great stake in the prestige, the respectability, and the gentility guaranteed by the politics of true womanhood. To identify with the issues and interests of poor and uneducated black women entailed a great risk. Cooper and her intellectual contemporaries would have to deal with their own class privilege and would undoubtedly alienate the very white women they felt they needed as allies. Burdened by the race's morality, black women could not be as free as white women or black men to think outside of these boundaries of "uplift"; every choice they made had tremendous repercussions for an entire race of women already under the stigma of inferiority and immorality.

When Cooper is willing to speak out of her own personal experience, to probe her own pain, anger, and victimization, as she does in one of the early essays in *A Voice*, "The Higher Education of Woman," her own real outrage surfaces. At the time she was writing *A Voice*, Cooper had been a self-supporting widow for nearly fourteen years, and she undoubtedly knew how difficult life was for a professional woman. As an intellectually curious and exceptionally bright young girl, she had already experienced the discouragements planted in the way of the "exceptional" female: "I constantly felt (as I suppose many an ambitious girl has felt) a thumping from within unanswered by any beckoning from without."[38] With her own struggle for an education as a background, she understood what little encouragement there was for female development, and she was insulted by the advice to women of her class to "merely look pretty and appear well in society." Her own private poll of colleges that admitted black women

revealed a striking inequality between black men and black
women: By 1890 Fisk had graduated only twelve black
women; Oberlin, five; Wilberforce, four; Atlanta, one; Howard, none. Imagine how difficult it must have been for black
women intellectuals of Cooper's day to fight against the racism
that roadblocked almost every avenue to education for women
and to contend as well with the sexism in "their own little
world" that denigrated their attempts at intellectual growth.

Passionately committed to women's independence, Cooper
espoused higher education as the essential key to ending wom-
en's physical, emotional, and economic dependence on men:

> I grant you that intellectual development, with the self-
> reliance and capacity for earning a livelihood which it gives,
> renders woman less dependent on the marriage relationship
> for physical support (which, by the way, does not always
> accompany it). Neither is she compelled to look to sexual love
> as the one sensation capable of giving tone and relish, move-
> ment and vim to the life she leads. Her horizon is extended.
> Her sympathies are broadened and deepened and multiplied.[39]

Education, Cooper continues, will change woman's relationship to marriage, enabling her to see herself as a power
broker and not merely as a grateful beneficiary. The question
shall not be " 'How shall I so cramp, stunt, simplify and
nullify myself as to make me eligible to the honor of being
swallowed up into some little man?' " The question instead
"now rests with the man as to how he can so develop his
God-given powers as to reach the ideal of [this] generation
of women. . ."?[40] The humor and irony she brings to the
question of how intellectual women will fare in the matrimonial market makes Cooper seem remarkably progressive
for a nineteenth-century woman. When asked if higher edu-

cation would make women less desirable to men, she first says, tongue-in-cheek, that she realizes that only men think this a most weighty and serious argument. Then she dismisses the question with the sarcastic rejoinder that "strong-minded women could be, when they thought it worth their while, quite endurable. . . ."[41]

If there is a serious flaw in this feminist position, it is that it often bears so little relation to the lives of black women of the 1890s, most of whom were sharecroppers, struggling farmers, or domestic servants, few of whom could aspire to anything beyond an elementary education. But it was typical of black publications and black writers of this period to treat black women's lives as though they were merely reflections of leisured white women's. In *We Are Your Sisters: Black Women in the Nineteenth Century,* Dorothy Sterling reports that there were articles in the black press on the latest fashions and advice on how to be a submissive wife.[42] Although her sympathies were with the poor and uneducated, Cooper's images in *A Voice* are almost entirely of privileged women: the struggling, ambitious intellectual, those fatally beautiful Southern mulatto women, a "cream-colored" aspirant to a white culture club, and an artist whose application to the Corcoran museum school was rejected because of her race.

Cooper and her contemporaries saw themselves in the 1890s, "the Women's Era," as avatars of the progress of black women. As "representative" women, they had dual and con-flicting roles: They had to "represent" as advocates that class of American women who were victimized by every social and political policy created by the American power structure, and they had to "represent" the progress that black women were making toward greater refinement, good taste, intelligence, and religious development.[43] And even these efforts were met with contempt and obstructions. Fannie Barrier Williams, in a speech to the 1893 World's Congress of Representative Women, addressed black women's intellectual progress since the Emancipation and declared that every movement of black American women toward intellectual and cultural growth was met with hostility: "If we seek the sanctities of religion, the enlightenment of the university, the honors of politics, and the natural recreations of our common country, the social alarm is instantly given and our aspirations are insulted."[44] Sensing perhaps that she was addressing a sympathetic audience, Cooper also spoke before this same congress and broached a sensitive and potentially damaging subject—the sexual violation of black women. In a speech that could not have taken more than five minutes to deliver, Cooper revealed what is often concealed in *A Voice:* her passionate concern for the poorest black women and her unshakable belief that they were waging a heroic struggle for the necessities of life—for knowledge, for bread, for dignity, and for the simple right of possession of their own bodies.

Without women like Fannie Barrier Williams, Ida B. Wells, Fannie Jackson Coppin, Victoria Earle Matthews, Frances Harper, Mary Church Terrell, and Anna Julia Cooper, we would know very little about the conditions of nineteenth-century black women's lives, and yet the black intellectual tradition, until very recently, has virtually ignored them and devalued their scholarship as clearly subordinate to that produced by black men.[45] These women were activists as well as intellectuals: They worked as teachers, lecturers, social workers, journalists, and in women's clubs. They were more committed to the idea of uplift than to their own personal advancement, partly because they could not isolate themselves from the problems of poor black women. If at times their language betrays their elitism, they were nevertheless forced to give expression to the needs and problems of the least privileged in this society.[46] Cooper wrote in a college questionnaire in 1932 that her chief cultural interest was "the education of the underprivileged," and indeed the fullest expression of her feminism and her intellectual life is to be found in her work as an educator. Still, I do not want to minimize the accomplishment of *A Voice From the South*. It is the most precise, forceful, well-argued statement of black feminist thought to come out of the nineteenth century. Ironically Cooper and other black women intellectuals were very much like poor black women who were engaged in the most difficult and poorly rewarded physical labor: They did the work that no one else was willing to do.

NOTES

1. Interview with Dr. Paul Phillips Cooke, Washington, D.C., May 1985.

2. Louise Daniel Hutchinson, staff historian, Anacostia Neighborhood Museum of the Smithsonian Institution. Mrs. Hutchinson told me this story in a telephone interview, May 1985.

3. Anna Julia Cooper, *A Voice From the South by a Black Woman of the South* (New York: Negro Universities Press, 1969), p. 136. (Originally published in Xenia, Ohio: Aldine Printing House, 1892.)

4. *A Voice From the South*, p. 31.

5. Ibid., p. 75.

6. Mary Church Terrell, in D. W. Culp, ed., *Twentieth-Century Negro Literature; or, a Cyclopedia of Thought on the Vital Topics Relating to the American Negro, by One Hundred of America's Greatest Negroes* (Naperville, Ill., and Toronto, 1902), pp. 174–75. Cited

in Bert Loewenberg and Ruth Bogin, eds., *Black Women in Nineteenth-Century American Life: Their Words, Their Thoughts, Their Feelings* (University Park and London: The Pennsylvania University Press, 1976), p. 23.

7. An excellent discussion of the pressure felt by nineteenth-century black women to defend themselves against the charge of immorality is found in Paula Giddings, *When and Where I Enter: The Impact of Black Women on Race and Sex in America* (New York: William Morrow and Company, Inc., 1984).

8. An undated autobiographical account of her birth by Anna J. Cooper, Courtesy Moorland-Spingarn Research Center, Howard University. Reprinted in Louise D. Hutchinson, *Anna J. Cooper: A Voice From the South* (Washington, D.C.: Smithsonian Press, 1982), p. 4.

9. Anna Julia Cooper papers, courtesy Moorland-Spingarn Research Center, Howard University.

10. *A Voice From the South*, p. 77.

11. Ibid., p. 49.

12. Among the distinguished graduates of Dunbar High School were Benjamin O. Davis, the first black U.S. general; Judge William Hastie, a U.S. appeals court judge and the first black governor of the Virgin Islands; Dr. Charles Drew, who devised the method of storing blood plasma in banks; Senator Edward Brooks of Massachusetts, the first black U.S. senator since Reconstruction; Robert Weaver, secretary of the U.S. Department of Housing and Urban Development under President Kennedy; and Eleanor Holmes Norton, chair of the federal Equal Employment Opportunity Commission under President Carter.

13. Letter from Annette Eaton to Leona C. Gabel, 1977. Smith College Archives.

14. Letter from Annette Eaton to Leona Gabel, October 11, 1977. Smith College Archives.

15. Louise D. Hutchinson, *Anna J. Cooper*, pp. 67–84.

16. Letter from Annette Eaton to Leona Gabel, September 4, 1977. Smith College Archives.

17. Telephone interview with Louise D. Hutchinson, May 1985.

18. Anna J. Cooper, *The Third Step*. Anna Julia Cooper Papers, courtesy Moorland-Spingarn Research Center, Howard University, p. 5.

19. Ibid., p. 6.

20. *A Voice From the South*, pp. 78, 79.

21. Letter from Frederick Douglass to M. A. Majors, August 26, 1892. Reprinted in Dorothy Sterling, ed., *We Are Your Sisters: Black Women in the Nineteenth Century* (New York: W. W. Norton & Company, 1984), p. 436.

22. Alfred A. Moss, Jr., *The American Negro Academy: Voice of the Talented Tenth* (Baton Rouge: Louisiana State University Press, 1981), p. 38.

23. Letter to W. E. B. Du Bois, 1929. Anna Julia Cooper Papers.

24. Letter to W. E. B. Du Bois, October 27, 1929. Anna Julia Cooper Papers.

25. W. E. B. Du Bois, "On the Damnation of Women," in *Darkwater: Voices From Within the Veil* (New York: Schocken Books, 1969), p. 173.

26. *A Voice From the South*, p. 74.

27. Letter to Francis Grimké, April 9, 1936. Anna Julia Cooper Papers.

28. *A Voice From the South*, p. 186.

29. News article on Wright and Hughes. Anna Julia Cooper Papers.

30. Hazel Carby, " 'On the Threshold of Woman's Era': Lynching, Empire, and Sexuality in Black Feminist Theory." *Critical Inquiry* 12 (Autumn 1985):262–77.

31. *A Voice From the South*, pp. 254–55.

32. Ibid., p. 116.

33. Ibid., p. 123.

34. Ibid., p. 144.

35. Ibid., pp. 137–38.

36. For a discussion of the ideology of true womanhood, see

Barbara Welter, "The Cult of True Womanhood: 1800–1860," in *Dimity Convictions: The American Woman in the Nineteenth Century* (Athens: Ohio University Press, 1976), pp. 21–41.

37. *A Voice From the South*, p. 141.

38. Ibid., p. 76.

39. *A Voice From the South*, pp. 68–69.

40. Ibid., pp. 70–71.

41. Ibid., p. 72.

42. Sterling, *We Are Your Sisters*, p. 434.

43. This list of attributes is suggested by a speech given by Fannie Barrier Williams to the World's Congress of Representative Women in 1893 entitled "The Intellectual Progress of the Colored Women of the United States Since the Emancipation Proclamation," in Loewenberg and Bogin, *Black Women in Nineteenth-Century American Life*, p. 272.

44. Loewenberg and Bogin, *Black Women in Nineteenth-Century American Life*, p. 277.

45. The first contemporary documentation of the intellectual tradition of nineteenth-century black women was Loewenberg and Bogin's *Black Women in Nineteenth-Century American Life* in 1976.

46. Ibid., p. 21.

A VOICE FROM THE SOUTH.

" WITH REGRET
I FORGET
IF THE SONG BE LIVING YET,
    YET REMEMBER, VAGUELY NOW,
    IT WAS HONEST, ANYHOW."

To

BISHOP BENJAMIN WILLIAM ARNETT,

WITH PROFOUND REGARD FOR HIS
HEROIC DEVOTION TO

GOD AND THE RACE,

both in Church and in State,—and with sincere
esteem for his unselfish espousal of the cause
of the Black Woman and of every human interest
that lacks a Voice and needs a Defender, this,
the primary utterance of my heart and pen,

Is AFFECTIONATELY INSCRIBED.

A VOICE FROM THE SOUTH.

BY

A BLACK WOMAN OF THE SOUTH.

XENIA, OHIO
THE ALDINE PRINTING HOUSE.
1892

CONTENTS.

OUR RAISON D'ÊTRE.

———

IN the clash and clatter of our American Conflict, it has been said that the South remains Silent. Like the Sphinx she inspires vociferous disputation, but herself takes little part in the noisy controversy. One muffled strain in the Silent South, a jarring chord and a vague and uncomprehended cadenza has been and still is the Negro. And of that muffled chord, the one mute and voiceless note has been the sadly expectant Black Woman,

> An infant crying in the night,
> An infant crying for the light;
> And with *no language—but a cry.*

The colored man's inheritance and apportionment is still the sombre crux, the perplexing *cul de sac* of the nation,—the dumb skeleton in the closet provoking ceaseless harangues, indeed, but little understood and seldom consulted. Attorneys for the plaintiff and attorneys for the defendant, with bungling *gaucherie* have analyzed and dissected, theorized and synthesized with sublime ignorance or pathetic misapprehension of counsel from the black client. One important witness has not yet been heard from. The summing up of the evidence deposed, and the charge to the jury have been made—but no word from the Black Woman.

It is because I believe the American people to be conscientiously committed to a fair trial and ungarbled evidence, and because I feel it essential to a perfect understanding and an equitable verdict that truth from *each* stand-point be presented at the bar,—that this little Voice has been added to the already full chorus. The " other side" has not been represented by one who "lives there." And not many can more sensibly realize and more accurately tell the weight and the fret of the "long dull pain " than the open-eyed but hitherto voice-less Black Woman of America.

The feverish agitation, the perfervid energy, the busy objectivity of the more turbulent life of our men serves, it may be, at once to cloud or color their vision somewhat, and as well to relieve the smart and deaden the pain for them. Their voice is in consequence not always temperate and calm, and at the same time radically corrective and sanatory. At any rate, as our Caucasian barristers are not to blame if they cannot *quite* put themselves in the dark man's place, neither should the dark man be wholly expected fully and adequately to reproduce the exact Voice of the Black Woman.

Delicately sensitive at every pore to social atmospheric conditions, her calorimeter may well be studied in the interest of accuracy and fairness in diagnosing what is often conceded to be a "puzzling" case. If these broken utterances can in any way help to a clearer vision and a truer pulse-beat in studying our Nation's Problem, this Voice by a Black Woman of the South will not have been raised in vain.

Tawawa Chimney Corner,
    Sept. 17, 1892.

SOPRANO OBLIGATO.

For they the *Royal-hearted Women* are
Who nobly love the noblest, yet have grace
For needy, suffering lives in lowliest place ;
Carrying a choicer sunlight in their smile,
The heavenliest ray that pitieth the vile.

* * *

Though I were happy, throned beside the king,
I should be tender to each little thing
With hurt warm breast, that had no speech to tell
Its inward pangs ; and I would sooth it well
With tender touch and with a low, soft moan
For company.

—George Eliot.

* WOMANHOOD A VITAL ELEMENT IN THE REGENERATION AND PROGRESS OF A RACE.

THE two sources from which, perhaps, modern civilization has derived its noble and ennobling ideal of woman are Christianity and the Feudal System.

In Oriental countries woman has been uniformly devoted to a life of ignorance, infamy, and complete stagnation. The Chinese shoe of to-day does not more entirely dwarf, cramp, and destroy her physical powers, than have the customs, laws, and social instincts, which from remotest ages have governed our Sister of the East, enervated and blighted her mental and moral life.

Mahomet makes no account of woman whatever in his polity. The Koran, which, unlike our Bible, was a product and not a

*Read before the convocation of colored clergy of the Protestant Episcopal Church at Washington, D. C., 1886.

growth, tried to address itself to the needs of Arabian civilization as Mahomet with his circumscribed powers saw them. The Arab was a nomad. Home to him meant his present camping place. That deity who, according to our western ideals, makes and sanctifies the home, was to him a transient bauble to be toyed with so long as it gave pleasure and then to be thrown aside for a new one. As a personality, an individual soul, capable of eternal growth and unlimited development, and destined to mould and shape the civilization of the future to an incalculable extent, Mahomet did not know woman. There was no hereafter, no paradise for her. The heaven of the Mussulman is peopled and made gladsome not by the departed wife, or sister, or mother, but by *houri*—a figment of Mahomet's brain, partaking of the ethereal qualities of angels, yet imbued with all the vices and inanity of Oriental women. The harem here, and—" dust to dust " hereafter, this was the hope, the inspiration, the *summum bonum* of the Eastern woman's life! With what result on the life of the nation, the "Unspeakable Turk," the "sick man" of modern Europe can to-day exemplify.

Says a certain writer: "The private life of

the Turk is vilest of the vile, unprogressive, unambitious, and inconceivably low." And yet Turkey is not without her great men. She has produced most brilliant minds; men skilled in all the intricacies of diplomacy and statesmanship; men whose intellects could grapple with the deep problems of empire and manipulate the subtle agencies which check-mate kings. But these minds were not the normal outgrowth of a healthy trunk. They seemed rather ephemeral excrescencies which shoot far out with all the vigor and promise, apparently, of strong branches; but soon alas fall into decay and ugliness because there is no soundness in the root, no life-giving sap, permeating, strengthening and perpetuating the whole. There is a worm at the core! The homelife is impure! and when we look for fruit, like apples of Sodom, it crumbles within our grasp into dust and ashes.

It is pleasing to turn from this effete and immobile civilization to a society still fresh and vigorous, whose seed is in itself, and whose very name is synonymous with all that is progressive, elevating and inspiring, viz., the European bud and the American flower of modern civilization.

And here let me say parenthetically that

our satisfaction in American institutions rests
not on the fruition we now enjoy, but springs
rather from the possibilities and promise that
are inherent in the system, though as yet,
perhaps, far in the future.

"Happiness," says Madame de Stael, "consists not in perfections attained, but in a sense
of progress, the result of our own endeavor
under conspiring circumstances *toward* a goal
which continually advances and broadens and
deepens till it is swallowed up in the Infinite."
Such conditions in embryo are all that we
claim for the land of the West. We have not
yet reached our ideal in American civilization.
The pessimists even declare that we are not
marching in that direction. But there can be
no doubt that here in America is the arena in
which the next triumph of civilization is to be
won; and here too we find promise abundant
and possibilities infinite.

Now let us see on what basis this hope for
our country primarily and fundamentally
rests. Can any one doubt that it is chiefly on
the homelife and on the influence of good
women in those homes? Says Macaulay:
"You may judge a nation's rank in the scale
of civilization from the way they treat their
women." And Emerson, "I have thought

that a sufficient measure of civilization is the influence of good women." Now this high regard for woman, this germ of a prolific idea which in our own day is bearing such rich and varied fruit, was ingrafted into European civilization, we have said, from two sources, the Christian Church and the Feudal System. For although the Feudal System can in no sense be said to have originated the idea, yet there can be no doubt that the habits of life and modes of thought to which Feudalism gave rise, materially fostered and developed it; for they gave us chivalry, than which no institution has more sensibly magnified and elevated woman's position in society.

Tacitus dwells on the tender regard for woman entertained by these rugged barbarians before they left their northern homes to over-run Europe. Old Norse legends too, and primitive poems, all breathe the same spirit of love of home and veneration for the pure and noble influence there presiding—the wife, the sister, the mother.

And when later on we see the settled life of the Middle Ages "oozing out," as M. Guizot expresses it, from the plundering and pillaging life of barbarism and crystallizing into the Feudal System, the tiger of the field is brought once more within the charmed circle of the goddesses of his castle, and his imagination weaves around them a halo whose reflection possibly has not yet altogether vanished.

It is true the spirit of Christianity had not yet put the seal of catholicity on this sentiment. Chivalry, according to Bascom, was but the toning down and softening of a rough and lawless period. It gave a roseate glow to a bitter winter's day. Those who looked out from castle windows revelled in its " amethyst tints." But God's poor, the weak, the unlovely, the commonplace were still freezing and starving none the less in unpitied, unrelieved loneliness.

Respect for woman, the much lauded chivalry of the Middle Ages, meant what I fear it still means to some men in our own day—respect for the elect few among whom they expect to consort.

The idea of the radical amelioration of womankind, reverence for woman as woman regardless of rank, wealth, or culture, was to come from that rich and bounteous fountain from which flow all our liberal and universal ideas—the Gospel of Jesus Christ.

And yet the Christian Church at the time

of which we have been speaking would seem to have been doing even less to protect and elevate woman than the little done by secular society. The Church as an organization committed a double offense against woman in the Middle Ages. Making of marriage a sacrament and at the same time insisting on the celibacy of the clergy and other religious orders, she gave an inferior if not an impure character to the marriage relation, especially fitted to reflect discredit on woman. Would this were all or the worst! but the Church by the licentiousness of its chosen servants invaded the household and established too often as vicious connections those relations which it forbade to assume openly and in good faith. "Thus," to use the words of our authority, "the religious corps became as numerous, as searching, and as unclean as the frogs of Egypt, which penetrated into all quarters, into the ovens and kneading troughs, leaving their filthy trail wherever they went." Says Chaucer with characteristic satire, speaking of the Friars:

'Women may now go safely up and doun,
   In every bush, and under every tree,
   Ther is non other incubus but he,
   And he ne will don hem no dishonour.'

Henry, Bishop of Liege, could unblushingly boast the birth of twenty-two children in fourteen years.*

It may help us under some of the perplexities which beset our way in "the one Catholic and Apostolic Church" to-day, to recall some of the corruptions and incongruities against which the Bride of Christ has had to struggle in her past history and in spite of which she has kept, through many vicissitudes, the faith once delivered to the saints. Individuals, organizations, whole sections of the Church militant may outrage the Christ whom they profess, may ruthlessly trample under foot both the spirit and the letter of his precepts, yet not till we hear the voices audibly saying "Come let us depart hence," shall we cease to believe and cling to the promise, "*I am with you to the end of the world.*"

> "Yet saints their watch are keeping,
> The cry goes up ' How long ! '
> And soon the night of weeping
> Shall be the morn of song."

However much then the facts of any particular period of history may seem to deny it, I for one do not doubt that the source of the vitalizing principle of woman's development

---

*Bascom.

and amelioration is the Christian Church, so far as that church is coincident with Christianity.

Christ gave ideals not formulæ. The Gospel is a germ requiring millennia for its growth and ripening. It needs and at the same time helps to form around itself a soil enriched in civilization, and perfected in culture and insight without which the embryo can neither be unfolded or comprehended. With all the strides our civilization has made from the first to the nineteenth century, we can boast not an idea, not a principle of action, not a progressive social force but was already mutely foreshadowed, or directly enjoined in that simple tale of a meek and lowly life. The quiet face of the Nazarene is ever seen a little way ahead, never too far to come down to and touch the life of the lowest in days the darkest, yet ever leading onward, still onward, the tottering childish feet of our strangely boastful civilization.

By laying down for woman the same code of morality, the same standard of purity, as for man; by refusing to countenance the shameless and equally guilty monsters who were gloating over her fall,—graciously stooping in all the majesty of his own spotlessness to wipe away the filth and grime of her guilty past and bid her go in peace and sin no more; and again in the moments of his own careworn and footsore dejection, turning trustfully and lovingly, away from the heartless snubbing and sneers, away from the cruel malignity of mobs and prelates in the dusty marts of Jerusalem to the ready sympathy, loving appreciation and unfaltering friendship of that quiet home at Bethany; and even at the last, by his dying bequest to the disciple whom he loved, signifying the protection and tender regard to be extended to that sorrowing mother and ever afterward to the sex she represented;—throughout his life and in his death he has given to men a rule and guide for the estimation of woman as an equal, as a helper, as a friend, and as a sacred charge to be sheltered and cared for with a brother's love and sympathy, lessons which nineteen centuries' gigantic strides in knowledge, arts, and sciences, in social and ethical principles have not been able to probe to their depth or to exhaust in practice.

It seems not too much to say then of the vitalizing, regenerating, and progressive influence of womanhood on the civilization of to-day, that, while it was foreshadowed among

Germanic nations in the far away dawn of their history as a narrow, sickly and stunted growth, it yet owes its catholicity and power, the deepening of its roots and broadening of its branches to Christianity.

The union of these two forces, the Barbaric and the Christian, was not long delayed after the Fall of the Empire. The Church, which fell with Rome, finding herself in danger of being swallowed up by barbarism, with characteristic vigor and fertility of resources, addressed herself immediately to the task of conquering her conquerers. The means chosen does credit to her power of penetration and adaptability, as well as to her profound, unerring, all-compassing diplomacy; and makes us even now wonder if aught human can successfully and ultimately withstand her far-seeing designs and brilliant policy, or gainsay her well-earned claim to the word *Catholic*.

She saw the barbarian, little more developed than a wild beast. She forbore to antagonize and mystify his warlike nature by a full blaze of the heartsearching and humanizing tenets of her great Head. She said little of the rule " If thy brother smite thee on one cheek, turn to him the other also;" but thought it sufficient for the needs of those times, to establish the so-called "Truce of God" under which men were bound to abstain from butchering one another for three days of each week and on Church festivals. In other words, she respected their individuality: non-resistance pure and simple being for them an utter impossibility, she contented herself with less radical measures calculated to lead up finally to the full measure of the benevolence of Christ.

Next she took advantage of the barbarian's sensuous love of gaudy display and put all her magnificent garments on. She could not capture him by physical force, she would dazzle him by gorgeous spectacles. It is said that Romanism gained more in pomp and ritual during this trying period of the Dark Ages than throughout all her former history.

The result was she carried her point. Once more Rome laid her ambitious hand on the temporal power, and allied with Charlemagne, aspired to rule the world through a civilization dominated by Christianity and permeated by the traditions and instincts of those sturdy barbarians.

Here was the confluence of the two streams we have been tracing, which, united now, stretch before us as a broad majestic river.

In regard to woman it was the meeting of two noble and ennobling forces, two kindred ideas the resultant of which, we doubt not, is destined to be a potent force in the betterment of the world.

Now after our appeal to history comparing nations destitute of this force and so destitute also of the principle of progress, with other nations among whom the influence of woman is prominent coupled with a brisk, progressive, satisfying civilization,—if in addition we find this strong presumptive evidence corroborated by reason and experience, we may conclude that these two equally varying concomitants are linked as cause and effect; in other words, that the position of woman in society determines the vital elements of its regeneration and progress.

Now that this is so on *a priori* grounds all must admit. And this not because woman is better or stronger or wiser than man, but from the nature of the case, because it is she who must first form the man by directing the earliest impulses of his character.

Byron and Wordsworth were both geniuses and would have stamped themselves on the thought of their age under any circumstances; and yet we find the one a savor of life unto life, the other of death unto death. " Byron, like a rocket, shot his way upward with scorn and repulsion, flamed out in wild, explosive, brilliant excesses and disappeared in darkness made all the more palpable."*

Wordsworth lent of his gifts to reinforce that " power in the Universe which makes for righteousness " by taking the harp handed him from Heaven and using it to swell the strains of angelic choirs. Two locomotives equally mighty stand facing opposite tracks; the one to rush headlong to destruction with all its precious freight, the other to toil grandly and gloriously up the steep embattlements to Heaven and to God. Who—who can say what a world of consequences hung on the first placing and starting of these enormous forces!

Woman, Mother,—your responsibility is one that might make angels tremble and fear to take hold! To trifle with it, to ignore or misuse it, is to treat lightly the most sacred and solemn trust ever confided by God to human kind. The training of children is a task on which an infinity of weal or woe depends. Who does not covet it? Yet who does not stand awe-struck before its momentous issues! It is a matter of small moment, it seems to

*Bascom's Eng. Lit, p. 253.

me, whether that lovely girl in whose accomplishments you take such pride and delight, can enter the gay and crowded salon with the ease and elegance of this or that French or English gentlewoman, compared with the decision as to whether her individuality is going to reinforce the good or the evil elements of the world. The lace and the diamonds, the dance and the theater, gain a new significance when scanned in their bearings on such issues. Their influence on the individual personality, and through her on the society and civilization which she vitalizes and inspires— all this and more must be weighed in the balance before the jury can return a just and intelligent verdict as to the innocence or banefulness of these apparently simple amusements.

Now the fact of woman's influence on society being granted, what are its practical bearings on the work which brought together this conference of colored clergy and laymen in Washington? "We come not here to talk." Life is too busy, too pregnant with meaning and far reaching consequences to allow you to come this far for mere intellectual entertainment.

The vital agency of womanhood in the re-

generation and progress of a race, as a general
question, is conceded almost before it is fairly
stated. I confess one of the difficulties for
me in the subject assigned lay in its obvious-
ness. The plea is taken away by the opposite
attorney's granting the whole question.

"Woman's influence on social progress"—
who in Christendom doubts or questions it?
One may as well be called on to prove that
the sun is the source of light and heat and
energy to this many-sided little world.

Nor, on the other hand, could it have been
intended that I should apply the position when
taken and proven, to the needs and responsibilities of the women of our race in the South.
For is it not written, "Cursed is he that
cometh after the king?" and has not the King
already preceded me in "The Black Woman
of the South"?*

They have had both Moses and the Proph-
ets in Dr. Crummell and if they hear not him,
neither would they be persuaded though one
came up from the South.

I would beg, however, with the Doctor's
permission, to add my plea for the *Colored
Girls* of the South:—that large, bright, promising fatally beautiful class that stand shiver-

---

*Pamphlet published by Dr. Alex. Crummell.

ing like a delicate plantlet before the fury of tempestuous elements, so full of promise and possibilities, yet so sure of destruction; often without a father to whom they dare apply the loving term, often without a stronger brother to espouse their cause and defend their honor with his life's blood; in the midst of pitfalls and snares, waylaid by the lower classes of white men, with no shelter, no protection nearer than the great blue vault above, which half conceals and half reveals the one Care-Taker they know so little of. Oh, save them, help them, shield, train, develop, teach, inspire them! Snatch them, in God's name, as brands from the burning! There is material in them well worth your while, the hope in germ of a staunch, helpful, regenerating womanhood on which, primarily, rests the foundation stones of our future as a race.

It is absurd to quote statistics showing the Negro's bank account and rent rolls, to point to the hundreds of newspapers edited by colored men and lists of lawyers, doctors, professors, D. D's, LL D's, etc., etc., etc., while the source from which the life-blood of the race is to flow is subject to taint and corruption in the enemy's camp.

True progress is never made by spasms.

Real progress is growth. It must begin in the seed. Then, "first the blade, then the ear, after that the full corn in the ear." There is something to encourage and inspire us in the advancement of individuals since their emancipation from slavery. It at least proves that there is nothing irretrievably wrohg in the shape of the black man's skull, and that under given circumstances his development, downward or upward, will be similar to that of other average human beings.

But there is no time to be wasted in mere felicitation. That the Negro has his niche in the infinite purposes of the Eternal, no one who has studied the history of the last fifty years in America will deny. That much depends on his own right comprehension of his responsibility and rising to the demands of the hour, it will be good for him to see; and how best to use his present so that the structure of the future shall be stronger and higher and brighter and nobler and holier than that of the past, is a question to be decided each day by every one of us.

The race is just twenty-one years removed from the conception and experience of a chattel, just at the age of ruddy manhood. It is well enough to pause a moment for retrospec-

tion, introspection, and prospection. We look
back, not to become inflated with conceit because of the depths from which we have
arisen, but that we may learn wisdom from
experience. We look within that we may
gather together once more our forces, and, by
improved and more practical methods, address
ourselves to the tasks before us. We look
forward with hope and trust that the same
God whose guiding hand led our fathers
through and out of the gall and bitterness of
oppression, will still lead and direct their children, to the honor of His name, and for their
ultimate salvation.

But this survey of the failures or achiev-
ments of the past, the difficulties and embar-
rassments of the present, and the mingled
hopes and fears for the future, must not degenerate into mere dreaming nor consume
the time which belongs to the practical and
effective handling of the crucial questions of
the hour; and there can be no issue more vital
and momentous than this of the womanhood
of the race.

Here is the vulnerable point, not in the heel,
but at the heart of the young Achilles; and
here must the defenses be strengthened and
the watch redoubled.

We are the heirs of a past which was not our fathers' moulding. " Every man the arbiter of his own destiny " was not true for the American Negro of the past: and it is no fault of his that he finds himself to-day the inheritor of a manhood and womanhood impoverished and debased by two centuries and more of compression and degradation.

But weaknesses and malformations, which to-day are attributable to a vicious schoolmaster and a pernicious system, will a century hence be rightly regarded as proofs of innate corruptness and radical incurability.

Now the fundamental agency under God in the regeneration, the re-training of the race, as well as the ground work and starting point of its progress upward, must be the *black woman*.

With all the wrongs and neglects of her past, with all the weakness, the debasement, the moral thralldom of her present, the black woman of to-day stands mute and wondering at the Herculean task devolving upon her. But the cycles wait for her. No other hand can move the lever. She must be loosed from her bands and set to work.

Our meager and superficial results from past efforts prove their futility ; and every attempt to elevate the Negro, whether undertaken by himself or through the philanthropy of others, cannot but prove abortive unless so directed as to utilize the indispensable agency of an elevated and trained womanhood.

A race cannot be purified from without. Preachers and teachers are helps, and stimulants and conditions as necessary as the gracious rain and sunshine are to plant growth. But what are rain and dew and sunshine and cloud if there be no life in the plant germ? We must go to the root and see that that is sound and healthy and vigorous; and not deceive ourselves with waxen flowers and painted leaves of mock chlorophyll.

We too often mistake individuals' honor for race development and so are ready to substitute pretty accomplishments for sound sense and earnest purpose.

A stream cannot rise higher than its source. The atmosphere of homes is no rarer and purer and sweeter than are the mothers in those homes. A race is but a total of families. The nation is the aggregate of its homes. As the whole is sum of all its parts, so the character of the parts will determine the characteristics of the whole. These are all axioms and so evident that it seems gratuitous to remark it;

and yet, unless I am greatly mistaken, most of the unsatisfaction from our past results arises from just such a radical and palpable error, as much almost on our own part as on that of our benevolent white friends.

The Negro is constitutionally hopeful and proverbially irrepressible; and naturally stands in danger of being dazzled by the shimmer and tinsel of superficials. We often mistake foliage for fruit and overestimate or wrongly estimate brilliant results.

The late Martin R. Delany, who was an unadulterated black man, used to say when honors of state fell upon him, that when he entered the council of kings the black race entered with him; meaning, I suppose, that there was no discounting his race identity and attributing his achievements to some admixture of Saxon blood. But our present record of eminent men, when placed beside the actual status of the race in America to-day, proves that no man can represent the race. Whatever the attainments of the individual may be, unless his home has moved on *pari passu*, he can never be regarded as identical with or representative of the whole.

Not by pointing to sun-bathed mountain tops do we prove that Phœbus warms the valleys. We must point to homes, average homes, homes of the rank and file of horny handed toiling men and women of the South (where the masses are) lighted and cheered by the good, the beautiful, and the true,—then and not till then will the whole plateau be lifted into the sunlight.

Only the BLACK WOMAN can say "when and where I enter, in the quiet, undisputed dignity of my womanhood, without violence and without suing or special patronage, then and there the whole *Negro race enters with me.*" Is it not evident then that as individual workers for this race we must address ourselves with no half-hearted zeal to this feature of our mission. The need is felt and must be recognized by all. There is a call for workers, for missionaries, for men and women with the double consecration of a fundamental love of humanity and a desire for its melioration through the Gospel; but superadded to this we demand an intelligent and sympathetic comprehension of the interests and special needs of the Negro.

I see not why there should not be an organized effort for the protection and elevation of our girls such as the White Cross League in England. English women are strengthened and protected by more than twelve centuries of Christian influences, freedom and civilization; English girls are dispirited and crushed down by no such all-levelling prejudice as that supercilious caste spirit in America which cynically assumes "A Negro woman cannot be a lady." English womanhood is beset by no such snares and traps as betray the unprotected, untrained colored girl of the South, whose only crime and dire destruction often is her unconscious and marvelous beauty. Surely then if English indignation is aroused and English manhood thrilled under the leadership of a Bishop of the English church to build up bulwarks around their wronged sisters, Negro sentiment cannot remain callous and Negro effort nerveless in view of the imminent peril of the mothers of the next generation. "*I am my Sister's keeper!*" should be the hearty response of every man and woman of the race, and this conviction should purify and exalt the narrow, selfish and petty personal aims of life into a noble and sacred purpose.

We need men who can let their interest and gallantry extend outside the circle of their æsthetic appreciation; men who can be a father, a brother, a friend to every weak, struggling unshielded girl. We need women who are so

sure of their own social footing that they need
not fear leaning to lend a hand to a fallen or
falling sister. We need men and women who
do not exhaust their genius splitting hairs on
aristocratic distinctions and thanking God they
are not as others; but earnest, unselfish souls,
who can go into the highways and byways,
lifting up and leading, advising and encouraging with the truly catholic benevolence of
the Gospel of Christ.

As Church workers we must confess our
path of duty is less obvious; or rather our ability to adapt our machinery to our conception
of the peculiar exigencies of this work as
taught by experience and our own consciousness of the needs of the Negro, is as yet not
demonstrable. Flexibility and aggressiveness
are not such strong characteristics of the
Church to-day as in the Dark Ages.

As a Mission field for the Church the Southern Negro is in some aspects most promising;
in others, perplexing. Aliens neither in language and customs, nor in associations and
sympathies, naturally of deeply rooted religious
instincts and taking most readily and kindly
to the worship and teachings of the Church,
surely the task of proselytizing the American
Negro is infinitely less formidable than that

which confronted the Church in the Barbarians of Europe. Besides, this people already look to the Church as the hope of their race. Thinking colored men almost uniformly admit that the Protestant Episcopal Church with its quiet, chaste dignity and decorous solemnity, its instructive and elevating ritual, its bright chanting and joyous hymning, is eminently fitted to correct the peculiar faults of worship —the rank exuberance and often ludicrous demonstrativeness of their people. Yet, strange to say, the Church, claiming to be missionary and Catholic, urging that schism is sin and denominationalism inexcusable, has made in all these years almost no inroads upon this semi-civilized religionism.

Harvests from this over ripe field of home missions have been gathered in by Methodists, Baptists, and not least by Congregationalists, who were unknown to the Freedmen before their emancipation.

Our clergy numbers less than two dozen* priests of Negro blood and we have hardly more than one self-supporting colored congregation in the entire Southland. While the organization known as the A. M. E. Church

---

*The published report of '91 shows 26 priests for the entire country, including one not engaged in work and one a professor in a non-sectarian school, since made Dean of an Episcopal Annex to Howard University known as King Hall.

has 14,063 ministers, itinerant and local, 4,069 self-supporting churches, 4,275 Sunday-schools, with property valued at $7,772,284, raising yearly for church purposes $1,427,000.

Stranger and more significant than all, the leading men of this race (I do not mean demagogues and politicians, but men of intellect, heart, and race devotion, men to whom the elevation of their people means more than personal ambition and sordid gain—and the men of that stamp have not all died yet) the Christian workers for the race, of younger and more cultured growth, are noticeably drifting into sectarian churches, many of them declaring all the time that they acknowledge the historic claims of the Church, believe her apostolicity, and would experience greater personal comfort, spiritual and intellectual, in her revered communion. It is a fact which any one may verify for himself, that representative colored men, professing that in their heart of hearts they are Episcopalians, are actually working in Methodist and Baptist pulpits; while the ranks of the Episcopal clergy are left to be filled largely by men who certainly suggest the propriety of a " *perpetual* Diaconate " if they cannot be said to have created the necessity for it.

Now where is the trouble? Something must be wrong. What is it?

A certain Southern Bishop of our Church reviewing the situation, whether in Godly anxiety or in " Gothic antipathy " I know not, deprecates the fact that the colored people do not seem *drawn* to the Episcopal Church, and comes to the sage conclusion that the Church is not adapted to the rude untutored minds of the Freedmen, and that they may be left to go to the Methodists and Baptists whither their racial proclivities undeniably tend. How the good Bishop can agree that all-foreseeing Wisdom, and Catholic Love would have framed his Church as typified in his seamless garment and unbroken body, and yet not leave it broad enough and deep enough and loving enough to seek and save and hold seven millions of God's poor, I cannot see.

But the doctors while discussing their scientifically conclusive diagnosis of the disease, will perhaps not think it presumptuous in the patient if he dares to suggest where at least the pain is. If this be allowed, a *Black woman of the South* would beg to point out two possible oversights in this southern work which may indicate in part both a cause and a remedy for some failure. The first is *not calcula-*

ting for the Black man's personality; not having respect, if I may so express it, to his manhood or deterring at all to his conceptions of the needs of his people. When colored persons have been employed it was too often as machines or as manikins. There has been no disposition, generally, to get the black man's ideal or to let his individuality work by its own gravity, as it were. A conference of earnest Christian men have met at regular intervals for some years past to discuss the best methods of promoting the welfare and development of colored people in this country. Yet, strange as it may seem, they have never invited a colored man or even intimated that one would be welcome to take part in their deliberations. Their remedial contrivances are purely theoretical or empirical, therefore, and the whole machinery devoid of soul.

The second important oversight in my judgment is closely allied to this and probably grows out of it, and that is not developing Negro womanhood as an essential fundamental for the elevation of the race, and utilizing this agency in extending the work of the Church.

Of the first I have possibly already presumed to say too much since it does not strictly come within the province of my subject. However, Macaulay somewhere criticises the Church of England as not knowing how to use fanatics, and declares that had Ignátius Loyola been in the Anglican instead of the Roman communion, the Jesuits would have been schismatics instead of Catholics; and if the religious awakenings of the Wesleys had been in Rome, she would have shaven their heads, tied ropes around their waists, and sent them out under her own banner and blessing. Whether this be true or not, there is certainly a vast amount of force potential for Negro evangelization rendered latent, or worse, antagonistic by the halting, uncertain, I had almost said, *trimming* policy of the Church in the South. This may sound both presumptuous and ungrateful. It is mortifying, I know, to benevolent wisdom, after having spent itself in the execution of well conned theories for the ideal development of a particular work, to hear perhaps the weakest and humblest element of that work asking " what doest thou ?"

Yet so it will be in life. The " thus far and no farther" pattern cannot be fitted to any growth in God's kingdom. The universal law of development is " onward and upward." It is God-given and inviolable. From the

unfolding of the germ in the acorn to reach
the sturdy oak, to the growth of a human
soul into the full knowledge and likeness of
its Creator, the breadth and scope of the
movement in each and all are too grand, too
mysterious, too like God himself, to be encompassed and locked down in human molds.

After all the Southern slave owners were
right: either the very alphabet of intellectual
growth must be forbidden and the Negro
dealt with absolutely as a chattel having
neither rights nor sensibilities; or else the
clamps and irons of mental and moral, as well
as civil compression must be riven asunder
and the truly enfranchised soul led to the entrance of that boundless vista through which
it is to toil upwards to its beckoning God as
the buried seed germ to meet the sun.

A perpetual colored diaconate, carefully
and kindly superintended by the white clergy;
congregations of shiny faced peasants with
their clean white aprons and sunbonnets cate-
chised at regular intervals and taught to recite the creed, the Lord's prayer and the ten
commandments—duty towards God and duty
towards neighbor, surely such well tended
sheep ought to be grateful to their shepherds
and content in that station of life to which it

pleased God to call them. True, like the old professor lecturing to his solitary student, we make no provision here for irregularities. " Questions must be kept till after class," or dispensed with altogether. That some do ask questions and insist on answers, in class too, must be both impertinent and annoying. Let not our spiritual pastors and masters however be grieved at such self-assertion as merely signifies we have a destiny to fulfill and as men and women we must *be about our Father's business*.

It is a mistake to suppose that the Negro is prejudiced against a white ministry. Naturally there is not a more kindly and implicit follower of a white man's guidance than the average colored peasant. What would to others be an ordinary act of friendly or pastoral interest he would be more inclined to regard gratefully as a condescension. And he never forgets such kindness. Could the Negro be brought near to his white priest or bishop, he, is not suspicious. He is not only willing but often longs to unburden his soul to this intelligent guide. There are no reservations when he is convinced that you are his friend. It is a saddening satire on American history and manners that it takes something to convince him.

That our people are not " drawn " to a church whose chief dignitaries they see only in the chancel, and whom they reverence as they would a painting or an angel, whose life never comes down to and touches theirs with the inspiration of an objective reality, may be " perplexing " truly (American caste and American Christianity both being facts) but it need not be surprising. There must be something of human nature in it, the same as that which brought about that " the Word was made flesh and dwelt among us " that He might " draw " us towards God.

Men are not " drawn " by abstractions. Only sympathy and love can draw, and until our Church in America realizes this and provides a clergy that can come in touch with our life and have a fellow feeling for our woes, without being imbedded and frozen up in their " Gothic antipathies," the good bishops are likely to continue " perplexed " by the sparsity of colored Episcopalians.

A colored priest of my acquaintance recently related to me, with tears in his eyes, how his reverend Father in God, the Bishop who had ordained him, had met him on the cars on his way to the diocesan convention and warned him, not unkindly, not to take a seat

in the body of the convention with the white
clergy. To avoid disturbance of their godly
placidity he would of cource please sit back
and somewhat apart. I do not imagine that
that clergyman had very much heart for the
Christly (!) deliberations of that convention.

To return, however, it is not on this broader
view of Church work, which I mentioned as a
primary cause of its halting progress with the
colored people, that I am to speak. My proper theme is the second oversight of which in
my judgment our Christian propagandists
have been guilty : or, the necessity of church
training, protecting and uplifting our colored
womanhood as indispensable to the evangelization of the race.

Apelles did not disdain even that criticism
of his lofty art which came from an uncouth
cobbler; and may I not hope that the writer's
oneness with her subject both in feeling and in
being may palliate undue obtrusiveness of
opinions here. That the race cannot be effectually lifted up till its women are truly elevated
we take as proven. It is not for us to dwell
on the needs, the neglects, and the ways of
succor, pertaining to the black woman of the
South. The ground has been ably discussed
and an admirable and practical plan proposed

by the oldest Negro priest in America, advising and urging that special organizations such as Church Sisterhoods and industrial schools be devised to meet her pressing needs in the Southland. That some such movements are vital to the life of this people and the extension of the Church among them, is not hard to see. Yet the pamphlet fell still-born from the press. So far as I am informed the Church has made no motion towards carrying out Dr. Crummell's suggestion.

The denomination which comes next our own in opposing the proverbial emotionalism of Negro worship in the South, and which in consequence like ours receives the cold shoulder from the old heads, resting as we do under the charge of not "having religion" and not believing in conversion—the Congregationalists—have quietly gone to work on the young, have established industrial and training schools, and now almost every community in the South is yearly enriched by a fresh infusion of vigorous young hearts, cultivated heads, and helpful hands that have been trained at Fisk, at Hampton, in Atlanta University, and in Tuskegee, Alabama.

These young people are missionaries actual or virtual both here and in Africa. They have learned to love the methods and doctrines of the Church which trained and educated them; and so Congregationalism surely and steadily progresses.

Need I compare these well known facts with results shown by the Church in the same field and during the same or even a longer time.

The institution of the Church in the South to which she mainly looks for the training of her colored clergy and for the help of the " Black Woman " and " Colored Girl " of the South, has graduated since the year 1868, when the school was founded, *five young women ;** and while yearly numerous young men have been kept and trained for the ministry by the charities of the Church, the number of indigent females who have here been supported, sheltered and trained, is phenomenally small. Indeed, to my mind, the attitude of the Church toward this feature of her work is as if the solution of the problem of Negro missions depended solely on sending a quota of deacons and priests into the field, girls being a sort of *tertium quid* whose development may be promoted if they can pay their way and fall in with the plans mapped out for the training of the other sex.

---

*Five have been graduated since '86, two in '91, two in '92.

Now I would ask in all earnestness, does not this force potential deserve by education and stimulus to be made dynamic? Is it not a solemn duty incumbent on all colored churchmen to make it so? Will not the aid of the Church be given to prepare our girls in head, heart, and hand for the duties and responsibilities that await the intelligent wife, the Christian mother, the earnest, virtuous, helpful woman, at once both the lever and the fulcrum for uplifting the race.

As Negroes and churchmen we cannot be indifferent to these questions. They touch us most vitally on both sides. We believe in the Holy Catholic Church. We believe that however gigantic and apparently remote the consummation, the Church will go on conquering and to conquer till the kingdoms of this world, not excepting the black man and the black woman of the South, shall have become the kingdoms of the Lord and of his Christ.

That past work in this direction has been unsatisfactory we must admit. That without a change of policy results in the future will be as meagre, we greatly fear. Our life as a race is at stake. The dearest interests of our hearts are in the scales. We must either break away from dear old landmarks and

plunge out in any line and every line that enables us to meet the pressing need of our people, or we must ask the Church to allow and
help us, untrammelled by the prejudices and
theories of individuals, to work agressively
under her direction as we alone can, with God's
help, for the salvation of our people.

The time is ripe for action. Self-seeking
and ambition must be laid on the altar. The
battle is one of sacrifice and hardship, but our
duty is plain. We have been recipients of
missionary bounty in some sort for twenty-
one years. Not even the senseless vegetable
is content to be a mere reservoir. Receiving
without giving is an anomaly in nature.
Nature's cells are all little workshops for manu-
facturing sunbeams, the product to be *given
out* to earth's inhabitants in warmth, energy,
thought, action. Inanimate creation always
pays back an equivalent.

Now, *How much owest thou my Lord?* Will
his account be overdrawn if he call for single-
ness of purpose and self-sacrificing labor for
your brethren? Having passed through your
drill school, will you refuse a general's commission even if it entail responsibility, risk
and anxiety, with possibly some adverse criticism? Is it too much to ask you to step for-

ward and direct the work for your race along those lines which you know to be of first and vital importance ?

Will you allow these words of Ralph Waldo Emerson ? " In ordinary," says he, " we have a snappish criticism which watches and contradicts the opposite party. We want the will which advances and dictates [acts]. Nature has made up her mind that what cannot defend itself, shall not be defended. Complaining never so loud and with never so much reason, is of no use. What cannot stand must fall; *and the measure of our sincerity and therefore of the respect of men is the amount of health and wealth we will hazard in the defense of our right."*

THE HIGHER EDUCATION OF WOMEN.

———

IN the very first year of our century, the year
1801, there appeared in Paris a book by
Silvain Marechal, entitled "Shall Woman
Learn the Alphabet." The book proposes a
law prohibiting the alphabet to women, and
quotes authorities weighty and various, to
prove that the woman who knows the alphabet has already lost part of her womanliness.
The author declares that woman can use the
alphabet only as Moliere predicted they would,
in spelling out the verb *amo;* that they have
no occasion to peruse Ovid's *Ars Amoris*, since
that is already the ground and limit of their
intuitive furnishing; that Madame Guion
would have been far more adorable had she
remained a beautiful ignoramus as nature
made her; that Ruth, Naomi, the Spartan
woman, the Amazons, Penelope, Andromache,
Lucretia, Joan of Arc, Petrarch's Laura, the
daughters of Charlemagne, could not spell

their names; while Sappho, Aspasia, Madame de Maintenon, and Madame de Stael could read altogether too well tor their good; finally, that if women were once permitted to read Sophocles and work with logarithms, or to nibble at any side of the apple of knowledge, there would be an end forever to their sewing on buttons and embroidering slippers.

Please remember this book was published at the *beginning* of the Nineteenth Century. At the end of its first third, (in the year 1833) one solitary college in America decided to admit women within its sacred precincts, and organized what was called a "Ladies' Course" as well as the regular B. A. or Gentlemen's course.

It was felt to be an experiment—a rather dangerous experiment—and was adopted with fear and trembling by the good fathers, who looked as if they had been caught secretly mixing explosive compounds and were guiltily expecting every moment to see the foundations under them shaken and rent and their fair superstructure shattered into fragments.

But the girls came, and there was no upheaval. They performed their tasks modestly and intelligently. Once in a while one or two were found choosing the gentlemen's course. Still no collapse; and the dear, careful, scrupulous, frightened old professors were just getting their hearts out of their throats and preparing to draw one good free breath, when they found they would have to change the names of those courses; for there were as many ladies in the gentlemen's course as in the ladies', and a distinctively Ladies' Course, inferior in scope and aim to the regular classical course, did not and could not exist.

Other colleges gradually fell into line, and to-day there are one hundred and ninety-eight colleges for women, and two hundred and seven coeducational colleges and universities in the United States alone offering the degree of B. A. to women, and sending out yearly into the arteries of this nation a warm, rich flood of strong, brave, active, energetic, well-equipped, thoughtful women—women quick to see and eager to help the needs of this needy world—women who can think as well as feel, and who feel none the less because they think—women who are none the less tender and true for the parchment scroll they bear in their hands—women who have given a deeper, richer, nobler and grander meaning to the word "womanly" than any one-sided masculine definition could ever have suggested or inspired—women whom the world has long waited for in pain and anguish till there should be at last added to its forces and allowed to permeate its thought the complement of that masculine influence which has dominated it for fourteen centuries.

Since the idea of order and subordination succumbed to barbarian brawn and brutality in the fifth century, the civilized world has been like a child brought up by his father. It has needed the great mother heart to teach it to be pitiful, to love mercy, to succor the weak and care for the lowly.

Whence came this apotheosis of greed and cruelty? Whence this sneaking admiration we all have for bullies and prize-fighters? Whence the self-congratulation of "dominant" races, as if "dominant" meant "righteous" and carried with it a title to inherit the earth? Whence the scorn of so-called weak or un-warlike races and individuals, and the very comfortable assurance that it is their manifest destiny to be wiped out as vermin before this advancing civilization? As if the possession of the Christian graces of meekness, non-resistance and forgiveness, were incompatible with a civilization professedly based on

Christianity, the religion of love! Just listen
to this little bit of Barbarian brag:

"As for Far Orientals, they are not of those who will sur-
-vive. Artistic attractive people that they are, their civilization is like their own tree flowers, beautiful blossoms destined never to bear fruit. If these people continue in their
old course, their earthly career is closed. Just as surely as
morning passes into afternoon, so surely are these races' of
the Far East, if unchanged, destined to disappear before the
advancing nations of the West. Vanish, they will, off the
face of the earth, and leave our planet the eventual posses.
sion of the dwellers where the day declines. Unless their
newly imported ideas really take root, it is from this whole
world that Japanese and Koreans, as well as Chinese, will
inevitably be excluded. Their Nirvana is already being realized; already, it has wrapped Far Eastern Asia in its
winding sheet."—*Soul of the Far East*—*P. Lowell.*

Delightful reflection for "the dwellers where
day declines." A spectacle to make the gods
laugh, truly, to see the scion of an upstart
race by one sweep of his generalizing pen consigning to annihilation one-third the inhabitants of the globe—a people whose civilization was hoary headed before the parent elements that begot his race had advanced beyond nebulosity.

How like Longfellow's Iagoo, we Westerners
are, to be sure! In the few hundred years,
we have had to strut across our allotted territory and bask in the afternoon sun, we im-

agine we have exhausted the possibilities of humanity. Verily, we are the people, and after us there is none other. Our God is power; strength, our standard of excellence, inherited from barbarian ancestors through a long line of male progenitors, the Law Salic permitting no feminine modifications.

Says one, "The Chinaman is not popular with us, and we do not like the Negro. It is not that the eyes of the one are set bias, and the other is dark-skinned; but the Chinaman, the Negro is weak—*and Anglo Saxons don't like weakness.*"

The world of thought under the predominant man-influence, unmollified and unrestrained by its complementary force, would become like Daniel's fourth beast: "dreadful and terrible, and *strong* exceedingly;" "it had great iron teeth; it devoured and brake in pieces, and stamped the residue with the feet of it;" and the most independent of us find ourselves ready at times to fall down and worship this incarnation of power.

Mrs. Mary A. Livermore, a woman whom I can mention only to admire, came near shaking my faith a few weeks ago in my theory of the thinking woman's mission to put in the tender and sympathetic chord in nature's grand symphony, and counteract, or better, harmonize the diapason of mere strength and might.

She was dwelling on the Anglo-Saxon genius for power and his contempt for weakness, and described a scene in San Francisco which she had witnessed.

The incorrigible animal known as the American small-boy, had pounced upon a simple, unoffending Chinaman, who was taking home his work, and had emptied the beautifully laundried contents of his basket into the ditch. "And," said she, "when that great man stood there and blubbered before that crowd of lawless urchins, to any one of whom he might have taught a lesson with his two fists, *I didn't much care.*

This is said like a man! It grates harshly. It smacks of the worship of the beast. It is contempt for weakness, and taken out of its setting it seems to contradict my theory. It either shows that one of the highest exponents of the Higher Education can be at times untrue to the instincts I have ascribed to the thinking woman and to the contribution she is to add to the civilized world, or else the influence she wields upon our civilization may be potent without being necessarily and always direct and conscious. The latter is the case. Her voice may strike a false note, but her whole being is musical with the vibrations of human suffering. Her tongue may parrot over the cold conceits that some man has taught her, but her heart is aglow with sympathy and loving kindness, and she cannot be true to her real self without giving out these elements into the forces of the world.

No one is in any danger of imagining Mark Antony "a plain blunt man," nor Cassius a sincere one—whatever the speeches they may make.

As individuals, we are constantly and inevitably, whether we are conscious of it or not, giving out our real selves into onr several little worlds, inexorably adding our own true ray to the flood of starlight, quite independently of our professions and our masquerading; and so in the world of thought, the influence of thinking woman far transcends her feeble declamation and may seem at times even opposed to it.

A visitor in Oberlin once said to the lady principal, "Have you no rabble in Oberlin? How is it I see no police here, and yet the streets are as quiet and orderly as if there were an officer of the law standing on every corner."

Mrs. Johnston replied, " Oh, yes; there are vicious persons in Oberlin just as in other towns—*but our girls are our police.*"

With from five to ten hundred pure-minded young women threading the streets of the village every evening unattended, vice must slink away, like frost before the rising sun : and yet I venture to say there was not one in a hundred of those girls who would not have run from a street brawl as she would from a mouse, and who would not have declared she could never stand the sight of blood and pistols.

There is, then, a real and special influence of woman. An influence subtle and often involuntary, an influence so intimately interwoven in, so intricately interpenetrated by the masculine influence of the time that it is often difficult to extricate the delicate meshes and analyze and identify the closely clinging fibers. And yet, without this influence—so long as woman sat with bandaged eyes and manacled hands, fast bound in the clamps of ignorance and inaction, the world of thought moved in its orbit like the revolutions of the moon ; with one face (the man's face) always out, so that the spectator could not distinguish whether it was disc or sphere.

Now I claim that it is the prevalence of the Higher Education among women, the making it a common everyday affair for women to reason and think and express their thought, the training and stimulus which enable and encourage women to administer to the world the bread it needs as well as the sugar it cries for; in short it is the transmitting the potential forces of her soul into dynamic factors that has given symmetry and completeness to the world's agencies. So only could it be consummated that Mercy, the lesson she teaches, and Truth, the task man has set himself, should meet together: that righteousness, or *rightness*, man's ideal,—and *peace*, its necessary ' other half,' should kiss each other.

We must thank the general enlightenment and independence of woman (which we may now regard as a *fait accompli*) that both these forces are now at work in the world, and it is fair to demand from them for the twentieth century a higher type of civilization than any attained in the nineteenth. Religion, science, art, economics, have all needed the feminine flavor; and literature, the expression of what is permanent and best in all of these, may be guaged at any time to measure the strength of the feminine ingredient. You will not find

theology consigning infants to lakes of unquenchable fire long after women have had a
chance to grasp, master, and wield its dogmas.
You will not find science annihilating personality from the government of the Universe
and making of God an ungovernable, unintel-
ligible, blind, often destructive physical force;
you will not find jurisprudence formulating
as an axiom the absurdity that man and wife
are one, and that one the man—that the married woman may not hold or bequeath her
own property save as subject to her husband's
direction; you will not find political econo-
mists declaring that the only possible adjustment between laborers and capitalists is that
of selfishness and rapacity—that each must
get all he can and keep all that he gets, while
the world cries *laissez faire* and the lawyers
explain, " it is the beautiful working of the
law of supply and demand;" in fine, you will
not find the law of love shut out from the affairs of men after the feminine half of the
world's truth is completed.

Nay, put your ear now close to the pulse of
the time. What is the key-note of the literature of these days? What is the banner cry
of all the activities of the last half decade?
What is the dominant seventh which is to add

richness and tone to the final cadences of this century and lead by a grand modulation into the triumphant harmonies of the next? Is it not compassion for the poor and unfortunate, and, as Bellamy has expressed it, "indignant outcry against the failure of the social machinery as it is, to ameliorate the miseries of men!" Even Christianity is being brought to the bar of humanity and tried by the standard of its ability to alleviate the world's suffering and lighten and brighten its woe. What else can be the meaning of Matthew Arnold's saddening protest, "We cannot do without Christianity," cried he, "and we cannot endure it as it is."

When went there by an age, when so much time and thought, so much money and labor were given to God's poor and God's invalids, the lowly and unlovely, the sinning as well as the suffering—homes for inebriates and homes for lunatics, shelter for the aged and shelter for babes, hospitals for the sick, props and braces for the falling, reformatory prisons and prison reformatories, all show that a "mothering" influence from some source is leavening the nation.

Now please understand me. I do not ask you to admit that these benefactions and vir-

tues are the exclusive possession of women, or
even that women are their chief and only advocates. It may be a man who formulates
and makes them vocal. It may be, and often
is, a man who weeps over the wrongs and
struggles for the amelioration : but that man
has imbibed those impulses from a mother
rather than from a father and is simply
materializing and giving back to the world
in tangible form the ideal love and tenderness,
devotion and care that have cherished and
nourished the helpless period of his own existence.

All I claim is that there is a feminine as
well as a masculine side to truth ; that these are
related not as inferior and superior, not as
better and worse, not as weaker and stronger,
but as complements—complements in one
necessary and symmetric whole. That as the
man is more noble in reason, so the woman is
more quick in sympathy. That as he is indefatigable in pursuit of abstract truth, so is she
in caring for the interests by the way—striv-
ing tenderly and lovingly that not one of the
least of these 'little ones' should perish. That
while we not unfrequently see women who
reason, we say, with the coolness and precision
of a man, and men as considerate of helpless-

ness as a woman, still there is a general con-
sensus of mankind that the one trait is essentially masculine and the other as peculiarly
feminine. That both are needed to be worked
into the training of children, in order that our
boys may supplement their virility by tenderness and sensibility, and our girls may round
out their gentleness by strength and self-reliance. That, as both are alike necessary in
giving symmetry to the individual, so a nation
or a race will degenerate into mere emotionalism on the one hand, or bullyism on the
other, if dominated by either exclusively;
lastly, and most emphatically, that the feminine factor can have its proper effect only
through woman's development and education
so that she may fitly and intelligently stamp
her force on the forces of her day, and add her
modicum to the riches of the world's thought.

"For woman's cause is man's: they rise or sink
Together, dwarfed or godlike, bond or free :
For she that out of Lethe scales with man
The shining steps of nature, shares with man
His nights, his days, moves with him to one goal.
If she be small, slight-natured, miserable,
How shall men grow ?
* * * Let her make herself her own
To give or keep, to live and learn and be
All that not harms distinctive womanhood.
For woman is not undeveloped man

But diverse: could we make her as the man
Sweet love were slain; his dearest bond is this,
Not like to like, but like in difference.
Yet in the long years liker must they grow;
The man be more of woman, she of man;
He gain in sweetness and in moral height,
Nor lose the wrestling thews that throw the world;
She mental breadth, nor fail in childward care,
Nor lose the childlike in the larger mind;
Till at the last she set herself to man,
Like perfect music unto noble words."

Now you will argue, perhaps, and rightly, that higher education for women is not a modern idea, and that, if that is the means of setting free and invigorating the long desired feminine force in the world, it has already had a trial and should, in the past, have produced some of these glowing effects. Sappho, the bright, sweet singer of Lesbos, " the violet-crowned, pure, sweetly smiling Sappho" as Alcaeus calls her, chanted her lyrics and poured forth her soul nearly six centuries before Christ, in notes as full and free, as passionate and eloquent as did ever Archilochus or Anacreon.

Aspasia, that earliest queen of the drawing-room, a century later ministered to the intellectual entertainment of Socrates and the leading wits and philosophers of her time. Indeed, to her is attributed, by the best critics, the authorship of one of the most noted speeches ever delivered by Pericles.

Later on, during the Renaissance period, women were professors in mathematics, physics, metaphysics, and the classic languages in Bologna, Pavia, Padua, and Brescia. Olympia Fulvia Morata, of Ferrara, a most interesting character, whose magnificent library was destroyed in 1553 in the invasion of Schweinfurt by Albert of Brandenburg, had acquired a most extensive education. It is said that this wonderful girl gave lectures on classical subjects in her sixteenth year, and had even before that written several very remarkable Greek and Latin poems, and what is also to the point, she married a professor at Heidelberg, and became a *help-meet for him.*

It is true then that the higher education for women—in fact, the highest that the world has ever witnessed—belongs to the past; but we must remember that it was possible, down to the middle of our own century, only to a select few; and that the fashions and traditions of the times were before that all against it. There were not only no stimuli to encourage·women to make the most of their powers and to welcome their development as a helpful agency in the progress of civilization, but their little aspirations, when they had any, were chilled and snubbed in embryo, and any attempt at thought was received as a monstrous usurpation of man's prerogative.

Lessing declared that "the woman who thinks is like the man who puts on rouge—ridiculous;" and Voltaire in his coarse, flippant way used to say, "Ideas are like beards —women and boys have none." Dr. Maginn remarked, "We like to hear a few words of sense from a woman sometimes, as we do from a parrot—they are so unexpected!" and even the pious Fenelon taught that virgin delicacy is almost as incompatible with learning as with vice.

That the average woman retired before these shafts of wit and ridicule and even gloried in her ignorance is not surprising. The Abbe Choisi, it is said, praised the Duchesse de Fontanges as being pretty as an angel and silly as a goose, and all the young ladies of the court strove to make up in folly what they lacked in charms. The ideal of the day was that "women must be pretty, dress prettily, flirt prettily, and not be too well informed;" that it was the *summum bonum* of her earthly hopes to have, as Thackeray puts it, "all the fellows battling to dance with

her;" that she had no God-given destiny, no
soul with unquenchable longings and inex-
haustible possibilities—no work of her own to
do and give to the world—no absolute and inherent value, no duty to self, transcending all
pleasure-giving that may be demanded of a
mere toy; but that her value was purely a
relative one and to be estimated as are the fine
arts—by the pleasure they give. "Woman,
wine and song," as "the world's best gifts to
man," were linked together in praise with as
little thought of the first saying, "What doest
thou," as that the wine and the song should
declare, "We must be about our Father's
business."

Men believed, or pretended to believe, that
the great law of self development was obli-
gatory on their half of the human family
only; that while it was the chief end of man
to glorify God and put his five talents to the
exchangers, gaining thereby other five, it was,
or ought to be, the sole end of woman to glorify
man and wrap her one decently away in a
napkin, retiring into "Hezekiah Smith's lady
during her natural life and Hezekiah Smith's
relict on her tombstone;" that higher education was incompatible with the shape of the
female cerebrum, and that even if it could be

acquired it must inevitably unsex woman destroying the lisping, clinging, tenderly helpless, and beautifully dependent creatures whom men would so heroically think for and so gallantly fight for, and giving in their stead a formidable race of blue stockings with corkscrew ringlets and other spinster propensities.

But these are eighteenth century ideas.

We have seen how the pendulum has swung across our present century. The men of our time have asked with Emerson, "that woman only show us how she can best be served;" and woman has replied: the chance of the seedling and of the animalcule is all I ask— the chance for growth and self development, the permission to be true to the aspirations of my soul without incurring the blight of your censure and ridicule.

> "Audetque viris concurrere virgo."

In soul-culture woman at last dares to contend with men, and we may cite Grant Allen (who certainly cannot be suspected of advocating the unsexing of woman) as an example of the broadening effect of this contest on the ideas at least of the men of the day. He says in his *Plain Words on the Woman Question*, recently published:

"The position of woman was not [in the [a past position which could bear the test of nineteenth-century scrutiny. Their education was inadequate, their social status was humiliating, their political power was nil, their practical and personal grievances were innumerable; above all, their relations to the family—to their husbands, their children, their friends, their property—was simply insupportable."

And again: "As a body we 'Advanced men' are, I think, prepared to reconsider, and to reconsider fundamentally, without prejudice or misconception, the entire question of the relation betwen the sexes. We are ready to make any modifications in those relations which will satisfy the woman's just aspiration for personal independence, for intellectual and moral development, for physical culture, for political activity, and for a voice in the arrangement of her own affairs, both domestic and national."

Now this is magnanimous enough, surely; and quite a step from eighteenth century preaching, is it not? The higher education of Woman has certainly developed the men; —let us see what it has done for the women.

Matthew Arnold during his last visit to

America in '82 or '83, lectured before a certain
co-educational college in the West. After the
lecture he remarked, with some surprise, to a
lady professor, that the young women in his
audience, he noticed, paid as close attention
as the men, *all the way through.*" This led, of
course, to a spirited discussion of the higher
education for women, during which he said to
his enthusiastic interlocutor, eyeing her philo-
sophically through his English eyeglass: "But
—eh—don't you think it—eh—spoils their
chawnces, you know!"

Now, as to the result to women, this is the
most serious argument ever used against the
higher education. If it interferes with marriage, classical training has a grave objection
to weigh and answer.

For I agree with Mr. Allen at least on this
one point, that there must be marrying and
giving in marriage even till the end of time.

I grant you that intellectual development,
with the self-reliance and capacity for earning
a livelihood which it gives, renders woman
less dependent on the marriage relation for
physical support (which, by the way, does not
always accompany it). Neither is she compelled to look to sexual love as the one sensa-
tion capable of giving tone and relish, move-

ment and vim to the life she leads. Her hor-
ison is extended. Her sympathies are broad-
ened and deepened and multiplied. She is in
closer touch with nature. Not a bud that
opens, not a dew drop, not a ray of light, not
a cloud-burst or a thunderbolt, but adds to
the expansiveness and zest of her soul. And
if the sun of an absorbing passion be gone
down, still 'tis night that brings the stars.
She has remaining the mellow, less obtrusive,
but none the less enchanting and inspiring
light of friendship, and into its charmed circle
she may gather the best the world has known.
She can commune with Socrates about the
daimon he knew and to which she too can
bear witness; she can revel in the majesty of
Dante, the sweetness of Virgil, the simplicity
of Homer, the strength of Milton. She can
listen to the pulsing heart throbs of passionate Sappho's encaged soul, as she beats her
bruised wings against her prison bars and
struggles to flutter out into Heaven's æther,
and the fires of her own soul cry back as she
listens. " Yes; Sappho, I know it all; I know
it all." Here, at last, can be communion
without suspicion; friendship without misun-
derstanding; love without jealousy.

We must admit then that Byron's picture,

whether a thing of beauty or not, has faded
from the canvas of to-day.

"Man's love," he wrote, "is of man's life a thing apart,
'Tis woman's whole existence.
Man may range the court, camp, church, the vessel and
the mart,
Sword, gown, gain, glory offer in exchange.
Pride, fame, ambition, to fill up his heart—
And few there are whom these cannot estrange.
Men have all these resources, we *but one*—
To love again and be again undone."

This may have been true when written. *It
is not true to-day.* The old, subjective, stag-
nant, indolent and wretched life for woman
has gone. She has as many resources as men,
as many activities beckon her on. As large
possibilities swell and inspire her heart.

Now, then, does it destroy or diminish her
capacity for loving?

Her standards have undoubtedly gone up.
The necessity of speculating in 'chawnces' has
probably shifted. The question is not now
with the woman "How shall I so cramp,
stunt, simplify and nullify myself as to make
me elegible to the honor of being swallowed
up into some little man?" but the problem, I
trow, now rests with the man as to how he
can so develop his God-given powers as to
reach the ideal of a generation of women who

demand the noblest, grandest and best
achievements of which he is capable; and this
surely is the only fair and natural adjustment
of the chances. Nature never meant that the
ideals and standards of the world should be
dwarfing and minimizing ones, and the men
should thank us for requiring of them the
richest fruits which they can grow. If it
makes them work, all the better for them.

As to the adaptability of the educated
woman to the marriage relation, I shall simply
quote from that excellent symposium of
learned women that appeared recently under
Mrs. Armstrong's signature in answer to the
"Plain Words" of Mr. Allen, already referred
to. " Admitting no longer any question as to
their intellectual equality with the men whom
they meet, with the simplicity of conscious
strength, they take their place beside the men
who challenge them, and fearlessly face the
result of their actions. They deny that their
education in any way unfits them for the duty
of wifehood and maternity or primarily renders these conditions any less attractive to
them than to the domestic type of woman.
On the contrary, they hold that their knowledge of physiology makes them better mothers
and housekeepers; their knowledge of chem-

istry makes them better cooks; while from their training in other natural sciences and in mathematics, they obtain an accuracy and fair-mindedness which is of great value to them in dealing with their children or employees."

So much for their willingness. Now the apple may be good for food and pleasant to the eyes, and a fruit to be desired to make one wise. Nay, it may even assure you that it has no aversion whatever to being tasted. Still, if you do not like the flavor all these recommendations are nothing. Is the intellectual woman *desirable* in the matrimonial market?

This I cannot answer. I confess my ignorance. I am no judge of such things. I have been told that strong-minded women could be, when they thought it worth their while, quite endurable, and, judging from the number of female names I find in college catalogues among the alumnae with double patronymics, I surmise that quite a number of men are willing to put up with them.

Now I would that my task ended here. Having shown that a great want of the world in the past has been a feminine force; that that force can have its full effect only through

the untrammelled development of woman;
that such development, while it gives her to
the world and to civilization, does not necessarily remove her from the home and fireside;
finally, that while past centuries have witnessed
sporadic instances of this higher growth, still
it was reserved for the latter half of the nineteenth century to render it common and general enough to be effective; I might close
with a glowing prediction of what the twentieth century may expect from this heritage
of twin forces—the masculine battered and
toil-worn as a grim veteran after centuries of
warfare, but still strong, active, and vigorous,
ready to help with his hard-won experience
the young recruit rejoicing in her newly found
freedom, who so confidently places her hand
in his with mutual pledges to redeem the ages.

> " And so the twain upon the skirts of Time,
> Sit side by side, full-summed in all their powers,
> Dispensing harvest, sowing the To-be,
> Self-reverent each and reverencing each."

Fain would I follow them, but duty is nearer
home. The high ground of generalities is
alluring but my pen is devoted to a special
cause: and with a view to further enlightenment on the achievements of the century for
THE HIGHER EDUCATION OF COLORED WOMEN, I
wrote a few days ago to the colleges which

admit women and asked how many colored women had completed the B. A. course in each during its entire history. These are the figures returned: Fisk leads the way with twelve; Oberlin next with five; Wilberforcè, four; Ann Arbor and Wellesley three each, Livingstone two, Atlanta one, Howard, as yet, none.

I then asked the principal of the Washington High School how many out of a large number of female graduates from his school had chosen to go forward and take a collegiate course. He replied that but one had ever done so, and she was then in Cornell.*

Others ask questions too, sometimes, and I was asked a few years ago by a white friend, " How is it that the men of your race seem to outstrip the women in mental attainment?" " Oh," I said, " so far as it is true, the men, I suppose, from the life they lead, gain more by contact; and so far as it is only apparent, I think the women are more quiet. They don't feel called to mount a barrel and harangue by the hour every time they imagine they have produced an idea."

But I am sure there is another reason which

---

* Graduated from Scientific Course, June, 1890, the first colored woman to graduate from Cornell.

I did not at that time see fit to give. The atmosphere, the standards, the requirements of
our little world do not afford any special stimulus to female development.

It seems hardly a gracious thing to say, but
it strikes me as true, that while our men seem
thoroughly abreast of the times on almost
every other subject, when they strike the
woman question they drop back into sixteenth century logic. They leave nothing to
be desired generally in regard to gallantry
and chivalry, but they actually do not seem
sometimes to have outgrown that old contemporary of chivalry—the idea that women may
stand on pedestals or live in doll houses, (if
they happen to have them) but they must not
furrow their brows with thought or attempt
to help men tug at the great questions of the
world. I fear the majority of colored men do
not yet think it worth while that women aspire to higher education. Not many will subscribe to the "advanced" ideas of Grant
Allen already quoted. The three R's, a little
music and a good deal of dancing, a first rate
dress-maker and a bottle of magnolia balm,
are quite enough generally to render charming any woman possessed of tact and the
capacity for worshipping masculinity.

My readers will pardon my illustrating my point and also giving a reason for the fear that is in me, by a little bit of personal experience. When a child I was put into a school near home that professed to be normal and collegiate, i. e. to prepare teachers for colored youth, furnish candidates for the ministry, and offer collegiate training for those who should be ready for it. Well, I found after a while that I had a good deal of time on my hands. I had devoured what was put before me, and, like Oliver Twist, was looking around to ask for more. I constantly felt (as I suppose many an ambitious girl has felt) a thumping from within unanswered by any beckoning from without. Class after class was organized for these ministerial candidates (many of them men who had been preaching before I was born). Into every one of these classes I was expected to go, with the sole intent, I thought at the time, of enabling the dear old principal, as he looked from the vacant countenances of his sleepy old class over to where I sat, to get off his solitary pun—his never-failing pleasantry, especially in hot weather—which was, as he called out " Any one ! " to the effect that " *any* one " then meant " *Annie* one."

Finally a Greek class was to be formed. My inspiring preceptor informed me that Greek had never been taught in the school, but that he was going to form a class *for the candidates for the ministry,* and if I liked I might join it. I replied—humbly I hope, as became a female of the human species—that I would like very much to study Greek, and that I was thankful for the opportunity, and so it went on. A boy, however meager his equipment and shallow his pretentions, had only to declare a floating intention to study theology and he could get all the support, encouragement and stimulus he needed, be absolved from work and invested beforehand with all the dignity of his far away office. While a self-supporting girl had to struggle on by teaching in the summer and working after school hours to keep up with her board bills, and actually to fight her way against positive discouragements to the higher education; till one such girl one day flared out and told the principal "the only mission opening before a girl in his school was to marry one of those candidates." He said he didn't know but it was. And when at last that same girl announced her desire and intention to go to college it was received with about the same incredulity and dismay as if a brass button on one of those candidate's coats had propounded a new method for squaring the circle or trisecting the arc.

Now this is not fancy. It is a simple unvarnished photograph, and what I believe was not in those days exceptional in colored schools, and I ask the men and women who are teachers and co-workers for the highest interests of the race, that they give the girls a chance! We might as well expect to grow trees from leaves as hope to build up a civilization or a manhood without taking into consideration our women and the home life made by them, which must be the root and ground of the whole matter. Let us insist then on special encouragement for the education of our women and special care in their training. Let our girls feel that we expect something more of them than that they merely look pretty and appear well in society. Teach them that there is a race with special needs which they and only they can help; that the world needs and is already asking for their trained, efficient forces. Finally, if there is an ambitious girl with pluck and brain to take the higher education, encourage her to make the most of it. Let there be the same flourish of trumpets and clapping of hands as when a boy announces his determination to enter the lists; and then, as you know that she is physically the weaker of the two, don't stand from under and leave her to buffet the waves alone. Let her know that your heart is following her, that your hand, though she sees it not, is ready to support her. To be plain, I mean let money be raised and scholarships be founded in our colleges and universities for self-supporting, worthy young women, to offset and balance the aid that can always be found for boys who will take theology.

The earnest well trained Christian young woman, as a teacher, as a home-maker, as wife, mother, or silent influence even, is as potent a missionary agency among our people as is the theologian; and I claim that at the present stage of our development in the South she is even more important and necessary.

Let us then, here and now, recognize this force and resolve to make the most of it—not the boys less, but the girls more.

"WOMAN VERSUS THE INDIAN."

IN the National Woman's Council convened
at Washington in February 1891, among a
number of thoughtful and suggestive papers
read by eminent women, was one by the Rev.
Anna Shaw, bearing the above title.

That Miss Shaw is broad and just and
liberal in principal is proved beyond contra-
diction. Her noble generosity and womanly
firmness are unimpeachable. The unwavering stand taken by herself and Miss Anthony
in the subsequent color ripple in Wimodaughsis
ought to be sufficient to allay forever any
doubts as to the pure gold of these two
women.

Of Wimodaughsis (which, being interpreted
for the uninitiated, is a woman's culture club
whose name is made up of the first few letters
of the four words wives, mothers, daughters,
and sisters) Miss Shaw is president, and a lady
from the Blue Grass State *was* secretary.

Pandora's box is opened in the ideal harmony of this modern Eden without an Adam when a colored lady, a teacher in one of our schools, applies for admission to its privileges and opportunities.

The Kentucky secretary, a lady zealous in good works and one who, I can't help imagining, belongs to that estimable class who daily thank the Lord that He made the earth that they may have the job of superintending its rotations, and who really would like to help "elevate" the colored people (in her own way of course and so long as they understand their places) is filled with grief and horror that any persons of Negro extraction should aspire to learn type-writing or languages or to enjoy any other advantages offered in the sacred halls of Wimodaughsis. Indeed, she had not calculated that there were any wives, mothers, daughters, and sisters, except white ones; and she is really convinced that *Whimo-daughsis* would sound just as well, and then it need mean just *white mothers, daughters and sisters*. In fact, so far as there is anything in a name, nothing would be lost by omitting for the sake of euphony, from this unique mosaic, the letters that represent wives. *Whi-wimodaughsis* might be a little startling, and on the whole wives would better yield to white; since clearly all women are not wives, while surely all wives are daughters. The daughters therefore could represent the wives and this immaculate assembly for propagating liberal and progressive ideas and disseminating a broad and humanizing culture might be spared the painful possibility of the sight of a black man coming in the future to escort from an evening class this solitary cream-colored applicant. Accordingly the Kentucky secretary took the cream-colored applicant aside, and, with emotions befitting such an epoch-making crisis, told her, "as kindly as she could," that colored people were not admitted to the classes, at the same time refunding the money which said cream-colored applicant had paid for lessons in type-writing.

When this little incident came to the knowledge of Miss Shaw, she said firmly and emphatically, NO. As a minister of the gospel and as a Christian woman, she could not lend her influence to such unreasonable and uncharitable discrimination; and she must resign the honor of president of Wimodaughsis if persons were to be proscribed solely on account of their color.

To the honor of the board of managers, be it

said, they sustained Miss Shaw; and the Kentucky secretary, and those whom she succeeded
in inoculating with her prejudices, resigned.

'Twas only a ripple,—some bewailing of lost
opportunity on the part of those who could
not or would not seize God's opportunity for
broadening and enlarging their own souls—
and then the work flowed on as before.

Susan B. Anthony and Anna Shaw are evidently too noble to be held in thrall by the
provincialisms of women who seem never to
have breathed the atmosphere beyond the con-
fines of their grandfathers' plantations. It is
only from the broad plateau of light and love
that one can see petty prejudice and narrow
priggishness in their true perspective; and it
is on this high ground, as I sincerely believe,
these two grand women stand.

As leaders in the woman's movement of to-
day, they have need of clearness of vision as
well as firmness of soul in.adjusting recalci-
trant forces, and wheeling into line the thousand and one none-such, never-to-be-modified,
won't-be-dictated-to banners of their somewhat mottled array.

The black woman and the southern woman,
I imagine, often get them into the predica-
ment of the befuddled man who had to take

singly across a stream a bag of corn, a fox and a goose. There was no one to help, and to leave the goose with the fox was death— with the corn, destruction. To re-christen the animals, the lion could not be induced to lie down with the lamb unless the lamb would take the inside berth.

The black woman appreciates the situation and can even sympathize with the actors in the serio-comic dilemma.

But, may it not be that, as women, the very lessons which seem hardest to master now, are possibly the ones most essential for our promotion to a higher grade of work?

We assume to be leaders of thought and guardians of society. Our country's manners and morals are under our tutoring. Our standards are law in our several little worlds. However tenaciously men may guard some prerogatives, they are our willing slaves in that sphere which they have always conceded to be woman's. Here, no one dares demur when her fiat has gone forth. The man would be mad who presumed, however inexplicable and past finding out any reason for her action might be, to attempt to open a door in her kingdom officially closed and regally sealed by her.

The American woman of to-day not only gives tone directly to her immediate world, but her tiniest pulsation ripples out and out, down and down, till the outermost circles and the deepest layers of society feel the vibrations. It is pre-eminently an age of organizations. The "leading woman," the preacher, the reformer, the organizer "enthuses" her lieutenants and captains, the literary women, the thinking women, the strong, earnest, irresistible women; these in turn touch their myriads of church clubs, social clubs, culture clubs, pleasure clubs and charitable clubs, till the same lecture has been duly administered to every married man in the land (not to speak of sons and brothers) from the President in the White House to the stone-splitter of the ditches. And so woman's lightest whisper is heard as in Dionysius' ear, by quick relays and endless reproductions, through every recess and cavern as well as on every hilltop and mountain in her vast domain. And her mandates are obeyed. When she says "thumbs up," woe to the luckless thumb that falters in its rising. They may be little things, the amenities of life, the little nothings which cost nothing and come to nothing, and yet can make a sentient being so comfortable or so miserable in this life, the oil of social machinery, which we call the courtesies of life, all are under the magic key of woman's permit.

The American woman then is responsible for American manners. Not merely the right ascension and declination of the satellites of her own drawing room; but the rising and the setting of the pestilential or life-giving orbs which seem to wander afar in space, all are governed almost wholly through her magnetic polarity. The atmosphere of street cars and parks and boulevards, of cafes and hotels and steamboats is charged and surcharged with her sentiments and restrictions. Shop girls and serving maids, cashiers and accountant clerks, scribblers and drummers, whether wage earner, salaried toiler, or proprietress, whether laboring to instruct minds, to save souls, to delight fancies, or to win bread,—the working women of America in whatever station or calling they may be found, are subjects, officers, or rulers of a strong centralized government, and bound together by a system of codes and countersigns, which, though unwritten, forms a network of perfect subordination and unquestioning obedience as marvelous as that of the Jesuits. At the head and center in this regime stands the Leading Woman in the principality. The one talis-manic word that plays along the wires from palace to cook-shop, from imperial Congress to the distant plain, is *Caste*. With all her vaunted independence, the American woman of to-day is as fearful of losing caste as a Brahmin in India. That is the law under which she lives, the precepts which she binds as frontlets between her eyes and writes on the door-posts of her homes, the lesson which she instils into her children with their first baby breakfasts, the injunction she lays upon husband and lover with direst penalties at-tached.

The queen of the drawing room is absolute ruler under this law. Her pose gives the cue. The microscopic angle at which her pencilled brows are elevated, signifies who may be re-cognized and who are beyond the pale. The delicate intimation is, quick as electricity, telegraphed down. Like the wonderful trans-formation in the House that Jack Built (or regions thereabouts) when the rat began to gnaw the rope, the rope to hang the butcher, the butcher to kill the ox, the ox to drink the water, the water to quench the fire, the fire to burn the stick, the stick to beat the dog, and the dog to worry the cat, and on, and on, and on,—when miladi causes the inner arch over her matchless orbs to ascend the merest trifle, *presto*! the Miss at the notions counter grows curt and pert, the dress goods clerk becomes indifferent and taciturn, hotel waiters and ticket dispensers look the other way, the Irish street laborer snarles and scowls, conductors, policemen and park superintendents jostle and push and threaten, and society suddenly seems transformed into a band of organized adders, snapping, and striking and hissing just because they like it on general principles. The tune set by the head singer, sung through all keys and registers, with all qualities of tone,—the smooth, flowing, and gentle, the creaking, whizzing, grating, screeching, growling—according to ability, taste, and temperament of the singers. Another application of like master, like man. In this case, like mistress, like nation.

It was the good fortune of the Black Woof the South to spend some weeks, not long since, in a land over which floated the Union Jack. The Stars and Stripes were not the only familiar experiences missed. A uniform, matter-of-fact courtesy, a genial kindliness, quick perception of opportunities for rendering any little manly assistance, a readiness to give information to strangers,—a hospitable, thawing-out atmosphere everywhere—in shops and waiting rooms, on cars and in the streets, actually seemed to her chilled little soul to transform the commonest boor in the service of the public into one of nature's noblemen, and when the old whipped-cur feeling was taken up and analyzed she could hardly tell whether it consisted mostly of self pity for her own wounded sensibilities, or of shame for her country and mortification that her countrymen offered such an unfavorable contrast.

Some American girls, I noticed recently, in search of novelty and adventure, were taking an extended trip through our country unattended by gentleman friends; their wish was to write up for a periodical or lecture the ease and facility, the comfort and safety of American travel, even for the weak and unprotected, under our well-nigh perfect railroad systems and our gentlemanly and efficient corps of officials and public servants. I have some material I could furnish these young ladies, though possibly it might not be just on the side they wish to have illuminated. The Black Woman of the South has to do considerable travelling in this country, often unat-

tended. She thinks she is quiet and unobtru-
sive in her manner, simple and inconspicuous
in her dress, and can see no reason why in any
chance assemblage of *ladies*, or even a promis-
cuous gathering of ordinarily well-bred and
dignified individuals, she should be signaled
out for any marked consideration. And yet
she has seen these same "gentlemanly and efficient" railroad conductors, when their cars
had stopped at stations having no raised plat-
forms, making it necessary for passengers to
take the long and trying leap from the car
step to the ground or step on the narrow little stool placed under by the conductor, after
standing at their posts and handing woman
after woman from the steps to the stool, thence
to the ground, or else relieving her of satchels
and bags and enabling her to make the
descent easily, deliberately fold their arms and
turn round when the Black Woman's turn
came to alight—bearing her satchel, and bearing besides another unnamable burden inside
the heaving bosom and tightly compressed
lips. The feeling of slighted womanhood is
unlike every other emotion of the soul. Happily for the human family, it is unknown
to many and indescribable to all. Its poign-
ancy, compared with which even Juno's

spretae injuria formae is earthly and vulgar, is holier than that of jealousy, deeper than indignation, tenderer than rage. Its first impulse of wrathful protest and proud self vindication is checked and shamed by the consciousness that self assertion would outrage still further the same delicate instinct. Were there a brutal attitude of hate or of ferocious attack, the feminine response of fear or repulsion is simple and spontaneous. But when the keen sting comes through the finer sensibilities, from a hand which, by all known traditions and ideals of propriety, should have been trained to reverence and respect them, the condemnation of man's inhumanity to woman is increased and embittered by the knowledge of personal identity with a race of beings so fallen.

I purposely forbear to mention instances of personal violence to colored women travelling in less civilized sections of our country, where women have been forcibly ejected from cars, thrown out of seats, their garments rudely torn, their person wantonly and cruelly injured. America is large and must for some time yet endure its out-of-the-way jungles of barbarism as Africa its uncultivated tracts of marsh and malaria. There are murderers and thieves and villains in both London and Paris. Humanity from the first has had its vultures and sharks, and representatives of the fraternity who prey upon mankind may be expected no less in America than elsewhere. That this virulence breaks out most readily and commonly against colored persons in this country, is due of course to the fact that they are, generally speaking, weak and can be imposed upon with impunity. Bullies are always cowards at heart and may be credited with a pretty safe instinct in scenting their prey. Besides, society, where it has not exactly said to its dogs "s-s-sik him!" has at least engaged to be looking in another direction or studying the rivers on Mars. It is not of the dogs and their doings, but of society holding the leash that I shall speak. It is those subtile exhalations of atmospheric odors for which woman is accountable, the indefinable, unplaceable aroma which seems to exude from the very pores in her finger tips like the delicate sachet so dexterously hidden and concealed in her linens; the essence of her teaching, guessed rather than read, so adroitly is the lettering and wording manipulated; it is the undertones of the picture laid finely on by woman's own practiced hand, the reflection of

the lights and shadows on her own brow; it
is, in a word, the reputation of our nation for
general politeness and good manners and of
our fellow citizens to be somewhat more than
cads or snobs that shall engage our present
study. There can be no true test of national
courtesy without travel. Impressions and
conclusions based on provincial traits and
characteristics can thus be modified and gen-
eralized. Moreover, the weaker and less influential the experimenter, the more exact and
scientific the deductions. Courtesy "for reve-
nue only" is not politeness, but diplomacy.
Any rough can assume civilty toward those
of "his set," and does not hesitate to carry it
even to servility toward those in whom he
recognizes a possible patron or his master in
power, wealth, rank, or influence. But, as
the chemist prefers distilled $H_2 O$ in testing
solutions to avoid complications and unwar-
ranted reactions, so the Black Woman holds
that her femineity linked with the impossibility of popular affinity or unexpected attraction through position and influence in her
case makes her a touchstone of American
courtesy exceptionally pure and singularly
free from extraneous modifiers. The man
who is courteous to her is so, not because of

anything he hopes or fears or sees, but because
he is a gentleman.

I would eliminate also from the discussion all
uncharitable reflections upon the orderly execution of laws existing in certain states of
this Union, requiring persons known to be
colored to ride in one car, and persons supposed to be white in another. A good citizen
may use his influence to have existing laws
and statutes changed or modified, but a public servant must not be blamed for obeying
orders. A railroad conductor is not asked to
dictate measures, nor to make and pass laws.
His bread and butter are conditioned on his
managing his part of the machinery as he is
told to do. If, therefore, I found myself in
that compartment of a train designated by the
sovereign law of the state for presumable Cau-
casians, and for colored persons only when
traveling in the capacity of nurses and maids,
should a conductor inform me, as a gentleman
might, that I had made a mistake, and offer to
show me the proper car for black ladies; I
might wonder at the expensive arrangements
of the company and of the state in providing
special and separate accommodations for the
transportation of the various hues of humanity,
but I certainly could not take it as a want of

courtesy on the conductor's part that he gave
the information. It is true, public sentiment
precedes and begets all laws, good or bad; and
on the ground I have taken, our women are to
be credited largely as teachers and moulders
of public sentiment. But when a law has
passed and received the sanction of the land,
there is nothing for our officials to do but en-
force it till repealed; and I for one, as a loyal
American citizen, will give those officials
cheerful support and ready sympathy in the
discharge of their duty. But when a great
burly six feet of masculinity with sloping
shoulders and unkempt beard swaggers in,
and, throwing a roll of tobacco into one corner of his jaw, growls out at me over the
paper I am reading, " Here gurl," (I am past
thirty) " you better git out 'n dis kyar 'f yer
don't, I'll put yer out,"—my mental annota-
tion is *Here's an American citizen who has
been badly trained. He is sadly lacking in
both ' sweetness' and ' light';* and when in the
same section of our enlightened and progressive country, I see from the car window, working on private estates, convicts from the state
penitentiary, among them squads of boys
from fourteen to eighteen years of age in a
chain-gang, their feet chained together and

heavy blocks attached—not in 1850, but in 1890, '91 and '92, I make a note on the fly-leaf of my memorandum, *The women in this section should organize a Society for the Prevention of Cruelty to Human Beings, and disseminate civilizing tracts, and send throughout the region apostles of anti-barbarism for the propagation of humane and enlightened ideas.* And when farther on in the same section our train stops at a dilapidated station, rendered yet more unsightly by dozens of loafers with their hands in their pockets while a productive soil and inviting climate beckon in vain to industry; and when, looking a little more closely, I see two dingy little rooms with "FOR LADIES" swinging over one and "FOR COLORED PEOPLE" over the other; while wondering under which head I come, I notice a little way off the only hotel proprietor of the place whittling a pine stick as he sits with one leg thrown across an empty goods box; and as my eye falls on a sample room next door which seems to be driving the only wide-awake and popular business of the commonwealth, I cannot help ejaculating under my breath, "What a field for the missionary woman." I know that if by any fatality I should be obliged to lie over at that station, and, driven by hunger, should be compelled to seek refreshments or the bare necessaries of life at the only public accommodation in the town, that same stick-whittler would coolly inform me, without looking up from his pine splinter, "We doan uccommodate no niggers hyur." And yet we are so scandalized at Russia's barbarity and cruelty to the Jews! We pay a man a thousand dollars a night just to make us weep, by a recital of such heathenish inhumanity as is practiced on Sclavonic soil.

A recent writer on Eastern nations says: "If we take through the earth's temperate zone, a belt of country whose northern and southern edges are determined by certain limiting isotherms, not more than half the width of the zone apart, we shall find that we have included in a relatively small extent of surface almost all the nations of note in the world, past or present. Now, if we examine this belt and compare the different parts of it with one another, we shall be struck by a remarkable fact. *The peoples inhabiting it grow steadily more personal as we go west.* So unmistakable is this gradation, that one is almost tempted to ascribe it to cosmical rather than to human causes. It is as marked as the

change in color of the human complexion ob-
servable along any meridian, which ranges
from black at the equator to blonde toward
the pole. In like manner the sense of self
grows more intense as we follow in the
wake of the setting sun, and fades steadily as
we advance into the dawn. America, Europe,
the Levant, India, Japan, each is less personal
than the one before. . . . . *That politeness
should be one of the most marked results of
impersonality* may appear surprising, yet a
slight examination will show it to be a fact.
Considered *a priori*, the connection is not far
to seek. Impersonality by lessening the interest in one's self, induces one to take an interest in others. Looked at *a posteriori*, we
find that where the one trait exists the other
is most developed, while an absence of the
second seems to prevent the full growth of the
first. This is true both in general and in detail. *Courtesy increases as we travel eastward
round the world, coincidently with a decrease in
the sense of self.* Asia is more courteous than
Europe, Europe than America. Particular
races show the same concomitance of characteristics. France, the most impersonal nation
of Europe, is at the same time the most polite.”
And by inference, Americans, the most per-

sonal, are the least courteous nation on the globe.

The Black Woman had reached this same conclusion by an entirely different route; but it is gratifying to vanity, nevertheless, to find one's self sustained by both science and philosophy in a conviction, wrought in by hard experience, and yet too apparently audacious to be entertained even as a stealthy surmise. In fact the Black Woman was emboldened some time since by a well put and timely article from an Editor's Drawer on the " Mannerless Sex," to give the world the benefit of some of her experience with the " *Mannerless Race* "; but since Mr. Lowell shows so conclusively that the entire Land of the West is a *mannerless continent*, I have determined to plead with our women, the mannerless sex on this mannerless continent, to institute a reform by placing immediately in our national curricula a department for teaching GOOD MANNERS.

Now, am I right in holding the American Woman responsible? Is it true that the exponents of woman's advancement, the leaders in woman's thought, the preachers and teachers of all woman's reforms, can teach this nation to be courteous, to be pitiful, having compassion one of another, not rendering evil for inoffensiveness, and railing in proportion to the improbability of being struck back; but contrariwise, being *all* of one mind, to love as brethren?

I think so.

It may require some heroic measures, and like all revolutions will call for a determined front and a courageous, unwavering, stalwart heart on the part of the leaders of the reform.

The " *all* " will inevitably stick in the throat of the Southern woman. She must be allowed, please, to except the ' darkey ' from the ' all '; it is too bitter a pill with black people in it. You must get the Revised Version to put it, " *love all white people* as brethren." She really could not enter any society on earth, or in heaven above, or in—the waters under the earth, on such unpalatable conditions.

The Black Woman has tried to understand the Southern woman's difficulties; to put herself in her place, and to be as fair, as charitable, and as free from prejudice in judging her antipathies, as she would have others in regard to her own. She has honestly weighed the apparently sincere excuse, " But you must remember that these people were once our slaves "; and that other, " But civility towards the Negroes will bring us on *social equality* with them.”

These are the two bugbears; or rather, the two humbugbears : for, though each is founded on a most glaring fallacy, one would think they were words to conjure with, so potent and irresistible is their spell as an argument at the North as well as in the South.

One of the most singular facts about the unwritten history of this country is the consummate ability with which Southern influence, Southern ideas and Southern ideals, have from the very beginning even up to the present day, dictated to and domineered over the brain and sinew of this nation. Without wealth, without education, without inventions, arts, sciences, or industries, without well-nigh every one of the progressive ideas and impulses which have made this country great, prosperous and happy, personally indolent and practically stupid, poor in everything but bluster and self-esteem, the Southerner has nevertheless with Italian finesse and exquisite skill, uniformly and invariably, so manipulated Northern sentiment as to succeed sooner or later in carrying his point and shaping the policy of this government to suit his purposes. Indeed, the Southerner is a

magnificent manager of men, a born educator.
For two hundred and fifty years he trained to
his hand a people whom he made absolutely
his own, in body, mind, and sensibility. He
so insinuated differences and distinctions
among them, that their personal attachment
for him was stronger than for their own
brethren and fellow sufferers. He made
it a crime for two or three of them to be
gathered together in Christ's name without a white man's supervision, and a felony
for one to teach them to read even the
Word of Life; and yet they would defend
his interest with their life blood; his smile
was their happiness, a pat on the shoulder
from him their reward. The slightest difference among themselves in condition, circumstances, opportunities, became barriers of
jealousy and disunion. He sowed his blood
broadcast among them, then pitted mulatto
against black, bond against free, house slave
against plantation slave, even the slave of one
clan against like slave of another clan; till,
wholly oblivious of their ability for mutual
succor and defense, all became centers of
myriad systems of repellent forces, having but
one sentiment in common, and that their entire subjection to that master hand.

And he not only managed the black man, he also hoodwinked the white man, the tourist and investigator who visited his lordly estates. The slaves were doing well, in fact couldn't be happier,—plenty to eat, plenty to drink, comfortably housed and clothed—they wouldn't be free if they could; in short, in his broad brimmed plantation hat and easy aristo- cratic smoking gown, he made you think him a veritable patriarch in the midst of a lazy, well fed, good natured, over-indulged tenantry.

Then, too, the South represented blood— not red blood, but blue blood. The difference is in the length of the stream and your dis- tance from its source. If your own father was a pirate, a robber, a murderer, his hands are dyed in red blood, and you don't say very much about it. But if your great great great grandfather's grandfather stole and pillaged and slew, and you can prove it, your blood has become blue and you are at great pains to establish the relationship. So the South had neither silver nor gold, but she had blood; and she paraded it with so much gusto that the substantial little Puritan maidens of the North, who had been making bread and can- ning currants and not thinking of blood the least bit, began to hunt up the records of the

Mayflower to see if some of the passengers
thereon could not claim the honor of having
been one of William the Conqueror's brigands,
when he killed the last of the Saxon kings
and, red-handed, stole his crown and his lands.
Thus the ideal from out the Southland brooded
over the nation and we sing less lustily than
of yore

> ' Kind hearts are more than coronets
> And simple faith than Norman blood.'

In politics, the two great forces, commerce
and empire, which would otherwise have
shaped the destiny of the country, have been
made to pander and cater to Southern notions.
"Cotton is King" meant the South must be
allowed to dictate or there would be no fun.
Every statesman from 1830 to 1860 exhausted
his genius in persuasion and compromises to
smooth out her ruffled temper and gratify her
petulant demands. But like a sullen younger
sister, the South has pouted and sulked and
cried: "I won't play with you now; so there!"
and the big brother at the North has coaxed
and compromised and given in, and—ended
by letting her have her way. Until 1860 she
had as her pet an institution which it was
death by the law to say anything about, except
that it was divinely instituted, inaugurated by

Noah, sanctioned by Abraham, approved by Paul, and just ideally perfect in every way. And when, to preserve the autonomy of the family arrangements, in '61, '62 and '63, it became necessary for the big brother to administer a little wholesome correction and set the obstreperous Miss vigorously down in her seat again, she assumed such an air of injured innocence, and melted away so lugubriously, the big brother has done nothing since but try to sweeten and pacify and laugh her back into a companionable frame of mind.

Father Lincoln did all he could to get her to repent of her petulance and behave herself. He even promised she might keep her pet, so disagreeable to all the neighbors and hurtful even to herself, and might manage it at home to suit herself, if she would only listen to reason and be just tolerably nice. But, no— she was going to leave and set up for herself; she didn't propose to be meddled with; and so, of course, she had to be spanked. Just a little at first—didn't mean to hurt, merely to teach her who was who. But she grew so ugly, and kicked and fought and scratched so outrageously, and seemed so determined to smash up the whole business, the head of the family got red in the face, and said: "Well, now, he

couldn't have any more of that foolishness.
Arabella must just behave herself or take the
consequences." And after the spanking, Arabella sniffed and whimpered and pouted, and
the big brother bit his lip, looked half ashamed,
and said: "Well, I didn't want to hurt you.
You needn't feel so awfully bad about it, I
only did it for your good. You know I
wouldn't do anything to displease you if I
could help it; but you would insist on making
the row, and so I just had to. Now, there—
there—let's be friends!" and he put his great
strong arms about her and just dared anybody
to refer to that little unpleasantness—he'd
show them a thing or two. Still Arabella
sulked,—till the rest of the family decided she
might just keep her pets, and manage her own
affairs and nobody should interfere.

So now, if one intimates that some clauses
of the Constitution are a dead letter at the
South and that only the name and support of
that pet institution are changed while the fact
and essence, minus the expense and responsibility, remain, he is quickly told to mind his
own business and informed that he is waving
the bloody shirt.

Even twenty-five years after the fourteenth
and fifteenth amendments to our Constitution,

a man who has been most unequivocal in his outspoken condemnation of the wrongs regularly and systematically heaped on the oppressed race in this country, and on all even most remotely connected with them—a man whom we had thought our staunchest friend and most noble champion and defender—after a two weeks' trip in Georgia and Florida immediately gives signs of the fatal inception of the virus. Not even the chance traveller from England or Scotland escapes. The arch-manipulator takes him under his special watch-care and training, uses up his stock arguments and gives object lessons with his choicest specimens of Negro depravity and worthlessness; takes him through what, in New York, would be called "the slums," and would predicate there nothing but the duty of enlightened Christians to send out their light and emulate their Master's aggressive labors of love; but in Georgia is denominated "our terrible problem, which people of the North so little understand, yet vouchsafe so much gratuitous advice about." With an injured air he shows the stupendous and atrocious mistake of reasoning about these people as if they were just ordinary human beings, and amenable to the tenets of the Gospel; and not long after the inoculation begins to work, you hear this old-time friend of the oppressed delivering himself something after this fashion: "Ah, well, the South must be left to manage the Negro. She is most directly concerned and must under- stand her problem better than outsiders. We must not meddle. We must be very care- ful not to widen the breaches. The Negro is not worth a feud between brothers and sisters."

Lately a great national and international movement characteristic of this age and country, a movement based on the inherent right of every soul to its own highest develop- ment, I mean the movement making for Woman's full, free, and complete emancipa- tion, has, after much courting, obtained the gracious smile of the Southern woman—I beg her pardon—the Southern *lady*.

She represents blood, and of course could not be expected to leave that out; and firstly and foremostly she must not, in any organiza- tion she may deign to grace with her pres- ence, be asked to associate with "these peo- ple who were once her slaves."

Now the Southern woman (I may be par- doned, being one myself) was never renowned for her reasoning powers, and it is not surprising that just a little picking will make her logic fall to pieces even here.

In the first place she imagines that because her grandfather had slaves who were black, all the blacks in the world of every shade and tint were once in the position of her slaves. This is as bad as the Irishman who was about to kill a peaceable Jew in the streets of Cork, —having just learned that Jews slew his Redeemer. The black race constitutes one-seventh the known population of the globe; and there are representatives of it here as elsewhere who were never in bondage at any time to any man,—whose blood is as blue and lineage as noble as any, even that of the white lady of the South. That her slaves were black and she despises her slaves, should no more argue antipathy to all dark people and peoples, than that Guiteau, an assassin, was white, and I hate assassins, should make me hate all persons more or less white. The objection shows a want of clear discrimination.

The second fallacy in the objection grows out of the use of an ambiguous middle, as the logicians would call it, or assigning a double signification to the term " *Social equality.*"

Civility to the Negro implies social equality. I am opposed to *associating* with dark persons

on terms of social equality. Therefore, I ab-
rogate civility to the Negro. This is like

> Light is opposed to darkness.
> Feathers are light.
> *Ergo*, Feathers are opposed to darkness.

The " social equality " implied by civility to
the Negro is a very different thing from forced
association with him socially. Indeed it
seems to me that the mere application of a
little cold common sense would show that un-
congenial social environments could by no
means be forced on any one. I do not, and
cannot be made to associate with all dark persons, simply on the ground that I am dark;
and I presume the Southern lady can imagine
some whose faces are white, with whom she
would no sooner think of chatting unreserved-
ly than, were it possible, with a veritable
' darkey.' Such things must and will always
be left to individual election. No law, human
or divine, can legislate for or against them.
Like seeks like; and I am sure with the
Southern lady's antipathies at their present
temperature, she might enter ten thousand
organizations besprinkled with colored women
without being any more deflected by them
than by the proximity of a stone. The social
equality scare then is all humbug, conscious

or unconscious, I know not which. And were it not too bitter a thought to utter here, I might add that the overtures for forced association in the past history of these two races were not made by the manacled black man, nor by *the silent and suffering black woman!*

When I seek food in a public café or apply for first-class accommodations on a railway train, I do so because my physical necessities are identical with those of other human beings of like constitution and temperament, and crave satisfaction. I go because I want food, or I want comfort—not because I want association with those who frequent these places; and I can see no more " social equality " in buying lunch at the same restaurant, or riding in a common car, than there is in paying for dry goods at the same counter or walking on the same street.

The social equality which means forced or unbidden association would be as much deprecated and as strenuously opposed by the circle in which I move as by the most hide-bound Southerner in the land. Indeed I have been more than once annoyed by the inquisitive white interviewer, who, with spectacles on nose and pencil and note-book in hand, comes to get some " points " about " *your people.*"

My "people" are just like other people—indeed, too like for their own good. They hate, they love, they attract and repel, they climb or they grovel, struggle or drift, aspire or despair, endure in hope or curse in vexation, exactly like all the rest of unregenerate humanity. Their likes and dislikes are as strong; their antipathies—and prejudices too I fear, are as pronounced as you will find anywhere; and the entrance to the inner sanctuary of their homes and hearts is as jealously guarded against profane intrusion.

What the dark man wants then is merely to live his own life, in his own world, with his own chosen companions, in whatever of comfort, luxury, or emoluments his talent or his money can in an impartial market secure. Has he wealth, he does not want to be forced into inconvenient or unsanitary sections of cities to buy a home and rear his family. Has he art, he does not want to be cabined and cribbed into emulation with the few who merely happen to have his complexion. His talent aspires to study without proscription the masters of all ages and to rub against the broadest and fullest movements of his own day.

Has he religion, he does not want to be

made to feel that there is a white Christ and a black Christ, a white Heaven and a black Heaven, a white Gospel and a black Gospel,— but the one ideal of perfect manhood and womanhood, the one universal longing for development and growth, the one desire for being, and being better, the one great yearning, aspiring, outreaching, in all the heart-throbs of humanity in whatever race or clime.

A recent episode in the Corcoran art gallery at the American capital is to the point. A colored woman who had shown marked ability in drawing and coloring, was advised by her teacher, himself an artist of no mean rank, to apply for admission to the Corcoran school in order to study the models and to secure other advantages connected with the organization. She accordingly sent a written application accompanied by specimens of her drawings, the usual *modus operandi* in securing admission.

The drawings were examined by the best critics and pronounced excellent, and a ticket of admission was immediately issued together with a highly complimentary reference to her work.

The next day my friend, congratulating her country and herself that at least in the republic of art no caste existed, presented her ticket of admission *in propria persona.* There was a little preliminary side play in Delsarte panto-mine, — aghast — incredulity — wonder; then the superintendent told her in plain unartistic English that of course he had not dreamed a colored person could do such work, and had he suspected the truth he would never have issued the ticket of admission; that, to be right frank, the ticket would have to be can-celled,—she could under no condition be ad-mitted to the studio.

Can it be possible that even art in America is to be tainted by this shrivelling caste spirit? If so, what are we coming to? Can any one conceive a Shakespeare, a Michael Angelo, or a Beethoven putting away any fact of simple merit because the thought, or the suggestion, or the creation emanated from a soul with an unpleasing exterior?

What is it that makes the great English bard pre-eminent as the photographer of the human soul? Where did he learn the uni-versal language, so that Parthians, Medes and Elamites, and the dwellers in Mesopotamia, in Egypt and Libya, in Crete and Arabia do hear every one in our own tongue the wonderful revelations of this myriad mind? How did he learn our language? Is it not that his own soul was infinitely receptive to Nature, the dear old nurse, in all her protean forms? Did he not catch and reveal her own secret by his sympathetic listening as she "would constantly sing a more wonderful song or tell a more marvellous tale" in the souls he met around him?

"Stand off! I am better than thou!" has never yet painted a true picture, nor written a thrilling song, nor given a pulsing, a soul-burning sermon. 'Tis only sympathy, another name for love,—that one poor word which, as George Eliot says, "expresses so much of human insight"—that can interpret either man or matter.

It was Shakespeare's own all-embracing sympathy, that infinite receptivity of his, and native, all-comprehending appreciation, which proved a key to unlock and open every soul that came within his radius. And *he received as much as he gave.* His own stores were infinitely enriched thereby. For it is decreed

Man like the vine supported lives,
The strength he gains is from th' embrace he gives.

It is only through clearing the eyes from bias and prejudice, and becoming one with the great all pervading soul of the universe that either art or science can

> " Read what is still unread
> In the manuscripts of God."

No true artist can allow himself to be narrowed and provincialized by deliberately shutting out any class of facts or subjects through prejudice against externals. And American art, American science, American literature can never be founded in truth, the universal beauty; can never learn to speak a language intelligible in all climes and for all ages, till this paralyzing grip of caste prejudice is loosened from its vitals, and the healthy sympathetic eye is taught to look out on the great universe as holding no favorites and no black beasts, but bearing in each plainest or loveliest feature the handwriting of its God.

And this is why, as it appears to me, woman in her lately acquired vantage ground for speaking an earnest helpful word, can do this country no deeper and truer and more lasting good than by bending all her energies to thus broadening, humanizing, and civilizing her native land.

" Except ye become as little children " is not a pious precept, but an inexorable law of the universe. God's kingdoms are all sealed to the seedy, moss-grown mind of self-satisfied maturity. Only the little child in spirit, the simple, receptive, educable mind can enter. Preconceived notions, blinding prejudices, and shrivelling antipathies must be wiped out, and the cultivable soul made a *tabula rasa* for whatever lesson great Nature has to teach.

This, too, is why I conceive the subject to have been unfortunately worded which was chosen by Miss Shaw at the Woman's Council and which stands at the head of this chapter.

Miss Shaw is one of the most powerful of our leaders, and we feel her voice should give no uncertain note. Woman should not, even by inference, or for the sake of argument, seem to disparage what is weak. For woman's cause is the cause of the weak; and when all the weak shall have received their due consideration, then woman will have her " rights," and the Indian will have his rights, and the Negro will have his rights, and all the strong will have learned at last to deal justly, to love mercy, and to walk humbly; and our fair land will have been taught the secret of universal courtesy which is after all nothing but the art, the science, and the religion of regarding one's neighbor as one's self, and to do for him as we would, were conditions swapped, that he do for us.

It cannot seem less than a blunder, whenever the exponents of a great reform or the
harbingers of a noble advance in thought and
effort allow themselves to seem distorted by a
narrow view of their own aims and principles.
All prejudices, whether of race, sect or sex,
class pride and caste distinctions are the be-
littling inheritance and badge of snobs and
prigs.

The philosophic mind sees that its own
" rights " are the rights of humanity. That
in the universe of God nothing trivial is or
mean; and the recognition it seeks is not
through the robber and wild beast adjustment
of the survival of the bullies but through the
universal application ultimately of the Golden
Rule.

Not unfrequently has it happened that the
impetus of a mighty thought wave has done
the execution meant by its Creator in spite of
the weak and distorted perception of its human
embodiment. It is not strange if reformers,
who, after all, but think God's thoughts after
him, have often " builded more wisely than
they knew; " and while fighting consciously
for only a narrow gateway for themselves,
have been driven forward by that irresistible
" Power not ourselves which makes for right-

eousness " to open a high road for humanity.
It was so with our sixteenth century reformers. The fathers of the Reformation had no
idea that they were inciting an insurrection of
the human mind against all domination. None
would have been more shocked than they at
our nineteenth century deductions from their
sixteenth century premises. Emancipation of
mind and freedom of thought would have
been as appalling to them as it was distasteful
to the pope. They were right, they argued,
to rebel against Romish absolutism—because
Romish preaching and Romish practicing were
wrong. They denounced popes for hacking
heretics and forthwith began themselves to
roast witches. The Spanish Inquisition in the
hands of Philip and Alva was an institution
of the devil; wielded by the faithful, it would
become quite another thing. The only "rights"
they were broad enough consciously to fight
for was the right to substitute the absolutism
of their conceptions, their party, their ' *ism* '
for an authority whose teaching they conceived to be corrupt and vicious. Persecution
for a belief was wrong only when the persecutors were wrong and the persecuted right.
The sacred prerogative of the individual to
decide on matters of belief they did not dream

of maintaining. Universal tolerance and its twin, universal charity, were not conceived yet. The broad foundation stone of all human rights, the great democratic principle " A man's a man, *and his own sovereign* for a' that" they did not dare enunciate. They were incapable of drawing up a Declaration of Independence for humanity. The Reformation to the Reformers meant one bundle of authoritative opinions vs. another bundle of authoritative opinions. Justification by faith, vs. justification by ritual. Submission to Calvin vs. submission to the Pope. English and Germans vs. the Italians.

To our eye, viewed through a vista of three centuries, it was the death wrestle of the principle of thought enslavement in the throttling grasp of personal freedom; it was the great Emancipation Day of human belief, man's intellectual Independence Day, prefiguring and finally compelling the world-wide enfranchisement of his body and all its activities. Not Protestant vs. Catholic, then; not Luther vs. Leo, not Dominicans vs. Augustinians, nor Geneva vs. Rome;—but humanity rationally free, vs. the clamps of tradition and superstition which had manacled and muzzled it.

The cause of freedom is not the cause of a

race or a sect, a party or a class,—it is the cause of human kind, the very birthright of humanity. Now unless we are greatly mistaken the Reform of our day, known as the Woman's Movement, is essentially such an embodiment, if its pioneers could only realize it, of the universal good. And specially important is it that there be no confusion of ideas among its leaders as to its scope and universality. All mists must be cleared from the eyes of woman if she is to be a teacher of morals and manners: the former strikes its roots in the individual and its training and pruning may be accomplished by classes; but the latter is to lubricate the joints and minimize the friction of society, and it is important and fundamental that there be no chromatic or other aberration when the teacher is settling the point, " Who is my neighbor ? "

It is not the intelligent woman vs. the ignorant woman; nor the white woman vs. the black, the brown, and the red,—it is not even the cause of woman vs. man. Nay, 'tis woman's strongest vindication for speaking that *the world needs to hear her voice*. It would be subversive of every human interest that the cry of one-half the human family be stifled. Woman in stepping from the pedestal of statue-like inactivity in the domestic shrine, and daring to think and move and speak,—to undertake to help shape, mold, and direct the thought of her age, is merely completing the circle of the world's vision. Hers is every interest that has lacked an interpreter and a defender. Her cause is linked with that of every agony that has been dumb—every wrong that needs a voice.

It is no fault of man's that he has not been able to see truth from her standpoint. It does credit both to his head and heart that no greater mistakes have been committed or even wrongs perpetrated while she sat making tatting and snipping paper flowers. Man's own innate chivalry and the mutual interdependence of their interests have insured his treating her cause, in the main at least, as his own. And he is pardonably surprised and even a little chagrined, perhaps, to find his legislation not considered "perfectly lovely" in every respect. But in any case his work is only impoverished by her remaining dumb. The world has had to limp along with the wobbling gait and one-sided hesitancy of a man with one eye. Suddenly the bandage is removed from the other eye and the whole body is filled with light. It sees a circle where before it saw a segment. The darkened eye restored, every member rejoices with it.

What a travesty of its case for this eye to become plaintiff in a suit, *Eye vs. Foot.* " There is that dull clod, the foot, allowed to roam at will, free and untrammelled; while I, the source and medium of light, brilliant and beautiful, am fettered in darkness and doomed to desuetude." The great burly black man, ignorant and gross and depraved, is allowed to vote; while the franchise is withheld from the intelligent and refined, the pure-minded and lofty souled white woman. Even the un- tamed and untamable Indian of the prairie, who can answer nothing but ' ugh ' to great economic and civic questions is thought by some worthy to wield the ballot which is still denied the Puritan maid and the first lady of Virginia.

Is not this hitching our wagon to something much lower than a star? Is not woman's cause broader, and deeper, and grander, than a blue stocking debate or an aristocratic pink tea? Why should woman become plaintiff in a suit versus the Indian, or the Negro or any other race or class who have been crushed under the iron heel of Anglo-Saxon power and selfishness? If the Indian has been

wronged and cheated by the puissance of this
American government, it is woman's mission
to plead with her country to cease to do evil
and to pay its honest debts. If the Negro has
been deceitfully cajoled or inhumanly cuffed
according to selfish expediency or capricious
antipathy, let it be woman's mission to plead
that he be met as a man and honestly given
half the road. If woman's own happiness has
been ignored or misunderstood in our country's legislating for bread winners, for rum sel-
lers, for property holders, for the family relations, for any or all the interests that touch
her vitally, let her rest her plea, not on Indian
inferiority, nor on Negro depravity, but on
the obligation of legislators to do for her as
they would have others do for them were relations reversed. Let her try to teach her
country that every interest in this world is
entitled at least to a respectful hearing, that
every sentiency is worthy of its own gratification, that a helpless cause should not be
trampled down, nor a bruised reed broken;
and when the right of the individual is made
sacred, when the image of God in human
form, whether in marble or in clay, whether
in alabaster or in ebony, is consecrated and
inviolable, when men have been taught to

look beneath the rags and grime, the pomp
and pageantry of mere circumstance and have
regard unto the celestial kernel uncontami-
nated at the core,—when race, color, sex, condition, are realized to be the accidents, not the
substance of life, and consequently as not ob-
scuring or modifying the inalienable title to
life, liberty, and pursuit of happiness,—then is
mastered the science of politeness, the art of
courteous contact, which is naught but the
practical application of the principal of benevolence, the back bone and marrow of all religion; then woman's lesson is taught and
woman's cause is won—not the white woman
nor the black woman nor the red woman, but
the cause of every man or woman who has
writhed silently under a mighty wrong. The
pleading of the American woman for the
right and the opportunity to employ the
American method of influencing the disposal
to be made of herself, her property, her children in civil, economic, or domestic relations
is thus seen to be based on a principle as
broad as the human race and as old as human
society. Her wrongs are thus indissolubly
linked with all undefended woe, all helpless
suffering, and the plenitude of her " rights "
will mean the final triumph of all right over

might, the supremacy of the moral forces of reason and justice and love in the government of the nation.

God hasten the day.

THE STATUS OF WOMAN IN AMERICA.

JUST four hundred years ago an obscure dreamer and castle builder, prosaically poor and ridiculously insistent on the reality of his dreams, was enabled through the devotion of a noble woman to give to civilization a magnificent continent.

What the lofty purpose of Spain's pure-minded queen had brought to the birth, the untiring devotion of pioneer women nourished and developed. The dangers of wild beasts and of wilder men, the mysteries of unknown wastes and unexplored forests, the horrors of pestilence and famine, of exposure and loneli-ness, during all those years of discovery and settlement, were braved without a murmur by women who had been most delicately con-stituted and most tenderly nurtured.

And when the times of physical hardship and danger were past, when the work of clearing and opening up was over and the struggle for accumulation began, again woman's inspiration and help were needed and still was she loyally at hand. A Mary Lyon, demanding and making possible equal advantages of education for women as for men, and, in the face of discouragement and incredulity, bequeathing to women the opportunities of Holyoke.

A Dorothea Dix, insisting on the humane and rational treatment of the insane and bringing about a reform in the lunatic asylums of the country, making a great step forward in the tender regard for the weak by the strong throughout the world.

A Helen Hunt Jackson, convicting the nation of a century of dishonor in regard to the Indian.

A Lucretia Mott, gentle Quaker spirit, with sweet insistence, preaching the abolition of slavery and the institution, in its stead, of the brotherhood of man; her life and words breathing out in tender melody the injunction

> " Have love. Not love alone for one
> But man as man thy brother call ;
> And scatter, like the circling sun,
> Thy charities *on all*."

And at the most trying time of what we have called the Accumulative Period, when internecine war, originated through man's love of gain and his determination to subordinate national interests and black men's rights alike to considerations of personal profit and loss, was drenching our country with its own best blood, who shall recount the name and fame of the women on both sides the senseless strife,—those uncomplaining souls with a great heart ache of their own, rigid features and pallid cheek their ever effective flag of truce, on the battle field, in the camp, in the hospital, binding up wounds, recording dying whispers for absent loved ones, with tearful eyes pointing to man's last refuge, giving the last earthly hand clasp and performing the last friendly office for strangers whom a great common sorrow had made kin, while they knew that somewhere—somewhere a husband, a brother, a father, a son, was being tended by stranger hands—or mayhap those familiar eyes were even then being closed forever by just such another ministering angel of mercy and love.

But why mention names? Time would fail to tell of the noble army of women who shine like beacon lights in the otherwise sordid wilderness of this accumulative period—prison reformers and tenement cleansers, quiet unnoted workers in hospitals and homes, among imbeciles, among outcasts—the sweetening, purifying antidotes for the poisons of man's acquisitiveness,—mollifying and soothing with the tenderness of compassion and love the wounds and bruises caused by his overreaching and avarice.

The desire for quick returns and large profits tempts capital ofttimes into unsanitary, well nigh inhuman investments,—tenement tinder boxes, stifling, stunting, sickening alleys and pestiferous slums; regular rents, no waiting, large percentages,—rich coffers coined out of the life-blood of human bodies and souls. Men and women herded together like cattle, breathing in malaria and typhus from an atmosphere seething with moral as well as physical impurity, revelling in vice as their native habitat and then, to drown the whisperings of their higher consciousness and effectually to hush the yearnings and accusations within, flying to narcotics and opiates— rum, tobacco, opium, binding hand and foot, body and soul, till the proper image of God is transformed into a fit associate for demons,— a besotted, enervated, idiotic wreck, or else a monster of wickedness terrible and destructive.

These are some of the legitimate products of the unmitigated tendencies of the wealth-producing period. But, thank Heaven, side by side with the cold, mathematical, selfishly calculating, so-called practical and unsentimental instinct of the business man, there comes the sympathetic warmth and sunshine of good women, like the sweet and sweetening breezes of spring, cleansing, purifying, soothing, inspiring, lifting the drunkard from the gutter, the outcast from the pit. Who can estimate the influence of these " daughters of the king," these lend-a-hand forces, in counteracting the selfishness of an acquisitive age?

To-day America counts her millionaires by the thousand; questions of tariff and questions of currency are the most vital ones agitating the public mind. In this period, when material prosperity and well earned ease and luxury are assured facts from a national standpoint, woman's work and woman's influence are needed as never before; needed to bring a heart power into this money getting, dollar-worshipping civilization; needed to bring a moral force into the utilitarian motives and interests of the time; needed to stand for God and Home and Native Land *versus gain and greed and grasping selfishness.*

There can be no doubt that this fourth centenary of America's discovery which we celebrate at Chicago, strikes the keynote of another important transition in the history of this nation; and the prominence of woman in the management of its celebration is a fitting tribute to the part she is destined to play among the forces of the future. This is the first congressional recognition of woman in this country, and this Board of Lady Managers constitute the first women legally appointed by any government to act in a national capacity. This of itself marks the dawn of a new day.

Now the periods of discovery, of settlement, of developing resources and accumulating wealth have passed in rapid succession. Wealth in the nation as in the individual brings leisure, repose, reflection. The struggle with nature is over, the struggle with ideas begins. We stand then, it seems to me, in this last decade of the nineteenth century, just in the portals of a new and untried movement on a higher plain and in a grander strain than any the past has called forth. It does not require a prophet's eye to divine its trend and image its possibilities from the forces we see already at work around us; nor is it hard to guess what must be the status of woman's work under the new regime.

In the pioneer days her role was that of a camp-follower, an additional something to fight for and be burdened with, only repaying the anxiety and labor she called forth by her own incomparable gifts of sympathy and appreciative love; unable herself ordinarily to contend with the bear and the Indian, or to take active part in clearing the wilderness and constructing the home.

In the second or wealth producing period her work is abreast of man's, complementing and supplementing, counteracting excessive tendencies, and mollifying over rigorous proclivities.

In the era now about to dawn, her sentiments must strike the keynote and give the dominant tone. And this because of the nature of her contribution to the world.

Her kingdom is not over physical forces. Not by might, nor by power can she prevail. Her position must ever be inferior where strength of muscle creates leadership. If she follows the instincts of her nature, however, she must always stand for the conservation of those deeper moral forces which make for the happiness of homes and the righteousness of the country. In a reign of moral ideas she is easily queen.

There is to my mind no grander and surer prophecy of the new era and of woman's place in it, than the work already begun in the waning years of the nineteenth century by the W. C. T. U. in America, an organization which has even now reached not only national but international importance, and seems destined to permeate and purify the whole civilized world. It is the living embodiment of woman's activities and woman's ideas, and its extent and strength rightly prefigure her increasing power as a moral factor.

The colored woman of to-day occupies, one may say, a unique position in this country. In a period of itself transitional and unsettled, her status seems one of the least ascertainable and definitive of all the forces which make for our civilization. She is confronted by both a woman question and a race problem, and is as yet an unknown or an unacknowl edged factor in both. While the women of the white race can with calm assurance enter upon the work they feel by nature appointed to do, while their men give loyal support and appreciative countenance to their efforts, recognizing in most avenues of usefulness the propriety and the need of woman's distinctive co-operation, the colored woman too often

finds herself hampered and shamed by a less
liberal sentiment and a more conservative attitude on the part of those for whose opinion
she cares most. That this is not universally
true I am glad to admit. There are to be
found both intensely conservative white men
and exceedingly liberal colored men. But as
far as my experience goes the average man of
our race is less frequently ready to admit the
actual need among the sturdier forces of the
world for woman's help or influence. That
great social and economic questions await her
interference, that she could throw any light
on problems of national import, that her in-
termeddling could improve the management
of school systems, or elevate the tone of public
institutions, or humanize and sanctify the far
reaching influence of prisons and reformatories and improve the treatment of lunatics
and imbeciles, — that she has a word worth
hearing on mooted questions in political economy, that she could contribute a suggestion
on the relations of labor and capital, or offer a
thought on honest money and honorable trade,
I fear the majority of " Americans of the colored variety " are not yet prepared to concede.
It may be that they do not yet see these
questions in their right perspective, being ab-

sorbed in the immediate needs of their own political complications. A good deal depends on where we put the emphasis in this world; and our men are not perhaps to blame if they see everything colored by the light of those agitations in the midst of which they live and move and have their being. The part they have had to play in American history during the last twenty-five or thirty years has tended rather to exaggerate the importance of mere political advantage, as well as to set a fictitious valuation on those able to secure such advantage. It is the astute politician, the manager who can gain preferment for himself and his favorites, the demagogue known to stand in with the powers at the White House and consulted on the bestowal of government plums, whom we set in high places and denominate great. It is they who receive the hosannas of the multitude and are regarded as leaders of the people. The thinker and the doer, the man who solves the problem by enriching his country with an invention worth thousands or by a thought inestimable and precious is given neither bread nor a stone. He is too often left to die in obscurity and neglect even if spared in his life the bitterness of fanatical jealousies and detraction.

And yet politics, and surely American politics, is hardly a school for great minds. Sharpening rather than deepening, it develops the faculty of taking advantage of present emergencies rather than the insight to distinguish between the true and the false, the lasting and the ephemeral advantage. Highly cultivated selfishness rather than consecrated benevolence is its passport to success. Its votaries are never seers. At best they are but manipulators—often only jugglers. It is conducive neither to profound statesmanship nor to the higher type of manhood. Altruism is its *mauvais succes* and naturally enough it is indifferent to any factor which cannot be worked into its own immediate aims and purposes. As woman's influence as a political element is as yet nil in most of the commonwealths of our republic, it is not surprising that with those who place the emphasis on mere political capital she may yet seem almost a nonentity so far as it concerns the solution of great national or even racial perplexities.

There are those, however, who value the calm elevation of the thoughtful spectator who stands aloof from the heated scramble; and, above the turmoil and din of corruption and selfishness, can listen to the teachings of

eternal truth and righteousness. There are
even those who feel that the black man's unjust and unlawful exclusion temporarily from
participation in the elective franchise in certain states is after all but a lesson "in the
desert" fitted to develop in him insight and
discrimination against the day of his own appointed time. One needs occasionally to stand
aside from the hum and rush of human interests and passions to hear the voices of God.
And it not unfrequently happens that the All-
loving gives a great push to certain souls to
thrust them out, as it were, from the distract-
ing current for awhile to promote their discipline and growth, or to enrich them by
communion and reflection. And similarly it
may be woman's privilege from her peculiar
coigne of vantage as a quiet observer, to
whisper just the needed suggestion or the
almost forgotten truth. The colored woman,
then, should not be ignored because her bark
is resting in the silent waters of the sheltered
cove. She is watching the movements of the
contestants none the less and is all the better
qualified, perhaps, to weigh and judge and advise because not herself in the excitement of
the race. Her voice, too, has always been
heard in clear, unfaltering tones, ringing the

changes on those deeper interests which make
for permanent good. She is always sound and
orthodox on questions affecting the well-being
of her race. You do not find the colored
woman selling her birthright for a mess of
pottage. Nay, even after reason has retired
from the contest, she has been known to cling
blindly with the instinct of a turtle dove to
those principles and policies which to her
mind promise hope and safety for children yet
unborn. It is notorious that ignorant black
women in the South have actually left their
husbands' homes and repudiated their support
for what was understood by the wife to be
race disloyalty, or " voting away," as she expresses it, the privileges of herself and little
ones.

It is largely our women in the South to-day
who keep the black men solid in the Republican party. The latter as they increase in intelligence and power of discrimination would
be more apt to divide on local issues at any
rate. They begin to see that the Grand Old
Party regards the Negro's cause as an outgrown issue, and on Southern soil at least
finds a too intimate acquaintanceship with
him a somewhat unsavory recommendation.
Then, too, their political wits have been sharp-

ened to appreciate the fact that it is good policy to cultivate one's neighbors and not depend too much on a distant friend to fight one's home battles. But the black woman can never forget—however lukewarm the party may to-day appear—that it was a Republican president who struck the manacles from her own wrists and gave-the possibilities of manhood to her helpless little ones ; and to her mind a Democratic Negro is a traitor and a time-server. Talk as much as you like of venality and manipulation in the South, there are not many men, I can tell you, who would dare face a wife quivering in every fiber with the consciousness that her husband is a coward who could be paid to desert her deepest and dearest interests.

Not unfelt, then, if unproclaimed has been the work and influence of the colored women of America. Our list of chieftains in the service, though not long, is not inferior in strength and excellence, I dare believe, to any similar list which this country can produce.

Among the pioneers, Frances Watkins Harper could sing with prophetic exaltation in the darkest days, when as yet there was not a rift in the clouds overhanging her people :

"Yes, Ethiopia shall stretch
Her bleeding hands abroad;
Her cry of agony shall reach the burning throne of God.
Redeemed from dust and freed from chains
Her sons shall lift their eyes,
From cloud-capt hills and verdant plains
Shall shouts of triumph rise."

Among preachers of righteousness, an un-answerable silencer of cavilers and objectors, was Sojourner Truth, that unique and rugged genius who seemed carved out without hand or chisel from the solid mountain mass; and in pleasing contrast, Amanda Smith, sweetest of natural singers and pleaders in dulcet tones for the things of God and of His Christ.

Sarah Woodson Early and Martha Briggs, planting and watering in the school room, and giving off from their matchless and irre-sistible personality an impetus and inspiration which can never die so long as there lives and breathes a remote descendant of their disciples and friends.

Charlotte Fortin Grimke, the gentle spirit whose verses and life link her so beautifully with America's great Quaker poet and loving reformer.

Hallie Quinn Brown, charming reader, earn-est, effective lecturer and devoted worker of unflagging zeal and unquestioned power.

Fannie Jackson Coppin, the teacher and organizer, pre-eminent among women of whatever country or race in constructive and executive force.

These women represent all shades of belief and as many departments of activity; but they have one thing in common—their sympathy with the oppressed race in America and the consecration of their several talents in whatever line to the work of its deliverance and development.

Fifty years ago woman's activity according to orthodox definitions was on a pretty clearly cut " sphere," including primarily the kitchen and the nursery, and rescued from the barrenness of prison bars by the womanly mania for adorning every discoverable bit of china or canvass with forlorn looking cranes balanced idiotically on one foot. The woman of to-day finds herself in the presence of responsibilities which ramify through the profoundest and most varied interests of her country and race. Not one of the issues of this plodding, toiling, sinning, repenting, falling, aspiring humanity can afford to shut her out, or can deny the reality of her influence. No plan for renovating society, no scheme for purifying politics, no reform in church or in state, no moral,

social, or economic question, no movement
upward or downward in the human plane is
lost on her. A man once said when told his
house was afire: " Go tell my wife; I never
meddle with household affairs." But no woman can possibly put herself or her sex outside any of the interests that affect humanity.
All departments in the new era are to be hers,
in the sense that her interests are in all and
through all; and it is incumbent on her to
keep intelligently and sympathetically *en rapport* with all the great movements of her time,
that she may know on which side to throw
the weight of her influence. She stands now
at the gateway of this new era of American
civilization. In her hands must be moulded
the strength, the wit, the statesmanship, the
morality, all the psychic force, the social and
economic intercourse of that era. To be alive
at such an epoch is a privilege, to be a woman
then is sublime.

In this last decade of our century, changes
of such moment are in progress, such new and
alluring vistas are opening out before us, such
original and radical suggestions for the adjustment of labor and capital, of government and
the governed, of the family, the church and the
state, that to be a possible factor though an

infinitesimal in such a movement is pregnant
with hope and weighty with responsibility.
To be a woman in such an age carries with it
a privilege and an opportunity never implied
before.   But to be a woman of the Negro race
in America, and to be able to grasp the deep
significance of the possibilities of the crisis, is
to have a heritage, it seems to me, unique in
the ages.   In the first place, the race is young
and full of the elasticity and hopefulness of
youth.   All its achievements are before it.   It
does not look on the masterly triumphs of
nineteenth century civilization with that *blasé*
world-weary look which characterizes the old
washed out and worn out races which have
already, so to speak, seen their best days.

Said a European writer recently: "Except
the Sclavonic, the Negro is the only original
and distinctive genius which has yet to come
to growth—and the feeling is to cherish and
develop it."

Everything to this race is new and strange
and inspiring.   There is a quickening of its
pulses and a glowing of its self-consciousness.
Aha, I can rival that!   I can aspire to that!
I can honor my name and vindicate my race!
Something like this, it strikes me, is the enthusiasm which stirs the genius of young

Africa in America; and the memory of past
oppression and the fact of present attempted
repression only serve to gather momentum for
its irrepressible powers. Then again, a race
in such a stage of growth is peculiarly sensitive
to impressions. Not the photographer's sensi-
tized plate is more delicately impressionable to
outer influences than is this high strung people
here on the threshold of a career.

What a responsibility then to have the sole
management of the primal lights and shadows!
Such is the colored woman's office. She must
stamp weal or woe on the coming history of
this people. May she see her opportunity and
vindicate her high prerogative.

TUTTI AD LIBITUM.

———

A *People* is but the attempt of many
To rise to the completer life of one.

* * *

The common *Problem*, yours, mine, every one's
Is—not to fancy what were fair in life
Provided it could be,—but, finding first
What may be, then find how to make it fair
Up to our means ; a very different thing !

     —*Robert Browning.*

 The greatest question in the world is how to give every man a man's share in what goes on in life—we want a freeman's share, and that is to think and speak and act about what concerns us all, and see whether these fine gentlemen who undertake to govern us are doing the best they can for us.—*Felix Holt.*

HAS AMERICA A RACE PROBLEM.; IF SO, HOW CAN IT BEST BE SOLVED?

——

THERE are two kinds of peace in this world. The one produced by suppression, which is the passivity of death; the other brought about by a proper adjustment of living, acting forces. A nation or an individual may be at peace because all opponents have been killed or crushed; or, nation as well as individual may have found the secret of true harmony in the determination to live and let live.

A harmless looking man was once asked how many there were in his family.

"Ten," he replied grimly; "my wife's a one and I a zero." In that family there was harmony, to be sure, but it was the harmony of a despotism—it was the quiet of a muzzled mouth, the smoldering peace of a volcano crusted over.

Now I need not say that peace produced by suppression is neither natural nor desirable. Despotism is not one of the ideas that man has copied from nature. All through God's universe we see eternal harmony and symmetry as the unvarying result of the equilibrium of opposing forces. Fair play in an equal fight is the law written in Nature's book. And the solitary bully with his foot on the breast of his last antagonist has no warrant in any fact of God.

The beautiful curves described by planets and suns in their courses are the resultant of conflicting forces. Could the centrifugal force for one instant triumph, or should the centripetal grow weary and give up the struggle, immeasurable disaster would ensue—earth, moon, sun would go spinning off at a tangent or must fall helplessly into its master sphere. The acid counterbalances and keeps in order the alkali; the negative, the positive electrode. A proper equilibrium between a most inflammable explosive and the supporter of combustion, gives us water, the bland fluid that we cannot dispense with. Nay, the very air we breathe, which seems so calm, so peaceful, is

rendered innocuous only by the constant conflict of opposing gases. Were the fiery, never-
resting, all-corroding oxygen to gain the mastery we should be burnt to cinders in a trice.
With the sluggish, inert nitrogen triumphant,
we should die of inanition.

These facts are only a suggestion of what
must be patent to every student of history.
Progressive peace in a nation is the result of
conflict; and conflict, such as is healthy, stim-
ulating, and progressive, is produced through
the co-existence of radically opposing or
racially different elements. Bellamy's ox-like
men pictured in *Looking Backward*, taking
their daily modicum of provender from the
grandmotherly government, with nothing to
struggle for, no wrong to put down, no reform
to push through, no rights to vindicate and
uphold, are nice folks to read about; but they
are not natural; they are not progressive.
God's world is not governed that way. The
child can never gain strength save by resistance, and there can be no resistance if all
movement is in one direction and all opposition made forever an impossibility.

I confess I can see no deeper reason than
this for the specializing of racial types in the
world. Whatever our theory with reference

to the origin of species and the unity of mankind, we cannot help admitting the fact that no sooner does a family of the human race take up its abode in some little nook between mountains, or on some plain walled in by their own hands, no sooner do they begin in earnest to live their own life, think their own thoughts, and trace out their own arts, than they begin also to crystallize some idea different from and generally opposed to that of other tribes or families.

Each race has its badge, its exponent, its message, branded in its forehead by the great Master's hand which is its own peculiar keynote, and its contribution to the harmony of nations.

Left entirely alone,—out of contact, that is with other races and their opposing ideas and conflicting tendencies, this cult is abnormally developed and there is unity without variety, a predominance of one tone at the expense of moderation and harmony, and finally a sameness, a monotonous dullness which means stagnation,—death.

It is this of which M. Guizot complains in Asiatic types of civilization; and in each case he mentions I note that there was but one race, one free force predominating.

In Lect. II. Hist. of Civ. he says:

" In Egypt the theocratic principle took possession of society and showed itself in its manners, its monuments and in all that has come
down to us of Egyptian civilization. In India
the same phenomenon occurs—a repetition of
the almost exclusively prevailing influence of
theocracy. In other regions the domination
of a conquering caste; where such is the case
the principle of force takes entire possession
of society. In another place we discover
society under the entire influence of the democratic principle. Such was the case in the
commercial republics which covered the coasts
of Asia Minor and Syria, in Ionia and Phœni-
cia. In a word whenever we contemplate the
civilization of the ancients, we find them all
impressed with *one ever prevailing character of
unity*, visible in their institutions, their ideas
and manners; *one sole influence seems to govern
and determine all things*. . . . . In one nation,
as in Greece, the unity of the social principle
led to a development of wonderful rapidity ;
no other people ever ran so brilliant a career
in so short a time. But Greece had hardly
become glorious before she appeared worn
out. Her decline was as sudden as her rise had
been rapid. It seems as if the principle which

called Greek civilization into life was exhausted. No other came to invigorate it or
supply its place. In India and Egypt where
again only one principle of civilization pre-
vailed (*one race predominant you see*) society
became stationary. Simplicity produced monotony. Society continued to exist, but there
was no progression. It remained torpid and
inactive."

Now I beg you to note that in none of these
systems was a RACE PROBLEM possible. The
dominant race had settled that matter forever.
Asiatic society was fixed in cast iron molds.
Virtually there was but one race inspiring and
molding the thought, the art, the literature,
the government. It was against this shrivelling caste prejudice and intolerance that the
zealous Buddha set his face like a flint. And
I do not think it was all blasphemy in Renan
when he said Jesus Christ was first of democrats, i. e., a believer in the royalty of the individual, a preacher of the brotherhood of
man through the fatherhood of God, a teacher
who proved that the lines on which worlds are
said to revolve are *imaginary*, that for all the
distinctions of blue blood and black blood and
red blood—*a man's a man for a' that.* Buddha
and the Christ, each in his own way, wrought

to rend asunder the clamps and bands of caste, and to thaw out the ice of race tyranny and exclusiveness. The Brahmin, who was Aryan, spurned a suggestion even, from the Sudra, who belonged to the hated and proscribed Turanian race. With a Pariah he could not eat or drink. They were to him outcasts and unclean. Association with them meant contamination; the hint of their social equality was blasphemous. Respectful consideration for their rights and feelings was almost a physical no less than a moral impossibility.

No more could the Helots among the Greeks have been said to contribute anything to the movement of their times. The dominant race had them effectually under its heel. It was the tyranny and exclusiveness of these nations, therefore, which brought about their immobility and resulted finally in the barrenness of their one idea. From this came the poverty and decay underlying their civilization, from this the transitory, ephemeral character of its brilliancy.

To quote Guizot again : " Society belonged to *one exclusive* power which could bear with no other. Every principle of a different tendency was proscribed. The governing principle would nowhere suffer by its side the

manifestation and influence of a rival principle. This character of unity in their civilization is equally impressed upon their literature
and intellectual productions. Those monuments of Hindoo literature lately introduced
into Europe seem all struck from the same
die. They all seem the result of one same
fact, the expression of one idea. Religious and moral treatises, historical traditions,
dramatic poetry, epics, all bear the same
physiognomy. The same character of unity
and monotony shines out in these works
of mind and fancy, as we discover in
their life and institutions." Not even Greece
with all its classic treasures is made an exception from these limitations produced by ex-
clusivness.

But the course of empire moves one degree
westward. Europe becomes the theater of the
leading exponents of civilization, and here we
have a *Race Problem*,—if, indeed, the confused
jumble of races, the clash and conflict, the din
and devastation of those stormy years can be
referred to by so quiet and so dignified a term
as "problem." Complex and appalling it
surely was. Goths and Huns, Vandals and
Danes, Angles, Saxons, Jutes—could any
prophet foresee that a vestige of law and order,

of civilization and refinement would remain after this clumsy horde of wild barbarians had swept over Europe?

"Where is somebody'll give me some white for all this yellow?" cries one with his hands full of the gold from one of those magnificent monuments of antiquity which he and his tribe had just pillaged and demolished. Says the historian: "Their history is like a history of kites and crows." Tacitus writes: "To shout, to drink, to caper about, to feel their veins heated and swollen with wine, to hear and see around them the riot of the orgy, this was the first need of the barbarians. The heavy human brute gluts himself with sensations and with noise."

Taine describes them as follows:

"Huge white bodies, cool-blooded, with fierce blue eyes, reddish flaxen hair; ravenous stomachs, filled with meat and cheese, heated by strong drinks. Brutal drunken pirates and robbers, they dashed to sea in their two-sailed barks, landed anywhere, killed everything; and, having sacrificed in honor of their gods the tithe of all their prisoners, leaving behind the red light of their burning, went farther on to begin again."

A certain litany of the time reads: "From

the fury of the Jutes, Good Lord deliver us."
"Elgiva, the wife of one of their kings," says
a chronicler of the time, "they hamstrung
and subjected to the death she deserved;" and
their heroes are frequently represented as
tearing out the heart of their human victim
and eating it while it still quivered with life.

A historian of the time, quoted by Taine,
says it was the custom to buy men and women
in all parts of England and to carry them to
Ireland for sale.   The buyers usually made the
women pregnant and took them to market in
that condition to ensure a better price.   "You
might have seen," continues the historian,
"long files of young people of both sexes and
of great beauty, bound with ropes and daily
exposed for sale.   They sold as slaves in this
manner, their nearest relatives and even their
own children."

What could civilization hope to do with
such a swarm of sensuous, bloodthirsty vipers?
Assimilation was horrible to contemplate.
They will drag us to their level, quoth the
culture of the times.   Deportation was out of
the question; and there was no need to talk
of their emigrating.   The fact is, the barbarians were in no hurry about moving.   They
didn't even care to colonize.   They had come

to stay. And Europe had to grapple with
her race problem till time and God should
solve it.

And how was it solved, and what kind of
civilization resulted?

Once more let us go to Guizot. " Take ever
so rapid a glance," says he, " at modern Europe
and it strikes you at once as diversified, confused, and stormy. All the principles of social
organization are found existing together within
it; powers temporal, and powers spiritual, the
theocratic, monarchic, aristocratic, and democratic elements, all classes of society *in a state
of continual struggle* without any one having
sufficient force to master the others and take
sole possession of society." Then as to the
result of this conflict of forces: "Incomparably more rich and diversified than the ancient,
European civilization 'has within it the promise of *perpetual progress*. It has now endured
more than fifteen centuries and in all that
time has been in a state of progression, not so
rapidly as the Greek nor yet so ephemeral.
While in other civilizations the exclusive
domination of a principle (*or race*) led to
tyranny, in Europe the diversity of social elements (*growing out of the contact of different
races*) the incapability of any one to exclude

the rest, gave birth to the LIBERTY which now prevails. This inability of the various principles to exterminate one another compelled each to endure the others and made it necessary for them in order to live in common to enter into a sort of mutual understanding. Each consented to have only that part of civilization which equitably fell to its share. Thus, while everywhere else the predominance of one principle produced tyranny, the variety and warfare of the elements of European civilization gave birth to *reciprocity and liberty.*"

There is no need to quote further. This is enough to show that the law holds good in sociology as in the world of matter, *that equilibrium, not repression among conflicting forces is the condition of natural harmony, of permanent progress, and of universal freedom.* That exclusiveness and selfishness in a family, in a community, or in a nation is suicidal to progress. Caste and prejudice mean immobility. One race predominance means death. The community that closes its gates against foreign talent can never hope to advance beyond a certain point. Resolve to keep out foreigners and you keep out progress. Home talent develops its one idea and then dies. Like the century plant it produces its one flower, brilliant and beautiful it may be, but it lasts only for a night. Its forces have exhausted themselves in that one effort. Nothing remains but to wither and to rot.

It was the Chinese wall that made China in 1800 A. D. the same as China in the days of Confucius. Its women have not even yet learned that they need not bandage their feet if they do not relish it. The world has rolled on, but within that wall the thoughts, the fashions, the art, the tradition, and the beliefs are those of a thousand years ago. Until very recently, the Chinese were wholly out of the current of human progress. They were like gray headed infants — a man of eighty years with the concepts and imaginings of a babe of eight months. A civilization measured by thousands of years with a development that might be comprised within as many days — arrested development due to exclusive living.

But European civilization, rich as it was compared to Asiatic types, was still not the consummation of the ideal of human possibilities. One more degree westward the hand on the dial points. In Europe there was conflict, but the elements crystallized out in isolated nodules, so to speak. Italy has her dominant principle, Spain hers, France hers, England hers, and so on. The proximity is close enough for interaction and mutual restraint, though the acting forces are at different points. To preserve the balance of power, which is nothing more than the equilibrium of warring elements, England can be trusted to keep an eye on her beloved step-relation-in-law, Russia,— and Germany no doubt can be relied on to look after France and some others. It is not, however, till the scene changes and America is made the theater of action, that the interplay of forces narrowed down to a single platform.

Hither came Cavalier and Roundhead, Baptist and Papist, Quaker, Ritualist, Freethinker and Mormon, the conservative Tory, the liberal Whig, and the radical Independent,— the Spaniard, the Frenchman, the Englishman, the Italian, the Chinaman, the African, Swedes, Russians, Huns, Bohemians, Gypsies, Irish, Jews. Here surely was a seething caldron of conflicting elements. Religious intolerance and political hatred, race prejudice and caste pride—

> " Double, double, toil and trouble ;
> Fire burn and cauldron bubble."

Conflict, Conflict, Conflict.

America for Americans! This is the white man's country! The Chinese must go, shrieks the exclusionist. Exclude the Italians! Colonize the blacks in Mexico or deport them to Africa. Lynch, suppress, drive out, kill out! America for Americans!

"*Who are Americans?*" comes rolling back from ten million throats. Who are to do the packing and delivering of the goods? Who are the homefolks and who are the strangers? Who are the absolute and original tenants in fee-simple?

The red men used to be owners of the soil, —but they are about to be pushed over into the Pacific Ocean. They, perhaps, have the best right to call themselves "Americans" by law of primogeniture. They are at least the oldest inhabitants of whom we can at present identify any traces. If early settlers from abroad merely are meant and it is only a question of squatters' rights—why, the Mayflower, a pretty venerable institution, landed in the year of Grace 1620, and the first delegation from Africa just one year ahead of that,—in 1819. The first settlers seem to have been almost as much mixed as we are on this point; and it does not seem at all easy to decide just what individuals we mean when we yell " America for the Americans." At least the cleavage cannot be made by hues and noses, if we are to seek for the genuine F. F. V.'s as the inhabitants best entitled to the honor of that name.

The fact is this nation was foreordained to conflict from its incipiency. Its elements were predestined from their birth to an irrepressible clash followed by the stable equilibrium of opposition. Exclusive possession belongs to none. There never was a point in its history when it did. There was never a time since America became a nation when there were not more than one race, more than one party, more than one belief contending for supremacy. Hence no one is or can be supreme. All interests must be consulted, all claims conciliated. Where a hundred free forces are lustily clamoring for recognition and each wrestling mightily for the mastery, individual tyrannies must inevitably be chiselled down, individual bigotries worn smooth and malleable, individual prejudices either obliterated or concealed. America is not from choice more than of necessity republic in form and democratic in administration. The will of the majority must rule simply because no class, no family, no individual has ever been able to prove sufficient political legitimacy to impose their yoke on the country. All attempts at establishing oligarchy must be made by wheedling and cajoling, pretending that not supremacy but service is sought. The nearest approach to outspoken self-assertion is in the conciliatory tones of candid compromise. " I will let you enjoy that if you will not hinder me in the pursuit of this " has been the American sovereign's home policy since his first Declaration of Independence was inscribed as his policy abroad. Compromise and concession, liberality and toleration were the conditions of the nation's birth and are the *sine qua non* of its continued existence. A general amnesty and universal reciprocity are the only *modus vivendi* in a nation whose every citizen is his own king, his own priest and his own pope.

De Tocqueville, years ago, predicted that republicanism must fail in America. But if republicanism fails, America fails, and somehow I can not think this colossal stage was erected for a tragedy. I must confess to being an optimist on the subject of my country. It is true we are too busy making history, and have been for some years past, to be able to write history yet, or to understand and in-

terpret it. Our range of vision is too short
for us to focus and image our conflicts. Indeed Von Holtz, the clearest headed of calm
spectators, says he doubts if the history of
American conflict can be written yet even by
a disinterested foreigner. The clashing of
arms and the din of battle, the smoke of can-
non and the heat of combat, are not yet
cleared away sufficiently for us to have the
judicial vision of historians. Our jottings are
like newspaper reports written in the saddle,
mid prancing steeds and roaring artillery.

But of one thing we may be sure: the God
of battles is in the conflicts of history. The
evolution of civilization is His care, eternal
progress His delight. As the European was
higher and grander than the Asiatic, so will
American civilization be broader and deeper
and closer to the purposes of the Eternal than
any the world has yet seen. This the last
page is to mark the climax of history, the
bright consummate flower unfolding *charity
toward all and malice toward none*,— the final
triumph of universal reciprocity born of universal conflict with forces that cannot be ex-
terminated. Here at last is an arena in which
every agony has a voice and free speech. Not
a spot where no wrong can exist, but where

each feeblest interest can cry with Themisto-
cles, " *Strike, but hear me!* " Here you will
not see as in Germany women hitched to a
cart with donkeys; not perhaps because men
are more chivalrous here than there, but because woman can speak. Here labor will not
be starved and ground to powder, because the
laboring man can make himself heard. Here
races that are weakest can, *if they so elect*, make
themselves felt.

The supremacy of one race,— the despotism
of a class or the tyranny of an individual can
not ultimately prevail on a continent held in
equilibrium by such conflicting forces and by
so many and such strong fibred races as there
are struggling on this soil. Never in America
shall one man dare to say as Germany's somewhat bumptious emperor is fond of proclaim-
ing : " There is only one master in the country
and I am he. I shall suffer no other beside
me. Only to God and my conscience am I
accountable." The strength of the opposition
tones down and polishes off all such ugly excrescencies as that. " I am the State," will
never be proclaimed above a whisper on a
platform where there is within arm's length
another just as strong, possibly stronger, who
holds, or would like to hold that identical

proposition with reference to himself. In this arena then is to be the last death struggle of political tyranny, of religious bigotry, and intellectual intolerance, of caste illiberality and class exclusiveness. And the last monster that shall be throttled forever methinks is race prejudice. Men will here learn that a race, as a family, may be true to itself without seeking to exterminate all others. That for the note of the feeblest there is room, nay a positive need, in the harmonies of God. That the principles of true democracy are founded in universal reciprocity, and that "A man's a man" was written when God first stamped His own image and superscription on His child and breathed into his nostrils the breath of life. And I confess I can pray for no nobler destiny for my country than that it may be the stage, however far distant in the future, whereon these ideas and principles shall ultimately mature; and culminating here at whatever cost of production shall go forth hence to dominate the world.

Methought I saw a mighty conflagration, plunging and heaving, surging and seething, smoking and rolling over this American continent. Strong men and wise men stand helpless in mute consternation. Empty headed babblers add the din of their bray to the crashing and crackling of the flames. But the hungry flood rolls on. The air is black with smoke and cinders. The sky is red with lurid light. Forked tongues of fiery flame dart up and lick the pale stars, and seem to laugh at men's feebleness and frenzy. As I look on I think of Schiller's sublime characterization of fire: "Frightful becomes this God-power, when it snatches itself free from fetters and stalks majestically forth on its own career—the free daughter of Nature." Ingenuity is busy with newly patented snuffers all warranted to extinguish the flame. The street gamin with a hooked wire pulls out a few nuggets that chanced to be lying on the outskirts where they were cooked by the heat; and gleefully cries "What a nice fire to roast my chestnuts," and like little Jack Horner, "what a nice boy am I!"

Meantime this expedient, that expedient, the other expedient is suggested by thinkers and theorizers hoping to stifle the angry, roaring, devouring demon and allay the mad destruction.

> "Wehe wenn sie losgelassen,
> Wachsend ohne Widerstand,
> Durch die volkbelebten Gassen
> Walzt den ungeheuren Brand!"

But the strength of the Omnipotent is in it.
The hand of God is leading it on. It matters
not whether you and I in mad desperation
cast our quivering bodies into it as our funeral
pyre; or whether, like the street urchins, we
pull wires to secure the advantage of the passing moment. We can neither help it nor
hinder; only

> " Let thy gold be cast in the furnace,
>   Thy red gold, precious and bright.
> Do not fear the hungry fire
>   With its caverns of burning light."

If it takes the dearest idol, the pet theory or
the darling 'ism', the pride, the selfishness,
the prejudices, the exclusiveness, the bigotry
and intolerance, the conceit of self, of race, or
of family superiority,— nay, if it singe from
thee thy personal gratifications in thy distinction by birth, by blood, by sex—everything,—
and leave thee nothing but thy naked manhood, solitary and unadorned,— let them go—
let them go!

> " And thy gold shall return more precious,
>   Free from every spot and stain,
>   For gold must be tried by fire."

And the heart of nations must be tried by
pain; and their polish, their true culture must
be wrought in through conflict.

Has America a Race Problem?

Yes.

What are you going to do about it?

Let it alone and mind my own business. It is God's problem and He will solve it in time. It is deeper than Gehenna. What can you or I do!

Are there then no duties and special lines of thought growing out of the present conditions of this problem?

Certainly there are. *Imprimis;* let every element of the conflict see that it represent a positive force so as to preserve a proper equipoise in the conflict. No shirking, no skulking, no masquerading in another's uniform. Stand by your guns. And be ready for the charge. The day is coming, and now is, when America must ask each citizen not " who was your grandfather and what the color of his cuticle," but " *What can you do?*" Be ready each individual element,—each race, each class, each family, each man to reply " *I engage to undertake an honest man's share.*"

God and time will work the problem. You and I are only to stand for the quantities *at their best*, which he means us to represent.

Above all, for the love of humanity stop the mouth of those learned theorizers, the expedient mongers, who come out annually with their new and improved method of getting the answer and clearing the slate: amalgamation, deportation, colonization and all the other ations that were ever devised or dreampt of. If Alexander wants to be a god, let him; but don't have Alexander hawking his patent plan for universal deification. If all could or would follow Alexander's plan, just the niche in the divine cosmos meant for man would be vacant. And we think that men have a part to play in this great drama no less than gods, and so if a few are determined to be white—amen, so be it; but don't let them argue as if there were no part to be played in life by black men and black women, and as if to become white were the sole specific and panacea for all the ills that flesh is heir to—the universal solvent for all America's irritations. And again, if an American family of whatever condition or hue takes a notion to reside in Africa or in Mexico, or in the isles of the sea, it is most un-American for any power on this continent to seek to gainsay or obstruct their departure; but on the other hand, no power or element of power on this continent, least of all a self-constituted tribunal of " recent arrivals," dossesses the right to begin figuring beforehand to calculate what it would require *to send* ten millions of citizens, whose ancestors have wrought here from the planting of the nation, to the same places at so much per head—at least till some one has consulted those heads.

We would not deprecate the fact, then, that America has a Race Problem. It is guaranty of the perpetuity and progress of her institutions, and insures the breadth of her culture and the symmetry of her development. More than all, let us not disparage the factor which the Negro is appointed to contribute to that problem. America needs the Negro for ballast if for nothing else. His tropical warmth and spontaneous emotionalism may form no unseemly counterpart to the cold and calculating Anglo-Saxon. And then his instinct for law and order, his inborn respect for authority, his inaptitude for rioting and anarchy, his gentleness and cheerfulness as a laborer, and his deep-rooted faith in God will prove indispensable and invaluable elements in a nation menaced as America is by anarchy, socialism, communism, and skepticism poured in with all the jail birds from the continents of Europe and Asia. I believe with our own Dr. Crummell that " the Almighty does not preserve, rescue, and build up a lowly people merely for ignoble ends." And the historian of American civilization will yet congratulate this country that she has had a Race Problem and that descendants of the black race furnished one of its largest factors.

ONE PHASE OF AMERICAN LITERATURE.

———

FOR nations as for individuals, a product, to be worthy the term literature, must contain something characteristic and *sui generis*.

So long as America remained a mere English colony, drawing all her life and inspiration from the mother country, it may well be questioned whether there was such a thing as American literature. " Who ever reads an American book? " it was scornfully asked in the eighteenth century. Imitation is the worst of suicides; it cuts the nerve of originality and condemns to mediocrity: and 'twas not till the pen of our writers was dipped in the life blood of their own nation and pictured out its own peculiar heart throbs and agonies that the world cared to listen. The nightingale and the skylark had to give place to the mocking bird, the bobolink and the whippoorwill, the heather and the blue bells of Britain, to our own golden-rod and daisy; the insular and monarchic customs and habits of thought of old England must develop into the broader, looser, freer swing of democratic America, before her contributions to the world of thought could claim the distinction of individuality and gain an appreciative hearing.

And so our writers have succeeded in becoming national and representative in proportion as they have from year to year entered more and more fully, and more and more sympathetically, into the distinctive life of their nation, and endeavored to reflect and picture its homeliest pulsations and its elemental components. And so in all the arts, as men have gradually come to realize that

> Nothing useless is or low
> Each thing in its place is best,

and have wrought into their products, lovingly and impartially and reverently, every type, every tint, every tone that they felt or saw or heard, just to that degree have their expressions, whether by pen or brush or rhythmic cadence, adequately and simply given voice to the thought of Nature around them. No man can prophesy with another's parable. For each of us truth means merely the re-presentation of the sensations and experiences of our personal environment, colored and vivified—fused into consistency and crytallized into individuality in the crucible of our own feelings and imaginations. The mind of genius is merely the brook, picturing back its own tree and bush and bit of sky and cloud ensparkled by individual salts and sands and rippling motion. And paradoxical as it may seem, instead of making us narrow and provincial, this trueness to one's habitat, this appreciative eye and ear for the tints and voices of one's own little wood serves but to usher us into the eternal galleries and choruses of God. It is only through the unclouded perception of our tiny " part " that we can come to harmonize with the " stupendous whole," and in order to this our sympathies must be finely attuned and quick to vibrate under the touch of the commonplace and vulgar no less than at the hand of the elegent and refined. Nothing natural can be wholly unworthy; and we do so at our peril, if, what God has cleansed we presume to call common or unclean. Nature's language is not writ in cipher. Her notes are always simple and sensuous, and the very meanest recesses and commonest byways are fairly deafening with her sermons and songs. It is only when we ourselves are out of tune through our pretentiousness and self-sufficiency, or are blinded and rendered insensate by reason of our foreign and unnatural " cultivation " that we miss her meanings and inadequately construe her multiform lessons.

For two hundred and fifty years there was in the American commonwealth a great *silent* factor. Though in themselves simple and unique their offices were those of the barest utility. Imported merely to be hewers of wood and drawers of water, no artist for many a generation thought them worthy the sympathetic study of a model. No Shakespeare arose to distil from their unmatched personality and unparalleled situations the exalted poesy and crude grandeur of an immortal Caliban. Distinct in color, original in temperament, simple and unconventionalized in thought and action their spiritual development and impressionability under their novel environment would have furnished, it might seem, as interesting a study in psychology for the poetic pen, as would the gorges of the Yosemite to the inspired pencil. Full of vitality and natural elasticity, the severest persecution and oppression could not kill them out or even sour their temper. With massive brawn and indefatigable endurance they wrought under burning suns and chilling blasts, in swamps and marshes,—they cleared the forests, tunneled mountains, threaded the land with railroads, planted, picked and ginned the cotton, produced the rice and the sugar for the markets of the world. Without money and without price they poured their hearts' best blood into the enriching and developing of this country. *They wrought but were silent.*

The most talked about of all the forces in this diversified civilization, they seemed the great American fact, the one objective reality, on which scholars sharpened their wits, at which orators and statesmen fired their eloquence, and from which, after so long a time, authors, with varied success and truthfulness have begun at last to draw subjects and models. Full of imagination and emotion, their sensuous pictures of the " New Jerusalem," " the golden slippers," " the long white robe," " the pearly gates," etc., etc., seem fairly to steam with tropical luxuriance and naive abandon. The paroxysms of religious fervor into which this simple-minded, child-like race were thrown by the contemplation of Heaven and rest and freedom, would have melted into sympathy and tender pity if not into love, a race less cold and unresponsive than the one with which they were thrown in closest contact. There was something truly poetic in their weird moanings, their fitful gleams of hope and trust, flickering amidst the darkness of their wailing helplessness, their strange sad songs, the half coherent ebullitions of souls in pain, which become, the more they are studied, at once the wonder and the despair of musical critics and imitators. And if one had the insight and the simplicity to gather together, to digest and assimilate these original lispings of an unsophisticated people while they were yet close—so close—to nature and to nature's God, there is material here, one might almost believe, as rich, as unhackneyed, as original and distinctive as ever inspired a Homer, or a Cædmon or other simple genius of a people's infancy and lisping childhood.

In the days of their bitterest persecution, their patient endurance and Christian manliness inspired Uncle Tom's Cabin, which revolutionized the thought of the world on the subject of slavery and at once placed its author in the front rank of the writers of her country and age. Here at last was a work which England could not parallel. Here was a work indigenous to American soil and characteristic of the country — a work which American forces alone could have produced. The subject was at once seen to be fresh and interesting to the world as well as national and peculiar to America; and so it has since been eagerly cultivated by later writers with widely varying degrees of fitness and success.

By a rough classification, authors may be separated into two groups: first, those in whom the artistic or poetic instinct is uppermost—those who write to please—or rather who write because *they* please; who simply paint what they see, as naturally, as instinctively, and as irresistibly as the bird sings— with no thought of an audience—singing because it loves to sing,—singing because God, nature, truth sings through it. For such writers, to be true to themselves and true to Nature is the only canon. They cannot warp a character or distort a fact in order to prove a point. They have nothing to prove. All who care to, may listen while they make the woods resound with their glad sweet carolling; and the listeners may draw their own conclusions as to the meaning of the cadences of this minor strain, or that hushed and almost awful note of rage or despair. And the myriad-minded multitude attribute their myriad-fold impressions to the myriad-minded soul by which they have severally been enchanted, each in his own way according to what he brings to the witching auditorium. But the singer sings on with his hat before his face, unmindful, it may be unconscious, of the varied strains reproduced from him in the multitudinous echoes of the crowd. Such was Shakespeare, such was George Eliot, such was Robert Browning. Such, in America, was Poe, was Bryant, was Longfellow; and such, in his own degree perhaps, is Mr. Howells.

In the second group belong the preachers,—whether of righteousness or unrighteousness,—all who have an idea to propagate, no matter in what form their talent enables them to clothe it, whether poem, novel, or sermon,—all those writers with a purpose or a lesson, who catch you by the buttonhole and pommel you over the shoulder till you are forced to give assent in order to escape their vociferations; or they may lure you into listening with the soft music of the siren's tongue—no matter what the expedient to catch and hold your attention, they mean to fetter you with their one idea, whatever it is, and make you, if possible, ride their hobby. In this group I

would place Milton in much of his writing,
Carlyle in all of his, often our own Whittier,
the great reformer-poet, and Lowell; together
with such novelists as E. P. Roe, Bellamy,
Tourgee and some others.

Now in my judgment writings of the first
class will be the ones to withstand the ravages
of time. 'Isms' have their day and pass away.
New necessities arise with new conditions and
the emphasis has to be shifted to suit the
times. No finite mind can grasp and give out
the whole circle of truth. We do well if we
can illuminate just the tiny arc which we occupy and should be glad that the next generation will not need the lessons we try so
assiduously to hammer into this. In the evolution of society, as the great soul of humanity
builds it "more lofty chambers," the old shell
and slough of didactic teaching must be left
behind and forgotten. The world for instance
has outgrown, I suspect, those passages of
Paradise Lost in which Milton makes the
Almighty Father propound the theology of a
seventeenth century Presbyterian. But a
passage like the one in which Eve with guile-
less innocence describes her first sensations
on awaking into the world is as perennial
as man.

"That day I oft remember, when from sleep
I first awaked and found myself reposed
Under a shade on flowers, much wondering where
And what I was, whence thither brought and how.
Not distant far from thence a murmuring sound
Of waters issued from a cave, and spread
Into a liquid plain, then stood unmoved
Pure as the expanse of Heaven;

        I thither went
With unexperienced thought and laid me down
On the green bank, to look into the clear
Smooth lake that to me seemed another sky.
As I bent down to look, just opposite
A shape within the watery gleam appeared,
Bending to look on me; I started back,
It started back; but pleased I soon returned,
Pleased it returned as soon with answering looks
Of sympathy and love; there I had fixed
Mine eyes till now,—and pined with vain desire,
Had not a voice thus warned me.

      'What thou seest,
What there thou seest, fair creature, is thyself;
With thee it came and goes; but follow me,
And I will bring thee where no shadow stays
Thy coming and thy soft embraces.'

        What could I do but follow straight
Invisibly thus led?
Till I espied thee, fair indeed and tall,
Under a plantain; yet methought less fair,
Less winning soft, less amiably mild
Than that smooth watery image; back I turned
Thou following criedst aloud, ' Return, fair Eve,
Whom fliest thou? whom thou fliest, of him thou art.
Part of my soul, I seek thee, and thee claim
My other half.' "

This will never cease to throb and thrill as long as man is man and woman is woman.

Now owing to the problematical position at present occupied by descendants of Africans in the American social polity,— growing, I presume, out of the continued indecision in the mind of the more powerful descendants of the Saxons as to whether it is expedient to apply the maxims of their religion to their civil and political relationships,— most of the writers who have hitherto attempted a portrayal of life and customs among the darker race have belonged to our class II: they have all, more or less, had a point to prove or a mission to accomplish, and thus their art has been almost uniformly perverted to serve their ends; and, to add to their disadvantage, most, if not all the writers on this line have been but partially acquainted with the life they wished to delineate and through sheer ignorance ofttimes, as well as from design occasionally, have not been able to put themselves in the darker man's place. The art of " thinking one's self imaginatively into the experiences of others " is not given to all, and it is impossible to acquire it without a background and a substratum of sympathetic knowledge. Without this power our portraits are but death's heads or caricatures and no amount of cudgeling can put into them the movement and reality of life. Not many have had Mrs. Stowe's power because not many have studied with Mrs. Stowe's humility and love. They forget that underneath the black man's form and behavior there is the great bed-rock of humanity, the key to which is the same that unlocks every tribe and kindred of the nations of earth. Some have taken up the subject with a view to establishing evidences of ready formulated theories and preconceptions; and, blinded by their prejudices and antipathies, have altogether abjured all candid and careful study. Others with flippant indifference have performed a few psychological experiments on their cooks and coachmen, and with astounding egotism, and powers of generalization positively bewildering, forthwith aspire to enlighten the world with dissertations on racial traits of the Negro. A few with really-kind intentions and a sincere desire for information have approached the subject as a clumsy microscopist, not quite at home with his instrument, might study a new order of beetle or bug. Not having focused closely enough to obtain a clear-cut view, they begin by telling you that all colored people look exactly alike and end by noting down every chance contortion or idiosyncrasy as a race characteristic. Some of their conclusions remind one of the enterprising German on a tour of research and self improvement through Great Britain, who recommended his favorite sauer kraut both to an Irishman, whom he found sick with fever, and to a Scotchman, who had a cold. On going that way subsequently and finding the Scotchman well and the Irishman dead, he writes: *Mem.—Sauer kraut good for the Scotch but death to the Irish.*

This criticism is not altered by our grateful remembrance of those who have heroically taken their pens to champion the black man's cause. But even here we may remark that a painter may be irreproachable in motive and as benevolent as an angel in intention, nevertheless we have a right to compare his copy with the original and point out in what respects it falls short or is overdrawn; and he should thank us for doing so.

It is in no captious spirit, therefore, that we note a few contributions to this phase of American literature which have been made during the present decade; we shall try to estimate their weight, their tendency, their truthfulness and their lessons, if any, for ourselves.

Foremost among the champions of the black man's cause through the medium of fiction must be mentioned Albion W. Tourgee. No man deserves more the esteem and appreciation of the colored people of this country for his brave words. For ten years he has stood almost alone as the enthusiastic advocate, not of charity and dole to the Negro, but of justice. The volumes he has written upon the subject have probably been read by from five to ten millions of the American people. Look over his list consecrated to one phase or another of the subject: "A Fool's Errand," "A Royal Gentleman," "Bricks without Straw," "An Appeal to Cæsar," "Hot Ploughshares," "Pactolus Prime,"—over three thousand pages —enough almost for a life work, besides an almost interminable quantity published in periodicals.

Mr. Tourgee essays to paint life with the coloring of fiction, and yet, we must say, we do not think him a novelist primarily; that is, novel making with him seems to be a mere incident, a convenient vehicle through which to convey those burning thoughts which he is constantly trying to impress upon the people of America, whether in lecture, stump speech, newspaper column or magazine article. His

power is not that already referred to of thinking himself imaginatively into the experiences
of others. He does not create many men of
many minds. All his offspring are little
Tourgees—they preach his sermons and pray
his prayers.

In "Pactolus Prime," for example, one of
his latest, his hero, a colored bootblack in a
large hotel, is none other than the powerful,
impassioned, convinced and convincing lecturer, Judge Tourgee himself, done over in
ebony. His caustic wit, his sledge hammer
logic, his incisive criticism, his righteous indignation, all reflect the irresistible arguments
of the great pleader for the Negro; and all
the incidents are arranged to enable this bootblack to impress on senators and judges, lawyers, and divines, his plea for justice to the
Negro, along with the blacking and shine
which he skillfully puts on their aristocratic
toes. And so with all the types which Mr.
Tourgee presents — worthy or pitiful ones
always—they uniformly preach or teach, convict or convert. Artistic criticism aside, it is
mainly as a contribution to polemic literature
in favor of the colored man that most of
Tourgee's works will be judged; and we know
of no one who can more nearly put himself in

the Negro's place in resenting his wrongs and pleading for his rights. In presenting truth from the colored American's standpoint Mr. Tourgee excels, we think, in fervency and frequency of utterance any living writer, white or colored. Mr. Cable is brave and just. He wishes to see justice done in the Freedman's case in equity, and we honor and revere him for his earnest manly efforts towards that end. But Mr. Cable does not forget (I see no reason why he should, of course,) that he is a white man, a Southerner and an ex-soldier in the Confederate army. To use his own words, he writes, "with an admiration and affection for the South, that for justice and sincerity yield to none; in a spirit of faithful sonship to a Southern state." Of course this but proves his sincerity, illustrates his candor, and adds weight to the axiomatic justice of a cause which demands such support from a thoroughly disinterested party, or rather a party whose interest and sympathy and affection must be all on the side he criticises and condemns. The passion of the partisan and the bias of the aggrieved can never be charged against him. Mr. Cable's is the impartiality of the judge who condemns his own son or cuts off his own arm. His attitude is judicial, convincing, irreproachable throughout.

Not only the Christian conscience of the South, but also its enlightened self-interest is unquestionably on the side of justice and manly dealing toward the black man; and one can not help feeling that a cause which thus enlists the support and advocacy of the "better self" of a nation must ultimately be invincible: and Mr. Cable, in my judgment, embodies and represents that Christian conscience and enlightened self-interest of the hitherto silent South; he vocalizes and inspires its better self. To him the dishonesty and inhumanity there practiced against the black race is a blot on the scutcheon of that fair land and doomed to bring in its wake untold confusion, disaster, and disgrace. From his calm elevation he sees the impending evil, and with loving solicitude urges his countrymen to flee the wrath to come. Mr. Tourgee, on the other hand, speaks with all the eloquence and passion of the aggrieved party himself. With his whip of fine cords he pitilessly scourges the inconsistencies, the weaknesses and pettiness of the black man's persecutors. The fire is burning within him, he cannot but speak. He has said himself that he deserves no credit for speaking and writing on this subject, for it has taken hold of him and possesses him to the exclusion of almost everything else. Necessity is laid upon him. Not more bound was Saul of Tarsus to consecrate his fiery eloquence to the cause of the persecuted Nazarene than is this white man to throw all the weight of his powerful soul into the plea for justice and Christianity in this American anomaly and huge inconsistency. Not many colored men would have attempted Tourgee's brave defense of Reconstruction and the alleged corruption of Negro supremacy, more properly termed the period of white sullenness and desertion of duty. Not many would have dared, fearlessly as he did, to arraign this country for an enormous pecuniary debt to the colored man for the two hundred and forty-seven years of unpaid labor of his ancestors. Not many could so determinedly have held up the glass of the real Christianity before these believers in a white Christ and these preachers of the gospel, "Suffer the little *white* children to come unto me." We all see the glaring inconsistency and feel the burning shame. We appreciate the incongruity and the indignity of having to stand forever hat in hand as beggars, or be shoved aside as intruders in a country whose resources have been opened up by the unrequited toil of our forefathers. We know that our bill is a true one—that the debt is as real as to any pensioners of our government. But the principles of patience and forbearance, of meekness and charity, have become so ingrained in the Negro character that there is hardly enough self-assertion left to ask as our right that a part of the country's surplus wealth be *loaned* for the education of our children; even though we know that our present poverty is due to the fact that the toil of the last quarter century enriched these coffers, but left us the heirs of crippled, deformed, frost-bitten, horny-handed and empty handed mothers and fathers. Oh, the shame of it!

A coward during the war gets a few scratches and bruises—often in *fleeing from the enemy*—and his heirs are handsomely pensioned by his *grateful* country! But these poor wretches stood every man to his post for two hundred and fifty years, digging trenches, building roads, tunneling mountains, clearing away forests, cultivating the soil in the cotton fields and rice swamps till fingers dropped off, toes were frozen, knees twisted, arms stiff and useless—and when their sons and heirs, with the burdens of helpless parents to support, wish to secure enough education to enable them to make a start in life, *their* grateful country sagely deliberates as to the feasibility of sending them to another undeveloped jungle to show off their talent for unlimited pioneer work in strange climes! The Indian, during the entire occupancy of this country by white men, has stood proudly aloof from all their efforts at development, and presented an unbroken front of hostility to the introduction and spread of civilization. The Negro, though brought into the country by force and compelled under the lash to lend his brawn and sturdy sinews to promote its material growth and prosperity, nevertheless with perfect amiability of temper and adaptability of mental structure has quietly and unhesitatingly accepted its standards and fallen in line with its creeds. He adjusts himself just as readily and as appreciatively, it would seem, to the higher and stricter requirements of freedom and citizenship; and although from beginning to end, nettled and goaded under unprecedented provocation, he has never once shown any general disposition to arise in his might and deluge this country with blood or desolate it with burning, as he might have done. It is no argument to charge weakness as the cause

of his peaceful submission and to sneer at the
" inferiority " of a race who would allow
themselves to be made slaves—unrevenged.
It *may* be nobler to perish redhanded, to kill
as many as your battle axe holds out to hack
and then fall with an exultant yell and savage
grin of fiendish delight on the hugh pile of
bloody corpses,—expiring with the solace and
unction of having ten thousand wounds all in
front. I don't know. I sometimes think it
depends on where you plant your standard
and who wears the white plume which your
eye inadvertently seeks. If Napoleon is the
ideal of mankind, I suppose 'tis only noble to
be strong; and true greatness may consist in
an adamantine determination never to serve.
The greatest race with which I am even partially acquainted, proudly boasts that it has
never met another race save as either enemy
or victim. They seem to set great store by
this fact and I judge it must be immensely
noble according to their ideals. But somehow
it seems to me that those nations and races
who choose the Nazarene for their plumed
knight would find some little jarring and
variance between such notions and His ideals.
There could not be at all times perfect una-
nimity between Leader and host. A good

many of his sayings, it seems to me, would have to be explained away; not a few of his injunctions quietly ignored, and I am not sure but the great bulk of his principles and precepts must after all lie like leaden lumps, an undigested and unassimilable mass on an uneasy overburdened stomach. I find it rather hard to understand these things, and somehow I feel at times as if I have taken hold of the wrong ideal. But then, I suppose, it must be because I have not enough of the spirit that comes with the blood of those grand old *sea kings* (I believe you call them) who shot out in their trusty barks speeding over unknown seas and, like a death-dealing genius, with the piercing eye and bloodthirsty heart of hawk or vulture killed and harried, burned and caroused. This is doubtless all very glorious and noble, and the seed of it must be an excellent thing to have in one's blood. But I haven't it. I frankly admit my limitations. I am hardly capable of appreciating to the full such grand intrepidity,—due of course to the fact that the stock from which I am sprung did not attain that royal kink in its blood ages ago. My tribe has to own kinship with a very tame and unsanguinary individual who, a long time ago when blue blood was a distilling in the

stirring fiery world outside, had no more heroic
and daring a thing to do than help a pale
sorrow-marked man as he was toiling up a
certain hill at Jerusalem bearing his own cross
whereon he was soon to be ignominiously
nailed. This Cyrenian fellow was used to
bearing burdens and he didn't mind giving a
lift over a hard place now and then, with no
idea of doing anything grand or memorable,
or that even so much as his name would be
known thereby. And then, too, by a rather
strange coincidence this unwarlike and insig-
nificant kinsman of ours had his home in a
country (the fatherland of all the family)
which had afforded kindly shelter to that
same mysterious Stranger, when, a babe and
persecuted by bloody power and heartless jealousy, He had to flee the land of his birth. And
somehow this same country has in its day done
so much fostering and sheltering of that kind
—has watched and hovered over the cradles
of religions and given refuge and comfort to
the persecuted, the world weary, the storm
tossed benefactors of mankind so often that
she has come to represent nothing stronger or
more imposing than the "eternal womanly"
among the nations, and to accept as her mission and ideal, *loving service* to mankind.

With such antecedents then the black race in America should not be upbraided for having no taste for blood and carnage. It is the fault of their constitution that they prefer the judicial awards of peace and have an eternal patience to abide the bloodless triumph of right. It is no argument, therefore, when I point to the record of their physical supremacy —when the homes and helpless ones of this country were absolutely at the black man's mercy and not a town laid waste, not a building burned, and *not a woman insulted*—it is no argument, I say, for you to retort: "*He was a coward; he didn't dare!*" The facts simply do not show this to have been the case.

Now the tardy conscience of the nation wakes up one bright morning and is overwhelmed with blushes and stammering confusion because convicted of dishonorable and unkind treatment of *the Indian;* and there is a wonderful scurrying around among the keepers of the keys to get out more blankets and send out a few primers for the "*wards.*" While the black man, a faithful son and indefeasible heir,—who can truthfully say, "Lo, these many years do I serve thee, neither transgressed I at any time thy commandment, and yet thou never gavest me a kid that I might make merry with my friends,"—is snubbed and chilled and made unwelcome at every merry-making of the family. And when appropriations for education are talked of, the section for which he has wrought and suffered most, actually defeats the needed and desired assistance for fear they may not be able to prevent his getting a fair and equitable share in the distribution.

Oh, the shame of it!

In Pactolus Prime Mr. Tourgee has succeeded incomparably, we think, in photographing and vocalizing the feelings of the colored American in regard to the Christian profession and the pagan practice of the dominant forces in the American government. And as an impassioned denunciation of the heartless and godless spirit of caste founded on color, as a scathing rebuke to weak-eyed Christians who cannot read the golden rule across the color line, as an unanswerable arraignment of unparalleled ingratitude and limping justice in the policy of this country towards the weaker of its two children, that served it so long and so faithfully, the book is destined to live and to furnish an invaluable contribution to this already plethoric department of American literature.

Mr. Cable and Mr. Tourgee represent possibly the most eminent as well as the most prolific among the writers on this subject belonging to the didactic or polemic class. A host of others there are—lesser lights, or of more intermittent coruscations—who have contributed on either side the debate single treatises, numerous magazine articles or newspaper editorials, advocating some one theory some another on the so-called *race problem.* In this group belongs the author of " An Appeal to Pharoah," advocating the deportation absurdity; also the writings of H. W. Grady; " In Plain Black and White," " The Brother in Black," " The South Investigated," " A Defense of the Negro Race," " The Prosperity of the South Dependent on the Elevation of the Negro," " The Old South and the New," " Black and White," etc., etc., among which are included articles from the pen of colored men themselves, such as Mr. Douglass, Dr. Crummell, Dr. Arnett, Dr. Blyden, Dr. Scarborough, Dr. Price, Mr. Fortune, and others. These are champions of the forces on either side. They stand ever at the forefront dealing desperate blows right and left, now fist and skull, now broad-sword and battle-axe, now with the flash and boom of artillery; while

the little fellows run out ever and anon from
the ranks and deliver a telling blow between
the eyes of an antagonist. All are wrought
up to a high tension, some are blinded with
passion, others appalled with dread, — all sincerely feel the reality of their own vision and
earnestly hope to compel their world to see
with their eyes. Such works, full of the fever
and heat of debate belong to the turmoil and
turbulence of the time. A hundred years
from now they may be interesting history,
throwing light on a feature of these days
which, let us hope, will then be hardly intelligible to an American citizen not over fifty
years old.

Among our artists for art's sweet sake, Mr.
Howells has recently tried his hand also at
painting the Negro, attempting merely a side
light in half tones, on his life and manners;
and I think the unanimous verdict of the subject is that, in this single department at least,
Mr. Howells does not know what he is talking about. And yet I do not think we should
quarrel with *An Imperative Duty* because it
lacks the earnestness and bias of a special
pleader. Mr. Howells merely meant to press
the button and give one picture from American life involving racial complications. The

kodak does no more; it cannot preach sermons or solve problems.

Besides, the portrayal of Negro characteristics was by no means the main object of the
story, which was rather meant, I judge, to be
a thumb nail sketch containing a psychological study of a morbidly sensitive conscience
hectoring over a weak and vacillating will and
fevered into increased despotism by reading
into its own life and consciousness the analyses
and terrible retributions of fiction,—a product
of the Puritan's uncompromising sense of
" *right though the heavens fall*," irritated and
kept sore by being unequally yoked with indecision and cowardice. Of such strokes Mr.
Howells is undoubtedly master. It is true there
is little point and no force of character about
the beautiful and irresponsible young heroine;
but as that is an attainment of so many of
Mr. Howells' models, it is perhaps not to be
considered as illustrating any racial characteristics. I cannot help sharing, however, the
indignation of those who resent the picture in
the colored church,—" evidently," Mr. Howells
assures us, " representing *the best colored
society* "; where the horrified young prig, Rhoda
Aldgate, meets nothing but the frog-like
countenances and cat-fish mouths, the musky

exhalations and the " bress de Lawd, Honey,"
of an uncultivated people. It is just here that
Mr. Howells fails—and fails because he gives
only a half truth, and that a partisan half
truth. One feels that he had no business to
attempt a subject of which he knew so little,
or for which he cared so little. There is one
thing I would like to say to my white fellow
countrymen, and especially to those who dab-
ble in ink and affect to discuss the Negro;
and yet I hesitate because I feel it is a fact
which persons of the finer sensibilities and
more delicate perceptions must know instinctively: namely, that it is an insult to humanity and a sin against God to publish any such
sweeping generalizations of a race on such
meager and superficial information. We
meet it at every turn—this obtrusive and offensive vulgarity, this gratuitous sizing up of
the Negro and conclusively writing down his
equation, sometimes even among his ardent
friends and bravest defenders. Were I not
afraid of falling myself into the same error
that I am condemning, I would say it seems
an *Anglo Saxon characteristic* to have such
overweening confidence in his own power of
induction that there is no equation which he
would acknowledge to be indeterminate, how-

ever many unknown quantities it may possess.

Here is an extract from Dr. Mayo, a thoroughly earnest man and sincerely friendly, as I believe, to the colored people.

> " Among these women are as many grades of native, intellectual, moral and executive force as among the white people. The plantations of the Gulf, the Atlantic coast and the Mississippi bottoms swarm with negro women who seem hardly lifted above the brutes I know a group of young colored women, many of them accomplished teachers, who bear themselves as gently and with as varied womanly charms as any score of ladies in the land. The one abyss of perdition *to this class* is the slough of unchastity in which, *as a race* they still flounder, half conscious that it is a slough —the double inheritance of savage Africa and slavery."

Now there may be one side of a truth here, yet who but a self-confident Anglo Saxon would dare make such a broad unblushing statement about a people *as a race?* Some developments brought to light recently through the scientific Christianity and investigating curiosity of Dr. Parkhurst may lead one to suspect the need of missionary teaching to " elevate" the white race; and yet I have too much respect for the autonomy of races, too much reverence for the collective view of God's handiwork to speak of any such condition, however general, as characterizing *the race.* The colored people do not object to the ade-

quate and truthful portrayal of types of their
race in whatever degree of the scale of civilization, or of social and moral development, is
consonant with actual facts or possibilities.
As Mr. Howells himself says, " A man can be
anything along the vast range from angel to
devil, and without living either the good
thing or the bad thing in which his fancy
dramatizes him, he can perceive it "—and I
would add, can appreciate and even enjoy its
delineation by the artist. The average Englishman takes no exception to the humorous
caricatures of Dickens or to the satires and
cynicisms of Thackeray. The Quilps and the
Bernsteins are but strongly developed nega-
tives of our universal human nature on the dark
side. We recognize them as genre sketches,—
and with the Agneses and Esthers and Aunt
Lamberts as foils and correctives, we can appreciate them accordingly : while we do not believe ourselves to be the original of the portrait, there is enough sympathy and fellow
feeling for the character to prevent our human
relationship from being outraged and insulted.
But were Dickens to introduce an average
scion of his countrymen to a whole congregation of *Quilps*, at the same time sagely inform-
ing him that these represented *the best there was*

of English life and morals, I strongly suspect
the charming author would be lifted out on
the toe of said average Englishman's boot, in
case there shouldn't happen to be a good
horsewhip handy.

Our grievance then is not that we are not
painted as angels of light or as goody-goody
Sunday-school developments; but we do
claim that a man whose acquaintanceship is
so slight that he cannot even discern diversi-
ties of individuality, has no right or authority
to hawk " the only true and authentic " pictures of a race of human beings.   Mr. Howells'
point of view is precisely that of a white man
who sees colored people at long range or only
in certain capacities.   His conclusions about
the colored man are identical with the impressions that will be received and carried
abroad by foreigners from all parts of the
globe, who shall attend our Columbian Exposition for instance, and who, through the impartiality and generosity of our white countrymen, will see colored persons only as boot-
blacks and hotel waiters, grinning from ear
to ear and bowing and courtesying for the
extra tips.   In the same way Mr. Howells has
met colored persons in hotels or on the com-
mons promenading and sparking, or else act-

ing as menials and lazzaroni. He has not seen, and therefore cannot be convinced that there exists a quiet, self-respecting, dignified class of easy life and manners (save only where it crosses the roughness of their white fellow countrymen's barbarity) of cultivated tastes and habits, and with no more in common with the class of his acquaintance than the accident of complexion,—beyond a sympathy with their wrongs, or a resentment at being socially and morally classified with them, according as the principle of altruism or of self love is dominant in the individual.

I respectfully submit that there is hardly a colored church in any considerable city in this country, which could be said in any sense to represent *the best colored society*, in which Rhoda Aldgate could not have seen, when she opened her eyes, persons as quietly and as becomingly dressed, as cultivated in tone and as refined in manner, as herself; persons, too, as sensitive to rough contact and as horribly alive as she could be (though they had known it from childhood) to the galling distinctions in this country which insist on *levelling down* all individuals more or less related to the Africans. So far from the cringing deference which Mr. Howells paints as exhibited to

"the young white lady," in nine cases out of
ten the congregation would have supposed
intuitively that she was a quadroon, so far
from the unusual was her appearance and
complexion. In not a few such colored
churches would she have found young women
of aspiration and intellectual activity with
whom she could affiliate without nausea and
from whom she could learn a good many
lessons—and, sadly I say it, even more outside
the churches whom bitterness at racial inconsistency of white Christians had soured into a
silent disbelief of all religion. In either class
she would have found no trouble in reaching
a heart which could enter into all the agony
of her own trial and bitter grief. Nor am I
so sure, if she had followed her first gushing
impulse to go South and "elevate" the race
with whom she had discovered her relationship, that she would have found even them so
ready to receive her condescending patronage.

There are numerous other inadvertent mis-
representations in the book—such as supposing
that colored people voluntarily and deliberately prefer to keep to themselves in all public
places and that from choice "they have their
own neighborhoods, their own churches, their
own amusements, their own resorts,"—the

intimation that there is a "*black* voice," a black character, easy, irresponsible and fond of what is soft and pleasant, a black ideal of art and a black barbaric taste in color, a black affinity—so that in some occult and dreadful way one, only one-sixteenth related and totally foreign by education and environment, can still feel that one-sixteenth race calling her more loudly than the fifteen-sixteenths. I wish to do Mr. Howells the justice to admit, however, that one feels his blunders to be wholly unintentional and due to the fact that he has studied his subject merely from the outside. With all his matchless powers as a novelist, not even he can yet "think himself imaginatively" into the colored man's place.

To my mind the quaintest and truest little bit of portraiture from low-life that I have read in a long time is the little story that appeared last winter in the Harpers, of the "*Widder Johnsing and how she caught the preacher.*" It is told with naive impersonality and apprecia-tive humor, and is quite equal, I think, both in subject and treatment to the best of Mrs. Stowe's New England dialect stories. It is idyllic in its charming simplicity and natural-ness, and delightfully fresh in its sparkling wit and delicious humor. We do not resent

such pictures as this of our lowly folk—such
a homely and honest

" Pomegranate, which, if cut deep down the middle,
 Shows a heart within blood tinctured of a *veined humanity*,"

is always sweet to the taste and dear to the
heart, however plain and humble the setting.

A longer and more elaborate work, Harold,
published anonymously, comes properly in
our group second, the didactic novel. It gives
the picture of a black Englishman cultured
and refined, brought in painful contact with
American,—or rather *un-American*, color prejudice. The point of the book seems to be to
show that education for the black man is a
curse, since it increases his sensitiveness to
the indignities he must suffer in consequence
of white barbarity. The author makes Harold, after a futile struggle against American
inequalities, disappear into the jungles of
Africa, "there to wed a dusky savage," at the
last cursing the day he had ever suspected a
broader light or known a higher aspiration ;
a conclusion which, to my mind, is a most il-
logical one. If the cultivated black man cannot endure the white man's barbarity—the
cure, it seems to me, would be to cultivate the
white man. Civilize both, then each will
know what is due from man to man, and that

reduces at once to a minimum the friction of their contact.

In the same rank as Harold belongs that improbability of improbabilities, Doctor Huguet, by the arch-sensationalist, Ignatius Donelly. As its purpose is evidently good, I shall not undertake to review the book. Suffice it to say the plot hinges on the exchange of soul between the body of a black chicken-thief and that of a cultivated white gentleman, and sets forth the indignities and wrongs to which the cultured soul, with all its past of refinement and learning, has to submit in consequence of its change of cuticle. The book is an able protest against that snobbishness which elevates complexion into a touchstone of aristocracy and makes the pigment cells of a man's skin his badge of nobility regardless of the foulness or purity of the soul within; the only adverse criticism from the colored man's point of view being the selection of a chicken thief as his typical black man; but on the principle of antitheses this may have been artistically necessary.

I shall pass next to what I consider the most significant contribution to this subject for the last ten years—a poem by Maurice Thompson in the New York Independent for

January 21, 1892, entitled *A Voodoo Prophecy*. From beginning to end it is full of ghoulish imagery and fine poetic madness. Here are a few stanzas of it:

"I am the prophet of the dusky race,
  The poet of wild Africa. Behold,
The midnight vision brooding in my face!
        Come near me,
        And hear me,
  While from my lips the words of Fate are told.

A black and terrible memory masters me,
  The shadow and the substance of deep wrong;
You know the past, hear now what is to be:
        From the midnight land,
        Over sea and sand,
  From the green jungle, hear my Voodoo-song:

A tropic heat is in my bubbling veins,
  Quintessence of all savagery is mine,
The lust of ages ripens in my reins,
        And burns
        And yearns,
  Like venom-sap within a noxious vine.

Was I a heathen? Ay, I was—am still
  A fetich worshipper; but I was free
To loiter or to wander at my will,
        To leap and dance,
        To hurl my lance,
  And breathe the air of savage liberty.

You drew me to a higher life, you say;
  Ah, drove me, with the lash of slavery!
Am I unmindful? Every cursed day
            Of pain
            And chain
Roars like a torrent in my memory.

You make my manhood whole with 'equal rights!'
  Poor empty words! Dream you I honor them?—
I who have stood on Freedom's wildest hights?
            My Africa,
            I see the day
When none dare touch thy garment's lowest hem.

You cannot make me love you with your whine
  Of fine repentance. Veil your pallid face
In presence of the shame that mantles mine;
            Stand
            At command
Of the black prophet of the Negro race!

I hate you, and I live to nurse my hate,
  Remembering when you plied the slaver's trade
In my dear land . . . How patiently I wait
            The day,
            Not far away,
When all your pride shall shrivel up and fade.

Yea, all your whiteness darken under me!
  Darken and be jaundiced, and your blood
Take in dread humors from my savagery,
            Uutil
            Your will
Lapse into mine and seal my masterhood.

You, seed of Abel, proud of your descent,
  And arrogant, because your cheeks are fair,
Within my loins an inky curse is pent,
        To flood
        Your blood
  And stain your skin and crisp your golden hair.

As you have done by me, so will I do
  By all the generations of your race;
Your snowy limbs, your blood's patrician blue
        Shall be
        Tainted by me,
  And I will set my seal upon your face!

Yea, I will dash my blackness down your veins,
  And through your nerves my sensuousness I'll fling;
Your lips, your eyes, shall bear the musty stains
        Of Congo kisses,
        While shrieks and hisses
  Shall blend into the savage songs I sing!

Your temples will I break, your fountains fill,
  Your cities raze, your fields to deserts turn;
My heathen fires shall shine on every hill,
        And wild beasts roam,
        Where stands your home;—
  Even the wind your hated dust shall spurn.

I will absorb your very life in me,
  And mold you to the shape of my desire;
Back through the cycles of all cruelty
        I will swing you,
        And wring you,
  And roast you in my passions' hottest fire.

You, North and South, you, East and West,
  Shall drink the cup your fathers gave to me;
My back still burns, I bare my bleeding breast,
        I set my face,
        My limbs I brace,
  To make the long, strong fight for mastery.

My serpent fetich lolls its withered lip
  And bares its shining fangs at thought of this:
I scarce can hold the monster in my grip.
        So strong is he,
        So eagerly
  He leaps to meet my precious prophecies.

Hark for the coming of my countless host,
  Watch for my banner over land and sea.
The ancient power of vengeance is not lost!
        Lo! on the sky
        The fire-clouds fly,
  And strangely moans the windy, weltering sea."

Now this would be poetry if it were only
truthful. Simple and sensuous it surely is, but
it lacks the third requisite—truth. The Negro is utterly incapable of such vindictiveness.
Such concentrated venom might be distilled
in the cold Saxon, writhing and chafing under
oppression and repression such as the Negro
in America has suffered and is suffering. But
the black man is in real life only too glad to
accept the olive branch of reconciliation. He
merely asks to be let alone. To be allowed to
pursue his destiny as a free man and an Ameri-

can citizen, to rear and educate his children in peace, to engage in art, science, trades or industries according to his ability,—and *to go to the wall if he fail.* He is willing, if I understand him, to let bygones be bygones. He does not even demand satisfaction for the centuries of his ancestors' unpaid labor. He asks neither pension, nor dole nor back salaries; but is willing to start from the bottom, all helpless and unprovided for as he is, with absolutely nothing as his stock in trade, with no capital, in a country developed, enriched, and made to blossom through his father's "sweat and toil,"—with none of the accumulations of ancestors' labors, with no education or moral training for the duties and responsibilities of freedom; nay, with every power, mental, moral, and physical, emasculated by a debasing slavery—he is willing, even glad to take his place in the lists alongside his oppressors, who have had every advantage, to be tried with them by their own standards, and to ask no quarter from them or high Heaven to palliate or excuse the ignominy of a defeat.

The Voodoo Prophecy has no interest then as a picture of the black, but merely as a revelation of the white man. Maurice Thompson in penning this portrait of the Negro, has, un-

consciously it may be, laid bare his own soul—
its secret dread and horrible fear. And this,
it seems to me, is the key to the Southern situation, the explanation of the apparent heart-
lessness and cruelty of some, and the stolid indifference to atrocity on the part of others, before which so many of us have stood paralyzed
in dumb dismay. The Southerner is not a
cold-blooded villain. Those of us who have
studied the genus in its native habitat can testify that his impulses are generous and kindly,
and that while the South presents a solid pha-
lanx of iron resistance to the Negro's advancement, still as individuals to individuals they
are warm-hearted and often even tender. And
just here is the difference between the Southerner and his more philosophical, less sentimental Northern brother. The latter in an abstract metaphysical way rather wants you to
have all the rights that belong to you. He
thinks it better for the country, better for him
that justice, universal justice be done. But
he doesn't care to have the blacks, in the con-
crete, too near him. He doesn't know them
and doesn't want to know them. He really
can't understand how the Southerner could
have let those little cubs get so close to him
as they did in the old days—nursing from the

same bottle and feeding at the same breast

To the Southerner, on the other hand, race antipathy and color-phobia *as such* does not exist. Personally, there is hardly a man of them but knows, and has known from childhood, some black fellow whom he loves as dearly as if he were white, whom he regards as indispensable to his own pleasures, and for whom he would break every commandment in the decalogue to save him from any general disaster. But our Bourbon seems utterly incapable of generalizing his few ideas. He would die for A or B, but suddenly becomes utterly impervious to every principle of logic when you ask for the simple golden rule to be applied to the class of which A or B is one. Another fact strikes me as curious. A Southern white man's regard for his black friend varies in inverse ratio to the real distance between them in education and refinement. Puck expresses it—"I can get on a great deal better with a nigger than I can with a Negro." And Mr. Douglass puts it: "Let a colored man be out at elbows and toes and half way into the gutter and there is no prejudice against him; but let him respect himself and be a man and Southern whites can't abide to ride in the same car with him."

Why this anomaly? Is it pride? Ordinarily, congeniality increases with similarity in taste and manners. Is it antipathy to color? It does not exist. The explanation is the white man's dread dimly shadowed out in this Voodoo Prophecy of Maurice Thompson, and fed and inspired by such books as Minden Armais and a few wild theorizers who have nothing better to do with their time than spend it advocating the fusion of races as a plausible and expedient policy. Now I believe there are two ideas which master the Southern white man and incense him against the black race. On this point he is a monomaniac. In the face of this feeling he would not admit he was convinced of the axioms of Geometry. The one is personal and present, the fear of Negro political domination. The other is for his posterity—the future horror of being lost as a race in this virile and vigorous black race. Relieve him of this nightmare and he becomes " as gentle as the sucking dove." With that dread delusion maddening him he would drive his sword to the hilt in the tender breast of his darling child, did he fancy that through her the curse would come.

Now argument is almost supersensible with a monomaniac. What is most needed is a

sedative for the excited nerves, and then a
mental tonic to stimulate the power of clear
perception and truthful cerebration. The
Southern patient needs to be brought to see,
by the careful and cautious injection of cold
facts and by the presentation of well selected
object lessons that so far as concerns his first
named horror of black supremacy politically,
the usual safeguards of democracy are in the
hands of intelligence and wealth in the South
as elsewhere. The weapons of fair argument
and persuasion, the precautionary bulwark of
education and justice, the unimpeachable
supremacy and insuperable advantage of intelligence and discipline over mere numbers—
are all in his reach. It is to his interest to
help make the black peasant an intelligent
and self-respecting citizen. No section can
thrive under the incubus of an illiterate, impoverished, cheerless and hopeless peasantry.
Let the South once address herself in good
faith to the improvement of the condition of
her laboring classes, let her give but a tithe of
the care and attention which are bestowed in
the North on its mercurial and inflammable
importations, let her show but the disposition
in her relative poverty merely to utter the
benediction, *Be ye warmed and fed and educated,*

even while she herself has not the wherewithal
to emulate the Pullman villages and the Carnegie munificence, let her but give him a fair
wage and an honest reckoning and a kindly
God-speed,—and she will find herself in possession of the most tractable laborer, the most
faithful and reliable henchman, the most invaluable co-operator and friendly vassal of
which this or any country can boast.

So far as regards the really less sane idea
that amicable relations subsisting between the
races may promote their ultimate blending and
loss of identity, it hardly seems necessary to
refute it. Blending of races in the aggregate
is simply an unthinkable thought, and the
union of individuals can never fall out by accident or haphazard. There must be the
deliberate wish and intention on each side;
and the average black man in this country is
as anxious to preserve his identity and transmit
his type as is the average white man. In any
case, hybridity is in no sense dependent on
sectional or national amity. Oppression and
outrage are not the means to chain the affec-
tions. Cupid, who knows no bolt or bars, is
more wont to be stimulated with romantic
sympathy towards a forbidden object unjustly
persecuted. The sensible course is to remove

those silly and unjust barriers which protect nothing and merely call attention to the possibilities of law-breaking, and depend instead on religion and common sense to guide, control and direct in the paths of purity and right reason.

The froth and foam, the sticks and debris at the watertop may have an uncertain movement, but as deep calleth unto deep the mighty ocean swell is always true to the tides; and whatever the fluctuations along the ragged edge between the races, the home instinct is sufficiently strong with each to hold the great mass true to its attractions. If Maurice Thompson's nightmare vision is sincere on his part, then, it has no objective reality; 'tis merely a hideous phantasm bred of his own fevered and jaundiced senses; if he does not believe in it himself, it was most unkind and uncalled for to publish abroad such inflaming and irritating fabrications.

After this cursory glance at a few contributions which have peculiarly emphasized one phase of our literature during the last decade or two, I am brought to the conclusion that an authentic portrait, at once æsthetic and true to life, presenting the black man as a free American citizen, not the humble slave of

Uncle Tom's Cabin — but the *man*, divinely struggling and aspiring yet tragically warped and distorted by the adverse winds of circumstance, has not yet been painted. It is my opinion that the canvas awaits the brush of the colored man himself. It is a pathetic—a fearful arraignment of America's conditions of life, that instead of that enrichment from the years and days, the summers and springs under which, as Browning says,

" The flowers turn double and the leaves turn flowers,"—

the black man's native and original flowers have in this country been all hardened and sharpened into thorns and spurs. In literature we have no artists for art's sake. Albery A. Whitman in " *Twasinta's Seminoles* " and " *Not a Man and Yet a Man* " is almost the only poet who has attempted a more sustained note than the lyrics of Mrs. Harper, and even that note is almost a wail.

The fact is, a sense of freedom in mind as well as in body is necessary to the appreciative and inspiring pursuit of the beautiful. A bird cannot warble out his fullest and most joyous notes while the wires of his cage are pricking and cramping him at every heart beat. His tones become only the shrill and poignant protest of rage and despair. And so the black man's vexations and chafing environment, even since his physical emancipation has given him speech, has goaded him into the eloquence and fire of oratory rather than the genial warmth and cheery glow of either poetry or romance. And pity 'tis, 'tis true. A race that has produced for America the only folk-lore and folk songs of native growth, a race which has grown the most original and unique assemblage of fable and myth to be found on the continent, a race which has suggested and inspired almost the only distinctive American note which could chain the attention and charm the ear of the outside world— has as yet found no mouthpiece of its own to unify and perpetuate its wondrous whisperings—no painter-poet to distil in the alembic of his own imagination the gorgeous dyes, the luxuriant juices of this rich and tropical vegetation. It was the glory of Chaucer that he justified the English language to itself—that he took the homely and hitherto despised Saxon elements and ideas, and lovingly wove them into an artistic product which even Norman conceit and uppishness might be glad to acknowledge and imitate. The only man who is doing the same for Negro folk-lore is one not to the manner born. Joel Chandler Harris has made himself rich and famous by simply standing around among the black railroad hands and cotton pickers of the South and compiling the simple and dramatic dialogues which fall from their lips. What I hope to see before I die is a black man honestly and appreciatively portraying both the Negro as he is, and the white man, occasionally, as seen from the Negro's standpoint.

There is an old proverb "The devil is always painted *black*—by white painters." And what is needed, perhaps, to reverse the picture of the lordly man slaying the lion, is for the lion to turn painter.

Then too we need the calm clear judgment of ourselves and of others born of a disenchantment similar to that of a little girl I know in the South, who was once being laboriously held up over the shoulders of a surging throng to catch her first glimpse of a real live president. "Why Nunny," she cried half reproachfully, as she strained her little neck to see—"*It's nuffin but a man!*"

When we have been sized up and written down by others, we need not feel that the last word is said and the oracles sealed. "It's nuffin but a man." And there are many gifts the giftie may gie us, far better than seeing ourselves as others see us—and one is that of Bion's maxim "*Know Thyself.*" Keep true to your own ideals. Be not ashamed of what is homely and your own. Speak out and speak honestly. Be true to yourself and to the message God and Nature meant you to deliver. The young David cannot fight in Saul's unwieldy armor. Let him simply therefore gird his loins, take up his own parable and tell this would-be great American nation "*A chile's amang ye takin' notes;*" and when men act the part of cowards or wild beasts, this great silent but open-eyed constituency has a standard by which they are being tried. Know thyself, and know those around at their true weight of solid intrinsic manhood without being dazzled by the fact that littleness of soul is often gilded with wealth, power and intellect. There can be no nobility but that of soul, and no catalogue of adventitious circumstances can wipe out the stain or palliate the meanness of inflicting one ruthless, cruel wrong. 'Tis not only safer, but nobler, grander, diviner,

> "To be that which we destroy
> Than, by destruction, dwell in doubtful joy."

With this platform to stand on we can with

clear eye weigh what is written and estimate what is done and ourselves paint what is true with the calm spirit of those who know their cause is right and who believe there is a God who judgeth the nations.

WHAT ARE WE WORTH?

———

I once heard Henry Ward Beecher make this remark: "Were Africa and the Africans to sink to-morrow, how much poorer would the world be? A little less gold and ivory, a little less coffee, a considerable ripple, perhaps, where the Atlantic and Indian Oceans would come together—that is all; not a poem, not an invention, not a piece of art would be missed from the world."

This is not a flattering statement; but then we do not want flattery if seeing ourselves as others see us is to help us in fulfilling the higher order, " know thyself." The world is often called cold and hard. I don't know much about that; but of one thing I am sure, it is intensely practical. Waves of sentiment or prejudice may blur its old eyes for a little while but you are sure to have your bill presented first or last with the inexorable " How much owest thou?" What have you produced, what consumed? What is your real value in the world's economy? What do you give to the world over and above what you have cost? What would be missed had you never lived? What are you worth? What ot actual value would go down with you if you were sunk into the ocean or buried by an earthquake to-morrow? Show up your cash account and your balance sheet. In the final reckoning do you belong on the debit or the credit side of the account? according to a fair and square, an impartial and practical reckoning. It is by this standard that society estimates individuals; and by this standard finally and inevitably the world will measure and judge nations and races.

It may not be unprofitable then for us to address ourselves to the task of casting up our account and carefully overhauling our books. It may be well to remember at the outset that the operation is purely a mathematical one and allows no room for sentiment. The good housewife's pet chicken which she took when first hatched, fed from her own hand and fondled on her bosom as lovingly as if it were a babe, is worth no more (for all the affection and care lavished on it) when sold in the shambles: and that never-to-be-forgotten black hen that stole into the parlor, flew upon the mantel looking for a nest among

those handsome curios, smashed the sèvers
vases and picked the buds from the lovely
tea rose — so exasperatingly that the good
woman could never again endure the sight of
her—this ill-fated bird is worth no less. There
are sections of this country in which the very
name of the Negro, even in homeopathic doses,
stirs up such a storm of feeling that men fairly
grow wild and are unfit to discuss the simplest
principles of life and conduct where the colored man is concerned; and you would think
it necessary for the Ethiopian actually to
change his skin before there can be any har-
monious living or lucid thinking: there are a
few nooks and crannies, on the other hand,
in another quarter of the same country, in
which that name embodies an idealized theory
and a benevolent sentiment; and the black
man (the blacker the better) is the petted
nursling, the haloed idea, the foregone conclusion. In these Arcadias, it is as good capital
as pushing selfishness and aspiring mediocrity
need ask, to be advertised as one of the oppressed race and probably born a slave.

But after all sentiment, whether adverse or
favorable, is ephemeral. Ever shifting and
unreliable, it can never be counted in estimating values. The sentiments of youth are out-

grown in age, and we like to-day what we despised or were indifferent to yesterday. Nine-tenths of the mis-called color prejudice or race prejudice in this country is mere sentiment governed by the association of ideas. It is not color prejudice at all. The color of a man's face *per se* has no more to do with his worthiness and companionableness than the color of his eyes or the shades of his hair. You admire the one or think the other more beautiful to rest the gaze upon. But every one with brains knows and must admit that he must look deeper than this for the man. Mrs. Livermore once said in my hearing: " It is not that the Negro is black; Spaniards, Portuguese, East Indians, enter our parlors, sup at our tables, and, if they have a sufficiently long bank account, they may marry our daughters: but the Negro is weak—and we don't like weakness."

Now this dislike it is useless to inveigh against and folly to rail at. We share it ourselves and often carry it to a more unjustifiable extent. For as a rule the narrower the mind and the more circumscribed the experience, the greater will be the exaggeration of accidents over substance, and of circumstance over soul. It does no good to argue with the poor sea-sick wretch who, even on land after the voyage, is nauseated by the sight of clear spring water. In vain you show the unreason of the feeling. This, you explain, is a different time, a different place, a different stage of progress in the circulation of waters. That was salt, this is fresh, and so on. You might as well be presenting syllogisms to Ætna. " Yes, my dear Fellow," he cries, " You talk admirably; but you don't know how I feel. You don't know how sick I was on that nasty ship!" And so your rhetoric cannot annihilate the association of ideas. He feels; *you know.* But he will outgrow his feeling,—and you are content to wait.

Just as impervious to reason is the man who is dominated by the sentiment of race prejudice. You can only consign him to 'the fatherly hand of Time; and pray that your own mental sight be not thus obscured and your judgment warped in your endeavors to be just and true.

Sentiment and cant, then, both being ruled out, let us try to study our subject as the world finally reckons it — not certain crevices and crannies of the earth, but the cool, practical, business-like world. What are we worth? not in Georgia nor in Massachusetts; not to our brothers and sisters and cousins and aunts, every one of whom would unhesitatingly declare us worth a great gold-lump; nor to the exasperated neighbor over the way who would be just as ready, perhaps, to write us down a most unmitigated nuisance. But what do we represent to the world? What is our market value. Are we a positive and additive quantity or a negative factor in the world's elements. What have we cost and what do we come to?

The calculation may be made in the same way and on the same principle that we would estimate the value of any commodity on the market. Men are not very unlike watches. We might estimate first the cost of material— is it gold or silver or alloy, solid or plated, jewelled or sham paste. Settle the relative value of your raw material, and next you want to calculate how much this value has been enhanced by labor, the delicacy and fineness, the honesty and thoroughness of the workmanship; then the utility and beauty of the product and its adaptability to the end and purpose of its manufacture; and lastly is there a demand in the market for such an article. Does it meet a want, *will it go* and *go right?* Is it durable and reliable. How often do you have to wind it before it runs

down, how often repair it. Does it keep good
time and require but little watching and looking after. And there is no radical difference,
after all, between the world's way of estimating men and our usual way of valuing watches.
In both the fundamental item is the question
of material, and then the refining and en-
hancement of that material through labor, and
so on through the list.

What then can we say for our raw material?

Again I must preface an apology for anything unpalatable in our menu. I promised,
you remember, to leave out the sentiment—
you may stir it in afterwards, mixing thoroughly according to taste. We must discuss
facts, candidly and bluntly, without rhetoric
or cant if we would have a clear light on our
problem.

Now whatever notions we may indulge on
the theory of evolution and the laws of atavism
or heredity, all concede that no individual
character receives its raw material newly created and independent of the rock from whence
it was hewn. No life is bound up within the
period of its conscious existence. No personality dates its origin from its birthday. The
elements that are twisted into the cord did

not begin their formation when first the tiny thread became visible in the great warp and filling of humanity. When first we saw the light many of the threads undoubtedly were spun and the color and fineness of the weft determined. The materials that go to make the man, the probabilities of his character and activities, the conditions and circumstances of his growth, and his quantum of resistance and mastery are the resultant of forces which have been accumulating and gathering momentum for generations. So that, as one tersely expresses it, in order to reform a man, you must begin with his great grandmother.

A few years ago a certain social scientist was struck by a remarkable coincidence in the name of a number of convicts in the State prison of New York. There were found thirty-five or forty men, of the same name with but slight modification in the spelling, all convicted of crimes similar in character. Looking into the matter, he traced them every one back to one woman of inferior character who had come from England in one of the first colonial ships. *And that woman had been a convict and charged with pretty nearly the same crime.*

Rightly to estimate our material, then, it is

necessary to go back of the twenty or thirty years during which we have been in possession, and find out the nature of the soil in which it has been forming and growing.

There is or used to be in England a system of entail by which a lot of land was fixed to a family and its posterity forever, passing always on the death of the father to his eldest son. A man may misuse or abuse, he may impoverish, mortgage, sterilize, eliminate every element of value—but he can never sell. He may cut down every tree, burn every fence and house, abstract by careless tillage, or by no tillage, every nutritive element from the soil, encumber it to two or three times its value and destroy forever its beauty and fertility — but he can never rid himself of it. That land with all its encumbrances and liabilities, its barrenness and squalidness, its poverty and its degradation is inexorably, inevitably, inalienably his; and like a shattered and debased personality it haunts him wherever he goes. An heir coming into an estate is thus often poorer than if he had no inheritance. He is chained to a life long possession of debt, toil, responsibility, often disgrace. Happier were it for him if he could begin life with nothing—an isolated but free man with no

capital but his possibilities, with no past and
no pedigree. And so it often is with men.
These bodies of ours often come to us mort-
gaged to their full value by the extravagance,
self-indulgence, sensuality of some ancestor.
Some man, generations back, has encumbered
his estate for strong drink, his descendants
coming into that estate have the mortgage to
pay off, principal and interest. Another cut
down the fences of character by debauchery
and vice,—and these have to ward off attacks
of the enemy without bulwarks or embattlements. They have burnt their houses of
purity and integrity, have rendered the soil
poor and unproductive by extravagance and
folly,—and the children have to shiver amid
the storms of passion and feed on husks till
they can build for themselves a shelter and
fertilize their farms. Not very valuable estates, you will say. Well, no, — nothing to
boast of, perhaps. But an energetic heir can
often pay off some of the liabilities and leave
the estate to his children less involved than
when he received it. At least he can arrest
the work of destruction and see to it that no
further encumbrances are added through his
folly and mismanagement.

In estimating the value of our material,

therefore, it is plain that we must look into the deeds of our estates and ferret out their history. The task is an individual one, as likewise its application. Certainly the original timber as it came from the African forests was good enough. No race of heathen are more noted for honesty and chastity than are the tribes of Africa. For one of their women to violate the laws of purity is a crime punishable with death; and so strictly honest are they, it is said, that they are wont to leave their commodities at the place of exchange and go about their business. The buyer coming up takes what he wishes to purchase and leaves its equivalent in barter or money. A returned missionary tells the story that certain European traders, when at a loss as to the safe keeping of their wares, were told by a native chief, " Oh just lay them down there. *They are perfectly safe, there are no Christians here.*"

Whatever may be said of its beauty, then, the black side of the stream with us is pretty pure, and has no cause to blush for its honesty and integrity. From the nature of the case the infusions of white blood that have come in many instances to the black race in this country are not the best that race afforded.

And if anything further is needed to account for racial irregularities—the warping and shrinking, the knotting and cracking of the sturdy old timber, the two hundred and fifty years of training here are quite sufficient to explain all. I have often thought, since coming in closer contact with the Puritan element in America, what a different planing and shaping this timber might have received under their hands!

As I compare the Puritan's sound, substantial, sanctified common sense with the Feudal froth and foam of the South; the Puritan's liberal, democratic, ethical and at the same time calculating, economical, stick-to-ative and go-ahead-ative spirit,—with the free and easy lavishness, the aristocratic notions of caste and class distinctions, the pliable consciences and unbending social bars amid which I was reared;—I have wished that it might have been ordered that as my race had to serve a term of bondage it might have been under the discipline of the successors of Cromwell and Milton, rather than under the training and example of the luxurious cavaliers. There is no doubt that the past two hundred and fifty years of working up the material we now inherit, has depreciated rather than enhanced its value. We find in it the foolish ideas of aristocracy founded on anything else than a moral claim; we find the contempt for manual labor and the horror of horny palms, the love of lavish expenditure and costly display, and —alas, that we must own it—the laxness of morals and easy-going consciences inherited and imitated from the old English gentry of the reigns of Charles and Anne. But to know our faults is one step toward correcting them, and there are, I trust, no flaws in this first element of value, *material*, which may not be planed and scraped and sand-papered out by diligent and strenuous effort. One thing is certain, the flaws that are simply ingrained in the timber are not our responsibility. A man is to be praised primarily not for having inherited fine tools and faultless materials but for making the most of the stuff he has, and doing his best in spite of disadvantages and poor material. The individual is responsible, not for what he has not, but for what he has; and the vital part for us after all depends on the use we make of our material.

Many a passable article has by diligent workmanship been made even from inferior material. And this brings us to our second item of value—Labor.

This is a most important item. It would seem sometimes that it is labor that creates all value. A gold mine is worth no more than common clay till it is worked. The simple element of labor bestowed on iron, the cheapest and commonest of metals, multiplies its value four hundred thousand times, making it worth sixty-five times its weight in gold, *e. g.:*

A pound of good iron is worth about . . . . . . 4 cts.
A pound of inch screws $1.00
A pound of steel wire from . . . . . . $3.00 to $7.00
A pound of sewing needles $14.00
A pound of fish hooks from . . . . . $20 00 to $50.00
A pound of jewel screws for watches $3,500.00
A pound of hair springs for watches $16,000.00
While a pound of fine gold in standard coin
    is worth only about $248.00

Now it is the same fundamental material in the hair springs valued at $16,000.00 which was sold in the rough at 4 cts. per pound. It is labor that has thus enhanced its value. Now let us see if there is a parallel rise of value in the material of which men are made.

No animal, the scientists tell us, is in infancy so utterly helpless, so completely destitute of the means of independent existence, so entirely worthless in itself as the world estimates values, as is man. The chick just out of the shell can pick up its own food and run away from approaching danger. Touch a snapping turtle just a moment after its birth, and it will bite at you. Cut off its head and it will still bite. Break open the egg of the young and the vivacious little creature will, even in the embryo, try to fight for its rights and maintain its independence. But the human babe can for weeks and months, do nothing but cry and feed and fear. It is a constant drain on the capital of its parents, both physically and mentally. It is to be fed, and worked for, and sheltered and protected. It cannot even defend itself against a draft of wind.

What is it worth? Unsentimentally and honestly,—it is worth just as much as a leak is worth to a ship, or what the mistletoe is worth to the oak. He is a parasite, a thief, a destroyer of values. He thrives at another's expense, and filches from that other every atom of his own existence. The infatuated mother, it is true, would not sell him, she will tell you, for his weight in gold; but that is sentiment —not business. Besides, there is no danger of her having the chance to make such a bargain. No one will ever tempt her with any such offer. The world knows too well what an outlay of time and money and labor must be made before he is worth even his weight in ashes. His present worth no one would accept even as a gift—and it is only the prospect of future development of worth that could induce any one, save that mother, to take up the burden. What an expenditure of toil and care, of heart power and brain power, what planning, what working, what feeding, what enriching, what sowing and sinking of values before one can tell whether the harvest is worth the output. Yet, how gladly does the mother pour out her strength and vitality, her energy, her life that the little bankrupt may store up capital for its own use. How anxiously does she hang over the lumpish little organism to catch the first awakening of a soul. And when the chubby little hands begin to swing consciously before the snapping eyes, and the great toe is caught and tugged towards the open mouth, when the little pink fists for the first time linger caressingly on her cheek and breast, and the wide open eyes say distinctly "I know you, I love you,"—how she strains him to her bosom as her whole soul goes out to this newly found intelligence in the impassioned cry of Carlyle: " *Whence— and Oh Heavens, whither!*"

> " How poor, how rich, how abject, how august,
> How complicate, how wonderful is man!"

It is labor, development, training, careful, patient, painful, diligent toil that must span the gulf between this vegetating life germ (now worth nothing but toil and care and trouble, and living purely at the expense of another)—and that future consummation in which "the elements are so mixed that Nature can stand up and say to all the world, ' *This is a man.*'"

It is a heavy investment, requires a large outlay of money on long time and large risk, no end of labor, skill, pains. Education is the word that covers it all—the working up of this raw material and fitting it into the world's work to supply the world's need—the manufacture of men and women for the markets of the world. But there is no other labor which so creates value. The value of the well developed man has been enhanced far more by the labor bestowed than is the iron in the watch springs. The value of the raw material was far below zero to begin with; but this "quintessence of dust" has become, *through labor*, "the beauty of the world, the paragon of animals,—noble in reason and infinite in faculty!"

What a piece of work, indeed!

Education, then, is the safest and richest investment possible to man. It pays the largest dividends and gives the grandest possible product to the world—a man. The demand is always greater than the supply—and the world pays well for what it prizes.

Now what sort of workmanship are we putting on our raw material. What are we doing for education? The man-factories among our people make, I think, a fairly good showing. Figures are encouraging things to deal with, and too they represent something tangible in casting up our accounts. There are now 25,530 colored schools in the United States with 1,353,352 pupils; the colored people hold in landed property for churches and schools $25,000,000. 2,500,000 colored children have learned to read and most of these to write also. 22,956 colored men and women are teaching in these schools. There are sixty-six academies and high schools and one hundred and fifty schools for advanced education taught by colored teachers, together with seven colleges administered by colored presidents and faculties. There are now one thousand college bred Negro ministers in the country, 250 lawyers, 749 physicians; while, according to Dr. Rankin, there are 247 colored students preparing themselves in the universities of Europe.

The African Methodists alone, representing the unassisted effort of the colored people for self-development, have founded thirty-eight institutes and colleges, with landed property valued at $502,650, and 134 teachers supported entirely by the self denying effort of the colored people themselves.

This looks like an attempt, to say the least, to do the best we can with our material. One feels there has not been much shirking here; the workmanship may be crude sometimes, when measured by more finished standards,— but they have done what they could; in their poverty and inexperience, through self denial and perseverance, they are struggling upward toward the light.

There is another item to be taken into account in estimating the value of a product, to which we must give just a thought in passing, *i. e.*, the necessary waste of material in the making

The Sultan of Turkey once sent to China to procure a *fac simile* of some elegant plates he had had, all of which were now broken but one and that, unfortunately, was cracked. He sent this one as a pattern and requested that the set be renewed exactly like the former ones. He was surprised on receiving the plates to note the fabulous sum charged for them,—but the Celestial explained that the cost was greatly increased by having *to put in the crack,*—so many had been lost in the making.

The anecdote is not my own, but it suggests a thought that may be useful to us and I borrow it for that purpose. They tell us that the waste of material is greater in making colored men and women than in the case of others— that a larger percentage of our children die under twenty-one years of age, especially in large cities, and that a larger number who reach that age and beyond, are to be classed among the world's invalids and paupers. According to the census of 1880 the average death rate throughout the country was, among the whites 14.74 per 1000; among colored 17.28 per 1000: the highest among whites being in New Mexico, 22.04, lowest in Arizona, 7.91 per 1000. Among colored, the mortality ranges from 35.25 in the District of Columbia where it is the highest, to 1.89 in Arizona, the lowest.

For 1889 the relative death-rate of the two races in the District of Columbia was: whites, 15.96 per 1000; colored, 30.48, about double. In 1888 they stood 18+ to 30+; in 1886 and '87, about 17 to 31; in '85 and '86, 17 to 32. Especially noticeable is the difference in the mortality of children. This is simply alarming. The report for 1889 shows that out of the 5,152 deaths occurring in the District of Columbia during that year, 634 were white infants under one year old, while 834, an excess of 200, within the same limits were colored. Yet the white population of the District outnumbers the colored two to one. The Health Commissioner, in his report for that year, says: "This material difference in mortality may be charged to a great extent to the massing of colored people in alleys and unhealthy parts of the city and to their unsanitary surroundings: while there is no doubt that a very large proportion of these children die in consequence of being fed improper and unhealthy food, especially cheap and badly prepared condensed milk, and cow's milk which has been allowed to stand to the point of acidity after having been kept in vessels badly or unskillfully cleaned." And he adds, "if the general statistics of infant mortality seem astounding to the public, the cause can most frequently be found in the reprehensible custom of committing little impoverished waifs to hired nurses and foul feeding bottles rather than allow them the food that nature has provided."

Now all this unquestionably represents a most wanton and flagrant *waste* of valuable material. By sapping out the possibilities of a healthy and vigorous existence it is deliberately and flagitiously breeding and multiplying paupers, criminals, idiots, drunkards, imbeciles and lunatics to infest and tax the commonwealth. The number spoiled in the making necessarily adds to the cost of those who survive. It is like the Sultan's cracked dinner-plates. It is no use to go into hysterics and explode in Ciceronian phillippics against life insurance companies for refusing to insure or charging a higher premium for colored policies. With them it is simply a question of dollars and cents. What are you worth? What are your chances, and what does it cost to take your risks in the aggregate? If thirty-five colored persons out of every thousand are, from any cause whatever, lost in the making, the remaining nine hundred and sixty-five will have to share the loss among them. This is an unavoidable law. No man can dissociate himself from his kind. The colored gentleman who keeps his horses, fares sumptuously, and lives in luxury is made to feel the death gasps of every squalid denizen of the alley and poor-house. It is God's own precaution to temper our self-seeking by binding our sympathies and interests indissolubly with the helpless and the wretched.

What our men of means need to do, then, is to devote their money, their enlightened interest, their careful attention to the improvement of sanitation among the poor. Let some of those who can command real estate in healthful localities build sweet and clean and wholesome tenements *on streets* and rent them at reasonable rates to the worthy poor who are at present forced into association with the vileness and foulness of alleys and filthy courts by the unfeeling discrimination of white dealers. Let some colored capitalists buy up a few of those immense estates in the South, divide them into single farms with neat, cheery, well-ventilated, healthsome cottages to be rented to the colored tenants who are toiling all these weary years in the one-room log hut, like their own cheerless mules—just to fodder themselves.

In cities, low priced houses on streets are almost uniformly kept for the white poor. I know of numerous houses in Washington the rent of which is no dearer than colored people are paying in alleys—but the advertisement says, " not rented to colored people." If the presence of a colored tenant in a neighborhood causes property to depreciate, it may be a question of sentiment,—it must be a question of business. The former it is superfluous to inveigh against or even to take cognizance of. It is possibly subject to enlightenment, and probably a sickness not unto death. But the practical reason underlying it is directly our concern and should command our energetic consideration. It is largely a question of what are we worth—and as such, subject to our immediate responsibility and amendment. If improvement is possible, if it is in our power to render ourselves *valuable* to a community or neighborhood, it should be the work of the earnest and able men and women among us, the moral physicians and reformers, to devise and apply a remedy. Sure it is that the burden rests on all till the deliverance comes. The richest and most highly favored cannot afford to be indifferent or to rest quietly complacent.

In rural districts, the relative mortality of colored people is not so excessive, still the poverty and destitution, the apparent dearth of accumulation notwithstanding ceaseless

drudging toil is something phenomenal in
labor statistics. I confess I have felt little
enthusiasm for the labor riots which seem
epidemic at the North. Carnegie's men at
Homestead, for instance, were among the best
paid workmen in the country, receiving many
of them $240 per month, living luxuriously,
dictating their own terms as to who should
work with them, how many hours, and what
special labor they will perform. Their em-
ployers are forced to hire so many and such
men—for these laboring despots insist on an
exact division of labor, no one must be called
on to work outside his specialty. Then they
must share profits, but be excused from all
concern in losses—a patent adjustable sliding
scale for wages which slides up beautifully, but
never down! If the Northern laboring man has
not become a tyrant, I would like to know
what tyranny is.

But I wonder how many know that there
are throughout the Southland able bodied,
hard working men, toiling year in and year
out, from sunrise to dusk, for fifty cents per
day, out of which they must feed and shelter
and clothe themselves and their families!
That they often have to take their wage in
tickets convertible into meat, meal and molas-

ses at the village grocery, owned by the same ubiquitous employer! That there are tenants holding leases on farms who toil sixteen hours to the day and work every chick and child in their posession, not sparing even the drudging wife—to find at the end of the harvesting season and the squaring up of accounts that their accumulations have been like gathering water in a sieve.

Do you ask the cause of their persistent poverty? It is not found in the explanation often vouchsafed by the white landlord—that the Negro is indolent, improvident and vicious. Taking them man for man and dollar for dollar, I think you will find the Negro, in ninety-nine cases out of a hundred, not a whit behind the Anglo-Saxon of equal chances. It is a fact which every candid man who rides through the rural districts in the South will admit, that in progressive aspirations and industry the Negro is ahead of the white man of his chances. Indeed it would not be hard to show that the white man *of his chances* does not exist. The "Crackers" and "poor-whites" were never slaves, were never oppressed or discriminated against. Their time, their earnings, their activities have always been at their own disposal; and pauperism in their case can

be attributed to nothing but stagnation,—
moral, mental, and physical immobility: while
in the case of the Negro, poverty can at least be
partially accounted for by the hard conditions
of life and labor,—the past oppression and
continued repression which form the vital
air in which the Negro lives and moves and
has his being.

One often hears in the North an earnest
plea from some lecturer for "our working
girls" (of course this means white working
girls). And recently I listened to one who
went into pious agonies at the thought of the
future mothers of Americans having to stand
all day at shop counters; and then advertised
with applause a philanthropic firm who were
giving their girls a trip to Europe for rest and
recreation! I am always glad to hear of the
establishment of reading rooms and social entertainments to brighten the lot of any women
who are toiling for bread—whether they are
white women or black women. But how
many have ever given a thought to the pinched
and down-trodden colored women bending
over wash-tubs and ironing boards — with
children to feed and house rent to pay, wood
to buy, soap and starch to furnish—lugging
home weekly great baskets of clothes for

families who pay them for a month's laundry-
ing barely enough to purchase a substantial
pair of shoes!

Will you call it narrowness and selfishness,
then, that I find it impossible to catch the fire
of sympathy and enthusiasm for most of these
labor movements at the North?

I hear these foreigners, who would boycott
an employer if he hired a colored workman,
complain of wrong and oppression, of low
wages and long hours, clamoring for eight-
hour systems and insisting on their right to
have sixteen of the twenty-four hours for rest
and self-culture, for recreation and social intercourse with families and friends—ah, come
with me, I feel like saying, I can show you
workingmen's wrong and workingmen's toil
which, could it speak, would send up a wail
that might be heard from the Potomac to the
Rio Grande; and *should it unite and act,* would
shake this country from Carolina to California.

But no man careth for their souls. The
labor interests of the colored man in this country are as yet dumb and limp. The unorganized mass has found neither tongue nor nerve.
In the free and liberal North, thanks to the
amalgamated associations and labor unions
of immigrant laborers, who cannot even speak

English,—the colored man is relegated to the
occupations of waiter and barber, unless he
has a taste for school teaching or politics. A
body of men who still need an interpreter
to communicate with their employer, will
threaten to cut the nerve and paralyze the
progress of an industry that gives work to an
American-born citizen, or one which takes
measures to instruct any apprentice not supported by the labor monopoly. A skilled
mechanic, a friend of mine, secured a job in
one of our cities and was seen by union men
at work on his house. He was immediately
ordered in murderous English to take down
his scaffolding and leave the town. Refusing
to do so, before night he was attacked by a
force that overwhelmed him and he was
obliged to leave. Such crushing opposition is
not alone against colored persons. These
amalgamated and other unions hold and are
determined to continue holding an impene-
trable monopoly on the labor market, assum-
ing supreme censorship as regards the knowledge and practice of their trade.

In the South, on the other hand, where the
colored man virtually holds the labor market,
he is too uncertain and unorganized to demand anything like a fair share of the pro-

ducts of his toil. And yet the man who thinks, must see that our labor interests lie at the foundation of our material prosperity. The growth of the colored man in this country must for a long time yet be estimated on his value and productiveness as a laborer. In adding up the account the aggregate of the great toiling mass largely overbalances the few who have acquired means and leisure. The nation judges us as workingmen, and poor indeed is that man or race of men who are compelled to toil all the weary years ministering to no higher want than that of bread. To feed is not the chief function of this material that has fallen to our care to be developed and perfected. It is an enormous waste of values to harness the whole man in the narrow furrow, plowing for bread. There are other hungerings in man besides the eternal all-subduing hungering of his despotic stomach. There is the hunger of the eye for beauty, the hunger of the ear for concords, the hungering of the mind for development and growth, of the soul for communion and love, for a higher, richer, fuller living—a more abundant life! And every man owes it to himself to *let nothing in him starve* for lack of the proper food. "What is man," says Shakespeare, "if his

chief good and market of his time be but to
sleep and feed!" Yet such slavery as that is
the settled lot of four-fifths the laboring men
of the Southland. This, I contend, is an
enormous, a profligate waste of the richest
possibilities and the divinest aptitudes. And
we owe it to humanity, we owe it pre-
eminently to those of our own household, to
enlarge and enrich, so far as in us lies, the
opportunity and grasp of every soul we can
emancipate. Surely there is no greater boon
we can bestow on our fellow-man in this life,
none that could more truly command his deepest gratitude and love, than to disclose to his
soul its possibilities and mend its opportunities,—to place its rootlets in the generous
loam, turn its leaves towards the gracious
dews and warm sunlight of heaven and let it
grow, let it mature in foliage, flower and fruit
for GOD AND THE RACE! Philanthropy will devise means—an object is not far to seek.

Closely akin to the value that may be said
to have been wasted through the inclemency
and barrenness of circumstance, through the
sickness, sin and death that wait on poverty
and squalor, a large item of worth has undoubtedly been destroyed by mistaken and
unscientific manufacture—foolhardy educators

rashly attempting to put in some theoretically desirable *crack*—the classical crack, or the professional crack, or the artistic-æsthetic-accomplishments crack—into material better fitted for household pottery and common every-day stone and iron ware. I want nothing I may say to be construed into an attack on classical training or on art development and culture. I believe in allowing every longing of the human soul to attain its utmost reach and grasp. But the effort must be a fizzle which seeks to hammer souls into pre-constructed molds and grooves which they have never longed for and cannot be made to take comfort in. The power of appreciation is the measure of an individual's aptitudes; and if a boy hates Greek and Latin and spends all his time whittling out steamboats, it is rather foolish to try to force him into the classics. There may be a locomotive in him, but there is certainly no foreshadowing evidence of either the teacher or preacher. It is a waste of forces to strain his incompetence, and smother his proficiencies. If his hand is far more cunning and clever than his brain, see what he can best do, and give him a chance according to his fitness; try him at a trade.

Industrial training has been hitherto neglected or despised among us, due, I think, as I have said elsewhere, to two causes: first, a mistaken estimate of labor arising from its association with slavery and from its having been despised by the only class in the South thought worthy of imitation; and secondly, the fact that the Negro's ability to work had never been called in question, while his ability to learn Latin and construe Greek syntax needed to be proved to sneering critics. "Scale the heights!" was the cry. "Go to college, study Latin, preach, teach, orate, wear spectacles and a beaver!"

Stung by such imputations as that of Calhoun that if a Negro could prove his ability to master the Greek subjunctive he might vindicate his title to manhood, the newly liberated race first shot forward along this line with an energy and success which astonished its most sanguine friends.

This may not have been most wise. It certainly was quite natural; and the result is we find ourselves in almost as ludicrous a plight as the African in the story, who, after a sermon from his missionary pleading for the habiliments of civilization, complacently donned a Gladstone hat leaving the rest of his body in its primitive simplicity of attire. Like him we began at the wrong end. Wealth must pave the way for learning. Intellect, whether of races or individuals, cannot soar to the consummation of those sublime products which immortalize genius, while the general mind is assaulted and burdened with "what shall we eat, what shall we drink, and wherewithal shall we be clothed." Work must first create wealth, and wealth leisure, before the untrammeled intellect of the Negro, or any other race, can truly vindicate its capabilities. Something has been done intellectually we all know. That one black man has written a Greek grammar is enough to answer Calhoun's sneer; but it is leisure, the natural outgrowth of work and wealth, which must furnish room, opportunity, possibility for the highest endeavor and most brilliant achievement. Labor must be the solid foundation stone—the *sine qua non* of our material value; and the only effective preparation for success in this, as it seems to me, lies in the establishment of industrial and technical schools for teaching our colored youth trades. This necessity is obvious for several reasons. First, a colored child, in most cases, can secure a trade in no other way. We had master mechanics while the Negro was a chattel, and the ingenuity of brain and hand served to enrich the coffers of his owner. But to-day skilled labor is steadily drifting into the hands of white workmen — mostly foreigners. Here it is cornered. The white engineer holds a tight monopoly both of the labor market and of the science of his craft. Nothing would induce him to take a colored apprentice or even to work beside a colored workman. Unless then trades are to fall among the lost arts for us as a people, they must be engrafted on those benevolent institutions for Negro training established throughout the land. The youth must be taught to use his trigonometry in surveying his own and his neighbor's farm; to employ his geology and chemistry in finding out the nature of the soil, the constituents drafted from it by each year's crop and the best way to meet the demand by the use of suitable renewers; to apply his mechanics and physics to the construction and handling of machinery— to the intelligent management of iron works and water works and steam works and electric works. One mind in a family or in a town may show a penchant for art, for literature, for the learned professions, or more bookish lore. You will know it when it is there. No need to probe for it. It is a light that cannot be hid under a bushel—and I would try to enable that mind to go the full length of its desires. Let it follow its bent and develop its talent as far as possible: and the whole community might well be glad to contribute its labor and money for the sustenance and cultivation of this brain. Just as earth gives its raw material, its carbons, hydrogen, and oxygen, for the tree which is to elaborate them into foliage, flower and fruit, so the baser elements, bread and money furnished the true brain worker come back to us with compound interest in the rich thought, the invention, the poem, the painting, the statue. Only let us recognize our assignment and not squander our portion in over fond experiments. James Russell Lowell says, " As we cannot make a silk purse out of a sow's ear, no more can we perform the opposite experiment without having a fine lot of spoiled silk on our hands."

With most of us, however, the material, such as it is, has been already delivered. The working of it up is also well under way. The gold, the silver, the wood, the hay, the stubble, whatever there was at hand has all gone in. Now can the world use it? Is there a demand for it, does it perform the functions for which it was made, and is its usefulness greater than the cost of its production? Does it pay expenses and have anything over.

The world in putting these crucial questions to men and women, or to races and nations, classifies them under two heads—as consumers or producers. The man who consumes as much as he produces is simply *nil*. It is no matter to the world economically speaking whether he is in it or out of it. He is merely one more to count in taking the census. The man who consumes more than he produces is a destroyer of the world's wealth and should be estimated precisely as the housekeeper estimates moths and mice. These are the world's parasites, the shirks, the lazy lubbers who hang around rum shops and enter into mutual relationships with lamp posts to bear each the other's burdens, moralizing all the while (wondrous moralists and orators they often are!) and insisting that the world owes them a living! To be sure the world owes them nothing of the kind. The world would consider it a happy riddance from bad rubbish if they would pay up their debt and move over to Mars. Every day they live their unproductive bodies sink and destroy a regular portion of the world's values. At the very lowest estimate, a boy who has reached the age of twenty, has already burned up between three and four thousand dollars of the world's possessions. This is on the very closest and most economical count; I charge him nothing for fuel or lights, allowing him to have warmed by fires that would have burned for others and estimating the cost simply of what he has eaten and worn, *i. e.* the amount which he has actually sunk of the world's wealth. I put his board at the moderate sum of ten dollars per month, and charge him the phenomenally small amount of thirty dollars a year for clothing and incidentals. This in twenty years gives him a debt of three thousand dollars, which no honest man should be willing to leave the world without settling. The world does not owe them a living then—the world only waits for them to square up and change their residence. It is only they who produce more than they consume, that the world owes, or even acknowledges as having any practical value.

Now to which class do we belong? The question must in the first place be an individual one for every man of whatever race: Am I giving to the world an equivalent of what it has given and is giving me? Have I a margin on the outside of consumption for surplus production? We owe it to the world to give out at least as much as we have taken in, but if we aim to be accounted a positive value we must leave it a little richer than we found it. The boy who dies at twenty leaving three thousand dollars in bank to help another, has just paid expenses. If he lives longer it increases his debit and should be balanced by a corresponding increase on the credit side. The life that serves to develop another, the mother who toils to educate her boy, the father who invests his stored-up capital in education, giving to the world the energies and usefulness of his children trained into a well disciplined manhood and womanhood has paid his debt in the very richest coin,— a coin which is always legal tender, a priceless gift, the most precious payment we can make for what we have received. And we may be sure, if we can give no more than a symmetric life, an inspiring thought, a spark caught from a noble endeavor, its value will not be lost.

Previous to 1793 America was able to produce unlimited quantities of cotton, but unable to free the fibre from the seeds. Eli Whitney came to the rescue of the strangled industry and perfected a machine which did the work needed. The deliverance which he wrought was complete. The following year America's exports of cotton to England were increased from not one pound in previous years to 1,600,000 pounds. He gave dollars.

Just before the battle of Quebec Wolf repeated and enjoyed Gray's Elegy saying he valued that gem more highly than the capture of the city before which he was encamped. The next day the city was taken and Wolf was laid to rest. But the world is in debt to both the poet and the soldier—a boundless debt, to the one for an eternal thought-gem, to the other for immortal heroism and devoted patriotism.

Once there lived among men One whom sorrowing millions for centuries since have joyed to call friend—One whose " come unto me ye that are heavy laden " has given solace and comfort to myriads of the human race. *He gave a life.*

We must as individuals compare our cost with what we are able to give. The worth of a race or a nation can be but the aggregate worth of its men and women. While we need not indulge in offensive boasting, it may not be out of place in a land where there is some adverse criticism and not a little unreasonable prejudice, quietly to take account of stock and see if we really represent a value in this great American commonwealth. The average American is never too prejudiced, I think, to have a keen appreciation for the utilities; and he is certainly not behind the rest of the world in his clear perception of the purchasing power of a dollar. Beginning here, then, I find that, exclusive of the billions of wealth *given* by them to enrich another race prior to the passage of the Thirteenth Amendment, the colored people of America to-day hold in their own right $264,000,000 of taxable property; and this is over and above the $50,000,000 which collapsed in the Freedman's Savings Bank when that gigantic iniquity paralyzed the hope and shocked the faith of an inexperienced and unfinancial people.

One would like to be able to give reliable statistics of the agricultural and mechanical products of the colored laborer, but so far I have not been able to obtain them. It is a modest estimate, I am sure, to ascribe fully two-thirds of the 6,940,000 bales of cotton produced in 1888 to Negro cultivation. The reports give estimates only in bulk as to the products of a state or county. Our efficient and capable census enumerators never draw the color line on labor products. You have no trouble in turning to the page that shows exactly what percentage of colored people are illiterate, or just how many have been condemned by the courts; no use taking the trouble to specify whether it was for the larceny of a ginger cake, or for robbing a bank of a cool half million and skipping off to Canada : it's all crime of course, and crime statistics and illiteracy statistics must be accurately detailed—and colored.

Similar commendable handling meets the colored producer from the managers of our Big American Show at Chicago which we are all so nervously anxious shall put the best foot foremost in bowing to the crowned heads and the gracious lords and ladies from over the waters. To allow any invention or mechanism, art or farm product to be accredited a black man would be drawing the color line! And our immaculate American could never be guilty of anything so vile as drawing a color line ! ! !

I am unable to say accurately, then, just how many bales of cotton, pounds of tobacco, barrels of molasses and bushels of corn and wheat are given to the world through Negro industry. The same difficulty is met in securing authentic information concerning their inventions and patents. The records of the

Patent Office at Washington do not show
whether a patentee is white or colored. And
all inventions and original suggestions made
by a colored man before emancipation were
necessarily accredited to some white individual, a slave not being able to take the oath
administered to the applicant for a patent.
Prof. Wright, however, by simply collecting
through personal inquiry the number of colored
patentees which could be remembered and
identified by examiners and attorneys practicing before the Patent Office authorities, published upwards of fifty in the A. M. E. Review
for April, 1886. Doubtless this number was
far within the truth, and many new patents
have been taken out since his count was made.
Almost daily in my walk I pass an ordinary
looking black man, who, I am told, is consid-
ering an offer of $30,000 for his patent rights
on a corn planter, which, by the way, has
been chosen as part of the Ohio exhibit for
the Columbian Exposition. He has secured
as many as half a dozen patents within a few
years and is carrying around a " new machine "
in his head every day.

Granville Wood, of Cincinnati, has given
valuable returns to the world as an electrician ;
and there is no estimating the money in the

outright gift of this people through unremu-
nerated toil. The Negro does not always
show a margin over and above consumption;
but this does not necessarily in his case prove
that he is not a producer. During the agitations for adverse legislation against the Chinese,
the charge was alleged that they spent nothing in the country. They hoarded their earnings, lived on nothing, and finally returned to
China to live in luxury and to circulate the
wealth amassed in this country. A similar
complaint can never be lodged against the
Negro. Poor fellow, he generally lives pretty
well up to his income. He labors for little
and spends it all. He has never yet gained
the full consent of his mind to " take his gruel
a little thinner " till his little pile has grown a
bit. He does not like to seem short. And
had he the wage of a thousand a year his big-
heartedness would immediately put him under
the painful necessity of having it do the entertainment of five thousand. He must eat,
and is miserable if he can't dress; and seems
on the whole internally fitted every way to
the style and pattern of a millionaire, rather
than to the plain, plodding, stingy old path
of common sense and economy. This is a
flaw in the *material* of the creature. The

grain just naturally runs that way. If our basal question of economics were put to him : *" What do you give — are you adding something every year to the world's stored up capital ? "* His ingenuous answer would be, as the ghost of a smile flits across his mobile lips—" Yea, Lord ; I give back *all*. I am even now living on the prospects of next year's income. I give my labor at accommodation rates, and forthwith reconvert my wages into the general circulation. Funds, somehow, don't seem to stick to me. I have no talents, or smaller coins either, hid in a napkin." It will be well for him to learn, however, that it is not what we make but what we save that constitutes wealth. The hod-carrier who toils for $1.50 a day, spending the dollar and laying up the half, is richer than the congressman with an annual income of $5000 and annual duns of $8000. What he most urgently needs to learn is systematic saving. He works hard enough generally—but does not seem able to retrench expenses—to cut off the luxuries which people of greater income and larger foresight, seeing to be costly and unnecessary would deny themselves. He wants to set to work vigorously to widen the margin outside the expenditures. He cannot be too deeply impressed with the fact that tobacco and liquors—even leaving out their moral aspects —are too costly to be indulged in by any who are not living on the interest of capital ready in store. A man living on his earnings should eschew luxuries, if he wishes to produce wealth. But when those luxuries deteriorate manhood, they impoverish and destroy the most precious commodity we can offer the world.

For after all, the highest gifts are not measurable in dollars and cents. Beyond and above the class who run an account with the world and merely manage honestly to pay *in kind* for what they receive, there is a noble army—the Shakespeares and Miltons, the Newtons, Galileos and Darwins, — Watts, Morse, Howe, Lincoln, Garrison, John Brown —a part of the world's roll of honor—whose price of board and keep dwindles into nothingness when compared with what the world owes them; men who have taken of the world's bread and paid for it in immortal thoughts, invaluable inventions, new facilities, heroic deeds of loving self-sacrifice; men who dignify the world for their having lived in it and to whom the world will ever bow in grateful worship as its heroes and benefactors. It may not be ours to stamp our genius in enduring characters—but we can give what we are *at its best*.

Visiting the slave market in Boston one day in 1761, Mrs. John Wheatley was attracted by the modest demeanor and intelligent countenance of a delicate looking black girl just from the slave ship. She was quite nude save for a piece of coarse carpet she had tied about her loins, and the only picture she could give of her native home was that she remembered her mother in the early morning every day pouring out water before the rising sun. The benevolent Mrs. Wheatley expended some labor in polishing up this crude gem, and in 1773 the gifted Phillis gave to the world a small octavo volume of one hundred and twenty precious pages, published in London and dedicated to the Countess of Huntingdon. In 1776, for some lines she had sent him, she received from the greatest American the following tribute dated at Cambridge:

Miss Phillis:— . . . I thank you most sincerely for your polite notice of me in the elegant lines you enclosed; and however undeserving I may be of such encomium and panegyric, the style and manner exhibit a striking proof of your poetical talents; in honor of which and as a tribute justly due to you, I would have published the poem had I not been apprehensive that, while I only meant to give the world this new instance of your genius, I might have incurred the imputation of vanity. This and nothing else determined me not to give it place in the public prints. If you should ever come to Cambridge or near headquarters, I shall be happy to see a person so favored by the Muses, and to whom nature has been so liberal and beneficent in her dispensations. I am, with great respect,

Your obedient humble servant,

GEORGE WASHINGTON.

That girl paid her debts *in song*.

In South Carolina there are two brothers, colored men, who own and conduct one of the most extensive and successful farms in this country for floriculture. Their system of irrigating and fertilizing is the most scientific in the state, and by their original and improved methods of grafting and cultivating they have produced a new and rich variety of the rose called *Loiseaux*, from their name. Their roses are famous throughout Europe and are specially prized by the French for striking and marvellous beauty. The Loiseaux brothers send out the incense of their grateful returns to the world in the *sweet fragrance of roses*.

Some years ago a poor and lowly orphan girl stood with strange emotions before a statue of Benjamin Franklin in Boston. Her bosom heaved and her eyes filled as she whispered between her clenched teeth, " Oh, how

I would like to make a stone man?" Wm.
Lloyd Garrison became her providence and
enlarged her opportunity; *she paid for it* in
giving to the world the *Madonna with the
Christ and adoring Angels,* now in the collection of the Marquis of Bute. From her studio
in Rome Edmonia Lewis, the colored sculpt-
ress, continues to increase the debt of the
world to her by her graceful thoughts in the
chaste marble.

On May 27, 1863, a mixed body of troops in
blue stood eagerly expectant before a rebel
stronghold. On the extreme right of the line,
a post of honor and of danger, were stationed
the Negro troops, the first and third regiments
of the Louisiana Native Guards. On going
into action, says an eye witness, they were
1080 strong, and formed into four lines, Lieut.-
Colonel Bassett, 1st Louisiana, forming the
first line, and Lieut.-Colonel Henry Finnegas
the second. Before any impression had been
made upon the earth works of the enemy, and
in full face of the batteries belching forth their
sixty-two pounders, the order to charge was
given,—and the black regiment rushed forward
to encounter grape, canister, shell and mus-
ketry, having no artillery but two small how-
itzers—which seemed mere pop-guns to their

adversaries—and with no reserve whatever. The terrible fire from the rebel guns upon the unprotected masses mowed them down like grass. Colonel Bassett being driven back, Colonel Finnegas took his place, and his men being similarly cut to pieces, Bassett reformed and recommenced. And thus these brave fellows went on from 7 o'clock in the morning till 3:30 p. m., under the most hideous carnage that men ever had to withstand. During this time they rallied and were ordered to make six distinct charges, losing thirty-seven killed, one hundred and fifty-five wounded, and one hundred and sixteen missing, " the majority, if not all of these," adds a correspondent of the New York Times, who was an eye witness of the fight, " being in all probability now lying dead on the gory field without the rights of sepulture! *for when, by flag of truce our forces in other directions were permitted to reclaim their dead, the benefit, through some neglect, was not extended to these black regiments.*"

" The deeds of heroism," he continues, " performed by these colored men were such as the proudest white men might emulate. Their colors are torn to pieces by shot, and literally bespattered by blood and brains. The color-sergeant of the 1st La. on being mortally wounded, hugged the colors to his breast when a struggle ensued between the two color-corporals on each side of him as to who should bear the sacred standard—and during this generous contention one of the corporals was wounded. One black lieutenant mounted the enemy's works three or four times, and in one charge the assaulting party came within fifty paces of them. If only ordinarily supported by artillery and reserve, no one can convince us that they would not have opened a passage through the enemy's works. Captain Callioux, of the 1st La., a man so black that he prided himself on his blackness, died the death of a hero leading on his men in the thickest of the fight. One poor wounded fellow came along with his arm shattered by a shell, jauntily swinging it with the other, as he said to a friend of mine: 'Massa, guess I can fight no more.' I was with one of the captains looking after the wounded, when we met one limping along toward the front. Being asked where he was going, he said, 'I been shot in de leg, cap'n, an' dey wants me to go to de hospital—but I reckon I c'n gib 'em some mo' yit.'"

Says Major-General Banks in the report from Headquarters of the Army of the Gulf, before Port Hudson, May 30, 1863, writing to Major-General Halleck, General-in-Chief at Washington: "The position occupied by the Negro troops was one of importance and called for the utmost steadiness and bravery in those to whom it was confided. It gives me pleasure to report that they answered every expectation. Their conduct was heroic. No troops could be more determined or more daring."

" 'Charge!' Trump and drum awoke,
    Onward the bondmen broke;
    Bayonet and sabre-stroke
    Vainly opposed their rush.
    Through the wild battle's crush,
    With but one thought aflush,
    Driving their lords like chaff,
    In the guns' mouths they laugh;
    Or at the slippery brands
    Leaping with open hands,
    Down they bear man and horse,
    Down in their awful course;
    Trampling with bloody heel
    Over the crashing steel,
    All their eyes forward bent,
    Rushed the black regiment.

    'Freedom!' their battle-cry—
    'Freedom! or leave to die!'
    Ah! and they meant the word,
    Not as with us 'tis heard,
    Not a mere party-shout:
    They gave their spirits out.

Trusted the end to God,
And on the gory sod
Rolled in triumphant blood!"

And thus they paid *their debt*. "They gave
—*their spirits out!*"

In the heart of what is known as the
"Black Belt" of Alabama and within easy
reach of the great cotton plantations of Georgia, Mississippi, and Florida, a devoted young
colored man ten years ago started a school
with about thirty Negro children assembled
in a comical looking shanty at Tuskegee. His
devotion was contagious and his work grew;
an abandoned farm of 100 acres was secured
and that gradually grew to 640 acres, largely
wood-land, on which a busy and prosperous
school is located; and besides a supply farm
was added, of heavy rich land, 800 acres, from
which grain and sugar cane are main products.
Since 1881, 2,947 students have been taught
here, of whom 102 have graduated, while 200
more have received enough training to fit
them to do good work as teachers, intelligent
farmers, and mechanics. The latest enroll-
ment shows girls, 247; boys, 264. Of the 102
graduates, 70 per cent. are teachers, ministers
and farmers. They usually combine teaching
and farming. Three are printers (learned the

trades at school), one is a tinner, one a black-
smith, one a wheel-wright, three are merchants, three are carpenters, others in the
professions or filling miscellaneous positions.

That man is paying his debt by giving to this
country *living, working, consecrated men and
women!*

Now each can give something. It may not
be a poem, or marble bust, or fragrant flower
even; it may not be ours to place our lives on
the altar of country as a loving sacrifice, or
even to devote our living activities so extensively as B. T. Washington to supplying the
world's need for strong and willing helpers.
But we can at least *give ourselves.* Each can
be *one* of those strong willing helpers—even
though nature has denied him the talent of
endlessly multiplying his force. And nothing
less can honorably cancel our debt. Each is
under a most sacred obligation not to squander
the material committed to him, not to sap its
strength in folly and vice, and to see at the
least that he delivers a product worthy the
labor and cost which have been expended on
him. A sound manhood, a true womanhood
is a fruit which the lowliest can grow. And
it is a commodity of which the supply never
exceeds the demand. There is no danger of

the market being glutted. The world will always want *men*. The worth of one is infinite. To this value all other values are merely relative. Our money, our schools, our governments, our free institutions, our systems of religion and forms of creeds are all first and last to be judged by this standard: what sort of men and women do they grow ? How are men and women being shaped and molded by this system of training, under this or that form of government, by this or that standard of moral action? You propose a new theory of education; *what sort of men does it turn out?* Does your system make boys and girls superficial and mechanical? Is it a producing of average percentages or a rounding out of manhood,—a sound, thorough, and practical development,—or a scramble for standing and marks?

We have a notion here in America that our political institutions,—the possibilities of a liberal and progressive democracy, founded on universal suffrage and in some hoped-for, providential way *compelling* universal education and devotion,—our peculiar American attainments are richly worth all they have cost in blood and anguish. But our form of government, divinely ordered as we dream it to be, must be brought to the bar to be tested by this standard. It is nothing worth of itself—independently of whether it furnishes a good atmosphere in which to cultivate men. Is it developing a self respecting freedom, a sound manliness on the part of *the individual*—or does it put into the power of the wealthy few the opportunity and the temptation to corrupt the many? If our vaunted " *rule of the people* " does not breed nobler men and women than monarchies have done—it must and will inevitably give place to something better.

I care not for the theoretical symmetry and impregnable logic of your moral code, I care not for the hoary respectability and traditional mysticisms of your theological institutions, I care not for the beauty and solemnity of your rituals and religious ceremonies, I care not even for the reasonableness and unimpeachable fairness of your social ethics,—if it does not turn out better, nobler, truer men and women,—if it does not add to the world's stock of valuable souls,—if it does not give us a sounder, healthier, more reliable product from this great factory of *men*—I will have none of it. I shall not try to test your logic, but weigh your results—and that test is the *measure of the stature of the fullness of a man.*

You need not formulate and establish the credibility and authenticity of Christian Evidences, when you can demonstrate and prove the present value of CHRISTIAN MEN. And this test for systems of belief, for schools of thought, and for theories of conduct, is also the ultimate and inevitable test of nations, of races and of individuals. What sort of men do you turn out? *How* are you supplying the great demands of the world's market? What is your true value? This, we may be sure, will be the final test by which the colored man in America will one day be judged in the cool, calm, unimpassioned, unprejudiced second thought of the American people.

Let us then quietly commend ourselves to this higher court—this final tribunal. Short sighted idiosyncracies are but transient phenomena. It is futile to combat them, and unphilosophical to be depressed by them. To allow such things to overwhelm us, or even to absorb undue thought, is an admission of weakness. As sure as time *is—these mists will clear away.* And the world—our world, will surely and unerringly see us as we are. Our only care need be the intrinsic worth of our contributions. If we represent the ignorance and poverty, the vice and destructiveness, the vagabondism and parasitism in the world's economy, no amount of philanthropy and benevolent sentiment can win for us esteem: and if we contribute a positive value in those things the world prizes, no amount of negrophobia can ultimately prevent its recognition. And our great " problem " after all is to be solved not by brooding over it, and orating about it, but by *living into it.*

THE GAIN FROM A BELIEF.

———

A SOLITARY figure stands in the market-
place, watching as from some lonely
tower the busy throng that hurry past him.
A strange contrast his cold, intellectual eye to
the eager, strained, hungry faces that surge by
in their never ending quest of wealth, fame,
glory, bread.

Mark his pallid cheek and haggard brow,
and the fitful gleam of those restless eyes like
two lone camp-fires on a deserted plain.

Why does that smile, half cynical, half sad,
flit across his countenance as he contemplates
these mighty heart-throbs of human passions
and woes, human hopes and human fears? Is
it pity—is it contempt—is it hate for this
struggling, working, believing humanity which
curls those lips and settles upon that hitherto
indifferent brow?

Who is he?

Earth's skepticism looking on at the protean

antics of earth's enthusiasms. Speculative un-
belief, curiously and sneeringly watching the
humdrum, common - place, bread-and-butter
toil of unspeculative belief. Lofty, unimpassioned agnosticism, *that thinks*—face to face
with hobbling, blundering, unscientific faith,
that works.

Dare we approach?

"Sir: I perceive you are not drawn into the
whirl-pool of hurrying desires that sweep over
earth's restless sons. Your philosophy, I presume, lifts you above the toils and anxieties
the ambitions and aspirations of the common
herd. Pardon me, but do you not feel called
to devote those superior powers of yours to the
uplifting of your less favored brethren? May
not you pour the oil of human kindness and
love on these troubled waters? May not your
wisdom shape and direct the channel of this
tortuous stream, building up here, and clearing out there, till this torrent become once
more a smiling river, reflecting Heaven's pure
love in its silvery bosom, and again this fruitful valley blossom with righteousness and
peace? Does not your soul burn within you
as you look on this seething mass of struggling,
starving, sinning souls? Are you not inspired
to lift up despairing, sinking, grovelling man,

—to wipe the grime and tears from his marred countenance, and bid him Look aloft and be strong, Repent and be saved, Trust God and live!"

Ah! the coldness of the look he turned on me! Methought 'twould freeze my soul. "Poor fool!" it seemed to say; and yet I could not but think I discovered a trace of sadness as he replied:—

"What is man?—A curiously fashioned clock; a locomotive, capable of sensations;—a perfected brute. Man is a plant that grows and thinks; the form and place of his growth and the product of his thought are as little dependent on his will or effort as are the bark, leaves, and fruit of a tree on its choice. Food, soil, climate,—these make up the man, —the whole man, his life, his soul (if he have one). Man's so-called moral sense is a mere dance of molecules; his spiritual nature, a pious invention. Remorse is a blunder, repentance is vain, self-improvement or reformation an impossibility. The laws of matter determine the laws of intellect, and these shape man's nature and destiny and are as inevitable and uncontrollable as are the laws of gravitation and chemical affinity. You would-be reformers know not the stupendous non-

sense you are talking. Man is as little responsible for vice or crime as for fever or an
earthquake. Those in whom the cerebrum
shows a particular formation, will make their
holidays in gambling, betting, drinking, horse-
racing—their more serious pursuits in stealing,
ravening, murdering. They are not immoral
any more than a tiger is immoral; they are
simply *un*moral. They need to be restrained,
probably, as pests of society, or submitted to
treatment as lunatics. Their fellows in whom
the white and gray matter of the brain cells
are a little differently correlated, will in their
merry moods sing psalms and make it their
habitual activity to reach out after the Unknown in various ways, trying to satisfy the
vague and restless longings of what they call
their souls by punishing themselves and pam-
pering the poor. I have neither blame nor
praise. Each class simply believe and do as
they must. And as for God — science finds
him not. If there be a God—He is unknown
and unknowable. The finite mind of man
cannot conceive the Infinite and Eternal. And
if such a being exists, he cannot be concerned
about the miserable wretches of earth. Searching after him is vain. Man has simply projected his own personality into space and

worshipped it as a God—a person—himself.
My utmost knowledge is limited to a series of
sensations within, aware of itself; and a possibility of sensations without, both governed
by unbending laws within the limits of experience and a reasonable distance beyond."

"And beyond that Beyond" I ask breath-
lessly—"beyond that Beyond?"

I am sure I detected just then a tremor as
of a chill running through that fragile frame;
and the eye, at first thoughtful and coldly
scornful only, is now unmistakably shaded
with sadness. "Beyond that Beyond?" he
repeated slowly,—beyond that Beyond, *if* there
be such,—*spaces of darkness and eternal silence!*

Whether this prolonged throb of consciousness exist after its external possibilities have
been dissolved—I cannot tell. That is to me
—a horrible plunge—*in the dark!* I stand at
the confluence of two eternities and three im-
mensities. I see, with Pascal, only infinities
in all directions which envelop me like an
atom—like a shadow which endures for a
moment and—will never return! All that I
know is that I must die, but what I know the
very least of is that very death—which I can
not avoid! *The eternal silence* of these infinite
paces maddens me!"

Sick at heart, I turn away and ask myself what is this system which, in the words of Richter, makes the universe an automaton, and man's future—a coffin! Is this the cold region to which thought, as it moves in its orbit, has brought us in the nineteenth century? Is this the germ of the "Philosophy of the future" — the exponent of our "advanced ideas," the "new light" of which our age so uproariously boasts? Nay rather is not this *monstruum horrendum* of our day but a renewal of the empiricism and skepticism of the days of Voltaire? Here was undoubtedly the nucleus of the cloud no bigger than a man's hand, which went on increasing in bulk and blackness till it seemed destined to enshroud earth and heaven in the gloom of hell.

David Hume, who, though seventeen years younger than Voltaire, died in 1776 just two years before the great French skeptic, taught skepticism in England on purely metaphysical grounds. Hume knew little or nothing about natural science; but held that what we call mind consists merely of successive perceptions, and that we can have no knowledge of anything but phenomena. His system afterwards passes through France, is borrowed and filtered through the brain of a

half crazy French schoolmaster, Auguste
Conte, who thus becomes the founder of the
Contist school of Positivism or Nescience or
Agnosticism as it is variously called. The
adherents of his school admit neither revelation, nor a God, nor the immortality of the
soul. Conte held, among other things, that
two hours a day should be spent in the worship of Collective Humanity to be symbolized
by some of the *sexe aimant*. On general principles it is not quite clear which is the *sexe
aimant*. But as Conte proceeds to mention
one's wife, mother, and daughter as fitting
objects of religious adoration because they
represent the present, past and future of Humanity—one is left to infer that he considered
the female the *loving sex* and the ones to be
worshipped; though he does not set forth who
were to be objects of woman's own adoring
worship. In this ecclesiastical system which
Prof. Huxley wittily denominates *Romanism
minus Christianity*, Conte made himself High
Pontiff, and his inamorata, the widow of a
galley slave, was chief saint. This man was
founder of the system which the agnostic
prefers to the teachings of Jesus ! However,
had this been all, the positivist would have
been as harmless as any other lunatic. But

he goes a step farther and sets up his system as the philosophy of *natural science*, originating in and proved by pure observation and investigation of physical phenomena; and scoffs at as presumptuous and unwarrantable all facts that cannot be discerned through the senses. In this last position he is followed by John Stuart Mill, Herbert Spencer, G. H. Lewes, and a noble army of physicists, naturalists, physiologists, and geologists. Says one: " We have no knowledge of anything but phenomena, and the essential nature of phenomena and their ultimate causes are unknown and inscrutable to us." Says another: " All phenomena without exception are governed by invariable laws with which no volitions natural or supernatural interfere." And another: " Final causes are unknown to us and the search after them is fruitless, a mere chase of a favorite will-o-the-wisp. We know nothing about any supposed purposes for which organs ' were made.' Birds fly because they have wings, a true naturalist will never say—he can never know they have wings *in order that* they may fly."

And Mr. Ingersoll, the American exponent of positivism, in his " Why I Am an Agnostic," winds up a glittering succession of epi-

grammatic inconsistencies with these words:
"Let us be honest with ourselves. In the
presence ot countless mysteries, standing beneath the boundless heaven sown thick with
constellations, knowing that each grain of
sand, each leaf, each blade of grass, asks of
every mind the answerless question ; knowing
that the simplest thing defies solution; feeling
that we deal with the superficial and the relative and that we are forever eluded by the
real, the absolute,—let us admit the limitations of our minds, and let us have the courage
and the candor to say : we do not know."

It is no part of my purpose to enter into
argument against the agnostics. Had I the
wish, I lack the ability. It is enough for me
to know that they have been met by foemen
worthy their steel and that they are by no
means invincible.

"The average man," says Mr. Ingersoll,
"does not reason — he feels." And surely
'twere presumption for an average woman to
attempt more. For my part I am content to
'feel.' The brave Switzer who sees the awful
avalanche stealing down the mountain side
threatening death and destruction to all he
holds dear, hardly needs any very correct
ratiocination on the mechanical and chemical

properties of ice. He *feels* there is danger nigh and there is just time for him to sound the tocsin of alarm and shout to his dear ones ' fly ! '

For me it is enough to know that by this system God and Love are shut out; prayer becomes a mummery; the human will but fixed evolutions of law ; the precepts and sanctions of morality a lie; the sense of responsibility a disease. The desire for reformation and for propagating conviction is thus a fire consuming its tender. Agnosticism has nothing to impart. Its sermons are the exhortations of one who convinces you he stands on nothing and urges you to stand there too. If your creed is that nothing is sure, there is certainly no spur to proselytize. As in an icicle the agnostic abides alone. The vital principle is taken out of all endeavor for improving himself or bettering his fellows. All hope in the grand possibilities of life are blasted. The inspiration of beginning now a growth which is to mature in endless development through eternity is removed from our efforts at self culture. The sublime conception of life as the seed-time of character for the growing of a congenial inner-self to be forever a constant conscious presence is changed into the base alternative conclusion, *Let us eat and drink for to-morrow we die.*

To my mind the essence of the poison is just here. As far as the metaphysical grounds for skepticism are concerned, they are as harmless to the masses as if they were entombed in Greek or Hebrew. Many of the terms, it is true, are often committed to memory and paraded pretty much in the spirit of the college sophomore who affects gold-bowed spectacles and stooping shoulders—it is scholarly, you know. But the real reasons for and against agnosticism rest on psychological and scientific facts too abstruse for the laity to appreciate. There is much subtle sophistry in the oracular utterances of a popular speaker like Mr. Ingersoll, which catch the fancy and charm the imagination of the many. His brilliant blasphemies like the winged seed of the thistle are borne on the slightest breath of wind and find lodgment in the shallowest of soils; while the refutation of them, undertaken in a serious and logical vein is often too conclusive to convince: that is, it is too different in kind to reach the same class of minds that have been inoculated with the poison germs.

My own object, however, is neither to argue nor to refute argument here. I want to utter

just this one truth:—The great, the fundamental need of any nation, any race, is for
heroism, devotion, sacrifice; and there cannot
be heroism, devotion, or sacrifice in a primarily skeptical spirit. A great man said of
France, when she was being lacerated with the
frantic stripes of her hysterical children,—
France needs a religion! And the need of
France during her trying Revolution is the
need of every crisis and conflict in the evolution of nations and races. At such times most
of all, do men need to be anchored to what
they *feel* to be eternal verities. And nothing
else at any time can propel men into those
sublime efforts of altruism which constitute
the moral heroes of humanity. The demand
for heroism, devotion and sacrifice founded on
such a faith is particularly urgent in a race at
almost the embryonic stage of character-build-
ing. The Hour is *now;*—where is the man?
He must *believe* in the infinite possibilities of
devoted self-sacrifice and in the eternal grandeur of a human idea heroically espoused. It
is the enthusiasms, the faiths of the world that
have heated the crucibles in which were
formed its reformations and its impulses
toward a higher growth. And I do not mean
by faith the holding of correct views and

unimpeachable opinions on mooted questions, merely; nor do I understand it to
be the ability to forge cast-iron formulas
and dub them TRUTH. For while I do not
deny that absolute and eternal truth *is*,
—still truth must be infinite, and as incapable
as infinite space, of being encompassed and
confined by one age or nation, sect or country
—much less by one little creature's finite
brain.

To me, faith means *treating the truth as true.*
Jesus *believed* in the infinite possibilities of an
individual soul. His faith was a triumphant
realization of the eternal development of *the
best* in man—an optimistic vision of the human
aptitude for endless expansion and perfecti-
bility. This truth to him placed a sublime
valuation on each individual sentiency — a
value magnified infinitely by reason of its immortal destiny. He could not lay hold of this
truth and let pass an opportunity to lift men
into nobler living and firmer building. He
could not lay hold of this truth and allow his
own benevolence to be narrowed and distorted
by the trickeries of circumstance or the color-
ings of prejudice.

Life must be something more than dilettante
speculation. And religion (ought to be if it

isn't) a great deal more than mere gratification
of the instinct for worship linked with the
straight - teaching of irreproachabla credos.
Religion must be *life made true;* and life is
action, growth, development—begun now and
ending never. And a life made true cannot
confine itself—it must reach out and twine
around every pulsing interest within reach of
its uplifting tendrils. If then you *believe* that
intemperance is a growing vice among a people
within touch of your sympathies; if you see
that, whereas the "Lord had shut them in,"
so that from inheritance there are but few
cases of alcoholized blood,—yet that there is
danger of their becoming under their changed
circumstances a generation of inebriates — if
you believe this, then this is your truth. Take
up your parable and in earnestness and faith
give it out by precept and by example.

Do you *believe* that the God of history often
chooses the weak things of earth to confound
the mighty, and that the Negro race in America has a veritable destiny in His eternal purposes,—then don't spend your time discussing
the 'Negro Problem' amid the clouds of your
fine havanna, ensconced in your friend's well-
cushioned arm-chair and with your patent
leather boot-tips elevated to the opposite

mantel. Do those poor "cowards in the South" need a leader—then get up and lead them! Let go your purse-strings and begin to *live* your creed. Or is it your modicum of truth that God hath made of one blood all nations of the earth; and that all interests which specialize and contract the broad, liberal, cosmopolitan idea of universal brotherhood and equality are narrow and pernicious, then treat that truth as true. Don't inveigh against lines of longitude drawn by others when at the same time you are applying your genius to devising lines of latitude which are neither race lines, nor character lines, nor intelligence lines—but certain social-appearance circlets assorting your "universal brotherhood" by shapes of noses and texture of hair. If you object to imaginary lines — don't draw them ! Leave only the real lines of nature and character. And so whatever the vision, the revelation, the idea, vouchsafed *you,*

Think it truly and thy thoughts shall the soul's famine feed.
Speak it truly and each word of thine shall be a fruitful seed;
Live it truly and thy life shall be a grand and holy creed!

Macaulay has left us in his masterly description of Ignatius Loyola a vivid picture of the power of a belief and its independence of material surroundings.

'On the road from the Theatine convent in Venice might have been seen once a poor crippled Spaniard, wearily but as fast as his injured limbs can carry him making his way toward Rome. His face is pinched, his body shrunken, from long fast and vigil. He enters the City of the Cæsars without money, without patrons, without influence! but there burns a light in his eye that recks not of despair. In a frequented portion of a busy street he stops and mounts a stone, and from this rude rostrum begins to address the passers by in barbarous Latin. Lo, there is contagion in the man! He has actually imparted of his spirit to that mottled audience! And now the same fire burns in a hundred eyes, that shone erewhile from his. Men become his willing slaves to do his bidding even unto the ends of the earth. With what courage, what zeal, what utter self-abnegation, with what blind devotion to their ends regardless of means do they preach, teach, write, act! Behind the thrones of kings, at the bedside of paupers, under every disguise in every land, mid pestilence and famine, in prisons oft, in perils by land and perils by sea, the Jesuit, undaunted, pursues his way.'

Do you seek to know the secret charm of

Ignatius Loyola, the hidden spring of the
Jesuit's courage and unfaltering purpose? It
is these magic words, " *I believe.*" That is
power. That is the stamping attribute in
every impressive personality, that is the fire
to the engine and the moter force in every
battery. That is the live coal from the altar
which at once unseals the lips of the dumb—
and that alone which makes a man a positive
and not a negative quantity in the world's
arithmetic. With this potent talisman man
no longer " abideth alone." He cannot stand
apart, a cold spectator of earth's pulsing struggles. The flame must burst forth. The idea,
the doctrine, the device for betterment must
be imparted. " *I believe,*"—this was strength
and power to Paul, to Mohammed, to the
Saxon Monk and the Spanish Zealot,—and
they must be our strength if our lives are to
be worth the living. They mean as much to-
day as they did in the breast of Luther or of
Loyola. Who cheats me of this robs me of
both shield and spear. Without them I have
no inspiration to better myself, no inclination
to help another.

It is small service to humanity, it seems to
me, to open men's eyes to the fact that the
world rests on nothing. Better the turtle of

the myths, than a *perhaps*. If "fooled they must
be, though wisest of the wise," let us help to
make them the fools of virtue. You may
have learned that the pole star is twelve degrees from the pole and forbear to direct your
course by it—preferring your needle taken
from earth and fashioned by man's device.
The slave brother, however, from the land of
oppression once saw the celestial beacon and
dreamed not that it ever deviated from due
North. He *believed* that *somewhere* under its
beckoning light, lay a far away country where
a man's a man. He sets out with his heavenly
guide before his face—would you tell him he
is pursuing a wandering light? Is he the
poorer for his ignorant hope? Are you the
richer for your enlightened suspicion?

Yes, I believe there is existence beyond our
present experience; that that existence is
conscious and culturable; and that there is a
noble work here and now in helping men to
live *into* it.

> " Not in Utopia,—subterraneous fields,—
> Or some secreted island, Heaven knows where !
> But in this very world, which is the world
> Of all of us—the place where in the end
> We find our happiness, or not at all ! "

There are nations still in darkness to whom

we owe a light. The world is to be moved one generation forward—whether by us, by blind force, by fate, or by God! If thou believest, all things are possible; and *as* thou believest, so be it unto thee.

FINIS.

ANCIENT CULTURE

THE COMIC THEATRE OF
GREECE AND ROME

ANCIENT CULTURE AND SOCIETY

General Editor
M. I. FINLEY

Master of Darwin College and
Professor of Ancient History
in the University of Cambridge

THE
COMIC THEATRE
OF GREECE AND
ROME

F. H. SANDBACH

Emeritus Professor of Classics
in the University of Cambridge

W · W · NORTON & COMPANY · INC · NEW YORK

Copyright © 1977 by F. H. Sandbach
Printed in the United States of America.
All Rights Reserved.

Library of Congress Cataloging in Publication Data

Sandbach, F   H
    The comic theatre of Greece and Rome.

    (Ancient culture and society)
    Bibliography: p.
    Includes index.
    1. Classical drama (Comedy)—History and criticism.
I. Title.
PA3161.S2   882   77-3141
ISBN 0-393-04483-1

1 2 3 4 5 6 7 8 9 0

CONTENTS

FIGURES

PLATES

Preface

THE prime object of this book is not simply to evaluate the comedies that survive from the ancient world, but to explain what sort of plays were written and why they were written, how and where they were produced, and how they were related to the world in which they were performed.

Information about the conditions of drama, whether it is to be gathered from the authors of antiquity or from archaeological evidence, is patchy and often uncertain. Experts disagree about the inferences that can be drawn, not least on how to interpret the remains of ancient theatres. To avoid overburdening my text with the word 'probably', I have at times been more dogmatic than is fully justified, but hope that uncertainty over important issues has not been concealed.

Transliteration of Greek names is always a problem, and no doubt inconsistencies remain. My aim has been to anglicise or latinise those of historical personages and places, that being their most familiar form, but to retain Greek spelling for characters in and titles of plays, except for three by Aristophanes which have long had a latinised termination.

Drafts have been read by Dr Colin Austin, Mr Michael Meyer, and Professor Moses Finley, to all of whom I am greatly indebted for corrections, information, and suggestions. For errors which remain I alone am responsible.

F.H.S.

Introduction

THE names are known of nearly 250 authors of Greek comedy, dating from the sixth century BC to the second century AD. At the end of that century Athenaeus, a learned man with access to the great library of Alexandria at the mouth of the Nile, claimed to have read 800 comedies which had been composed in a period roughly corresponding to the years 400–325 BC. How much of all this vast and continuing production, testimony to the place of comedy in Greek civilisation, still survives today?

The plays of just one author of comedies were copied and read by the scholars of the later Byzantine Empire, to whom the preservation of classical Greek literature is owed. He was Aristophanes, whose power and versatility won him fame in Athens at the end of the fifth century BC, that period of astonishing creativity, literary, artistic and philosophical, the time of Euripides and Pheidias, Thucydides and Socrates; he had then worked on in the drabber years of the early fourth century when comedy set out on a road of development to a new form. Eleven of his comedies were all that these scholars found remaining out of a total of at least forty. But copies of them were taken to Italy, and so when Byzantium fell to the Turks in 1453 these eleven plays were not in danger of being lost to the world.

From the others, which had disappeared during the Dark Ages of the seventh and eighth centuries, when pagan literature was suspect, hated, neglected and destroyed, nothing was preserved but odd words, lines and short passages, few of more than eight or nine verses; these had been quoted by other authors whose works for some reason survived, particularly by grammarians and lexicon-makers who were interested in his copious vocabulary, much of which was by their time obsolete. Similar flotsam from the works of about 120 other comic authors survived in the same way. Some of

9

these comedians attracted the attention of anthologists in search of moral maxims and well-turned sentiments, while Athenaeus fished widely in their waters for passages connected with food, drink, cooks and dinner-parties.

The material gathered from such sources and first assembled in a publication of 1839–41 unavoidably gave a distorted picture of these lost dramas. But there is other evidence which could do something to correct it. Twenty plays by Plautus and six by Terence, Latin dramatists of the second century BC, are adaptations of Greek comedies, most of which indubitably belonged to the period 325–250. These Latin versions survive because some manuscripts written in the fourth or fifth centuries AD, when there were still educated laymen to read them, were kept and copied in medieval monasteries. From them a very good idea can be formed of the plots at any rate of the originals.

But until the twentieth century direct knowledge of Greek comedy was, with trifling exceptions, confined to what had been transmitted through the Byzantines. Now, however, a new source was found. Books in the ancient world were mostly written on papyrus, a material made from a reed which grows in Egypt. It was less durable than good modern paper, but it can survive well in very dry conditions, such as are provided by the rubbish-heaps and collapsed houses of parts of that country, which had come to have a partly hellenised population after its conquest by Alexander the Great. The possible rewards of excavating on suitable sites became apparent a hundred years ago, and a great deal of material was collected, mainly between 1895 and 1914.

Among this material many scraps have turned up from numerous different manuscripts which contained comedies, attesting the popularity of this form of literature among the inhabitants of these small Egyptian towns. The majority are from the works of Menander, (342–292), whose name was in antiquity coupled by some critics with that of Homer. More important, however, was the find in 1905 of nineteen leaves (some damaged) and other fragments of a manuscript which made it possible to form a picture of three of his plays. A still greater discovery came to light in 1958, when the existence was first reported of a manuscript which has proved to contain

three plays by Menander; one is complete, while far the greater part of the second and more than half of the third are intact. Several other extensive texts also have been published since 1965. This new evidence has greatly extended understanding of his work and at the same time provided a wider and sounder basis for estimating the originality of the Latin dramatists.

In Greece public performances of drama were usually part of a religious festival, included in the official proceedings. The arrangements were in the hands of the authorities responsible for the festival. It was also usual that plays should be presented in competition with one another and that prizes should be awarded to those judged to be the best.

Drama was not necessarily an original feature of the festivals at which it was performed. No doubt it was immediately part of the programme at some festivals that were comparatively late institutions, like those established at many places during the century that followed the death of Alexander the Great. But at Athens, although comedy was presented at festivals of great antiquity, it was not taken under official patronage before the fifth century B C; this step was taken as late as about 440 at the Lenaia, where it always overshadowed tragedy, whereas the City Dionysia, where it was subordinate, included it as early as 486. To recapture the religious feelings of past civilisations may be impossible, but perhaps these old Athenians thought that their god Dionysus would share their pleasure in dramatic performances.

Competition was dear to the Greeks. The athletic contests at the court of Alcinous in the *Odyssey* appear to be purely secular, but the four great religious panhellenic festivals at Olympia, Delphi, Nemea and the Isthmus of Corinth, centred on a variety of races and other contests; at Delphi athletic events were an addition to original musical competitions for pipers, lyre-players and singers who accompanied themselves on the lyre. At Athens a torch-race was held at more than one festival, and after Peisistratus' expansion of the Panathenaia in the sixth century prizes were offered there for the recital of Homer and for performances with pipe and lyre as well as for

athletics and horse-racing. Consequently it is not surprising that when drama became part of two Dionysiac festivals, it too was made the occasion for competition.

The festival of the Lenaia was so-called after the *lēnai*, a name for ecstatic women experiencing possession by the god Dionysus. There is no evidence to show that they still played a part in its celebration in the fifth century. All that is certain is that there was a procession and, after 440, dramatic contests. Procession and plays were under the care of the 'king', one of the nine annual magistrates, the residual heir of a former monarchy. To him dramatists who wished to have their plays performed 'applied for a chorus', and he allotted choruses for two tragedies and five comedies. It is not known on what grounds he exercised his choice; poets certainly had not completed their plays at this point; occasionally two plays by the same author were selected. The duty of providing the choruses fell upon well-to-do citizens, one for each play, who became its *chorēgos*, literally 'chorus-leader', although he took no part in the actual performance; his task was to recruit its members, able to sing and to dance, provide their costumes, and pay a trainer and a piper who accompanied their songs. This was one of the 'liturgies', or public services, required of the wealthier citizens, whom civic and personal pride often forbade to stint their expenditure; it was easy to lay out fifteen minae on a comedy, the price of ten able-bodied slaves, even although the 'king' was responsible for hiring and paying the leading actor from public funds; he in his turn may have engaged the rest of the cast.

Arrangements were much the same at the City Dionysia, the other Athenian festival at which plays were presented. But the magistrate in charge was the *archōn epōnymos*, not the 'king'; he too was annually appointed and given his title because his name was used in the Athenian calendar to identify the year in which he held office. In contrast with the Lenaia, tragedy here had first place, occupying the theatre for three days, on each of which were performed three tragedies and a satyr-play. An earlier day may have seen five comedies[1] and before

[1] It is orthodox to suppose that during the Peloponnesian War the number of comedies was reduced for reasons of economy to

that at least a day must have been given to dithyrambs, songs in honour of gods, sung by choirs of fifty; each of the ten 'tribes', into which the citizens were divided, provided two choirs, one of men and one of boys.

These singers of dithyrambs cannot have been professionals, and it is a striking fact that such a large number of citizens were actively engaged as competitors at this festival. The chorusmen of tragedy and comedy were also citizens and there is nothing to show that in the fifth century they received any pay, apart from some possible 'fringe benefits'. We should probably see most of them as what we should call 'experienced amateurs'.

Every dramatist whose work was performed received a payment; it is not known whether the winner had any reward beyond a garland of ivy; there is a little evidence to show that second and third were also places of honour, as they are in modern athletic events. Not only were the poets in competition, but often the leading actors also; at the Lenaia a prize for the best comic actor seems to have been instituted at the same time as comedy, but there was none at the City Dionysia until some date between 329 and 312, although tragic actors had competed there from about 450. The successful actor did not by any means always appear in the winning play. It may be added that there is no record at any time, whether in literature or in inscriptions, of any man who acted both in tragedy and in comedy on the Greek stage. Nor were dramatists active in both fields; when Socrates at the end of Plato's *Symposium* forces the tragic poet Agathon and Aristophanes the comedian to admit that it is the same man who can write tragedy and comedy, that was an outrageous paradox.

---

three, and that one was performed after each satyr-play. A strong case against this has been made by W. Luppe, *Philologus* 116 (1972) pp. 53–75. We do not know that the comedies normally came between the dithyrambs and the tragedies, but official records always give the winners in the order boys' dithyramb, men's dithyramb, comedy, tragedy.

An Athenian Comedy

To say that we possess eleven plays by Aristophanes, the Athenian writer of comedies, is a half-truth. We have the words of eleven plays. But the text is not the play. The play was a single performance in the theatre at Athens, spoken and acted by costumed actors and in part sung by a chorus of dancers to the music of a piper. There is no record that any of the eleven plays was performed more than once except *Frogs* of 405 B C, and that was mentioned because it was exceptional. The experience of that original audience cannot be recaptured; the melodies they heard are lost for ever, and many of the jokes need explanation, which may give understanding, but does not encourage laughter. Yet imagination can do something to reconstruct the scene and, aided by information and hints to be found in ancient authors, do much to revivify the words. The stage can be before the mind's eye and the actors seen to move upon it; although these ghostly figures can do little to re-create that rapport with the audience and elicit that response from it without which a play is a failure, although the infectious laughter of the spectators is now silent and the topical allusions stir no emotions, the attempt must be made to transport ourselves back from the isolated chair in our house or library to a seat on a crowded Athenian hillside.

The year is 425 B C. It is midwinter, although the days have begun to lengthen. The festival of the Lenaia has returned to cheer the people. The Peloponnesian War has been in progress for more than five years, and farms have suffered the ravages of annual invasions; crops have been destroyed, here and there vines slashed, olives cut down, houses burnt. Every year the country population has been obliged to take refuge behind the walls which connect the city with its port, the Peiraeus. But command of the sea secures Athenian property in the Aegean islands, widespread trade, and tribute from the subject 'allies'.

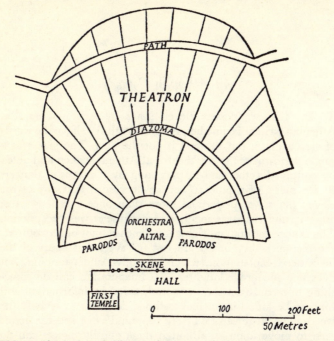

FIG. 1 *Sketch-plan of Theatre of Dionysus in the time of Aristophanes*

Let us go with the crowds at daybreak to the theatre (see Fig. 1), not forgetting a cushion and some food, for the performances will proceed without pause for the whole day. The auditorium has been formed in a hollow on the south side of the Acropolis; it is possible to reach the higher tiers by a path part way up, but we will enter at the lowest level by one of the *parodoi* or ways-in, which lead past the ends of the roughly semi-circular rows of wooden seating, and then climb up by one of the sets of steeply rising steps which intersect them. From our seats we look down on a circular area of hard-trodden earth, across which we have come; this is the *orchēstra*, or dancing-floor, about 22 yards in diameter, the length of a cricket-pitch, with an altar for Dionysus in the centre. Touching (or is it overlapping?) the far side runs a low platform; we can but guess its dimensions, perhaps 25 feet wide and 9

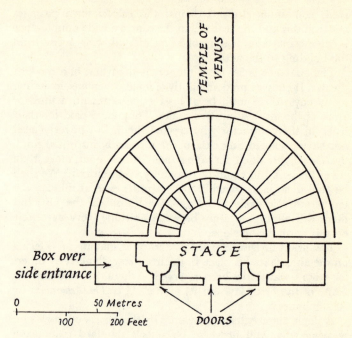

FIG. 2 *Sketch-plan of Pompey's Theatre at Rome*

feet deep.[1] A few steps connect this platform with the orchestra; we shall be interested to see whether they form a kind of short stairway or run all the way round. Behind and extending to the sides far beyond it is a building of thick timbers, the

[1] The description of the theatre depends on archaeological evidence difficult to interpret and much disputed. My text gives what I think to be a very probable account that is widely but not unanimously held. There are even those who argue that the performances at the Lenaia, unlike those at the City Dionysia (see p. 26), were not given in the theatre at all. This is typical of the problems which face the historian of ancient drama. The earlier writers of antiquity often fail to record what they suppose everyone must know, while later ones may be suspected of knowing no more than we do and of resorting, like us, to guesswork.

skēnē, containing dressing-rooms; the *parodoi* form passages between this and the seating. In the centre a wide double-door is the most striking feature of its façade, allowing access from the building to the acting area.

The audience is far more numerous than that of a modern theatre. It consists predominantly of male Athenians, including many boys; there must be at least 15,000 present, a third or more of the city's adult free males. They have paid for their seats, to the contractor who erected them. But poverty need not have excluded any citizen, for a recently instituted fund, the *theōric*, provided for a payment that would more than cover the cost and could be drawn by every citizen.[1] We shall be glad to sit close together, for warmth; even at midday the temperature is likely to be about 11 °C out of the sun; but there will almost certainly be some sunshine, very agreeable on this south-facing slope.

The priest of Dionysus enters and after making an offering on the altar takes his place in the front row, flanked by others for whom seats have been reserved. A herald announces the name of the first play and its author. It is *The Acharnians* by Aristophanes.[2]

A single actor enters the *orchestra* by the *parodos* on our right, wearing what will prove to be actor's standard costume, a mask that covers the whole face and flesh-coloured tights that reach to the wrists and ankles, with padded belly and buttocks; to these tights is attached an exaggerated phallus, revealed by an unnaturally short tunic. From his words, spoken in verse, as all the play will be, it soon appears that he is to be thought of as in the Pnyx, the open space on a low hill where there was held, at least three times a month, a general assembly of the Athenian people. He begins with some jokes at the expense

[1] This is a probability only. Theoric payments are explicitly attested only for the City Dionysia, the other festival at which there were dramatic performances.

[2] This is an arbitrary assumption. The play was presented at the Lenaia of 425, but its place in the programme is not known. Moreover, although its text assumes the audience to be aware that Aristophanes is the author, the producer was, as for his two earlier plays, his friend Callistratus; he and not Aristophanes may have been named by the herald.

of the politician Cleon, of Theognis, a writer of tragedies, of two singers and a piper, then complains of the dilatoriness of the people to attend the meeting; even its officers come pushing in at the last moment and never give a thought to making peace. He himself is always the first to arrive and sits there 'groaning, yawning, stretching, farting, puzzling, doodling, pulling out hairs and doing sums, looking towards his farm, longing for peace'. Today he has come prepared to create a scene unless peace is discussed.

Suddenly the assembly is filling; a herald calls for speakers. The first is Amphitheos, who presents himself as the goddess Demeter's grandson and complains that, although an immortal, he has been refused a grant of travelling-expenses to go to Sparta, where he proposes to conclude peace. In spite of protests by Dikaiopolis—that proves later to be the name of the character who had first appeared on the stage—he is seized by the police, who in Athens were slaves from Scythia. Next come ambassadors back from a visit to the King of Persia; they complain of their hardships, paid a mere two drachmas a day (four times a normal rate), forced to drink their wine neat out of golden cups, and fed on whole roast oxen. Dikaiopolis annotates their story with indecent comments. An ambassador then introduces Pseudartabas; in Greek the first part of this Persian-sounding name means 'false'. His mask has a huge eye, and he is alleged to be the official known as 'The King's Eye'. He speaks two lines; the first is gibberish, interpreted by the ambassador as promise of a subsidy; the second is broken Greek: 'no get money.' Dikaiopolis intervenes: 'Tell me, or I'll beat you black and blue, will the King send us money?'. The Eye indicates a negative. 'Then the ambassadors are fooling us?' Two 'eunuchs', who accompany the Eye, nod, so giving themselves away as Greeks. Dikaiopolis recognises them as two notorious supposed catamites, often ridiculed in comedies. The herald then announces that the Council invite the Eye to dinner, and Dikaiopolis gives Amphitheos eight drachmas to go to Sparta and bring back a private peace for him and his family.

The herald calls on an envoy who has been to the Thracian chief Sitalces. He introduces a troop of Thracian savages to be enlisted as mercenaries. They pounce upon Dikaiopolis, to

steal and devour the garlic he has brought to go with his lunch. Protesting against this and crying that he has felt a drop of rain, he causes the assembly to be suspended. Amphitheos rushes in, saying that he is being pursued by the men of Acharnae, a large village north of the city, because he is bringing *spondai* from Sparta, literally wine for libation, but also a word for a treaty of peace. Dikaiopolis tastes three varieties, chooses that with the longest validity and by going through a door into the stage-building, enters his farmhouse, now suddenly represented by the stage-building; he has the intention of celebrating the country Dionysia. Amphitheos makes off by the *parodos* opposite that by which he had entered.

No sooner has he gone than the Acharnians, who form the chorus of this play, surge into the *orchestra*, twenty-four of them, dressed in masks and tights, tunics and cloaks, intent on lynching the traitor; but they draw aside at the appearance of a religious procession—such as had a place at the rural Dionysia—formed by Dikaiopolis and his daughter, who bears the sacred basket, and a slave carrying high and erect the emblematic phallus. Dikaiopolis sings of his joy at returning to his village and the even greater pleasure of having his way with a slave-girl caught stealing his wood. The Acharnians rush at him; his daughter and the slave must run in.

The metre changes: the lines are now not iambic trimeters but mostly long trochaics with some cretics and a few anapaests.[1] The exchanges between Dikaiopolis and the chorus or its leader are for sixty-two verses almost exactly balanced, and they may have been spoken to the music of a long-robed piper who has come in with the chorus. He has twin pipes, supported and held to his mouth by a band which passes round the back of his head. Dikaiopolis saves the situation by running into his house and coming out with a bag of charcoal as a hostage. Many Acharnians were charcoal burners and his device parodies Euripides' *Telephus*, produced thirteen years earlier, in which the hostage was a child. They are forced to allow him to put his case, which he proposes to do with his head upon a block; Telephus had said that even if his neck

---

[1] For these metrical terms see Glossary, p. 157.

were threatened by an axe, he would not keep silent. Dikaiopolis turns this figure of speech into a literal realisation.

The actor now turns to the audience and, reverting to
iambic trimeters, reminds them how Cleon had dragged him
before the Council on account of last year's comedy, perhaps
a hint not to show such an absurd touchiness if they do not
like what they are about to hear. For the moment he has taken
on the person of the author. Then, making fun of a common
practice of defendants in a court of law, he says that he must
dress himself to look as wretched as possible; for this he will
go to Euripides, who was notorious for introducing into his
tragedies ragged heroes down on their luck. The central door
now represents Euripides' house: a servant answers 'he is at
home not at home'. Dikaiopolis persists and the poet, interrupted in composing a drama, consents to be wheeled out on
the *ekkyklēma*, a device by which in tragedies a platform was
pushed through the stage-door to reveal an interior tableau.
In tragic language he grants requests made one by one for
properties from his plays, until finally he exclaims: 'There all
my plays are gone!' But his tormentor has not finished: 'I've
forgotten the one thing on which everything depends. Sweetest
and dearest little Euripides, may I be damned if I ask you for
anything more, except one single thing, just this one thing,
this one thing: let me have some chervil you got from your
mother.'[1]

Dressed as a beggar, Dikaiopolis lays his head on the block
and puts his case. He hates the Spartans, but this is a war
about trifles. There had been an import ban, he says, on goods
from Megara and a prostitute kidnapped from that town; the
Megarians had retaliated by stealing two prostitutes from the
establishment of Aspasia, Pericles' mistress. Thereupon
Pericles carried a measure to outlaw Megarians by land and
sea; the Spartans had then come to the aid of their allies, just
as the Athenians would have rushed to arms to defend the
least of *their* allies.

This speech divides the Acharnians. Those who are still
indignant summon Lamachus, a popular general, who enters

[1] Aristophanes was fond of alleging that Euripides' mother had
once sold vegetables on the market.

in battle array. Dikaiopolis simulates terror, but then accuses him of making a good thing out of war, unlike the honest men who serve in the ranks. 'O Democracy! can we stand this?' cries Lamachus and departs, declaring that he will always fight the Spartans everywhere. Dikaiopolis goes into his own house.

What follows brings a surprise. The Acharnians announce that they have been won over, but that they must strip for their anapaests. Dropping their cloaks, they advance towards us, the spectators, and their leader delivers a long speech in anapaestic metre:

> Never before, since he had charge of a comic chorus, has our author come forward to the spectators to tell them how clever he is. But now, being slandered by his enemies among the Athenians, quick in their judgments, he must make his answer to the Athenians, who are quick to repent of their judgments. He says that your poet is to have credit for many good services, having stopped you from being taken in too much by what foreigners say, or having pleasure from their flatteries, or belonging to Suckertown. Previously ambassadors from other cities used to take you in; they began calling you 'violet-garlanded', and as soon as that word was uttered, those garlands had you sitting on the tips of your backsides. And if to flatter you anyone called Athens 'glittering', that 'glittering' would get him anything he wanted, an epithet fit for praising sardines.

The speech goes on to say that the poet's reputation had reached the King of Persia, who had told the Spartans that the side which that man vituperated would win the war. That is why they are asking the Athenians to surrender Aegina; his home is there and they want to capture him. The anapaests end with six short lines, uttered without pause for breath, which defy and insult Cleon.

Resuming their character, the chorus sings, accompanied by the piper, an invocation to the Muse of Acharnae, followed by sixteen trochaic lines of declamation: adopting the guise of veterans of the Persian Wars they complain that clever young

men entrap and entangle them in the law-courts. After a second song, which protests that those who fought at Marathon are now prosecuted by rascals, another sixteen lines continue the complaint about what happens in the courts.

Dikaiopolis briefly reappears to establish a market where Peloponnesians, Megarians and Boeotians can trade with him. The first to come is a starving Megarian, who hopes to sell his two daughters, disguised as piglets. An amusing scene follows, spiced by the fact that the word for 'piglet' was also a slang term for the female pudenda and by other ambiguities. An informer comes on, threatening to denounce the pigs as contraband, but is driven away. The chorus congratulate Dikaiopolis on the absence from his market of various Athenians, whom they accuse of unpleasant crimes and vices. A Boeotian, wishing to sell eels and other delicacies, is welcomed and his goods paid for by presenting him with another informer, who is trussed and packed up to be carried away as if he were a pottery vase, a familiar Athenian export. A messenger arrives from Lamachus, asking to buy some of the Boeotian fare with which to celebrate the festival of Anthesteria—a couple of months must have passed without our noticing—and is refused. Dikaiopolis carries the good things in, leaving the chorus to sing another pair of balanced songs, one rejecting war, the other welcoming Conciliation, who comes out in the guise of a beautiful woman.

As Dikaiopolis, out once more, makes preparations for a feast, a farmer, who has been ruined by the war, unavailingly asks for a drop of peace; then an emissary from a bridegroom brings a dish of meat from the wedding-feast, hoping for a cupful of peace in return, so that he may not have to leave his bride; he too is refused, but a bridesmaid, who comes with a whispered message, is more successful. Next a messenger arrives calling Lamachos to serve on the frontier, while another brings Dikaiopolis an invitation to dine with the priest of Dionysus. Line by line Lamachos calls for items of military equipment and Dikaiopolis for items of tasty food. Then they leave, one for the front, the other for dinner. After another pair of choral songs directed against a *choregos* who had failed to reward his singers with a dinner-party, a messenger announces (in a nonsensical parody of tragic style) that

Lamachus is a casualty. The general himself follows immediately, lamenting his wound in tragic language, while
Dikaiopolis comes back from his dinner with a girl on either
arm, and happily makes antiphonal responses, until he finally
leads the chorus out, raising a chant of victory for their play.

Victory is not yet assured; there are competing plays to
follow. At the end of the day the judges will give their decision.
They have been appointed by an elaborate method. Before
the contest the Council selected a number of names from each
of the ten 'tribes' between which the citizenry was divided,
and placed them in jars, one for each tribe. These were sealed
in the presence of the *choregoi*, to be reopened in the theatre
just before the performance. The presiding officer drew one
name from each jar and the ten chosen men swore to judge
impartially. When all the plays have been performed, each
man will write down his verdict, putting them in order of
merit, and cast it into another jar, from which the 'king' will
draw five at random. These will decide the issue, and in fact
Aristophanes, a young man in his early twenties, will be
crowned with the victor's wreath of ivy, beating into second
place Cratinus, the greatest of the dramatists of the earlier
generation. Eupolis, another rising young man, is third.

By making it uncertain whose voice would be effective, the
procedure was designed to minimise the possibility of bringing
threats or inducements to bear. Yet in the early fourth century,
at least, it was recognised that committed partisans might be
placed on the original panel. And since the judges' several
votes were made known, they were sometimes led to abandon
their own preferences by the way in which the plays were
popularly received. A philosopher like Plato might condemn
this, but they were judging not five plays *sub specie aeternitatis*
but particular performances of five plays: one of the aims of
the dramatist is to please his audience, and if he fails to do so,
there is something wrong with the play for that occasion.

The account of the play we have been watching has necessarily
been incomplete. Pure guesswork is the only way of supplying
many details. For instance, how much of the action took place

on the platform and how much did actors move on the space before it? Did all the extras, who played non-speaking parts, wear the comic actor's costume? Did they wear masks? When the chorus dropped their cloaks to come forward to address the audience, what was done with them? This part of the play was called the *parabasis*, or 'stepping-forward'. The name is applied both to the first element, usually anapaests, and more widely to the whole system including the songs and the trochaic addresses. The purpose of the stripping is generally supposed to be that of freeing their wearers for dancing. But if one wishes to imagine how and when they danced, there is neither agreement nor significant evidence. Movement of the arms and body was important, movement of the feet perhaps unnecessary. Even so, it is difficult to dance and speak at once. Hence some modern authors confidently state that the songs were sung by half-choruses, while the other half-chorus danced, that the anapaests were delivered by the chorus leader solo, and the trochaics by the leaders of half-choruses. It may have been standard practice so to divide the chorus, but evidence for it is frail.

There are, however, some uncertainties about which more can be said, and these are discussed in an appendix.

Aristophanes

The play at which we have imagined ourselves to be spectators is in a sense typical of the nine plays that survive from about thirty which Aristophanes wrote before the end of the fifth century. Its principal elements recur again and again. Sometimes they are modified and they are not all to be found in all plays. There is no lack of novelty and experiment. But although *The Acharnians* was written when the poet was in his early twenties, it already clearly reveals his style and methods.

What may seem most important to the modern reader is the subject about which least need be said. This is not a place to insist on all the literary merits: the fantasy, the variety of incident, the abundance of jokes, their timing, their unexpectedness. Much, though not all, will come over in an English translation. Nevertheless there are other things which must be lost: the plays upon words; the parody of contemporary tragedy, often now only to be suspected, because the original is not preserved; and above all the charm of some of the lyric passages.

The primary object of this chapter is to look at Aristophanes' plays, not as timeless parts of world literature, but as constituents of life in Athens during the Peloponnesian War. The Athenians thought comedy important. It was publicly organised, supported by private generosity, given the incitement of competition for prizes between both authors and leading actors, and made part of two old religious festivals. *The Acharnians*, as we have seen, was produced at the midwinter Lenaia; the other festival, the City Dionysia, was held about the end of March. Since the sailing season began in the spring, there were in Athens at the time of the Dionysia men from the 'allied' states all over the Aegean; many would find a place in the theatre, including those who had brought the annual tribute. In his *Babylonians*, shown at the Dionysia in the year before *The Acharnians*, Aristophanes had criticised Athenian

magistrates in the presence of these 'allies' and this caused Cleon, who was ridiculed in the play, to summon him before the Council on a charge of bringing the city into disrepute. No penalty seems to have been imposed, but one may notice that *Clouds* and *Birds*, other plays produced at the Dionysia, and *Women at the Thesmophoria*,[1] which may have been produced there, keep more or less clear of politically sensitive subjects, and *Peace* (421) is not critical of Athens (see below p. 34).

Clouds (423) is an attack on Socrates, but the play could be fully enjoyed by those who did not know him, for this dramatic Socrates is an individual who engages in all the antics that popular prejudice associated with intellectuals and keeps a school in which one can learn how to make a case, even in the law-courts, for cheating and violence. *Birds* (414), the most delightful of the plays, shows two men, Peisthetairos[2] and Euelpides, who wish to escape from life in the great city Athens. They come to the land of the birds, who form the chorus, dressed not uniformly but to represent twenty-four different species. The birds attack them but desist when persuaded that they can build a city in the sky which will sever communications between men and the gods, whose place they will take. This is done; Cloudcuckooland is founded and in the second half of the play Peisthetairos is pestered by a series of visitors from earth, not specifically from Athens, offering unwanted services or making requests. Emissaries come from the gods: Iris, who is contumeliously driven away; Prometheus, not an emissary, but a traitor, under cover of a sunshade, conveying a warning that the birds must insist on the surrender to them of the Queen, a lovely girl who guards Zeus' thunderbolts; finally a plenipotentiary embassy, consisting of the aristocratic Posidon, Heracles ready to accept any terms to get a dinner, and the barbarian Triballian god, who speaks gibberish. Posidon is outvoted, and Peisthetairos returns to the strains of a wedding-song with the Queen as his bride.

---

[1] The Thesmophoria was a religious festival.

[2] I do not share the confidence with which some scholars uphold their various normalisations of this name: Peithetairos, Peisetairos, Pisthetairos or Pithetairos.

Euripides, the main subject of the *Women at the Thesmophoria* (411), was well known outside Athens. He disguises a kinsman as a woman to make his way into the feminine festival, where he has heard that the celebrants are to conspire against him in retaliation for his having exposed their vices through the evil women he had put upon the stage. The kinsman goes and speaks up ridiculously for Euripides, claiming that the dramatist had suppressed some of the most damaging facts. He is of course discovered, stripped, and fastened to a plank. The second half of the play contains a number of attempts by Euripides to rescue him, all involving parody of scenes from Euripidean tragedy. Finally the Scythian policeman who guards him and who speaks amusing broken Greek is lured away by a dancing-girl[1] introduced by Euripides in the disguise of an old bawd.

The plays from the Lenaia, on the other hand, generally have a close association with Athenian political life. In *Knights* (424) an elderly man Demos, who is the Athenian people, has fallen under the domination of his Paphlagonian slave, obviously Cleon, who manages him by bribery and bluster. Paphlagonia was a district of Asia Minor, and the name suggests the verb *paphlazein*, 'to bubble and splutter'. Another slave, whom it is tempting to identify with the general Demosthenes, calls in the help of the well-to-do young men who formed the Athenian cavalry, and they enter, riding pick-a-back on others who represent their horses. To depose the Paphlagonian it is necessary to find someone who will outdo him in vulgarity and lack of honesty. A suitable person is found in a sausage-seller, who wins a long contest with the Paphlagonian in reciprocal abuse and rival promises. Installed

[1] Although female speaking actors were unknown, it is possible that this silent character was played by a naked slave-girl. There are in Aristophanes several such silent characters whose part involves the excitation or (offstage) satisfaction of sexual desire. Sometimes the text implies that their private parts are visible and attractive. If they were played by men in tights, this might have raised a laugh. But a producer might have thought the titillation of real nudity more welcome. Some fourth-century vases made for the Greeks of Italy show naked female dancers or gymnasts in association with male actors who wear tights and masks.

28

in power, he rejuvenates Demos by boiling him in a cauldron, a traditional method of magicians. Thus the man who was the demagogue to beat all demagogues unexpectedly and inconsistently becomes a reformer who revives the glorious people of the young uncorrupted democracy, which was just, sensible and peace-loving.

Wasps (422) is a satire on the Athenian system of law. Philokleon, 'Cleon-lover', is shut up by his son Bdelykleon, 'Cleon-loather', to prevent him from going to sit as a juryman in the courts. Athenian juries were huge, normally having 501 members for public prosecutions, sometimes twice that number, drawn from a body of some 6,000 citizens registered as available for service, men to whom pay for sitting in court was often a valued source of income. They determined not only the verdict but also the sentence. Philokleon loves the power this gives him over the accused. His attempts to escape from his house occupy the opening of the play. Then his fellow-jurymen, who form the chorus, come to bring him away to the courts. Finding him imprisoned, they cast off their cloaks for action, revealing themselves as having the form of wasps with menacing stings. They are repulsed and Bdelykleon compensates his father by allowing him to try a domestic case at home, that of a dog accused of stealing food. As evening comes on and the courts are closed, Philokleon is encouraged to go out to a party, from which he returns drunk, bringing a girl he has stolen and pursued by a man and a woman he has assaulted, who threaten him with the law.

The repeated attacks upon Cleon invite a number of questions. Were they due to rancour over his reaction to the *Babylonians*, or to disagreement with his policies? Were they likely to be welcomed by the majority of the audience? Did Aristophanes intend to influence public opinion or simply to amuse his hearers by a caricature?

In theory it is unjustifiable to assume that any opinions expressed in a play are those of the dramatist himself; much erroneous interpretation of ancient drama has been advanced by critics who have ascribed to the author views which he put into the mouth of a character. Nevertheless Aristophanic comedy has features by which some opinions can be identified as being his own, or at the least as being those he wished his

audience to believe he held. One is the fact that in the anapaests which introduce the *parabasis* the chorus usually does
not speak in its own character, but openly claims to be the
poet's mouthpiece (see p. 22). Another is the repeated
introduction of certain sentiments and the repeated ridicule of
certain politicians, while contrary views are discredited, if
mentioned at all, and politicians of another kind escape attack;
the poet does not seem to be politically unprejudiced. We may
be sure that Aristophanes appeared and wished to appear to
hold certain views; we cannot prove that this was not a cynical
pretence, but nothing suggests such dishonesty.

There was a tradition that a poet was a teacher, and more
than once Aristophanes makes the claim for himself in serious
contexts. The first occasion is in *The Acharnians*, where the
chorus declares that 'he will teach you many good lessons to
bring you happiness, not flattering, nor holding out hopes of
pay, nor deceiving you', that is, not acting like the crooked
politicians (656). The last is in *Frogs*, written when defeat
in the war was imminent; the chorus of deceased initiates into
the holy mysteries of Eleusis, who enjoy a favoured lot in the
next world, say that it is right that the sacred chorus should
give the city good advice: all citizens should have the same civic
rights, there should be an amnesty for past offences, and
citizenship given to all who will man the ships. The advice
ascribed to these honourable and disinterested figures must be
advice with which the poet associates himself. It is said to have
been so popular that the play was, quite exceptionally, given a
second performance.

Here we see Aristophanes making liberal and generous
proposals certainly intended to influence opinion. But this
was consistent with attachment to some social concepts that
were current among upper-class conservatives. He follows them
in dividing the citizens into *chrēstoi*, or 'good men', and
ponēroi, or 'bad men'. The former were on the whole men of
means, of 'good' family, of good education in the traditional
athletic and literary disciplines, and it was they who ought to
be elected as 'generals'[1] and be the policy-makers whose

---

[1] The ten generals, elected annually and eligible for re-election,
not only provided military and naval commanders but also had a

advice the people should follow. The latter were the upstarts; some had made money by trade or the employment of slaves as artisans; they entered politics for their own enrichment and secured power by posing as champions of the people, whose favour they secured by making them payments from state funds.

Aristophanes' political sympathies were with these conservatives. The chorus of *Frogs*, quoted above, continues:

> Among the citizens there are some we know to be well-born, well-behaved honest gentlemen, educated in the wrestling-schools and in dancing and the arts of the Muses; these we ill-treat but use for all purposes foreigners and red-heads and rascally sons of rascally fathers, new arrivals, men whom the city would once not have been willing to use even as scapegoats. But even now, O ye foolish men, use the good sort once again.

Twenty years earlier, in *Knights*, he had declared the same sympathies. The rich young cavalrymen assert that 'our poet hates the men we hate and he dares to speak the right'. Cleon was the butt of that play because he was one of the new men of the people who had broken the dominance of the old families.

In the year when *Knights*, later claimed by Aristophanes as 'a blow in the belly', won first prize Cleon was re-elected general. The play did not succeed in undermining his popular support. It may cause surprise that Aristophanes, writing for a mass audience, so consistently turned his ridicule against the new men who had the favour of so large a part of the citizenry. It may be guessed that, although the audience for comedy was very large, it was not proportionately representative, but that the half of the people who were absent from the theatre were on the whole the poorer half, who preferred to spend the payment from the theoric fund on food and drink; the followers of men like Cleon and Hyperbolus may there have been in

---

general influence on policy because of a wide responsibility for finance and the right to summon the assembly and put proposals to it.

a minority. Some support for this guess may be found in the fact that Aristophanes' rival Eupolis shared his social outlook, if his own view is to be seen in a fragment which asserts that 'our generals once were chosen from the greatest families, men pre-eminent by wealth and birth . . . so our affairs went without mishap. Now we elect scum as generals and our campaigns go as they do.'

There is another consideration. The followers of the demagogues did not necessarily admire them without reservation. They may have believed them to be in politics for what they could make, but have supported them because of their promises. This would not preclude envy and they may have enjoyed any personal discomfort suffered in the theatre by those for whom it would profit them to vote.

The other two plays belonging to the Lenaia, *Lysistrata* (411) probably and *Frogs* (405) certainly, were written in times of crisis, when partisan politics would have been out of place. *Lysistrata* is discussed below (p. 36); in *Frogs* the poet turns his back on the world of impending defeat and possible destruction to a most entertaining critique of the tragedians Aeschylus and Euripides, who was but recently dead. Missing him, Dionysus goes to the underworld to bring him back. The first part of the play has the god's adventures on a sometimes perilous journey, which include having to pull an oar in Charon's boat on the Styx and to compete as he does so with a chorus of frogs.[1] After further difficulties, arising from the fact that he has disguised himself as Heracles, he finally enters the palace of Pluto, and the chorus, now dressed as Eleusinian initiates, deliver the *parabasis*. Next news comes that Euripides has laid claim to the tragic throne of Aeschylus and that Dionysus, with his long experience of the theatre, has been appointed judge. There follows a lengthy contest between the two poets over the merits of their art, a contest punctuated by inept comments from Dionysus. He cannot decide between them, but Pluto urges him to pick one of the two and take him back to earth. Thus we return to the original purpose of his descent

---

[1] There is to my mind a strong case for believing the frogs to have appeared in the orchestra; see K. J. Dover, *Aristophanic Comedy* (London, 1972), pp. 177–8.

to the underworld. He determines to take the one who offers the city the better advice. Euripides is not at a loss for a rhetorical antithesis and a far-fetched stratagem; Aeschylus is more reluctant but more realistic and unexpectedly gets Dionysus' verdict.

It is a striking fact that the mass audience was able to appreciate a play with this literary subject. More than that its abnormal structure makes them no concessions. Disconnected scenes of knockabout humour usually succeeded the *parabasis*, while the more serious part of the play came before it. In *Frogs* the pattern is reversed: Dionysus' misadventures have a large physical element, while the latter part of the play is on an intellectual level and concerned with a single subject.

But there is some danger of exaggerating the crowd's literary understanding. Although some serious points are made, they are not made by themselves in isolation. The parody of Euripides' monodies scores some undoubted hits on his style and metrical liberties. But to enjoy the parody a knowledge of Euripides' more recent plays or the niceties of metre would not have been necessary; it would have been enough to understand that the language of the tragic stage was being used to lament a trivial domestic loss. Even so Aeschylus was made to bring on the 'Muse of Euripides', either a highly made-up man or a naked slave-girl, who postured for the audience's diversion while he sang his travesty.

Consider by contrast the attack on Euripides' prologues. Aeschylus alleges that the phrase 'lost his little oil-flask' can be interpolated into their first sentences. He demonstrates this by using the phrase to complete the third line of three plays, the second of two, and the first of another. This is very amusing, as the fatal words are introduced earlier and earlier, but it has no value as literary criticism. No aesthetic sensibility is required to see the joke.

The praises of peace are sung by Aristophanes in several of his plays, but to praise peace and to be a pacifist are different things. 'War is for the sake of peace,' wrote Aristotle (*Pol.* 1333 a 35). Most people always want peace, but not peace at

any price. They want peace with victory or at least with safety. The route to peace may lie through war. Men can regret that, but they recognise it.

To see *The Acharnians* as a manifesto in favour of peace is too simple. Most Athenians wanted peace, but they wanted it on their own terms. There was at this time no hope of a compromise, as had been made plain when in 430 they had tried to open negotiations. The coalition opposing them wished and hoped to destroy the Athenian Empire; the Athenians were determined to maintain it. For anything we know, Aristophanes shared this ambition. In his next play, *Knights*, the rejuvenated people is hailed as 'monarch of Greece'. He had no suggestion of how to make peace a practical policy. All he does is to play with a fantasy of peace. His Dikaiopolis has no care for national interests, or indeed for any interests but his own. How delightful it is to imagine oneself for a moment as enjoying the pleasures of selfishness! But this is no more than a holiday escape from reality. It is impossible for an individual to contract out of his country's war and, even if it were possible, peace cannot be made, as Dikaiopolis made it, without any terms except that it is to last for thirty years.

Yet in a way *The Acharnians* had a political purpose. The Athenians were not agreed about the terms on which they would be ready to make peace. Aristophanes seems to have been one of those who believed that the Peloponnesian War ought to have been avoided and ought to be brought to an end. He suggested therefore that its origins had been trivial, that the blame did not rest entirely with Sparta, and that if the two great powers co-operated, they could rule the Greek world. If his play could exert any influence, it would be in favour of moderates who were ready to accept some compromise if the opportunity offered. At the same time he tried to discredit those who favoured fighting on for decisive victory by accusing them of making personal gains from the war.

Peace, of 421, may have been begun to urge an end to hostilities, but concluded to celebrate it. The war had lasted for ten years; the coalition had failed to reduce Athens and its Spartan leaders were anxious to recover the 120 front-line soldiers taken prisoner in 425 and used by the Athenians as hostages to keep their farms free from further invasion. On the

34

other hand the Athenian attempt to instigate a revolution in Boeotia, their northern neighbour, had led to their army's rout at Delium. The contest might seem to be drawn and peace on terms of the *status quo* possible. By the time that Aristophanes' play was acted, it was known that formal ratification of a treaty was on the point of taking place. But it proved to be a fragile peace, since the issue had not been settled. Although some, both in Athens and in Sparta, hoped that the two states would co-operate to impose order on the other Greeks, the Athenians took every opportunity to weaken the Spartan position, while for various reasons the Boeotians, Megarians and Corinthians refused to adhere to the treaty.

The hero of the play, Trygaios, flies up to heaven on the back of a giant dung-beetle—a crane will have lifted him up from behind the *skene* to deposit him in front of it—and there finds that Zeus has gone and that the god War is preparing to pound the Greeks to pieces. Advised by Hermes, he calls for a panhellenic effort to draw the goddess Peace out of the cave in which she has been incarcerated. No doubt Aristophanes realised that the right way to peace lay through unity and was sincere in raising his voice in its favour. But he knew quite well that the way would not be followed. When the chorus enter and begin to haul upon ropes to draw Peace out, it soon appears that the Boeotians, the Argives, the military party among the Spartans, the Megarians and many Athenians are not joining in the effort. The work is left to the farmers, who finally succeed in extricating her.

The rest of the play consists predominantly of a protracted celebration of peace with praise of the joys of country life, now once again possible. Sacrifice is made to the goddess and the climax is a wedding-party, the marriage of Trygaios and Opōra, 'Harvest', one of her attendants, the other, Theōria or 'Spectacle', having been given to the Council.

Clearly this is no more than an agreeable fantasy. Co-operation between the Greek cities was necessary to secure peace; it was not to be won by the efforts of farmers, let alone by those of the Athenian farmers, with whom the chorus becomes identified. Perhaps simple-minded members of the audience might regard the second half of the play as a celebration of the peace that was about to be concluded, and the

35

author may have been ready to make use of the short-sighted enthusiasm for it, but the first half shows that he had no illusions about its prospects.

It is interesting that the blessings of peace are those of country life. At least three-quarters of Athenian citizens owned some land (Dion. Hal. *Lysias* 32). For many it may have been no more than a patch which could not provide a living, but which gave them a basis that could be supplemented, preferably by pay for activities proper for citizens, attendance at the assembly, service on juries or in the navy. So the majority of the spectators will have had connections with the country and been ready to place themselves on the side of the larger farmers.

Perhaps *Lysistrata*, produced early in 411, was designed to exert a real influence for peace. In the summer of 413 the disastrous end of the expedition to Syracuse had inflicted immense losses both of men and of ships. During the following winter neutral states hastened to join what they thought was the winning side, the Athenian 'allies' revolted, and there was a general expectation that the summer of 412 would see final victory (Thucydides 8.1). But it did not; the Athenians made heroic efforts and, although they had lost their undisputed command of the sea, succeeded in keeping control of Samos and of the essential passage of corn-ships from the Black Sea. Yet although their enemies had failed to press home their advantage, the outlook was threatening. If immediate peace had been possible, it would surely have been welcomed. But was peace on tolerable terms available? The rather inadequate evidence of Thucydides' unfinished eighth book suggests that whereas some thought that negotiations should be opened at once, others considered that this would be taken as a sign of weakness (this was indeed to be the reaction of the Spartan king Agis) and that the war should for the time be continued. In these circumstances to call attention to the hardships suffered by women, separated from their husbands who were on active service, may have been intended to aid the peace-party.

Yet Aristophanes cannot have supposed that an acceptable peace was to be had for the asking, any more than he can have supposed that his suggested method of bringing the Greeks

to their senses was anything other than a fantasy. And a hilarious fantasy it is. The citizen women of the warring states enter, with some reluctance, into a compact to refuse their husbands sexual relations until they make peace. This is inconsequential, for shortly before they were complaining that they were deprived of sex by their husbands' absence. But such inconsequentiality is typical of Aristophanic comedy. Unhampered by need to be consistent, the dramatist can freely develop each idea with which his imagination presents him.

The Athenian women go further, seizing the Acropolis, which they hold against the police and the old men, who try to re-establish masculine authority. The deprived men, who for the purposes of the play seem never to have heard of slave prostitutes or even of masturbation, to which the more practical women intended to resort, are immediately afflicted by continuous erection, which the phallus of the comic actor's costume could represent in exaggerated form. An embassy, racked by this torment, comes from Sparta and the two sides, reminded of how they had in earlier times aided one another, quickly agree; they hardly trouble to argue about territorial claims, being more concerned with the attractions of a beautiful girl whose name is Reconciliation. The play ends with a joyful song and dance. This is nothing but a fanciful wish in a dream world. The Athenians would have been happy if their ambitions for empire could have been wiped from the Greek memory, to be replaced by a sentimental regard for old and better days. But when the festival was over, they had to face reality.

We do not know how *Lysistrata* was received. To argue from silence is dangerous, but it may be that the reason why there is no record is that it was not placed among the first three comedies at the Lenaia of 411.

Like other authors of Old Comedy, Aristophanes made it his practice to ridicule and malign living contemporaries. Was this intended to hurt and to damage, to excite the laughter of contempt? It is quite possible to make friendly fun of others, who may enjoy the joke. Politicians collect caricatures of

themselves drawn in this spirit. But I doubt whether many of Aristophanes' butts relished the prominence he gave them, or that he was not moved by malice. 'Taking pleasure in what goes wrong for others' is a feeling for which the Greeks had a word (*epichairekakia*), and one which his audience will have known and enjoyed. His victims are accused of frigid writing, cowardice, effeminacy, passive homosexuality, adultery, stench, blackmail, peculation and other acts and qualities which are not subjects of kindly fun. This makes one suppose that allusions to ugliness, obesity and poverty were intended to raise a laugh at the man's expense and one in which he would not readily join. The runner in the torch-race who had let himself go flabby and came trailing in distressed, urged on by a rain of slaps from the spectators, would not welcome being reminded of that spectacle as much as the Athenians who had been amused by his humiliation (*Frogs* 1089 ff.).

There are three persons often attacked by Aristophanes who are still living figures for us: Cleon, Euripides and Socrates. No doubt can exist that he hated Cleon, both for personal reasons, since the politician had attempted to retaliate when first assailed, and because he saw in him an upstart demagogue who won power by bribing the people from public funds, and was moreover a man who preferred war to peace. Cleon's reprisals suggest that he thought the attacks dangerous. But he need not have worried, since the Athenian populace was not fickle in its favour to him.

Whereas it is not possible to detect any sympathy for Cleon in the works of Aristophanes, the case is not so clear with regard to Euripides. The most serious complaints he levels against him are that his dramas are full of sexually immoral women and that his characters, male and female, free and slave, talk and talk and argue and get new ideas. This is not only untragic; it also sets a bad example. Euripides would not feel this to be adverse criticism; he intended his plays to be like that and a great many people liked them like that.

For the rest, the frequent use of Euripidean lines in new and unsuitable contexts or their quotation in some distorted form could be taken as a compliment. It showed with what attention Aristophanes heard or read his plays and how it could be assumed that many of the audience were familiar with them

too. The repeated joke about ragged heroes, used by other writers of comedy also, becomes funny by virtue of repetition, and Euripides may almost have acquired credit by having provided its occasion. Intellectually Aristophanes probably disapproved of his way of writing tragedy, but he would have been ready to echo Dionysus: 'I think Aeschylus wise, but my delight is in Euripides.'

Since Socrates is an established hero to the modern world, Aristophanes' treatment of him is sometimes not taken at its face value. Plato's fictional account in the *Symposium*, which makes them both present at a party in honour of the tragic poet Agathon, another man of whom Aristophanes made fun, is said to show that all three were good friends. But in the *Apology* Plato declares his belief that the *Clouds* had been a cause of prejudice against Socrates, contributory to his condemnation. And it is hard to avoid the conclusion that the play was intended to damage him. It was harmless ridicule to represent him as running a school whose pupils were shut up away from the fresh air, explaining which end of a gnat was responsible for its whine, investigating the path of the moon, and riding in a suspended basket because:

> If from the ground below I had researched on
> What lies above, I'd never have found it. No,
> The earth attracts by force to its own self
> The moisture of one's thought. The same thing happens
> With cress.

All this is a caricature of the intellectual, imagined by the ordinary man to be an unhealthy and eccentric crackpot pursuing useless enquiries. The picture was simply untrue of Socrates, but it did not represent him as dangerous. More serious was the accusation that he worshipped, not Zeus, but Clouds and Air and Cosmic Whirl. Even worse was to make him the owner of an Immoral Argument which defeated Moral Argument. It does not matter that the contest between the two is conducted and concluded in comic terms: Immoral Argument wins when Moral Argument is forced to admit that every man in the audience has been a catamite, and impulsively deserts to join the overwhelming majority. Audiences enjoy

being made the subject of preposterously exaggerated insults, and the Athenians would not suppose that Aristophanes approved the result of the contest. Its consequences are seen when the young Pheidippides is made a pupil of the victor, unwillingly consenting but traditionally obedient, and returns to beat his father and to prove it right to do so. This is what comes of Socratic education. The play ends with the setting fire, at the instigation of the god Hermes, to Socrates' house, in an attempt on his life and that of his pupils. This scene, not harmless ridicule but incitement to violence, was first introduced into the unfinished revised version of the play, which had had only limited success at its original performance, coming third. It looks as if Aristophanes hoped, by sharpening his attack upon Socrates, to win greater favour. He may or may not have shared popular misconceptions about him, but as a dramatist he saw that they could be used to make an entertaining play.

Old Comedy

The term 'Old Comedy' means comedy produced in Athens during the fifth century BC. Antiquity regarded Eupolis, Cratinus and Aristophanes as its leading exponents, but had no doubt that Aristophanes was the greatest of the three. We are not in a position to test that judgment, which led to the survival of eleven of his plays and none of theirs. But Eupolis was still being copied and read in Egypt in the fourth century AD and Cratinus in the second or third. This must surely have been due to literary merit as well as the interest they had for admirers of classical Greece.

In *Knights* (424 BC) Aristophanes paid tribute to the power of Cratinus in his prime, when like a river in flood, he had 'swept away oaks and planes and had uprooted his enemies', while his lyrics were sung at every dinner-party. But he had gone to pieces with advancing years and drink. He deserved to be pensioned off, Aristophanes suggested, with free wine in the prytaneum and a seat in the theatre alongside Dionysus himself. The next year however Cratinus made his come-back, when his *Pytinē* or *Flask* beat Aristophanes' *Clouds*. In it he introduced himself as married to Comedy, who complained that he was deserting her for Drink; 'once I was his wife, but am no longer'. His friends came and urged her not to bring an action against him for ill-treatment. A few surviving lines suggest a project of reforming the erring poet:

> Now how could one put an end to his drinking, to his drinking too much? I know. I will break his bottles and smash his flagons to pieces, as if they were hit by a thunderbolt, and every single other vessel too that he uses for drinking; he shan't keep even a saucer with a taste of wine.

But a reconciliation seems to have followed, when someone urged that a poet's inspiration was in wine, not water.

O Lord Apollo, how his verses flow! There is splashing from his fountains, his mouth is the Twelve Springs themselves, Ilissus is in his throat. What more can one say? Unless someone puts a gag in his mouth, he will swamp the whole place with his lines.

Eupolis' dramatic career fell entirely within the course of the Peloponnesian War. Fourteen plays by him were known to later scholars and of these no fewer than seven had won the first prize. He seems to have shared the dislike shown by Aristophanes, of whom he was an almost exact contemporary, for the new lower-class leaders of the democracy. He claimed indeed to have helped in the composition of *Knights*, perhaps an accusation of plagiarism, while Aristophanes charged him, in the revised version of *Clouds* (553–6), with having villain-ously distorted *Knights* to attack the 'demagogue' Hyperbolus in his play *Marikās*, 'to which he had added a drunken old woman to dance the kordax,[1] a character produced long ago by Phrynichus'. Phrynichus was another contemporary, whose first play was performed in 429.

One cannot help asking whether the surviving plays of Aristophanes can be taken as typical of those of 'Old Comedy'. Scanty as are the remains of its other authors, there is enough to show that in many ways he either followed previous practice, or did what other poets of his time were doing.

In the first place it is clear that the Aristophanic choruses were in an established tradition. Most frequently the chorus gave the comedy its name. We know of plays entitled *Goats*, *Griffins*, *Ants*, *Bees*, etc. which correspond to his *Wasps*, *Birds* and *Frogs*. In others the chorusmen were, as in some of his, made to represent women, *Runaway Women*, *Women from Thrace*, *Old Women*. Then there were personifications, to be compared with the *Clouds*: *Wealths*, *Demes*, *Costumes*.

Nor was the *parabasis*, that interruption of the action when the chorus addresses itself to the spectators, his invention; it appeared in some plays by Cratinus, who belonged to the previous generation, as well as by his contemporary Eupolis and others with whom he competed. There is enough evidence to show that Aristophanes was not the originator of the

[1] A vulgar dance.

symmetrical scheme that is most fully displayed in his four earliest plays and in *The Birds*. It has five elements: (1) anapaests; (2) a song (*ōdē*); (3) sixteen or twenty long trochaic lines (*epirrhēma*); (4) another song (*antōdē*) metrically corresponding to the first; (5) sixteen or twenty long trochaic lines (*antepirrhēma*).

The other poets used the introductory anapaests, as he usually did, to speak in their own person, praising themselves and attacking their rivals. There are several passages which apologise for this and suggest that this use was an innovation. It is certainly not likely to have been a primitive feature, but was more probably the consequence of competition between dramatists in the theatre. Nor were anapaests *de rigeur* metrically; Eupolis sometimes substituted, as did Aristophanes in *Clouds*, a metre which goes by his name, and there are traces of other variants.

It may be guessed that another formal pattern found in many of Aristophanes' plays, although not in *The Acharnians*, did not originate with him. This pattern belongs to what modern scholars call the *Agōn* or Contest. Representatives of opposed points of view are pitted against one another and put their case in turn, interrupted by heckling mainly from their adversary, but also from a character who acts the buffoon. Their speeches, which often end with a *pnīgos* or passage delivered without pause for breath, are each introduced by a song and encouragement from the chorus, which sometimes concludes the *Agōn* by giving a verdict. In its most perfected form this *Agōn* is almost exactly symmetrical. Thus in *Birds* the two songs correspond syllable for syllable, the speeches of encouragement each consist of two anapaestic tetrameters, and each of the subsequent speeches, heckling counted, occupies sixty-one anapaestic tetrameters followed by sixteen anapaestic dimeters. To be accurate, that play shows what may be called the form of the *Agōn* without providing a true contest, since Peisthetairos champions the same cause in both halves. But in *Knights*, where the Paphlagonian and the sausage-seller are genuine opponents, correspondence is only marginally less strict.

Most plays by Aristophanes contain allusions to politics; several are based on the contemporary situation and would be

unthinkable without it. That he was not alone in this involve-
ment with the affairs of the city is illustrated by the *Demes* of
Eupolis. Written for production in 412, soon after the disaster
at Syracuse had faced Athens with the prospect of destruction,
it showed the great statesmen of the past called up from the
underworld to advise the city in her hour of need. There are
some enigmatic but significant fragments from the *parabasis*.
First from the *antōdē*:

> Then they say that Peisandros was twisted[1] yesterday
> when at breakfast, because he refused to provide meals
> for a foreigner who had no food.
> And Pauson went up to Theogenes as he was making his
> dinner to his heart's content off one of his own ships,
> gave him a hiding once for all, and a good twisting;
> and Theogenes lay paralysed and farting all night.
> Now Callias ought to be twisted and those in the Long
> Walls with him, for they breakfast better than we do.

Clearly this was a time of food-shortage; the first two men
attacked were well-known gluttons, and the third was rich,
whereas Pauson is twice mentioned by Aristophanes as a
starveling and once called a 'thorough villain'.

The *antepirrhēma* accuses some demagogue, perhaps Hyperbolus, of not being of Attic birth, of having been a male
prostitute, and of having proposed to treat as criminals
certain generals who had wished to pay heed to divine warnings against sending an expedition to Mantinea, probably the
unsuccessful one of 418.

The ridicule of individuals was a feature common to all the
dramatists about whom there is any quantity of evidence.
Many of Aristophanes' victims are to be found also in the
fragments of his rivals. At least three other comic poets made a
butt of Socrates. Eupolis frag. 352 runs:

> I hate Socrates too, that beggarly chatterer, who has
> thought of everything except where his next meal is
> coming from.

[1] The meaning of the Greek word is disputed. It may refer to a
method of torture, but some plausibly think it means 'buggered'.

Politicians—Pericles, Cleon, Hyperbolus and others—are lampooned. Later critics constantly refer to these personal attacks as a prime characteristic of Old Comedy. Not only that, but they tend to regard them as justified and salutary. Horace writes (*Satires* 1.4.1–5):

> The poets Eupolis and Cratinus and Aristophanes and the other great men who created antique comedy felt no restraint against branding anyone who deserved to be noticed because he was a bad character and a thief, or an adulterer or assassin or of ill-repute in any other way.

This description seems particularly suited to Cratinus who, according to a late anonymous author, 'added utility to the charm of comedy, by denouncing evil-doers and punishing them by a public flogging in his comedies'. Although Horace gives an exaggerated impression of the poets' moral purpose and the wickedness of those they attacked, he does not fall into the error of treating their attitude as one of affectionate raillery. They wished to exploit unpopularity and eccentricity.

It is a fact to be insisted upon that not only did Aristophanes relate the alleged vices or ridicule the habits and actions of the same persons in play after play, but the other dramatists also pursued them. They had become stock figures of comic drama and references to them were for that reason the more effective with the audience. Men like novelty, but they also like what is familiar. In the end they can tire of the latter, but its attraction is far from ephemeral. It pleased the Athenian audience to be reminded of their contempt for Cleonymus, who was said to have dropped his shield and run, and they will not have minded how often they heard of his disgrace.

Similarly there were stock motifs repeated from play to play. Here it is easy to find modern parallels from the more undemanding plays and cartoons—the interfering mother-in-law and the henpecked husband forced to wash up at the kitchen sink. Several times Aristophanes pretends that he did not descend to such elementary material. For example:

> If it is reasonable to honour someone who has become the best and most famous producer of comedy of all mankind, our poet declares himself to be worthy of great praise.

First of all he is the only man who has put a stop to his rivals always making fun of rags and waging war on lice; and then those Heracleses kneading their bread and always hungry, he was the first to bring them into disrepute and drive them out of the theatre, and he got rid of those slaves they used to bring on howling, so that a fellow-slave could jeer at their stripes and then put a question like this: 'You poor wretch, what has happened to your skin? You don't say that a whip has invaded your ribs in force and used your back for some practice in tree-felling?'

These particular motifs did not occur in *Peace*, from which this passage is taken (734–47), but most of them can be found in other plays by him. Aristophanes did not dispense with the stock themes used by comic dramatists; he knew that his audience loved them. It may be that he relied less on their intrinsic funniness, and preferred to use them as an element in other jokes. The beginning of *Frogs* illustrates this. Dionysus enters with his slave Xanthias, who rides on a donkey, carrying a huge bundle on a pole over his shoulder.

> *Xanthias.* Master, shall I say one of the usual things, at which the spectators always laugh?
> *Dionysus.* Anything you like, except 'It's crushing me'. Keep off that. It makes me quite sick.
> *Xanthias.* No other witty remark?
> *Dionysus.* Anything but 'I'm being squeezed'.
> *Xanthias.* What then? Shall I make that really funny joke?
> *Dionysus.* By all means. Go ahead. There's just one thing you're not to say.
> *Xanthias.* What?

Dionysus bans a couple of indecent jokes, after which Xanthias continues: 'Why had I to carry all these traps, if I'm not going to do any of the things Phrynichus and Lycis and Ameipsias used to do?' No doubt when Xanthias shortly afterwards exclaimed: 'It's crushing my shoulder', that got a laugh.

There is in Aristophanes a great deal of sexual, and some scatological, obscenity. The fragments we have of his con-

temporaries' plays confirm his assertion that they too indulged in it. Some modern writers have tried to palliate this by finding a religious origin in ritual obscenity and maintaining that it was traditional and proper at the festival of Dionysus. If there is any truth in the theory, the spectators will have expected to be entertained in this way, because it had always been part of the programme. But what they expected was entertainment, not a religious ceremony.

The Greek sense of propriety will not have coincided with our own, but for many, if not for most, some sense of shame attached to sexual acts and to defecation. If it had not, there would have been no need to use euphemisms in literature to replace what correspond to our four-letter words. In so far as Greek Old Comedy talks openly about bodily parts and normal acts which were probably not usual subjects of general conversation, it may have provided a relief from inhibitions. The relief will have been all the greater if these acts could be made to appear absurd and laughable by exaggeration and by attaching jokes to them. There is much of this in Aristophanes.

But there is another side. Clearly a fifth-century audience, or a large part of it, was ready to laugh at things in which most readers of this book probably do not find a source of amusement such as incontinence of the bowels and sodomy. We may enjoy jokes about them, but do not regard them as funny in themselves. Similarly we can jest about madmen, but do not, like our eighteenth-century ancestors, visit madhouses for our entertainment.

Aristophanes was not alone in providing much entertainment by parody of tragedy and allusions to it. His methods are still used by comedians, but he had the advantage that his audience was an audience of tragedy-goers, who would see tragedies at the same festival and in the same theatre as his comedies. The simplest form of parody was the introduction of vocabulary drawn from tragedy, which used much language that was not ordinary Attic speech. Put in the mouth of a down-to-earth character, this was comically inappropriate, especially if he mixed it with everyday phrases and colloquialisms. Sometimes metres were used whose traditional place was in serious poetry and even the iambic trimeter, the most common metre for dialogue, could be made to adhere to the

stricter rules employed in tragedy and so suggest an incongruous elevation of style.

Parody becomes more specific when actual lines are borrowed from a tragedian, either verbatim, when the fun lies in their transference to the comic contest, or with the substitution or addition of a word or phrase with ridiculous effect. The more apposite the line in its new setting, the sharper is the impact of the joke, and the greater the admiration for the cleverness of the comic poet. A most successful and sustained instance is in *Frogs*, when Euripides is discomfited by Dionysus' use of lines which he had himself written.

Dionysus.	My choice shall fall on him my soul desires.	1468
Euripides.	Remembering the gods and solemn oath You swore to bring me home, now choose your friend.	1470
Dionysus.	My tongue is sworn—but I'll choose Aeschylus.	
Euripides.	What have you done, man? You foul blackguard!	
Dionysus.	I? I judged a win for Aeschylus. Why not?	
Euripides.	How can you face me, wreaking a deed of shame?	
Dionysus.	What's shameful, if the audience think not so?	1475
Euripides.	Will you do nothing, wretch, and see me dead?	
Dionysus.	Who knows if life be death and death be life, To breathe to dine, and sleep a sheepskin rug?	

Lines 1471 and 1475 distort verses from Euripides' plays that had become notorious:

> My tongue is sworn—my mind did never swear

and

> What's shameful, if the doers think not so?

1477 is known to be taken verbatim. 1469–70 look like another distortion and it would not be surprising if 1468 and 1474 proved also to be from him.

There is, however, one way in which Aristophanes' surviving plays do not give a fair picture of Old Comedy. They do not fully represent its range of theme; in particular they include no example of a play that treated a story from mythology in a comic manner. Such became increasingly popular and Aristophanes himself wrote several which have not survived. Fortunately much of the plot of Cratinus' *Dionysalexandros* is known. In it part of the story usually attached to the Trojan prince Paris, *alias* Alexander, was transferred to the god Dionysus. The summary given in a papyrus runs as follows:

> ... Hermes leaves. They (probably satyrs) talk with the spectators (i.e. the audience) about the poets and make fun of Dionysus when he comes on the scene ... Hera offers him an unshaken despotic rule, Athena good luck in war, Aphrodite promises that he should be very beautiful and attractive. He adjudges her the winner, and then sailing to Lacedaemon he returns with Helen to Ida (the Trojan mountain). Shortly afterwards he hears that the Achaeans (Greeks) are burning the country ... Alexander. Quickly hiding Helen in a basket, he transforms himself into a ram and awaits events. Alexander comes on the scene, discovers them, and orders them both to be taken to the ships, intending to hand them over to the Achaeans. Helen is unwilling to go; pitying her, he keeps her to be his wife, but sends Dionysus off to be surrendered. The satyrs follow the god, telling him to be of good cheer and promising never to desert him.

The summary concludes with the words: 'Pericles is ridiculed by innuendo as having brought war on the Athenians.' This note, which suggests 430 as the date, is valuable evidence that mythological subjects did not exclude contemporary

political references. Another example of this is provided by the same author's *Cheirones*, or *Cheiron and Co.*, fragments from which refer to Pericles and his mistress Aspasia, but without naming them. 'Discord and old Cronos lay together and engendered a mighty despot, whom the gods called head-raiser ... and Lewdness bore Hera for him, a bitch-eyed mistress.' Zeus was called 'cloud-raiser' (*nephelēgeretās*) and Pericles, who had a very high skull, is here suggested by *kephalēgeretās*, 'head-raiser'; Hera was *boōpis*, 'cow-eyed', replaced here by *kynōpis*, 'bitch-eyed'.

There seem also to have been plays which included realistic scenes from contemporary life, to be contrasted with Aristophanic fantasy; they are marked by quiet humour rather than broad jests.

A. I've come from the bath-house quite boiled, and my throat's parched.

B. I'll give you something to drink.

A. My God, my spittle's sticky.

B. What shall I use to mix your drink in? The little cup?

A. No, no! Not the little one. It makes me feel sick at once, ever since I drank medicine out of one like that. Fill up mine now, the bigger one.

* * *

A. Undrinkable, Glyke!

Glyke. Did she put in too much water?

A. Worse! It's nothing but water!

Glyke. What have you done? Damn you, what measures did you use?

B. Two of water, mamma.

Glyke. And of wine?

B. Four.

Glyke. Devil take you! Frogs are what you should mix drinks for.[1]

This comes from Pherecrates' *Corianno*, probably written during the Peloponnesian War. Corianno, in all likelihood to be

---

[1] A normal mixture would have been two of water to *one* of wine. To drink wine neat or as good as neat was a mark of dissipation.

identified with 'A' in these lines, was a courtesan, but it is uncertain whether she was a real inhabitant of Athens or a fictitious person. Pherecrates is said not to have indulged in personal abuse, but to have been 'inventive of plots'. This suggests that he was a forerunner of the direction which was to be taken by comedy in the following century.

An immense amount has been written about the origins of Old Comedy. Some critics, with whom I incline to agree, consider that this has been largely misdirected effort, because there is so little hard evidence. The earliest plays to survive were written fifty years after the introduction of comedy at the City Dionysia and their form may to some extent be not traditional but invented by poets of the fifth century or even earlier. On the other hand, Comedy did not come into being simultaneously with official recognition. Aristotle knew, or guessed, that previously there had been plays presented by private enterprise and that these already had characteristic forms. But what these were he does not say (*Poetics* 1449 b 1–3).

He seems to have looked for the origins of Athenian comedy in two places, on the one hand in dialogue between the chorus of 'phallic songs' and its leader, on the other in the influence of Sicilian drama, in which he saw the source of 'plot'. He clearly had in mind Epicharmus, who wrote plays in verse for performance in Syracuse towards the end of the sixth century and the beginning of the fifth. There is nothing in the fragmentary remains to suggest that Epicharmus used a chorus except a few plural titles, for example *Persians, Dancers, Citizens, Sirens,* and these may just as well refer to characters in a play. Many of his personages were drawn from mythology: Alcyoneus, Amycus, Busiris, Philoctetes, the Sphinx, etc. Nearly half, perhaps more, were of this kind. Heracles was a character who lent himself to comedy; a hero of great strength must also be a great eater:

> May you die (?) if you should see him eating. There's a roar from his gullet, his jaw clatters, his molars grate, his canines squeak, he whistles through his nostrils, and wobbles his ears (frag. 21).

Other plays were concerned with the life of Epicharmus' own times, as appears from this extract from a play entitled *Hope* (or alternatively *Wealth*); it anticipates Athenian comedy of Aristotle's time in picturing the type of man who was later to be given the name of *parasite*:

> Dining with the man who wants me—he need only invite me—and with the man who don't—I've no need of any invitation. And then I'm witty and cause a lot of laughter and sing the host's praises; and if anyone tries to contradict him, I pitch into the fellow, and that's how I got myself disliked. And then when I've put plenty of food and plenty of drink inside me, I go. There's no slave to carry a torch for me; I creep along, slipping, and all alone in the dark. If I meet the watch, I count it a blessing from heaven that they want nothing more than to use their whips on me. But when I have got home, quite done in, I sleep without blankets; and I don't drop off at once (frag. 35).

Epicharmus was slightly older than the first Athenian writers of comedy whose names are preserved, and he may therefore have exerted an influence upon them. That is all that can be said. There is nothing to confirm a belief that he did affect them.

Aristotle's second source for comedy, namely dialogue between a 'phallic' chorus and its leader, has at least the merit of explaining the large part played by the chorus in Athenian comedy. There were ceremonies in Attica at which a large erect phallus, symbol of fertility, was displayed and songs were sung. The participants themselves did not wear phalli, any more than did the chorusmen of comedy. Such a ceremony is represented in *The Acharnians*, but only incidentally, and it plays no part in any other play. Semus, an author from the island of Delos, writing perhaps in the second century BC, described the entry of phallus-bearers into a theatre (it is not said in what town), where after reciting some verses, they ran forward and jeered at persons they picked on. This reminds one of the large element of mockery in Old Comedy. But there is nothing to show that any 'phallic' choruses ever conducted a

dialogue with a leader, or that they ever 'acted', that is to say represented characters not their own. One may suspect that Aristotle, believing tragedy to have arisen from a dialogue between a dithyrambic chorus and its leader, imagined a parallel origin for comedy.

Elsewhere Aristotle reports that the Megarians, both those who shared a frontier with Athens and those of Sicily, claimed to have originated comedy. The latter seem to have asserted that Epicharmus had originally been one of them before moving to Syracuse, and the mainland Megarians certainly had comic performances in his time. One of the slaves whose conversation opens *Wasps* may allude to such when he tells the spectators 'not to expect any laughs stolen from Megara'. Similarly Eupolis wrote: 'Herakles, this mockery of yours is outrageous, Megarian, and quite frigid: as you see, the children are laughing at it.'

To act and to act for laughs is a widespread human activity. Children do it spontaneously. It is *prima facie* likely that some form of comic acting took place in many cities. Even at Sparta 'there was an old manner of comic play . . . a man would represent harvest-thieves or a foreign doctor, using simple ordinary language . . . and those who pursued this sort of game were called *deikelistai* [*deikeliktai* in the local Dorian dialect].' Athenaeus, who reports this, adds that there were similar performers at Sicyon, at Thebes, in Italy, and elsewhere, who had various names, which include 'improvisers' and 'volunteers'. At Sicyon they were 'phallus-bearers', or did the word there mean 'phallus-wearers', to be compared with the actors at Athens? The claim of Megara to be the source of comedy may have rested on the persistence there of a primitive form of drama, whereas at Athens primitive drama had been superseded and forgotten; with the result that the native origin of Athenian comedy was no longer remembered.

The word comedy is in Greek *Kōmoidia*, or *kōmos*-singing. An alternative ancient derivation from *kōmē* 'village' is linguistically false, but it is likely enough that villages knew *kōmoi*, or 'revels'. Revels took the form of dancing, singing and processions; they could be attached to the worship of a god, particularly of Dionysus; they were easily connected with feasting and drinking. Revellers are likely to adopt many varied ways

of amusing themselves; it can be fun to go and sing ribaldries outside the house of someone who is unpopular, or to gratify the widespread human desires to imitate and to parody. From such beginnings a plausible origin for comedy can be sought. It would explain the association of singers and dancers with actors and the prominence given to ridicule of individuals.

There is a little evidence from art which may be relevant. Several Athenian vases of the late sixth or early fifth century show a group of men identically disguised, sometimes masked, moving to the music of a piper. They are dressed as birds, or women, or joined in pairs as horses and riders; others are mounted upon dolphins or ostriches, or walk on stilts, wearing Scythian caps. Such disguised groups were probably a feature of some festival or other, and can be seen as forerunners of many choruses of Old Comedy.

New Comedy

NEW Comedy is the name we give, adopting the practice of the later ancient critics, to the Greek plays (other than tragedies) written in the period following the death of Alexander the Great. Plays of this genre seem to have had a recognisable basic form, generally accepted by their authors, and reached by a process of development from Old Comedy. They were composed in five acts, divided by interludes irrelevant to the action. These were performed by the chorus which took no part in the play proper. Published texts recorded the presence of these interludes but not their content. The actors' padding and phalli were things of the past; they were now dressed in decent conventional contemporary clothes and represented the men and women, free and slave, whom one might have met in an Athenian street or home. But masks were still worn; those of young men and women were handsome, but those of the elderly and of slaves were grotesque exaggerations of the human features. The stories were mostly set in Athens, because that was the dramatic centre of the Greek world. Playwrights and actors came there from other cities. But the plays they wrote had few references to individual Athenians or to events at Athens. They treated universal, not local, themes and the plots were, by comparison with those of Old Comedy, realistic.

The transition to the new form took place during the first three-quarters of the fourth century, and the plays of that period came to be given the name of Middle Comedy. But they were a very varied lot. It was a time of change and experiment. No firm line can be drawn between Middle Comedy and Old on the one hand or between Middle and New on the other. Of necessity some writers produced plays during more than one period. In fact the only two extant Greek dramas to which the label of Middle Comedy can be attached are by Aristophanes.

These plays, *Women at the Assembly* (392?) and *Plutus* or *Wealth* (388), retain the element of fantasy that was later to disappear; in the former the Athenian women, disguised as men, pack the assembly and pass a resolution to hand over the direction of the country to themselves, whereupon they try to deal with economic problems by ordering the community of property and with sexual ones by giving the oldest women first turn of the men. Neither reform, as may readily be imagined, proves a success. *Plutus* has a happier, although less hilarious, ending; the god of Wealth is cured of his blindness and gives his favours to men according to their deserts. The concern which both these plays show for the poor is no doubt related to economic conditions at Athens, a city which had lost a war and with it an empire. Comedy has not yet abandoned the characteristic of being topical; there are also lines which jeer, somewhat half-heartedly, at individuals, often politicians. Fragments from contemporary writers of comedy show that this interest in politics and personalities was still quite usual. In later times it was not realised that the disappearance of personalities was a gradual process and it was ascribed to some new law. 'Freedom,' wrote Horace, 'slipped into violence, a fault which deserved regulation by law; the law was accepted and the right to injure was removed' (*Ars Poetica* 282–3). Of such a law there is neither record nor trace. Perhaps poets thought it prudent not to attack powerful men who might find some cause for arraigning them in the courts, but the only public action to restrain them was in 439, the time of the revolt of Samos, when a resolution was passed forbidding the ridicule of individuals. It was repealed two years later, the crisis being over. Something similar was attempted in 415, but, if the proposal was passed, it must have been reversed before *Birds* was staged in 414. The right to ridicule and satirise may have been unwelcome to politicians, but it was valued and guarded by the poets and the people.

Comedy in fact never surrendered the right to criticise in this way, although it was exercised less and less as time went on. Menander glanced occasionally in his earliest plays at men who were established butts and in the last decade of the century Philippides dared to write these lines of Stratocles,

agent of Demetrius the Besieger of Cities, whose army kept the 'democratic' faction in power:

> He who took the acropolis for an inn and lodged courtesans with the virgin goddess . . . he because of whom the frost nipped our vines, he because of whose impiety the sacred robe was split, when he transferred the gods' honours to a man. This, not our comedy, is what destroys the people.

But Aristophanes' two plays show other features that were new and were to be developed. The language has become more restricted than that of his earlier work; the vocabulary of the streets is giving way to that of literature. Another self-imposed restriction is that the place of the dramatic action no longer shifts with arbitrary freedom. As already in the *Clouds*, the scene is permanently outside houses belonging to characters of the play. This was to become the standard practice, being part of the movement towards naturalism.

In *Women at the Thesmophoria* and *Frogs* the *parabasis* had been truncated; in these plays it has been dropped altogether. It was moreover thought unnecessary to preserve the words of some of the choric songs, which are represented in our manuscripts by the phrase 'Little piece by chorus', or by abbreviation just 'By chorus'. What was sung must have been essentially, perhaps totally, irrelevant to the play. One cannot even be sure that the poet troubled to write any words for these songs; he may have left it to his chorusmen to sing whatever they fancied. This growing irrelevance of the chorus is illustrated by the first songs of *Plutus*, which are quite extraneous and could be sung by any band of revellers. But the verses spoken by the leader of the chorus in these plays, although no longer numerous, are still integrated into the text; the chorus was not yet simply a device, as it was to be in New Comedy, for creating a break in the action.

The plot based on mythology, not uncommon in Old Comedy, became still more popular in Middle Comedy. Aristophanes' last plays (now lost), *Aiolosikon* and *Kōkalos*, which were produced by his son, were of this kind. The former represented Aeolus, king of the winds, as a cook, while the latter seems to have involved the story that Minos of Crete,

having pursued Daedalus to the court of Cocalus, king of a town in Sicily, was drowned in a hot bath. But audiences must have come to tire of such burlesques, for to judge by surviving titles, they occurred but rarely among the dramas of New Comedy.

Mythological plays will, however, have had an influence on the development of comedy. Just as the stories of mythology were the subjects of tragedy, travesties of them will have been affected by its structure. Whereas Old Comedy often presented a series of scenes loosely strung together in an arbitrary sequence, tragedy tended towards a more integrated form of plot, in which each incident grew with seeming inevitability out of what had gone before. The humorous treatment of mythological stories no doubt led to the introduction from the comic tradition of scenes unnecessary to the progress of the story, but it is also probable that basically there was an adherence to the tragic pattern. Comedies of this sort, by telling a unified continuous tale, of which the decisive outcome or climax was not reached until the end, will have helped to make this construction popular. The first steps towards it can already be seen in Aristophanes. One may compare *The Acharnians*, where Dikaiopolis obtains and establishes his peace before the *parabasis* and thereafter merely enjoys its blessings, with *Knights*, in which the struggle to free Demos from the clutches of the Paphlagonian (i.e. Cleon) is not resolved until shortly before the end. Again, the early recovery of the goddess in *Peace* can be contrasted with the postponement of a solution until the penultimate scene of *Lysistrata*.

Comedy also profited from tragedy by the borrowing of motifs. Satyrus, the biographer of Euripides, wrote:

> ... confrontations of husband and wife, father and son, slave and master, unexpected reversals of circumstance, raping of virgins, supposititious children, recognitions by means of rings and necklaces; these are, no doubt, the main constituents of the more recent comedy, and it was Euripides who brought them to the highest pitch of development.

By 'more recent comedy' he probably meant all that succeeded Old Comedy. To call these things the 'main constituents',

even of New Comedy, is an exaggeration, but they were certainly frequent constituents. It is possible that some of them were first used by way of parody, just as Aristophanes parodied a scene from Euripides' *Telephus* in his *Acharnians*, and were then found convenient for the more realistic and more romantic plots that gradually became established as the norm.

Whereas Plato could still see in comedy an element that excited envy and spite (*Philebus* 51 C), a generation later Aristotle described it as the representation of inferior characters whose ugliness was of a kind to excite laughter rather than distress (*Poetics* 1449 a 32). Plato was of course hostile to drama, while Aristotle examined it with sympathy,[1] but the difference is also significant of a change in comedy's nature during the fourth century. The personal attacks that were once typical of it gave way to caricature of invented personages. A feature of many plays of Middle Comedy was their satire of certain social types that were of growing importance in the fourth century. The most frequently ridiculed were the professional soldier, the professional cook and the independent courtesan. They seem first to have appeared as comic treatments of real living persons, but these were succeeded by fictitious characters who followed those trades.

The employment of mercenary soldiers was increasing, and men whose profession it was to command them attracted attention. The comic poet loved to represent them as vain, boastful and vulgar in their ostentation of wealth newly gained from booty. They could be associated with another stock character, the flatterer or toady, sometimes called 'parasite'. Literally this word meant 'one who feeds alongside', and was the title of certain priests, who shared the meals offered to their gods; it was then applied in jest to persons who obtained their dinners by the bounty of rich patrons whom they served. Not only the toady, but also the courtesan might attach herself to

---

[1] Unfortunately his detailed treatment of comedy does not survive.

the soldier. She was represented as greedy, unreliable and insincere. The less-demanding soldier might be content with the wares of the owner of slave-prostitutes, a man who belonged to another calling whose followers were despised and disliked.

The cook is the character about whom most is known, because Athenaeus quoted many speeches by cooks in his *Deipnosophists*, or *Learned Men at Dinner*. The ancient Greek did not have a servant who specialised in cooking. His daily food was simple, and when a man who could afford it wanted a more elaborate meal he called in a professional cook. These persons were, in comedy at least, not slaves but self-employed men of low social status. They were obliged to work with slaves, either their own assistants or members of the household where they were employed. Some, if not all, were not of Attic birth and may have come from Asia Minor or Sicily, places of gastronomic renown.

Their characteristics in drama were inquisitiveness, loquacity, and pride in their cuisine. They remained popular with many poets of New Comedy, who allowed long speeches by cooks to hold up the progress of their plots. Aristophanes' plays had often ended with a festive dinner, a fitting climax to a light-hearted story, and this tradition of conviviality lived on. Many plots of New Comedy led up to a marriage and attendant marriage-feast; or if a young man was entangled with a courtesan, he would wish to entertain her. So there was often place for a cook among the dramatis personae.

Many statuettes from the first half of the fourth century represent slaves in actors' costume, masked, padded and phallic—evidence of their increased importance in plays of that period. Aristophanes had not made great use of them, although there are instances foreshadowing what was to come. In *Frogs* the opening scenes are built round the relation between Dionysus and his slave Xanthias, who is put upon but finally turns the tables on his master. In *Plutus* the slave Karion, described by his master as 'most faithful and most thieving', has a larger part than any other of the human characters; the unity of the play depends on him. From such beginnings the role of the comic slave was developed. No doubt there were in real life slaves who cheated their masters and others who exercised influence over them. The audience in the theatre

liked to see such things exaggerated; they were entertained by the slave's cunning wiles and the importance he arrogated to himself. Of course not all slaves in drama will have been of this type; there will doubtless have been others more simple-minded to act as foils.

We have now in our mind's eye a set of characters round whom it was possible to construct the plots of plays, the incidents of which, although perhaps unlikely, were not in themselves completely incredible, as were so many in Aristophanic comedy. One such plot is known from the *Persa* or *Persian* of the Latin author Plautus, if as seems likely he adapted it from a Greek drama written when Persia was still an independent country (506 ff.), that is before 334. A slave Toxilus, whose master is abroad, is in love with a girl, Lemniselenis, who is in the hands of a brothel-keeper named Dordalus. Another slave, Sagaristio, whose master has entrusted him with money to purchase oxen, gives it to Toxilus, enabling him to buy her. Meanwhile Toxilus has been planning a stratagem; he persuades a poor parasite, Saturio, to lend him his daughter to be dressed up as an Arabian girl, whom Sagaristio, disguised as a Persian, proceeds to sell to Dordalus, thus recouping the price paid for Lemniselenis. Thereupon Saturio appears and hauls Dordalus off to charge him with the crime of buying a free Athenian. The slaves, joined by Lemniselenis and a third young slave, settle down to drink, invite the discomfited Dordalus to join them, and subject him to verbal insults and physical indignities.

There were probably better plays than this. But it contains elements to be paralleled in other works. A slave carries through a stratagem to obtain money. A 'parasite' acts dishonestly. A foreigner, with the disreputable trade in women, gets into trouble and is humiliated. The hero is left in possession of the woman he loves, who has protested her love for him. The final scene is one of revelry. But no parallel can be adduced for Saturio's daughter who acts her part as a noble Arab captive most plausibly, provided one accepts the Arab's ability to speak a foreign tongue. Such deceit looks unusual in a young Athenian girl; but like father, like daughter.

The plots of New Comedy made much use of motifs and characters which we know to have been introduced by writers

of an earlier period. Doubtless there were also novelties, but they did not remain the property of their inventors. Again and again we meet soldiers, flatterers or parasites, courtesans, bawds, slavers and brothel-keepers, cooks and their assistants, young men in love, strict or miserly old men, cunning slaves, loyal slaves, elderly wives, nurses and merchants. Again and again motifs are repeated: rich young men rape poor girls, but obstacles to marrying them are in the end removed; newly born children are exposed if unwanted (this was true to life), and rescued to be brought up by substitute parents, usually of humble station (probably this was of less frequent occurrence); older children are kidnapped by pirates; these exposed or stolen offspring are finally recognised and welcomed back by their true parents; impecunious young men want girls who are in the hands of traders who make or intend to make them prostitutes; slaves help to find the cash needed to buy them by stratagems directed against the owner or against their own master; slaves come running on the stage either in fright or with unexpected news; brides are given handsome dowries. 'Nothing,' wrote the Roman dramatist Terence, 'is said, that has not been said before.'

These are facts that must be faced. Some critics have seen fit to condemn New Comedy as sterile and dreary repetition. They misunderstand the nature of Greek art, which did not seek to impress by shrill novelty and denunciations of the successes of the previous generation, but to discover new ways of treating old themes. One does not complain that houses are so often built of red bricks, tiles, mortar, glass and deal, and wish architects to show originality by using other materials, bricks of plastic, aluminium sheeting, old bottles and balsa wood. The stock motifs had been found useful for the making of comedies and were not abandoned; but the poets tried to use them in new ways and in new combinations, or would sometimes modify them in an unexpected direction. Part of the spectator's pleasure, if he had seen many plays, lay in noticing how traditional features were altered and in recognising allusions to them. But if he were new to the theatre, old themes would be new for him.

Apart from that, these standard elements, only a few of which are found in any one play, form no more than part of

its material. In the best work of New Comedy the real concern is with the individuality of the characters, on the one hand, and their relation one to another, and to the evolution of the plot, on the other hand, to be seen as determined by the reactions of these characters to the initial circumstances.

It has already been observed that Greek dramatists liked to associate certain qualities with certain professions or callings. Some remarks made by the novelist Fielding in his own defence are relevant here:

> Thou art to know, friend, that there are certain characteristics in which most individuals of every profession and occupation agree. To be able to preserve these characteristics, and at the same time to diversify their operations, is one talent of a good writer. Again to mark the nice distinction between two persons actuated by the same vice or folly is another; and as this last talent is found in very few writers, so is the true discernment of it found in as few readers (*Tom Jones*, Book X, chap. 1).

The Greek dramatist appears to have been more hopeful of finding true discernment among his spectators; he has not always been treated with it by his modern critics.

It is a remarkable feature of New Comedy that the same name is given to different characters in various plays. Where slaves are concerned this is less surprising, since even in real life there was no great stock of names for them. They were most frequently called after their place of origin, e.g. Syros, 'Syrian', or Getas, from the Thracian tribe the Getae. Thus there was a Daos, whose name indicates a Phrygian background, in at least eight of the seventeen identifiable plays by Menander of which papyrus fragments have been found. It is more remarkable that there is a similar duplication of names for citizens, who in real life used a great variety. The same seventeen plays have four young men called Moschion and three called Gorgias. The former is a 'speaking' name, 'Little Bull-calf', while each Gorgias is a country lad. Similarly more than one old man has the name of Demeas, or Laches, or

Smikrines, the last being given to men who are too much attached to money.

Perhaps these stock names are parallel to the use of stock masks. It would not have been possible to invent a distinctively individual mask for each of the thousands of slaves who were characters in the various comedies of this period. A thousand real men have a thousand different faces, but masks are simplified reproductions of the human face, emphasising certain features. So it was natural, as well as convenient, that certain types of mask, found to be effective, should be used over and over again. The encyclopaedist Pollux describes forty-four types which he assigns some to slaves, some to old men, some to youths and so on. Many of these types can be recognised in statuettes and other artistic representations. Just as the audience knew that a Daos was a slave, they would also recognise the wearer of certain kinds of mask as being a slave, for example if he had receding red hair, a ruddy complexion, a large thick-lipped mouth and a squint. But it may be hasty to suppose that the mask-makers were strictly confined to Pollux's list.

This failure to give individual names may confirm a prejudice that the characters of New Comedy lack individuality, but it will do so unjustly. A name that indicates no more than age or status does not inhibit the dramatist from conceiving the character as an individual personality; and a love of money can take many forms and be combined with a multitude of other traits. Menander's Moschions have little in common beyond sexual experience or appetite. Moschion of *Perikeiromene* (*Shorn Tresses*) is a conceited youngster who fancies himself as a lady-killer, he of *A Samian Woman* is ashamed of himself and eager to marry the girl he has wronged. What is strange is that the writer who conceived these individualised personalities did not give them names of their own. This was not a matter of principle, since sometimes he did use names that were uncommon in real life and so far as we know unique in comedy: Knemon, Kichesias, Thrasonides.

Probably all that can be said is that there was a tendency to give metrically convenient names that had in theatrical tradition become associated with characters of a particular status, old men, or young men, or married women, or nurses, or

hetairai. But this was not made into a rule. Some of the unusual names are of themselves suited to their characters: Polemon from *polemos*, 'war', and Stratophanes from *stratos*, 'army', will clearly be soldiers. The name Knemon may have carried some hint that now escapes us, and Kichesias may be intended to refer to his 'hitting on' (*kichein*) his lost daughter. But if these names have an appropriate meaning, they are all taken from life, and to be compared with Fielding's Alworthy rather than with Sheridan's Lady Sneerwell or Ben Jonson's Sir Politick Would-Be.

Many plays of New Comedy had a 'prologue'; perhaps it was usual. This was an address to the audience, which might be spoken by a character in the play, but was more frequently given to a divine figure, this a practice borrowed from tragedy. Its function was to inform the spectators of the situation at the time when the action began. The modern dramatist is obliged to smuggle these facts into his dialogue; some succeed in concealing what they are doing, but there are plays in which long passages stand out as being 'exposition', for the audience's sake, not that of the characters themselves. Because of the tradition in which he wrote, the author of New Comedy had no need to resort to expedients of this kind.

In pantomime today some characters, notably the Dame, openly recognise the presence of the audience; she even calls on it to sing, and may invite children on the stage. In *Peter Pan* they are challenged to shout their belief in fairies. The actors of Greek comedy had a similar relation to their audiences. They accepted their presence and their interest in the events going forward on the stage. There was a strange make-believe involved in this, for no one expected the spectators to intervene, to shout warnings of danger, or to give ill-informed characters facts that would be useful to them. But the actors had to give the spectators the facts they needed to understand the play, and this was done openly and without embarrassment. A man who is in a quandary can simply inform the audience of his difficulty and of his reflections about it. A man who has failed in an errand will just tell the audience on his

return how he has failed; the dramatist is not required to bring on the stage someone else to whom he may explain his failure.

That is not to say that dramatists spurned, if it was suitable, the modern method of making a man talk to himself. Sometimes also they wrote speeches that could as well be soliloquy as address to the audience; but it may be suspected that ancient actors preferred to treat them in the second way.

This practice of one-sided conversation with the public made natural the use of the prologue for exposition. That the speaker should represent a divine personage was often necessary. The plot might be such that no character was in possession of all the facts necessary to understand the situation; the discovery of some that were previously unknown could indeed bring the dénouement of the play. But although they were unknown to the characters whose affairs had formed the subject of the play, the prologue had seen to it that they were not hidden from the spectators.

In this must be recognised an important and striking feature of many plays of New Comedy. The dramatist did not use the device of keeping up his sleeve facts with which to surprise the audience. Instead he gave them a share in divine omniscience. They could enjoy their superior knowledge as they understood the misapprehensions and the blindness of the men and women whose fortunes they watched. At the same time they knew that the materials existed, if only they could be assembled, which would secure a happy ending. The fears and distresses which afflicted the characters could win sympathy, to be sure, but had no need to cause anxiety among spectators who knew them to be unfounded.

For not only did they know that a happy ending was possible, but the divine prologue sometimes concluded by promising it. Even if that reassurance had not been given, they had gone to the theatre to watch a comedy, and comedies always turned out happily. One might be uncertain how a 'tragedy' would end; a comedy had to be cheerful; it could not bring final discomfiture or disaster for those characters who had engaged sympathy, although the humiliation of villains would be greeted with pleasure. So by putting his cards on the table, as it were, from the beginning the dramatist did not surrender a

major means of suspense. The conclusion could not be in doubt. All that he lost was the power to leave the audience in the dark about a missing piece of the puzzle, and this he was in any case bound to lose with anyone who saw or read the play for a second time. For the loss of this simple one-time effect he gained a rich field for dramatic irony and for contrasts between truth and ignorance or false beliefs, features which give continuing pleasure.

But although the spectator was in no suspense about the result, although he knew that father and child would be re-united, and that the young hero would obtain the girl he loved, he enjoyed another kind of suspense, that of not know-ing how this result would be brought about, what would be the train of events to achieve it. This is another way in which comedy learned from tragedy. Almost everyone in the theatre will have known that Orestes killed his mother and her lover Aegisthus; what excited interest were the steps he took to achieve their deaths. One could not even be certain that his first plan would be successful. In Aeschylus' *Choephoroe* Orestes explains how he expects to gain access to Aegisthus (560–76); in the event nothing goes according to his expectations, but he kills him nevertheless. In their plays entitled *Electra* Soph-ocles and Euripides handled the same story as Aeschylus, but each in his own way. Similarly, if many comedies had a con-clusion which had been prophesied or could be predicted, that did not rob them of interest; the interest lay in seeing how that conclusion would be reached.

The leading dramatists of New Comedy worked in its initial period, about 320 to 280 BC. The Athenian Menander, Diphilus from Sinope on the Black Sea, and Philemon, who was probably a Syracusan, were all writing at this time, and the long-lived Alexis, native of Thurii in southern Italy, who had begun his career about 350, was still active. It is important to recognise that this was not a time of political quiet at Athens, but one of crises and upheaval. Her attempt after the death of Alexander the Great once again to play a leading role in military affairs by uniting Greek resistance to the Macedonians proved a failure, and in 322 she had to

surrender unconditionally to Antipater of Macedon. But that did not mean the end of political activity.

Fundamentally the people were divided between those who wished for security, which they expected to maintain by loyal acceptance of Macedonian protection, and those who hoped to regain independence by allying themselves with others among the powers who disputed Alexander's inheritance. The former party had the support of most of the wealthier members of the community, the latter that of the poorer and of the supporters of democracy, or equal rights for all citizens.

At first the presence of a Macedonian garrison at the Peiraeus enforced a revolution which limited the franchise to those who owned property to the value of twenty minae, not a large sum, but one which appears to have excluded more than half the citizens, who were also disbarred from sitting on juries; juries, it must be remembered, decided many cases which had political origins or political objects. There was a brief restoration of democracy in 318, lasting about a year. Ten more years of limited franchise ended in 307, when the democrats, regaining power with the help of Demetrius, Besieger of Cities, son of Antigonus, ruler of Asia Minor, attempted military action against Macedon, first successfully, then disastrously. He rescued them, but later his defeat at Ipsus in 301 led to a pro-Macedonian swing. In 198 he began to interfere again and his opponents began to kill his supporters. Previous changes of power had been marked by the execution, exile, or suicide of prominent leaders. Now there was open civil war: the democrats held the Peiraeus, while the so-called moderates, under dictatorial leadership, supported a long siege in the city, until starved into surrender in 294. But the see-saw between the pro-Macedonian and the nationalist forces, which was also one between rich and poor, continued, not in isolation but in association with the struggle between Alexander's heirs, who now controlled the major military forces. It ended only in 262 when, defeated in the war she had launched by the decree of Chremonides, Athens finally accepted Macedonian dominance and conservative government by men of means.

To these events there are few allusions in New Comedy. Because politics has so little part in the plays, some have

supposed that they also had little in most men's lives. That is a
hasty conclusion. Menander himself is said narrowly to have
escaped death in the revolution of 307, and one of his plays
missed performance because the civil war caused the cancella-
tion of the festival at which it would have appeared. Athens
was no longer a major power, and the politics of Athens were
no longer such as to be of prime interest to the historian of the
Greek-speaking world. But they did not lack importance for
the Athenians whose lives they determined. They were bitter
and sometimes deadly. They were not a suitable subject for
entertainment on a holiday. Even Aristophanes had shut his
eyes to many unpleasant political facts; the authors of New
Comedy shut their eyes, generally speaking, to politics as a
whole. In this they did no more than follow a tendency clearly
visible from the beginning of the fourth century; poets seem
more and more to have found their material in everyday non-
political life, and more and more to have eliminated references
to active politicians.

The changes of the late fourth century did not, however,
leave comedy untouched. The lifting from the rich of the
burden of 'liturgies', not reversed by the restored democracy of
307, meant that the chorus was no longer paid for by a private
individual; production was put in the hands of a public official,
the *agōnothetēs* or 'competition-manager'. It is not known
whether this had any consequences for the dramatists. But the
cessation of payments from the theoric fund to the disen-
franchised probably resulted in the absence from the theatre
of the poorer and on the whole simpler and less educated and
less critical members of the public. This would encourage the
elimination of vulgarity and obscenity in favour of the literary
merits which characterise New Comedy.

Having abandoned public affairs, the dramatists turned to
the representation of some aspects of private life. The society
of which they give a picture is one in which a leading part is
played by men of what we today call the higher income groups.
They own at least one household slave, frequently several.
Often they have a farm, where manual work is socially acceptable; but their main residence is not necessarily on it; the
better off will have a house in the city as well. Vaguely
described business abroad is another source of income;

journeys to trade or collect debts are convenient motifs to explain the absence from home of the head of the family.

Families are small; there is rarely mention of more than two children, often a boy and a girl. If both parents are still alive, there is frequently friction between them. A girl is brought up in the seclusion of the women's quarters, from which she escapes only to attend religious festivals. She will be given a dowry and married off to a husband chosen for her by her father, who may have her happiness in view or may wish merely to further his own interests.

A son may be required by a strict father to work on the farm, but most seem to lead an idle life about town. They may see a citizen girl at a festival, fall in love at sight, and finally achieve marriage. It is more usual that they associate with a hetaira; this requires money, which may be provided by an indulgent father or deceitfully obtained from a stingy one, with the aid of the slave who is attached to the service of the young master. Between these extremes are young men who form a relation with a citizen girl to whom they have access, either because she has lost her parents and other relatives or because she is the daughter of a poor widow or grass-widow, who is unable to provide the seclusion usual in a richer household and is willing to allow visits by the lover. The young man may doubt that his father would give consent to a marriage with her; consent may have been legally required, and was in any case necessary in practice, since he was financially dependent.

It would be vain to pretend that the society depicted is that of an average Athenian household. But it is a picture of possible and perhaps not altogether unusual households. It is far from a complete picture even of them. It concentrates on activities, aspects, and human relations which had become established as profitable subjects for the dramatist. One must also remember that, although this kind of society is a norm, dramatists may introduce characters who do not conform to it.

Menander is said to have written over a hundred plays; the titles are known of more than 200 by Antiphanes, a writer of the early half of the fourth century. Even if these poets obtained

a chorus on every occasion both for the Lenaia and for the Dionysia, it would seem that not half these plays can have been performed there. How is this to be explained? Some of the titles may have been alternatives, and occasionally a poet may have succeeded in having two plays accepted for one festival, as Anaxandrides did in 375 and Diodorus in 286, but these possibilities are not enough to solve the problem. It is not likely that anyone wrote comedies for no purpose but that of selling the text to a bookseller. Accordingly it is probable that plays were written in the hope of having them produced on some other occasion than those of the great Athenian festivals.

One possibility is that they were intended for other towns, which had built themselves theatres but lacked local dramatic talent; the great theatre at Megalopolis, dating from about 350, and the magnificent one at Epidaurus, constructed about 330, must have been designed for full-scale developed drama, which those places would have been obliged to import. Another outlet for the dramatists may have been the local festivals in Attica, where several of the country *demes* or villages possessed theatres by the end of the fourth century.

Information is scanty, but in some of these places plays were probably to be seen already in the fifth century. An inscription at Eleusis strongly suggests that both Sophocles and Aristophanes produced plays there. Were these first performances or revivals? And if they were first performances, were they later repeated at one of the city festivals? Unfortunately the questions cannot be answered, but there is no *a priori* reason why some plays should not have been performed in the country, but never in the city.

There is evidence for the performance of comedies at seven places in Attica outside Athens. The actors were probably paid professionals, but the chorus may have been composed of amateurs. As at Athens, the plays were in competition; the contest was organised by the *demarch*, or elected headman of the village, and the choruses were assembled and trained by *choregoi*. As at Athens, there were prizes and seats of honour. At the Peiraeus a contractor who provided seating kept the entrance-fees in the early fourth century; at Acharnae towards the end of it they seem to have gone to the *deme*. It would not

be surprising if new plays were sometimes written for these elaborately organised festivals.

In Athens itself New Comedy was produced in a reconstruction of the old theatre, carried out under the influence of Lycurgus, a leading political figure, between 336 and 326, a period when Macedonian ascendancy inhibited military expenditure. Permanent stone seating was installed and the stage building replaced by one in stone. There were now without a doubt three doors in it, opening on a stage a few feet above the orchestra and about 66 feet in length. At each end an open pillared building projected from the back wall, enclosing the acting area; through these structures actors could reach the stage from the *parodoi*.[1] Most comedies required the use of two of the doors to represent the entrance to two houses; the third door might be covered, if it was not needed as the entrance to a cave or temple or conceivably a third house. Modern notions of symmetry cause some scholars to assume that when there were two houses the two side doors were used; for what it is worth the ancient evidence states that the larger central door was used for the house of the 'protagonist' or leading actor (Pollux 4. 124).

In some towns soon after Lycurgus' time theatres were built on a different plan, to which his theatre was later adapted. The stage was for some reason unknown raised to the level of the upper storey of the two-floored stage-building and supported on columns which stood in front of the lower storey. It seems, sometimes at least, to have been protected by a projecting roof. The chorus may have remained in the orchestra, its irrelevance to contemporary plays symbolised by its separation from the actors; yet, reduced to a handful of members, it may have performed like them on the elevated stage.

It seems that scene-painting, in the modern sense of the word, was introduced during the period of the elevated stage. Large painted panels were placed between the doors which opened on it, with different sets for tragedy and comedy. It may be relevant that the 66-foot width of the stage could be

[1] These structures must have obstructed the view of some parts of the stage from the ends of the auditorium. This suggests that the full capacity of the theatre, estimated at 17,000, was not needed for dramatic performances.

extended in imagination. The doors were those of houses to
be thought of as opening on a street in a town, a lane in a
village, or an open space in the country. Occasionally there
was also a temple or the mouth of a cave. The houses or other
places were to be imagined as near one another, but not
necessarily cheek by jowl. The scenery between the doors
would give a suggestion of distance between them.

To match this elasticity of space there was a limited elasticity of time. A longer period must often be supposed to elapse
during the interval between acts than was in fact taken up by
the performance of the chorus. But it was unusual for the
action of the play to exceed the time between dawn and night-
fall; the words often call attention to how much has been
done, or must be done, in one day.

Inscriptional evidence shows that dramatic contests continued
at Athens both for comic poets and for comic actors until
143 BC at least; they may have been ended only by Sulla's
sack of the city in 86. One may doubt whether many of the
later dramatists, none of whom won any great reputation,
did much more than rework traditional elements. That seems
to be true of Apollodorus of Carystus, who wrote the originals
of Terence's *Phormio* and *Hecyra*.

The popularity of comedy is attested by the fact that in the
late third century the number of new plays at the Dionysia
was increased from five to six. One old comedy was also
regularly revived, not in competition with the new; the first
occasion was in 339, and from 311 when *The Treasure* by
Anaxandrides, a poet of the Middle Comedy, was presented,
it was the customary procedure. In one year about the middle
of the third century there was even a contest for old comedies,
won by a drama of Diphilus, with one of Menander's in second
place.

But in the mid-second century it became impossible to carry
out the full programme annually; on the average in half of the
years no contest took place at the Dionysia. This heralds the
virtual end of new work in comedy; very few names are
preserved of writers active in the first century, and of almost

none in the Christian era. Yet the playing of old comedies was not extinct; Menander's *Theophorumene* was probably to be seen in the theatre of Dionysus as late as AD 267.

Athens was not the only place to know dramatic contests. Whether evidence of them survives is very much a matter of accident and a record of a competition between tragedies need not mean that there was one for comedies also. But, to confine the list to certainties, comedies are known to have been in competition at more than a dozen places, including Delphi (from about 275 until the first century BC), Delos (284–170), Samos (second century), and the Boeotian town of Orchomenos (first century). Performances by comic actors are recorded at several other cities without explicit mention of a competition. Plutarch's question: 'Why should an educated man go to the theatre except to see Menander?' implies opportunities for seeing his plays in the latter part of the first century AD. In the middle of the second century AD Aelius Aristides deprecates in an address to the people of Ephesus their practice of allowing actors to ridicule individual members of their community. He had a capacity for avoiding hard facts, but makes it appear that topical references were there inserted into comedies, new or old.

This widespread and continued dramatic activity, 'the most popular and influential form of culture for several hundred years',[1] was associated with the rise of guilds of theatre per-

[1] A. W. Pickard-Cambridge, *The Dramatic Festivals of Athens*, 2nd edn., p. 241. Numerous fragments of papyrus rolls or codices, i.e. books with leaves, found in Egypt, show that Menander was widely read there until the fifth century or even later. It is remarkable that many texts paid little attention to the reader's convenience. Stage directions were rarely given; an initial list of dramatis personae was far from universal and, what is more surprising, the practice of inserting the names of speakers made slow progress. This is first known from a manuscript not earlier than the end of the first century AD, but although it becomes more common and more systematic as time goes on, the old way also persisted of doing no more to indicate a change of speaker than the placing of a short line, which projected into the margin, below the initial letters of the verse in which or at the end of which the change occurred and a pair of dots (:) where it occurred. Some texts do not have the dots, but only a small space. No wonder that Dion of Prusa (early second

sonnel, who called themselves Artists of Dionysus, and who are often known to have provided the performers for various festivals. The most important of these guilds were the Athenian and the Isthmian–Nemean, rivals formed in the first quarter of the third century, and the Ionian–Hellespontine, which arose later in that century. There were also minor guilds elsewhere. Membership was not confined to actors, but included poets and chorusmen, harpists and pipers, trainers and costumiers; their activities were not restricted to drama, but extended to all the musical events of the festivals.

These guilds were important and respected institutions. Their members were granted such privileges as exemption from taxation and from liability to military service. Their priests, who were chosen from their own number, were about 125 BC given the right to wear golden chaplets and purple robes in all cities. The Roman Senate intervened in their disputes. For their own part they fined members who refused to perform where the guild directed them or to keep their engagements. Later the separate guilds appear to have combined to create a single 'world-wide' organisation, first heard of in a letter of AD 43 from the emperor Claudius, which shows however that it was already recognised by Augustus. It was still active as late as the time of Diocletian (285–305) who, to prevent tax-evasion through the buying by rich men of nominal membership, restricted exemption to true professionals.

---

century AD), when recommending an ambitious man to study Menander, advises him not to try to read the plays himself but to have them acted for him and so avoid the preoccupation involved in reading (18.6).

Menander

LATER generations had no doubt that Menander was the greatest writer of New Comedy and condemned the taste of his contemporaries; he was awarded the first prize eight times only. Perhaps the broader strokes of Diphilus from Sinope and Philemon from Syracuse, whom later critics joined with him to constitute a leading trio in this form of comedy, made a greater appeal to the mass audience. Yet there is no evidence that these poets won any more victories than he did; they are credited with no more than three apiece at the Lenaia.[1] Nor is there any record of how often he competed; one cannot assume that his plays were always chosen by the archon for production on the occasions, about fifty in number, when he was theoretically eligible. Artistic merit may not have been the sole consideration which guided that official's choice.

It is known, however, that the judges placed him fifth and last at the Dionysia of 312 and 311, and these are decisions which one suspects it would be hard to defend. A great artist is not necessarily under-estimated in his own lifetime, so that one is encouraged to speculate on the causes of Menander's inadequate success. Possibly his friendship with Demetrius of Phalerum, the unpopular 'Supervisor of the City', imposed by the Macedonians from 319 to 307, created prejudice against his plays. It may be more likely that they suffered because their merits do not all appear at first sight.

A well-known anecdote gives Menander's answer to a friend who expressed surprise that although the Dionysia were approaching he had not written his comedy. 'Indeed I have composed my comedy! The plot is worked out, but I have to add the spell of the verses.' This reply is not to be regarded as a depreciation of the words of the play; they are spoken of as if they were an incantation to charm the hearer.

---

[1] *I.G.* ii². 2325 col. x.

Menander did in fact write with superb skill, which can unfortunately be appreciated only by those able to read the original Greek. He subtly varied his speed and his rhythms and the levels of his language to correspond with the psychology of his characters and their emotional changes. And although he constantly used the verse form to reinforce the meaning, he maintained the illusion that they were speaking as men speak in reality, colloquially and individually; they do not fall, as Philemon's personages seem to have done, into literary Greek, unless of deliberate purpose. This is even to some extent true of his trochaic tetrameters, although these tend to a more regular movement than the commoner iambic trimeters. But the excellence of the writing need not imply that composition was a slow affair. It may be that he was one of those authors from whom there comes a spontaneous and easy flow of admirable language.

What the anecdote does convey is the primary importance of plot. This does not mean simply the events. Of far more weight are the means by which those events are brought about; they include the psychology of the persons in the play, since the way in which they choose to act determines its course. Hence the imaginative creation of characters is part of the playwright's business, and at this too Menander was outstanding. His people are credible, consistent and lifelike; their emotions and thoughts are often not explicitly expressed but to be inferred from the clues given by their words; and the words are rich in suggestion. The action is then carried forward by doings and speeches suitable to the characters thus depicted.

A good plot gives further pleasure by its formal merits, that is to say by contrasts between successive scenes or between characters and pairs of characters, by symmetry and by mirror-image, by the balanced proportion of the parts. These must not be obtrusive, or they will appear contrived. Analysis of Menander's plays brings many instances of such elegance to light. One difficulty in constructing a plot is to provide natural exits and entrances, as some dramatists have confessed. In Menander they are always plausible. The *moment* at which a character enters or leaves is of course determined by the dramatist, but the *motive* is rarely in doubt or, if not explicitly

indicated, can be surmised. Movements are natural reactions to the situation which has arisen by the development of the plot. There are no extraneous, arbitrary factors, like the famous bear which causes Autolycus' exit in *The Winter's Tale*. The difficulty involved in so contriving the progress of the play must have been greatly increased if Menander was under the handicap of having to employ no more than three actors. This is a question on which there is no agreement.

In no surviving scene do more than three characters speak, although sometimes one or more others, who have spoken elsewhere, are on the stage. These silent characters were played by 'supers', who wore the masks that had previously been worn by actors. This restriction to three speakers appears also in the plays by Menander which Plautus adapted, and may have applied to those adapted by Terence; the changes, however, which the latter introduced are too much disputed to allow him to provide unchallenged evidence. The restriction has been explained by some scholars as self-imposed and due either to the difficulty, which can surely be exaggerated, of writing four-part dialogue or to that of recognising in a great open-air theatre which of a number of masked actors was speaking or to an artistic preference for simplicity.

The last explanation is the most difficult to combat, for its supposition that Menander would have found that four speakers offended against his aesthetic sensibility must be intuitively accepted or rejected; it cannot be usefully discussed. Masks certainly prevented the lips from providing any clue to the speaker, but gesture may often have accompanied words, as it does today more usually among southern peoples than with us, and so have served as an indication. If this was so, to pick out the right speaker would not be significantly more difficult if the choice were between four characters rather than three, particularly if the four were divided into pairs, perhaps at opposite ends of the stage, each pair engaged in its own conversation. But there is no such scene. It may also be observed that there is no scene where one of three characters who have been in conversation departs and is immediately replaced by a fourth; yet such a scene would never require the audience to discriminate between more than three actors at once.

The most obvious explanation of the absence of more than three speaking actors from any scene is that Menander wrote so that he could be performed by a company of three actors. It is known that companies who visited Delphi in the third century were so composed; they had three comic actors, five or seven chorusmen and a piper. He may have had such troupes in mind, although it is only a guess that they existed in his time. But he fashioned many of his plays for a première at one of the great Athenian festivals and it is possible that the same limitation was in force there. The travelling companies may have had three actors because that was the number engaged in the original performance.

It is generally agreed that tragedy was performed by three actors: Aristotle is the explicit authority for that and it is confirmed in various ways. On the other hand some plays of Aristophanes require a minimum of five. But did comedy come to accept the limitation traditional in tragedy? It is possible that such a rule was introduced in order to equalise conditions for the competitors; no dramatist was to gain an advantage by being able to employ a larger number of actors. The principal actor, assigned to the author by lot, was paid from state funds and probably used them to hire his assistants. It may have been thought fair that a rich actor or rich author should not be allowed to exceed a standard provision.

This, it must be confessed, is speculation. But if plays were written so that they could be performed by three actors, we have an explanation of the way in which certain exits are managed. For example, in *Dyskolos* (*The Curmudgeon*) Daos does not accompany his master Gorgias and Sostratos to the fields, but goes off first, telling them to follow. This is in character; he is a hard worker and wants to get to his labours. But it does not advance the action. The actor, however, is needed to return shortly as Sikon. Then Sostratos does not go off with Gorgias, but hangs back and talks to the audience. That is because Gorgias' actor must also play Getas, Sikon's companion; he is given time to return in his new role, because Getas is found to have fallen behind under the weight of the baggage he carries. In the *Sikyonios* Theron goes in to tell Stratophanes that the father of the girl the other loves has been found but, although an inquisitive man, does not come

back with him. The actor was needed to play Stratophanes himself.

A limitation of actors to three was feasible only if parts were sometimes shared, if for example in *Samia* (*The Woman from Samos*) the part of Parmenon was taken by one actor in Acts I and V and by another in Act III. In a completely realistic theatre this would be impossible, but the theatre of Menander was not of that sort. The fact that the actors were masked is enough to show that the audience looked for no more than a limited realism. By wearing A's mask an actor would become A, for it was by mask rather than voice or stature that A was recognised.

Apart from that, any offence caused by discrepancies between actors playing the same man could be minimised, if it was thought desirable. Notably tall or notably short men may have been regarded as unsuitable for the profession of acting. The art of mimicry, today somewhat out of fashion, which effects the disguise of one's own voice, must have been used by the ancient actor if he distinguished the voices of the different persons he represented in the same play; the same art could have been called upon by the different actors who played a single part; they could both or all three speak in a similar way, just as they could also assimilate their movements and gestures.

In conclusion it must be emphasised that the case for a limitation of actors to three is not cogent. The fact that a play could be performed by three actors does not prove that it was so performed. And even if it was a rule kept at Athens, it may not have been operative in some other place, or even enforced without exception at the Athenian festivals. The find of a new papyrus might establish a breach of the rule, and there are two or three Latin plays, adapted from Diphilus and Apollodorus, in which no simple change suffices to re-establish it.

In those plays, more than a dozen in number, where one can judge, it is either certain or highly probable that Menander used the five-act structure with an expository prologue. The

scarcity of information about Middle Comedy makes it impossible to decide whether these were already established and regularly used conventions or whether his example confirmed what had previously been experimental. But in any case here as elsewhere he must be seen as the inheritor of a tradition within which he worked but within which he created novelty. It may have been on his own initiative that in several plays he gave a surprising place to the 'prologue', putting it after an opening dialogue; surprising, but effective. The audience's attention was immediately gripped by a striking scene, which partially revealed the situation with which the play began, but which was also designed to mislead. It showed the circumstances as they appeared to one or more of the characters. But they were ignorant of some pertinent fact, recognition of which would work a complete change in the spectator's response to what he had seen. The divinity who speaks the prologue is better informed and able to put him right.

In the opening scene of *Aspis* (*The Shield*) the slave Daos reports the death on a campaign of his young master, whose avaricious uncle fails to conceal an interest in his very considerable booty. Then the goddess of Luck, the speaker of the 'prologue', not only spells out the family relationships, and explains the uncle's plans to acquire the dead nephew's estate by exercising a legal right to marry his sister, although another wedding for her was imminent, but also reveals that the young man is in fact alive and, having been taken prisoner, is on the point of returning home; all the miser's efforts will be trouble wasted.

Similarly in *Perikeiromene* (*Shorn Tresses*) the 'prologue' is postponed. The opening scene does not survive, but can be reconstructed in outline with fair certainty. A soldier, returning from an expedition, was met by his servant who had gone ahead; he reported that he had surprised the girl with whom the soldier lived allowing herself to be kissed and hugged by a young man on her doorstep. In a fury of jealousy the soldier hacked off her long hair. The goddess Misapprehension then puts a different face on the affair. The girl knew the young man to be her brother, although he was ignorant of the fact. There is an explanation of how they had come to meet and why she could not reveal their relationship. Finally there is a

promise that they will find the family to which they belong and that good will come of the present imbroglio.

Menander was not slow to make use of the traditional figures caricatured in Middle Comedy, soldiers, courtesans, cooks and so on. But he was not content simply to repeat their traditional qualities; when he used old themes he made them a part only of an individual character, or he modified them; sometimes he even contradicted tradition, to create an effect by the unexpectedness of his treatment.

The cook had been inquisitive, talkative and self-important. Sikon in *Dyskolos* shows curiosity as he questions Getas on his mistress's dream; he is not long-winded, but he talks to himself, using a vocabulary rich in oaths and in metaphors; he boasts, not of his cuisine, but of his large clientele and his technique in borrowing utensils; his conceit is shown by his reaction to Knemon's falling into the well:

> Now the Nymphs have given him the punishment he deserves on my account. No one who wrongs a cook ever gets off unscathed. Our art has something sacred about it.

By contrast the cook in *Aspis*, who is seen leaving, not as usual entering, his place of employment, complains that things always go wrong for him. The cook in *Samia* enters in full flow of talk and questions, but is cut short. Later he tries with officious benevolence to interfere as Demeas turns Chrysis out of his house. All these cooks display or contradict traditional characters, but they do it briefly and in sentences woven into the texture of plot and dialogue.

The stupidity, arrogance and vulgarity of the professional soldier, together with his habit of romancing about his exploits, were certainly all displayed in Bias of *Kolax* (*The Flatterer*), the origin of Terence's Thraso in *Eunuchus*. But the three soldiers who appear in the partially surviving plays are sympathetically drawn. Thrasonides of *Misumenos* (*Hated*), wild with love for the captive girl within his power, not laying a hand on her when she shows her repulsion, and generously freeing her

without ransom when her father appears, is the hero of the play. Yet he had talked of his exploits, a traditional motif, but it may be guessed, one made essential to the play, for it will have been one of these tales which made the girl suspect him of having killed her brother. Nor is there any reason to think that he exaggerated, for the prologue told that he had served with distinction.

There is no sign of any of the traditional defects in Stratophanes of *Sikyonios* (*The Man from Sikyon*). On the contrary his actions are practical and decisive, nor does he forget, at the moment when he seems about to secure the girl he loves, to issue orders for the quartering of the men for whom he is responsible. One can believe that he was a good officer. Polemon, on the other hand, in *Perikeiromene* displays neither the traditional qualities of the caricatured soldier nor those that are required in the field. He is hasty, uncertain of himself and impulsive, but he attracts sympathy by his bewilderment at the situation he has created by the outrage on the mistress he loves, his despair at the prospect of her leaving him, and his pleasure at her discovery of her father.

Similarly the selfish, acquisitive, lying and faithless courtesan, although no doubt a common figure in real life, was not according to Menander the sole type to be found in her profession. He brought into his plays a wide range of hetairai. Habrotonon in *Epitrepontes* (*The Arbitrants*) is still quite young and still a slave; clever and good-natured, but ready to deceive, not merely to help others but also in the hope of winning her own freedom by the trickery. Chrysis in *Samia* is older and attached to the child she passes off as her own; her lie is told with the best of intentions but infringes the loyalty she otherwise shows towards the man who is keeping her. For others we must go to Latin adaptations. Bacchis of *Heautontimorumenos* (*The Man Who Punished Himself*) is an unprincipled gold-digger, but Thais of *Eunuchus* acts with dignity when imposed upon and apparently thwarted in her sustained effort to return Pamphila unharmed to her family. To be sure her motives are not purely altruistic, she hopes to secure their friendship and protection. But Menander's world, like the real world, is not one of people blind to their own interests.

He was not the first to abandon the stereotype of the wicked hetaira. Already Antiphanes had written:

> The man of whom I speak saw a hetaira who lived next door to him and fell in love with her. She was of citizen birth, but without guardian or relatives, and had a character of gold for goodness—a true 'companion'.[1] Other women damage that name, really a fine one, by their behaviour.

The innovation is here excused by the woman's citizen birth; Menander extended his sympathy more widely. Yet he followed what seems to have been a rule in New Comedy: a girl of citizen birth must either remain a virgin before marriage, or be faithful to her first lover and marry him when marriage becomes possible.

Menander is also remarkable for presenting a great range of individualised and sympathetically treated slaves; he thought of them neither as mere instruments of their masters' wishes nor as vehicles for comic interludes; they act with their own motivation within a framework provided by the actions, characters, and intentions of their owners; they affect what happens, but do not direct it. This, it may be supposed, does not misrepresent the situation in many Athenian households.

This method of writing, which gives large parts to slaves and develops their personalities on much the same scale as those of their masters, is a testimonial to Menander's range of interest and sympathy: he did not regard slaves as a different kind of creature from the free; all men were human beings and he would give any man the artist's attention. He can fairly be contrasted with many dramatists of the Western world, in whose plays about households of the employing classes servants usually have a quite subsidiary role. Exceptions like Barrie's *Admirable Crichton* and Beaumarchais' *Figaro* were protests against the view that all members of the lower orders are inferior beings, but these characters are not made typical representatives of their status: they are exceptions and remain exceptional.

---

[1] 'Companion' is the literal meaning of the word 'hetaira'.

The recent discoveries which have enriched knowledge of Menander have made it more and more difficult to generalise about him in an absolute manner. His plays are like a large family of brothers and sisters, all recognisable as his work, each sharing features with some of the others, but each individually characterised. Plutarch, however, saw in them one common element, *Eros*, love. The Greek word overlaps the English, but does not coincide with it. It has a stronger association with sexual passion and desire, and is sometimes nothing more than these things. But it easily becomes allied with more altruistic urges, respect, loyalty, generosity, a wish for the welfare of the beloved. 'I know,' says Kallippides in *Dyskolos*, 'that what gives a young man's marriage security is that Eros prompted him to it.'

Yet although Eros is a force in all the plays, it is, usually at least, not their principal subject. As a main interest it would have been narrow and constricting for the dramatist, who would have been further limited by the social customs of his time, which almost entirely prevented contact between young men and marriageable girls. Eros often sets a play in motion, for example, *Dyskolos*, *Perikeiromene*, or *Samia*, but it is not necessarily even the initiating cause. In *Aspis* that is the avarice of Smikrines, which is then resisted because of its threat to the *eros* of Chaireas.

The major subject of *Dyskolos* is the misanthropy of Knemon, which is shown to be disadvantageous to himself as well as to others; a minor subject is the desirability of friendship between rich and poor, and the reciprocal aid they can give one to the other. In *Samia* the recurring theme is the relation between father and son, the strains to which it is subjected and its final survival. *Adelphoi B*, so called to distinguish it, since two of Menander's plays had the title *Adelphoi* (*Brothers*), the origin of Terence's *Adelphoe*, is another play in which much attention is given to the problem of relations between father and son and in which alternative methods of upbringing are contrasted. *Epitrepontes* is a play of extraordinarily rich content; its varied scenes are developed for their own sakes, yet this threat to the unity of action is nullified by their skilful attachment to the central situation, the difficulty that has arisen between Charisios and his wife. He has found that she had been pregnant when

he married her and had in his absence exposed the child. He has then retreated into a friend's house and hired a hetaira, perhaps with the object of causing his wife to divorce him; thus their marriage would be ended but her good name protected. Her father, who knows nothing of the child, urges this course on her but, in a lost scene which Charisios overhears, she refuses. He has previously learned that he had himself before marriage got a child by rape at a festival and he comes to feel how despicable is his conduct towards his wife, and is convinced that he must hold to her. Only when he has had this change of heart does it come to light that she had been the victim of his rape and that the child, which had been rescued, was theirs. Charisios is on the stage for a mere eighty lines at the end of Act IV, yet the whole of the play revolves around him and the theme of loyalty in marriage.

Yet the importance in some plays of themes which transcend the particular interests of the individuals who illustrate them must not tempt us to look for them everywhere. Menander was a dramatist, not a sociologist. His first concern was to write entertaining plays with a good story, like *Synaristosal (A Women's Lunch-party)* or *Dis Exapaton (A Double Deceit)*, the originals of Plautus' *Cistellaria (A Little Box)* and *Bacchides (The Bacchis Sisters)*.

There are many different ways of writing an entertaining play and there is considerable variety of form in Menander. *Sikyonios* seems to be almost entirely serious, an exciting drama full of incident and rising at times to a style more elevated than was common in comedy. In *Perikeiromene* the scene in which the father recognises his long-lost daughter is composed in stichomythia, or alternate lines, intended at once to be a mark of their emotion and a source of amusement by its borrowing of phrases from tragedy. In neither of these plays is there anything to excite sustained laughter, like Daos' deliberately absurd quotations from tragedy in *Aspis*.

Samia has only six characters, of whom one has no effect on the plot; *Synaristosai* seems to have had eleven, not counting the god who spoke the prologue, and six of them were women, who dominated the play, which is in that respect unique. Some plays reach as early as the fourth act a point where the satisfaction of Eros seems assured; the early *Dyskolos* and the

late *Epitrepontes* are examples of this. Thereafter there are scenes which carry on other themes and which conclude with hilarity. But in *Misumenos* and *Sikyonios* the happy ending for the lover is postponed until very near the termination of the play and there is no sign of a conclusion which gave cause for laughter.

This variety may lead one to wonder whether Plautus' *Stichus* has a closer relation to Menander's *Adelphoi A*, alleged to be its original, than most scholars have thought. It is a play almost without plot, consisting of eight scenes or sketches, very tenuously connected. Yet these scenes are clearly divided into five acts, which suggests that Plautus, who wrote for continuous performance, derived them from his Greek original. If so, Menander may for some reason, haste or experiment, have abandoned his usual care for the construction of a plot.

Impossible though it is to find a 'typical' play by Menander, *Samia* may serve as an example of the kind of thing to be expected in his writing. The following account of that play, being largely a summary, can provide only a diminished idea of its merits; even passages of translation can do no more than give the basic sense of the words; they cannot reproduce the skill of the versification. Even if a rendering in verse had been attempted, it must have been inadequate. Blank verse is the only possible form to represent the Greek iambic trimeter but, in comparison, it has few rules.

Samia has no need of a god to let the audience into secrets not known to the human characters; for there are none. A nearly complete explanation of the background is given in an opening monologue by the young Moschion. He has no hesitation about accepting the spectators' presence, but without ado tells them that (he is an adopted child of a rich father),[1] brought up in style and able to help poorer friends. Demeas, his father, had made him a full human being and he

---

[1] There are some lacunae in the text as it survives. I use brackets to enclose matter which may be guessed to have stood in them.

had responded by being well-behaved. Then his father had been taken by desire for a woman from Samos, a hetaira, and ashamed of this passion had tried to conceal it. Moschion had however become aware of it and seen that his father would have trouble from young rivals unless he got the woman under his own control. (So he encouraged him to establish the woman, whose name was Chrysis, in his house. Demeas had left her there when he had gone abroad with their neighbour, a poor man called Nikeratos. Nikeratos had a daughter in her teens and a wife who became friendly with the Samian woman.)

> Running down from our farm, [continues Moschion] I found them all collected in our house with some other women to celebrate the feast of Adonis ... Their noise made it difficult to sleep: they were taking plants up on the roof, and dancing, and making a night of it, scattered through the house. I hesitate to go on with the story, although perhaps it does no good to be ashamed. All the same I am ashamed. The girl became pregnant. By telling you that I make it clear what happened. I was to blame and I did not deny it. I went to the girl's mother of my own accord and promised marriage as soon as my father should return; I swore a solemn oath. When the child was born, I took charge of it, not so long ago. By a lucky chance it happened that Chrysis (had a little earlier given birth to a child who had died; she took the girl's baby in substitution, and so we were able to keep it.

Moschion then left and Chrysis came out of the house; she shortly) sees Moschion returning with their slave Parmenon, whom he seems to have met by accident. Parmenon tells him that he has seen Demeas and Nikeratos; they are back from their travels; Moschion must be brave and raise the question of his marriage at once. 'How? I am turning coward now that the moment comes; I am ashamed to face my father.' 'And what of the girl you have wronged and her mother?' Chrysis makes her presence known, and while Parmenon explains his own reasons for wanting the marriage to take place, Moschion pulls himself together and promises to keep his oath. They

confirm the plan that Chrysis should say that she is the child's mother. Demeas will be angry,[1] says Moschion, but she is confident that he will soon get over that; he's enamoured of her, and she will do anything to prevent the child's being put out to nurse in some tenement. (Parmenon and she enter the house, while) Moschion goes off to some quiet place to practise what he will have to say in the coming interview with his father. The stage is empty. There enter Demeas, Nikeratos and slaves with their luggage. They talk about the pleasure of being home again in Athens; Byzantium and the Black Sea were terrible places.

> *Nikeratos.* What surprised me most about that region, Demeas, was that sometimes one could not see the sun for days on end. It seemed as if a thick mist obscured it.
> *Demeas.* No; old Sun could see nothing worth looking at there, and so he gave the inhabitants of those parts just the minimum of sunshine.
> *Nikeratos.* By Dionysus, you are right.
> *Demeas.* Well, we'll let other people bother about that. Now what do you think should be done with regard to that matter we were talking about?

Demeas of course does not believe in his own anthropomorphic meteorology, but amuses himself by passing it off on Nikeratos, whose simplicity is thereby immediately indicated at his first appearance. The passage also prepares the way for a similar move, but in a serious situation, at the end of Act IV. But all this travel talk is primarily designed to form the background from which will suddenly spring the answer to that last question.

> *Nikeratos.* You mean our talk about your boy's marriage?
> *Demeas.* Quite.
> *Nikeratos.* My mind's the same. Let us fix a day and hope it turns out well.
> *Demeas.* Is that agreed then?

[1] He would not expect her to allow the child to live without his authority. But the time for infanticide is past.

Nikeratos. By me, it is.

Demeas. And by me too; and I thought of it first.

Only one conclusion can be drawn from these exchanges: the two fathers have agreed on a match between their children. The rich Demeas insists that the scheme had originated with himself and tactfully allows his poor friend to feel that it is his consent that is required. Moschion's fears are then groundless. The play seems to be as good as over (as the two fathers enter their houses).

Act II is badly mutilated, but whereas complications might be expected to set in at this point, difficulties seem hardly to have arisen before they were solved, and once again the play seems threatened by a premature end. Moschion, returning from an unsuccessful rehearsal of his confession, meets his father, greets him, and asks what makes him pull a long face. Demeas replies that he seems to have got a wife in his hetaira, who has provided him with a son without his consent; but she can get to hell out of his house, and take the child with her. Moschion protests with some fine sentiments: 'who of us in Heaven's name is legitimate and who a bastard when he's born a man?' (Demeas was quickly persuaded to keep Chrysis and the child supposed to be his, and as quickly discovered to his surprise that Moschion loved the girl intended for him.) He undertakes to ask Nikeratos to agree to the marriage's taking place that very day and, Moschion having retired, hurries his surprised friend into agreement and sends a puzzled Parmenon to fetch a cook and foodstuffs from the market. Nikeratos must go and tell his wife, who is thought likely to make difficulties, before following Parmenon to the market.

Act III. Demeas comes out and in a long speech of over eighty lines tells the audience of an unexpected development, that has left him in a turmoil of doubt. He describes the busy scene in his house as the slaves were in confusion caused by his orders to prepare for the unexpected wedding. The child was pushed out of the way on a couch, where it lay yelling, and the servants were calling for flour, water, olive oil, charcoal. He himself was giving a hand and went into a store-room, and while he was there an old woman, once his slave and Moschion's

nurse, came down from the upper floor by a stair which led into the weaving-room from which the store opened, and

> seeing the baby yelling there with no one to pay it any attention, and not knowing that I was at home, thought she could chatter safely: she goes up to it and says the usual stuff: 'Darling child!' and 'What a treasure! But where's mummy?'; she kissed him and walked him up and down. And when he stopped crying she said to herself 'Oh dear me! It's only yesterday that I was nursing Moschion himself and loving him, and he was just like this baby, and now he has already got a child of his own for me to hold'. A girl came running in from outside. 'Wash the baby,' she says to her, 'What's this? Can't you attend to the little one, when his father's getting married?' The other replied quickly: 'How loud you're talking! Master's at home.' 'You don't say! Where?' 'In the store-room', and then with a change of voice 'Mistress is calling you, nurse' and 'Get a move on! Hurry!—He hasn't heard a thing. What luck!' 'Oh dear me!' she said, 'How I chatter!' and took herself off, I don't know where. I emerged from the store exactly in the way I came out here just now, quite quietly, as if I'd heard nothing and noticed nothing, and I saw her, the Samian woman, outside by herself, holding it in her arms and giving it her breast. So one can know that it is hers, but who is its father, is it my child or is it—no, gentlemen, I'm not saying it, I won't suspect it, I'm just putting the facts before you, what I heard with my own ears, and I feel no resentment—not yet. I know that the lad has always been well-behaved and as loyal to me as could be. But on the other hand, when I remember that the woman who talked was his nurse, and that she was speaking behind my back, and then think of the woman who loves it and has insisted on rearing it against my wishes—I am utterly beside myself.

This speech is beautifully constructed. The initial sentences foreshadow some catastrophe, but the vivid details which follow do nothing to elucidate it, until it bursts as unexpectedly

on the audience as it had on Demeas himself. Then, ironically, the one thing he believes he knows is exactly where he is wrong. He forces himself to be calm, but his indignation is too strong and finally explodes. This pattern of behaviour will be repeated.

Now he recovers his self-control, as Parmenon comes home from the market with food and a cook, whose loquacity the slave checks before taking him indoors. Demeas, who has told him to return, has meanwhile let the audience know that he intends to have the truth out of him and so when he comes out full of self-confidence, giving instructions to Chrysis, they can relish his sudden dismay at Demeas' opening words, 'Listen now, Parmenon, there are many reasons why I don't want to flog you,' followed by a demand to know whose the child is. 'It belongs to Chrysis.' 'And who is the father?' 'You are, so she says.' At this Demeas bursts out that he knows perfectly well that it is Moschion's baby and that Parmenon knows it too. Everybody says so. Parmenon sees no hope of keeping up the pretence and is on the point of explaining everything, but unfortunately begins 'We wanted to keep it quiet'. Demeas supposes him to mean 'keep the liaison of Moschion and Chrysis quiet', and in fury proposes to have him branded [lit. tattooed] on the spot. In terror the slave takes to his heels, leaving Demeas to regain control of himself with a mighty effort. Once again he addresses the audience: Moschion must have been seduced by Chrysis; his eagerness for marriage is not due to his being in love, but to escape from her. His past conduct shows him not to be one to behave immorally and disloyally.

> But the creature's a damnable strumpet. Demeas, you must be a man. Forget your desire for her, put an end to love, and do all you can to keep this unlucky affair hidden, for your son's sake, yes, but throw that beautiful Samian head first out of your house and let her go to hell. You have your excuse, that she kept the child. Give no sign that there is anything else; bite your lip and bear it; be brave and see it out.

The cook comes out to look for the missing Parmenon; Demeas pushes past him with a cry of 'Get out of the way!'.

The cook, bewildered, hears shouting inside, and then Chrysis emerges, carrying the baby and followed by Demeas. With violent language he turns her away; twice he is on the point of letting the true reason slip, but checks himself. She of course cannot understand this sudden rage, and well-intentioned attempts on the part of the cook to interfere give a comic condiment to this tragic scene. Finally Demeas re-enters the house and locks the door. Nikeratos, returning from market with a skinny sheep, about which he makes wry jokes, makes a striking contrast to the weeping Chrysis. But when he sees her and learns of Demeas' conduct, he takes her in to his wife.

Act IV. Nikeratos comes out, angry at the lamentations in which the women are indulging, an ill-omen for the wedding: he intends to give Demeas a piece of his mind, but almost immediately meets Moschion, who returning impatient for the wedding learns from him that Chrysis has been turned out because of the baby. Then Demeas emerges and tells the audience that he intends to swallow his anger with Moschion and push on with the marriage. Moschion, who has meanwhile been consulting with Nikeratos, approaches him and a brilliant scene ensues, comic for the audience, grim earnest for the participants. Demeas knows Moschion to be the father, but wishes to conceal his knowledge, Moschion still believes Demeas to think the child his own and Chrysis to be the mother.

Moschion. Tell me, why has Chrysis left and gone?

Demeas. (*aside*) She is sending him to treat with me. This is dreadful. (*aloud*) It's none of your business. It's my affair entirely. Stop your nonsense. (*aside*) Yes, dreadful. He's in it with her to injure me.

Moschion. What did you say?

Demeas. (*aside*) Clearly. Why does he approach me on her behalf? He ought to have been glad at what has happened.

Moschion. What do you think your friends will say when they hear of this?

Demeas. I expect my *friends*, Moschion, to—Leave me alone!

Moschion. I should be a coward if I let you have your way.

93

to admit a thing. She is clinging to the baby and refuses to let it go. So don't be surprised if I murder her.' 'Murder my woman?' 'Yes, she knows all about it.' 'No, Nikeratos, you must not.' 'But I wanted to tell you first.' 'The man's mad,' concludes Demeas as Nikeratos rushes back in. [But he was in his own way logical. He wanted to cover up the affair by destroying the child. If that made it necessary to kill Chrysis he would at the same time eliminate a possible witness. Being slow-minded he had not as yet connected Moschion with his daughter.]

Demeas thinks it will be best to tell him the truth. But before he can move to do so, Chrysis rushes out with the baby, pursued by Nikeratos; when Demeas calls to her to run into his house, she cannot believe her ears. He has to repeat the order twice, while he grapples with Nikeratos and claims that the child is his. Thwarted, Nikeratos proposes to kill his own wife; Demeas stops him, and offers to tell him the facts. At long last this puts into his head the suspicion that his friend's son had been responsible for his daughter's misfortune. Demeas, wishing to shield his son from the other's resentment and to soften the blow to the other's pride, assures him that the boy, though innocent, will marry her; she must have been, like Danaë, the victim of a god. Nikeratos is not convinced but does not know how to argue against this theory; accepting necessity, he goes in to complete the preparations for the wedding.

Once again nothing seems to stand in the way of the marriage.

Act V. But now Moschion returns home and declares that although he had at first felt nothing but relief at being cleared of suspicion, on thinking things over he had become so angry with his father that he had quite lost control of himself. If it were not that he was so attached to the girl, he would not give him another chance of a similar misjudgment, but go off to the wars. That he cannot do, but he will pretend to do it, to give his father a fright and teach him to behave better in future. Taking himself very seriously, he speaks in an elaborate style approaching that of tragedy. He stops at the entrance of Parmenon, who also reflects. He had been foolish to run away; he had done nothing wrong; he had nothing to do with

the birth of the child; Moschion it was who had brought it to the house; one of the household had claimed to be its mother. 'He threatened to brand me. There you've got it. There's not a straw to choose between suffering that justly or unjustly; it's not a nice thing, however it is done.'

Moschion interrupts his ruminations with an order to fetch him out a sword and a military cloak, and as the puzzled slave goes in forecasts that his father will beg him to stay, and that he will refuse for a time but at length give in. But Parmenon returns without having fulfilled his task. He has found that they are both behind the times; the wedding-feast is going forward and it is time to fetch the bride. Moschion loses his temper, hits him in the face and drives him back; then the horrid thought strikes him that his father may not play the part assigned, but angrily let him go.

But there is no opportunity for reconsideration. Parmenon returns with the sword and cloak, and reports that not a soul had noticed him on his errand; so let Moschion get on his way. The stratagem has miscarried; play-acting has not attracted the desired audience. Yet no sooner has the expectation of the father's appearance been dashed, than he does come out, with a different motive, namely to look for the missing bridegroom. 'What's the idea of dressing like that?' he exclaims on seeing him, and then takes neither of the courses that Moschion had envisaged.

He says that he likes him for being angry, but that he should remember all that had been done for him from childhood. 'I accused you unjustly. I was under a misapprehension, I made mistakes, I was mad. But while I treated others wrongly, you see how I cared for your interests; I remained silent about those false suspicions, one and all, I kept them to myself, and did not exhibit them for our enemies' glee. But you are now making my mistake public and calling others to witness my folly. It's not what I expect, Moschion. Don't remember the one day of my life when I was utterly wrong and forget all the days that went before. I could say more but will not.'

Moschion is too young to match the candour of this sympathetic reproof. He is saved from making a reply by the appearance of Nikeratos, escaping from the fuss made by his wife over the preparations for the wedding. Seeing Moschion

apparently prepared to leave home, he proposes to arrest him for the rape of his daughter. The boy with vain attempts to maintain his dignity welcomes this as a way of escape from his false position, but Demeas intervenes, telling Nikeratos to bring out the bride at once. Reassured, he does so and the happy ending, so long desired and so often postponed, is reached at last.

That is the plot of *Samia*. Let us now consider some of its features. First, although the play is called after her, and although she is an essential and often prominent piece in its structure, she makes only three brief appearances on the stage. This gives little opportunity for drawing her character, yet she is designed to arouse keen sympathy. In the first scene her readiness to help the young pair and her concern for the baby's welfare are made more prominent than her willingness to father a child on Demeas, and it is not pointed out that she will so further her own interests. The insults with which Demeas expels her, ignorant as she is of their cause, win her our support. Later, threatened by Nikeratos, she shows loyal courage in sticking to the story concocted with Moschion and the other women.

With the fifth act she fades into the background; Moschion's marriage, preparations for which have been a constantly recurring theme throughout the play, becomes an increasingly important motive. The play had an alternative title, *Kedeia*, or *Connection by Marriage*, and this has the justification that one theme is the manner in which this marriage, universally desired, is frustrated over and over again by the emotions of those closely concerned.

Alternate acts open with monologues addressed to the audience, by Moschion in Acts I and V, by Demeas in Act III. That in Act V is considerably shorter than that in Act I, in accord with the increasing pace of the play as it progresses. Like Moschion, Demeas has two monologues, but in the same act, and for him too the second is the shorter. Acts II and IV are mainly dialogue, but begin with short monologues by two persons who enter one after the other and are not immediately aware of one another's presence; in Act IV the scheme is extended by the entry of a third person who gives his short monologue while the other two converse apart.

In the second half of the play the rapid succession of events and situations, which often cheats expectation, is noteworthy. Menander's writing is often very economical and requires of the spectator a quick and sympathetic recognition of what is afoot. More modern dramatists often proceed in a more leisurely way. Consider for example these exchanges from the opening of a scene in Goldsmith's *She Stoops to Conquer*:

> *Mrs Hardcastle*. Confusion! thieves! robbers! we are cheated, plundered, broke open, undone.
> *Tony*. What's the matter, what's the matter, mamma? I hope nothing has happened to any of the good family!
> *Mrs Hardcastle*. We are robbed. My bureau has been broken open, the jewels taken out, and I'm undone.

In Menander that *might* have run:

> *Mrs Hardcastle*. Thieves! We are plundered, broke open.
> *Tony*. What's the matter, mamma? I hope none of the family——
> *Mrs Hardcastle*. The jewels are taken and I'm undone.

Yet Menander varies his pace and sometimes disguises his speed by otiose oaths and parenthetical phrases, 'by the gods' and 'tell me now'. He can make a woman enter with the line

Oh what a misfortune! what a misfortune! what a misfortune!

Samia offers no profound study of character. But each individual is lifelike. For the most part he does not explain himself, but one can guess the emotions and considerations which lie behind his words and his actions. This is the way one reacts to people in real life, if one has any interest in them. To do it requires some imagination, but the spoken word is more revealing than the written, and no doubt the actor interpreted and reinforced his text.

Demeas is a man who tries to act calmly, but it is an effort for him to do so, and the forcible repression of his temper makes its explosion more powerful when it comes. Towards his social equals, that is those of citizen status, he is considerate; he

amuses himself, to be sure, by playing with the ingenuous Nikeratos, but again and again he treats him tactfully, being aware of his irascibility. But the slave Parmenon is for him an inferior being for whom he has no respect; he is to be handled with the threat of a whipping and with a lie. Moschion shares his father's attitude; made impatient by the slave's well-meaning attempt to convey a piece of good news, he cuts his lip with a blow.

It is not clear that the play has any moral or is anything but a very successful entertainment. It might be regarded as a warning against deceit. The passing-off of the child is the cause of all the trouble that assails Demeas, Chrysis, Moschion and even Nikeratos. The pretence of going off to the wars lands Moschion in an awkward place. But if it was intended as such a warning, the effect is weakened by the fact that without the deceit the young people's baby would have doubtless been exposed in order to conceal the illegitimate birth. Thus the final result is better than it would have been if all had honourably refused to father the child on Demeas. Even Moschion's pretence leads to a useful clearing of the air between him and his father.

Similar observations can be made about other plays. *Perikeiromene* may discourage outrages caused by jealousy; but without that perpetrated on Glykera she would not have found her father or achieved marriage with Polemon. *Epitrepontes* may suggest that a man should be as loyal to his wife as she to him; but if Charisios had taken that advanced view from the beginning, he would never have recovered his child.

Menander's plays always involve at least one well-to-do household, and the obtaining of a wife or lover by one of its members. Money is important, intellectual pursuits, literature, art or philosophy are not. Hence he is sometimes accused of being confined to the interests and morality of a bourgeois society.

Some critics have gone further with such judgments as that he depicts an imaginary society, 'a world outside time and space, which knows only seduced girls and frivolous youths, crafty slaves, depraved procurers, stupid fathers and so on, a world in which there is only love and money.' The untruth of these words, which were indefensible even when they were

written, has been underlined by every discovery of new Menandrean texts. It would be as true, and as false, to say that his world knows only innocent girls and hard-working young men, loyal slaves and understanding fathers. There are, it must be admitted, no high-minded procurers. Menander's world is a real world, in that it contains a whole spectrum of characters ranging from good to bad, and there are few of the bad without some redeeming feature and few of the good without some human fault. Nor is it true that it contains nothing but love and money. It contains friendship, loyalty, jealousy, determination, pique, malice, respect, all the web of emotions that colour human relations.

What is true is that Menander's is a selective world in the sense that if we take all his surviving work as constituting a 'world', it is one in which certain events, notably rape, kidnapping, and the recovery of long-lost children, and perhaps certain characters, like hetairai, soldiers and slave-traders, occurred more frequently than they did in the life of contemporary Athenians. A single play may associate a number of these over-represented factors and their association will be statistically improbable. But it is not impossible; these were all things that happened and persons who could exist and meet in reality. A dramatist is not a statistician.

Aristophanes had claimed that he would 'teach' or 'advise' his hearers; there was a long tradition in Greece that the poet was an educator. Was it still living in Menander's day? Could he have claimed, in Horace's words, to mix what was useful with what was pleasant? A speaker in Plutarch's *Table-Talk* (712 B) thinks that he could have done, praising his 'good simple maxims, which slip in to soften even the most rigid character and bend it to a better shape'. Such maxims, often single lines, were collected by anthologists for the sake of their sentiments, and may have exerted an influence on those who heard them spoken on the stage. Yet, as Plutarch's speaker noticed, in their context they do not call attention to themselves but arise naturally; indeed even a close search brings to light fewer than might have been expected. Sometimes they

are not without a touch of irony, as the man who utters the sentiment does so with comical earnestness or inappropriately or maliciously.

The phrase:

> Whom the gods love, die young

could be interpreted as resigned pessimism or beautiful consolation, if we did not know that it was in fact spoken to infuriate an old man. The line:

> I am a man; and think nothing that is human to be not mine

often sentimentally praised for its nobility, was spoken by an inquisitive man, who proves to be unaware of his son's love-affair and unsympathetic when he learns of it.

More important is the general moral atmosphere of the plays. Crime does not pay; greed is ugly; kindness and understanding are primary virtues. The human being is a weak creature, liable to make mistakes, and the sport of chance; yet there is nothing finer than a man, that is one who lives up to what a man should be, who knows his limits and his possibilities, who is generous to forgive and to help his friends. The virtues that belong to private life are required of everybody, and the plays give their approval to those who practise them and withhold it from those who fall short, reserving ridicule for the avaricious, the pompous, the insincere, and for fathers who have forgotten what it is like to be young.

Drama at Rome

ALTHOUGH the Romans eventually dominated Italy, they began as one of many peoples, some of whom were culturally more advanced than they. They took the opportunity to become great borrowers, in art, in religion and in literature. More often than not they were able to give a new turn and a Roman character to what they borrowed.

Around the coasts of Sicily and southern Italy Greeks had settled from the eighth century onwards and their cities, although politically independent, shared the civilisation of the old country. The most important communities were Syracuse, where one can still sit in their great theatre, and Taras, or Tarentum as the Romans called it (modern Taranto), the chief city in Apulia. Nearest to Rome was Naples (Neapolis), from which Greek influence spread northwards and no doubt reached Rome, whose protection the Neapolitans had accepted by the beginning of the third century BC. The Tarantines were more obstinate and were conquered, perhaps as early as 272; the Syracusans entered into treaties with Rome but, having deserted her during the Second Punic War, were subjected in 212.

Even nearer to Rome were the Etruscans, generally thought to have been invaders from Asia Minor, who formed the ruling classes in Etruria, the territory on the other side of the Tiber. Their language remains a mystery, although they wrote in Greek characters. They became great customers for the finest Greek pottery and grew familiar with Greek mythology, which was illustrated not only on that but also on metal work; local craftsmen then imitated these models.

Although the Etruscans were finally conquered and their culture was extinguished, for a long time it exercised a powerful influence on Rome. A passage in Livy (7.2), although it may be suspected of having a large element of guess-work, seems to preserve a memory of an Etruscan origin for early

performances intended to entertain the crowd. There was at Rome an old annual festival, the *Ludi Romani*,[1] held in September to reverence Jupiter; a procession was held in his honour, followed by a chariot-race and exhibitions of equestrian skill. In 363 B C, according to Livy, in the hope of mollifying the gods, who had inflicted a pestilence upon the city,

> players were introduced from Etruria who, dancing to the music of a piper, but not singing themselves or miming any representation of song, moved not ungracefully in the Etruscan manner. Young men began to imitate them, bandying jokes in rough verses, and their movements did not discord with their voices. Native Roman professional performers were given the name of *histriones* because a player was in Etruscan called *ister*; they did not follow the earlier practice (? of the young amateurs) which alternated irregular unpolished improvised lines similar to the Fescennine verses,[2] but presented medleys rich in music, with song fitted to the strains of the pipe and suitable movements to go with it.

All these entertainments are thought of as preceding true drama. Some support for the belief that they had an origin in Etruria is given by the probability that the Latin words for stage, *scaina*, and mask, *persona*, are Etruscan deformations of the Greek *skene* and *prosopon*.

Livy's references to the improvised jesting of the young amateurs look like an attempt to provide a Roman ancestry for the so-called Atellan plays. Named after the town Atella in Campania, they are proved by allusions in Plautus to have been familiar at Rome at the end of the third century; they may have been imported much earlier. Originally they were in Oscan, an Italic language but one which cannot have been intelligible to many in Rome; on being adopted there they must have changed their language to Latin, or at least modified

---

[1] *Ludi*, traditionally and inadequately translated as 'Games', were public holidays with a kernel of religious ceremonial. But as 'holy days' developed into 'holidays', the amusement of the crowds became of increasing importance.

[2] These may have had their name from the Etruscan town of Fescennium; their nature is obscure.

their dialect. Like the Commedia dell' Arte they had a nucleus of stock characters; all of them wore grotesque masks and were marked by greed, gluttony and folly. Some names are known: Maccus, Bucco, Pappus, Manducus, Dossennus. At first the dialogue seems to have been largely impromptu; a situation will have been invented, which the amateur actors developed with rough jokes and raillery. It was only in the early first century that Pomponius and Novius wrote texts for the Atellan performers, apparently short pieces which were used to close the proceedings after a day given over to tragedies; typical titles are *Maccus the Innkeeper*, *Maccus the Soldier*, *Maccus in Exile*, *Bucco Adopted*, *Pappus' Bride*, *A Nanny-goat*, *The Fullers*. The surviving fragments from these plays rarely exceed a single line, are often coarse, and contain much unusual vocabulary, for the sake of which they have been preserved; alliteration is insistently noticeable.

Another kind of local drama seems to be represented on many vases painted in southern Italy, particularly Apulia, for the most part during the fourth century B C. Many of them show a low stage, often with access in the centre by steps, five to seven in number; when no steps are drawn, the artist may just have omitted them to simplify his picture. The stage is usually supported by plain square timber props, but occasionally stands on round pillars with capitals. The space below it is sometimes concealed by draperies. The stage does not appear to be a wide one, but that may be due to the limitations imposed by painting on a vase; sometimes it is protected by an overhanging roof. On several vases the wooden wall behind it has first floor windows, from which women look out; characters may bring ladders to reach them. Sometimes there is a highly decorated door, placed at the side, perhaps for artistic convenience, to leave the centre free for figures; masks, garlands, bowls and jugs seem to hang on the wall. It is possible, however, that the artist did not intend a realistic picture, but simply filled empty spaces with objects used in the play. A similar problem attends the small trees which he sometimes draws; he may merely have wished to indicate an outdoor scene, or there may have been saplings or branches thrust between the planks of the stage. But altars, chairs and tables will have been real stage properties.

The actors wear tights, usually ill-fitting, often a huge phallus, padding and an extremely grotesque mask. That they are servants of Dionysus seems to be shown by several vases which depict him on the stage with them. The scenes in which they appear are partly travesties of mythology and partly taken from contemporary life. An old man tries to drag a woman away from a young man, who has however the better hold on her; a slave steals food; slaves are tied up and beaten. Heracles is a favourite figure in the mythological scenes, portrayed as a glutton or as a bully, threatening Apollo or even Zeus. An amusing fragment shows Ajax, traditionally the ravisher of Cassandra, clasping the statue of Athena in a terrified plea for sanctuary, as Cassandra drives her knee into his back and pulls off his helmet; a priestess recoils in horror.

Although these vases may have been inspired by Athenian plays imported into the West during the period of Middle Comedy, the actors are more generally supposed, with some plausibility, to be the *phlyakes* of southern Italy, who had some similarity to the *deikeliktai* of Sparta (see p. 53), and who were given literary standing by Rhinthon of Tarentum about 300 BC. He wrote plays in verse for them, which were called *hilarotragoidiai*, 'merry tragedies'.

Unfortunately there is nothing to show that the *phlyakes* had any influence on the development of drama at Rome. It is true that Livius Andronicus, who is credited by Livy with the decisive step of introducing plot into stage performances, perhaps was by origin a captive Greek from Tarentum, but his ambition seems to have been to introduce the Romans to good Greek literature. He translated the *Odyssey* into the old-established local metre of 'Saturnians', and when in 240 he exhibited a tragedy and a comedy at the *Ludi Romani*, the scanty evidence suggests that his models were classical Greek tragedy and New Comedy; certainly he used Greek metres for both kinds of drama.

His example was quickly followed by a native Italian, Gnaeus Naevius, from Campania; active from 235 to 204 or 201, he wrote an original epic on the First Punic War, a few tragedies on Greek subjects and one or two historical plays on themes from Roman history, but his dramatic work was mostly in comedy. The titles survive of more than thirty such

plays; nearly half are Greek words, often known to have been used as titles of Greek New Comedy. It is probable then that he usually translated Greek dramas, but possible that he also tried his hand at composing new comedies with a setting in Italy: *Ariolus*, or *The Soothsayer*, a fragment from which speaks of hosts at (or guests from) Praeneste and Lanuvium, towns near Rome, may have been one such (see p. 115).

It is not surprising that when the Romans began to develop a literature of their own, they should have been dependent on the highly advanced productions of the Greeks. What is not altogether clear is how knowledge of these works reached them and how they obtained them. Probably there were visitors and immigrants from the Greek cities of southern Italy, some of whom may even have originated in mainland Greece; they may have brought books with them. That not a few educated Romans could read Greek even as early as the late third century is suggested by the fact that Fabius Pictor, the first Roman historian, wrote in Greek, setting a fashion which lasted for a couple of generations.

However that may be, there was a ready audience for the plays of these early authors, which, being adapted from Greek models, dealt with Greek mythology, if they were tragedies, and represented Greek characters, if they were comedies. From 214 four days were devoted to stage-performances at the *Ludi Romani*. The 'Plebeian Holiday', instituted in 220 and held in November, the first of several festivals intended to keep up civilian morale in the Second Punic War, may have had a day of drama from the first, although the earliest recorded performance is that of Plautus' *Stichus* in 200. The 'Holiday of the Great Mother', a goddess brought from Phrygia in Asia Minor, was instituted in 204 and held in April; drama was probably a feature from the beginning. There is no evidence for the giving of plays at the 'Holiday of Apollo', begun in 212 with a date in July, at any time before 169, but this may be no more than an accident. Besides these regular festivals there were occasional opportunities for dramatic productions, perhaps at the 'Great Holidays', irregularly held for specific purposes, and certainly at some 'funeral games' in honour of eminent men. This growth of interest no doubt encouraged the ambitions of the most

original of all writers for the Roman theatre, known to later Romans by the name of Plautus, whose earliest plays belong to the last decade of the third century.

Many of the stages shown on the vases from Apulia (p. 115) look like temporary structures. It is certain that the plays of Naevius and Plautus were presented on a temporary wooden stage in front of a temporary wooden building with three doors; in this the actors assembled and dressed. Facing this there was seating, perhaps benches; but there is no evidence to indicate how extensive it was; probably some spectators had to stand at the back. From early in the second century the front rows were reserved for senators.

There was no permanent theatre at Rome before 55 BC, when one was built by Pompey (see Fig. 2); it was associated with a temple for Venus and colonnades where spectators could take refuge from a storm; there seem to have been seats for about 10,000 in the auditorium. An attempt had been made in 155 to erect a stone theatre, but it had foundered on the opposition of those who thought play-acting immoral. But in the first century the temporary theatres had become elaborate; linen awnings protected the spectators from the sun; there must have been rising tiers of scaffolded seating and the stage-building was lavishly decorated. The theatre built by the aedile Aemilius Scaurus in 58 became notorious for its extravagance; the elder Pliny's account, written some 125 years later, may be exaggerated, but even so is revealing. He alleges that it could seat 80,000 spectators, that it had a stage-building of three storeys, the lowest of marble, the middle one of glass, and the top one of gilded planks; standing between the 360 columns that decorated it were 300 bronze statues.

Clearly this stage-building was architecturally like those of later permanent theatres of which the best known is that of Orange in southern France. They had a semicircular *orchestra* in front of a stage longer than the diameter of the semicircle, which was used not for dancing, but for reserved seats; at Rome they were kept for senators and their families. Behind the stage rose a building decorated with tiers of columns and having doors in its lowest storey. It was as wide and often as high as the auditorium, to which it was joined at each end by a tall structure which spanned the entrances to the orchestra.

Thus the spectators sat in a space which was, in contrast to that of a Greek theatre, enclosed; even the sky above was excluded by the awnings; a small theatre could actually be roofed, like that at Pompeii, constructed about 80 BC. It may be guessed that this design was established at Rome before the year 68 BC, when the legislation of Otho gave the *equites* (men with a property qualification of 400,000 sesterces) the right to occupy the front fourteen rows behind the *orchestra*.

The audience of the first century was representative of all social classes, and the same seems to have been true in Plautus' days. Admission was free, expenses being borne by the aediles in charge of the festival, who disposed of some state funds but often supplemented them from their own pockets. They hoped that this liberality would have its reward when they presented themselves to the electors as candidates for higher office. In choosing to present plays adapted from the refined work of Greek dramatists they must have been trying to attract the favour of the more intelligent members of the population, for whom serious drama was a comparatively new experience. Others however were free to come and had to be reckoned with. The prologue to Plautus' *Poenulus* or *Little Carthaginian*, whether designed for its first performance or for a revival, shows what could happen. The attendants are asked not to walk in front of the spectators' faces nor to show anyone to a seat while an actor is on the stage, since latecomers ought to stand; slaves are not to grab seats, but leave room for the free men; it is in fact suggested that they will, if discovered, be driven out by blows from the rod-carrying officials. Nursemaids should look after their infant charges at home and not bring them to see the show, where they will cause annoyance by bleating like little goats. Married women are to watch silently and laugh silently, check the tinkle of their voices, and keep their chatter for their homes.

Not only was the audience one with less knowledge and appreciation of drama than was usual among the Greeks, it was also one with less respect for those who performed it. In Greece all in the cast were servants of Dionysus, and the leading actor in each play had his name preserved in the official records. At Rome, by the time of Cicero at least, most actors were slaves with Greek names, and this continued to be the

rule in the first century A D. They will have belonged to a free man, who may himself have appeared on the stage with them. This arrangement was perhaps already the custom at the end of the third century. The prologue to Plautus' *Asinaria*, speaking of the company and its master, uses words commonly applied to slaves and their owner, and jokes, if jokes they are, like that at the end of his *Cistellaria*—'they'll remove their costumes and any actor who has made a mistake will get a beating'—point the same way.

But free men played along with the slaves. Titus Publilius Pellio took the leading parts in Plautus' *Stichus* and *Epidicus* and Lucius Ambivius Turpio was well known in Terence's days. Actors were, however, regarded as somewhat disreputable; they were not allowed to serve in the army, were deprived of a vote,[1] and were subject to the *coercitio* of the magistrates, that is to say could be beaten, imprisoned, or exiled at will. Although the emperor Augustus restricted this power to the days of the festival, he used it to inflict a public flogging on a man who had caused a married Roman woman to cut her hair and take the role of a boy, perhaps in a mime (see p. 116). It is true that a few actors obtained a footing in society; the most famous was Publius Roscius Gallus, who won the favour of Sulla, receiving from him admission to the order of the *equites*, and who was defended by Cicero in a court case of 67 or 66 B C concerning a slave-actor of whom Roscius was part-owner. et Yin some quarters Sulla's association with a man of his profession was regarded as an enormity.

One might suppose that slaves with Greek names spoke Latin with a foreign accent. If this was so, it need not have been an unqualified handicap. The plays which were of greatest importance in the time of the Roman Republic, that is down to the middle of the first century B C, were adaptations of Greek and their characters were Greeks. It would then not have seemed altogether unnatural if they spoke their Latin like Greeks. Another relevant point is that actors did not attempt to give a close illusion of natural, ordinary speech as they declaimed their parts, which were written in verse, and large parts of which were delivered to a musical accompaniment. 'They do not utter their words,' writes Quintilian (*Inst. Or.*

[1] These disabilities did not apply to actors in Atellan plays.

2.10.13), 'quite in the manner in which we ordinarily speak, which would lack art, nor do they depart far from nature, a fault which would destroy mimicry.'

Among the Greeks, as has been seen (p. 78, plays of the New Comedy were sometimes, and perhaps normally, performed by three actors, who doubled the parts, assisted by mute supers. At Rome there was not such a strict limitation; there are many plays which require at least five speaking actors. It is not known how many were actually used since, although some doubling of parts is *a priori* likely, there is nothing to show its extent. All that is certain is that the speaker of the prologue might change his costume to appear as a character in the play proper.

Modern experience shows that it is possible for an audience to accept that a small change of costume, without any change in make-up, suffices to convert an actor from one role to another. Yet there is no doubt that in the Greek theatre the conversion was aided by the change of mask; the mask indicated what character was being played. Was doubling of parts similarly facilitated at Rome? Unfortunately it is disputed whether masks were worn in the Roman adaptations of Greek plays and the question, vital to the visualisation of the Roman theatre, admits of no confident answer.

There is no reason to doubt that the actors who performed Greek plays in Greek in the theatres of southern Italy and Sicily were masked. It would be natural to suppose that masks were worn in the Roman adaptations also, especially as this was the custom in the native Atellan drama. But Diomedes, a teacher of literature in the fourth century AD, reports that masks were introduced by Roscius to hide his squint; previously wigs had been worn. This may be derived from Varro, Roscius' scholarly contemporary, and it has been supported by an appeal to a passage of Cicero's dialogue *On the Orator* (3.221), where Crassus is made to say 'Everything depends on the face; there is the seat of all the mastery exerted by the eyes; and so those seniors of ours did better than us when they gave even Roscius no high praise when he wore a mask'. But an equally possible translation is 'because he wore a mask'; it is not necessary to suppose from this passage that he ever acted without one.

On the other hand the commentary derived from Donatus, which goes under his name and is contemporary with Diomedes, speaks of actors as 'still' being masked in the time of Terence. The contrast is with the conditions of the fourth century A.D. when masks had been abandoned and, it may be added, actresses played the female parts. Those who support the story about Roscius think that Donatus ignorantly believed masks had been used from the first.

Attempts to determine the credibility of Diomedes are inconclusive. References in the plays to change of facial expression are irrelevant; similar phrases are found in Greek plays; the audience can use its imagination. Roscius' alleged reason for adopting the mask (and making his company follow suit) seems frivolous and does not explain why other companies, who presumably did not squint, also took to wearing masks. It can only be thought that they found the practice in some way advantageous. But if it was advantageous, it is strange that it was not taken over from the Greeks originally.

In Plautus' *Amphitruo* Mercury and Jupiter take on the likenesses of Sosia and Amphitruo, and in order that the audience may distinguish them from the men they impersonate Mercury wears wings in his hat and Jupiter a golden lock of hair, signs which, it is explained, are invisible to the other characters. It can be argued with some plausibility that if no masks were worn these distinguishing marks would be unnecessary; yet perhaps they would be welcomed by the less keen-sighted or more distant spectators in a large theatre. Again, although masks would be even more convenient in this play, since no company would include two pairs of identical twins, than they would be in *Menaechmi*, Shakespeare's play *The Comedy of Errors* shows that they are not necessary.

None of the above considerations, nor others of even less force, suffice to settle the question. Many scholars have no hesitation in accepting the evidence of Diomedes. My own inclination is to disbelieve him; but if he got his story from Varro—and this is no more than an inference from the fact that he several times quotes Varro as an authority for other matters—one could not refuse him credence.

Fortunately there is no doubt about a change that really was made from Greek practice of the early third century.

Menander's plays were of five acts, separated by intermezzi provided by the chorus. The absence of a chorus from the Roman theatre meant that Plautus and Terence did not write in acts but for continuous performance. It is possible that their Greek contemporaries did the same; there is no evidence. In modern texts the plays of Plautus are divided into five acts, but these were first introduced in an edition of 1514 by Nicolà Angelio, who took up a proposal made by G. B. Pio in 1500. The division of Terence into acts dates from antiquity, although it puzzled scholars how to make him fit their scheme.

The disappearance of the five-act structure presented the Latin dramatists with problems. The plays they were adapting had used the intermezzi to mark the passage of time. How were they to mark it? More often than not they ignored the difficulty. This is perhaps not an adverse criticism. It is quite possible for an audience to understand that a momentarily empty stage represents a lapse of time. Shakespeare wrote for continuous performance and his audiences, modern or Elizabethan, accept or accepted this convention. But it is a convention easier to accept because successive scenes are normally to be thought of as occurring in different places; the spatial disruption facilitates the temporal disruption. Carried in imagination from one spot to another, the spectator can be easily carried also from one hour to another.

The action of the Greek play, however, took place in a single locality, usually outside the houses of two of the characters. If the text were translated into Latin without change, the audience would not know whether to think of an empty stage as empty for a time no longer than that during which the actors left it or whether it conventionally represented a longer period. Sometimes a phrase at the beginning of the scene that followed the break could indicate that time had passed. But the Latin authors seem often to have taken it for granted that this was not a thing over which spectators would bother their heads, or that they would have a clear sense of time.

This disregard is strikingly illustrated by Plautus' treatment in his *Bacchides* (*The Bacchis Sisters*) of the division between the first two acts of its original, *Dis Exapaton* (*A Double Deceit*). Plautus' play leaves no doubt that towards the end of the first act Menander's Moschos left for the market, and that shortly

afterwards the two girls whom he proposed to entertain prudently retreated indoors, having seen the approach of the rowdy chorus; its intermezzo covered the time of the shopping-expedition, from which Moschos returned at the beginning of the second act. In Plautus, Pistoclerus (his name for Moschos) leaves for the market at line 100, and is seen by the girls returning at 106; they mistake him for some unknown rowdy and retreat indoors, while he comes on the stage with his purchases at 110. It is true that Menander's plays require no strict correspondence of stage-time with that of events off-stage; five lines of a dialogue may cover happenings inside a house that would take at least five minutes to transact; but longer intervals, like those of a visit to the market or a journey to the country, are always covered by a choral interlude. There is never anything so offensive to a sense of time as this scene in Plautus.

But Plautus did on occasion take steps to overcome the difficulties caused by the absence of a chorus. His treatment of the division between Acts II and III of this same play is described below (p. 131). In *Curculio* he was faced with the problem that three characters left the stage at the end of the third act and entered again, some time having elapsed, at the beginning of the next. Their exit and immediate re-entry might have caused some bewilderment. The difficulty was solved by bringing on the man who provided costumes and properties, whether in person or represented by an actor. He says that one of the characters in the play, who has just left the stage, is such a scoundrel that he wonders whether he will get his properties back from him; after this joke, depending on identification of the character with the actor, he continues that while they wait for the man's return he will give the audience a kind of directory to Rome. In *Pseudolus* (537) the slave goes indoors to think out a plan of action, promising that he will soon be back and that meanwhile the audience will be entertained by the piper. The Greek original probably here had a division between acts and a choral interlude. Nothing suggests that such interludes were normally replaced at Rome by a piper's solo. This is a unique unrepeated experiment.

Such difficulties would of course not have arisen if the theatre had, like those of today, possessed a drop-curtain

which could have been lowered to indicate the passage of time. But unsophisticated spectators might have supposed the play to have ended. A curtain that could separate the audience from the stage seems not to have been invented before the end of the second century BC. Even then it was stowed in a slot in the floor from which it was raised at the end of a play. Cicero says that this was a convenient method of concluding a mime (see p. 116), which as a formless kind of entertainment had no natural end. That the curtain was invented for that purpose is no more than a guess; at Rome it was richly embroidered and it may have been introduced to provide a spectacle before or between plays. The modern method, by which the curtain is raised to reveal the stage, appears to have been discovered before the latter part of the second century AD.

Some attempts were made, perhaps even before the middle of the second century BC, to write comedies not only in Latin but also about Italian life and characters. These were called *fabulae togatae*, 'plays dressed in togas', in distinction from *fabulae palliatae*, 'plays in Greek cloaks'. Of course not all characters wore an outer garment in either genre, but enough did so to make the distinction effective.

These plays would have been informative to the social historian; it is our misfortune that nothing survives except some titles, some brief quotations, and occasional references made by the authors of antiquity. Apparently the scene was never in Rome, but always in some small Italian town. For the most part the characters were, in contrast with those of Greek New Comedy, drawn from the lower ranks of society. Nevertheless it was unusual to portray a slave as being cleverer than his master; that might occur among the Greeks; things were better ordered in Italy. Women may have played a more active part than they did in most Greek comedies; this would reflect the difference between Greek and Italian social life.

Seneca (*ep.* 8.8.) says that *togatae* had an element of seriousness and were on a level somewhere between comedy and tragedy. The fragments quoted by grammarians for the sake of their colloquial language do not suggest any elevation of

style. Perhaps he refers to a fondness for moral maxims. Lucius Afranius, more or less a contemporary of Terence's, was the best remembered of these authors; he admitted borrowing phrases from Menander, and he may have borrowed incidents also. His drama then was not of purely Italian inspiration, but drew on the traditions of Greek comedy.

Afranius' plays were still acted long after his death. The audience at Rome would often cheer a line in a play old or new, if it could be given some topical application, and actors might try to elicit such a response. Cicero alleges that in the year 57, when Clodius was sitting in the theatre, the whole company in unison directed against him a line from Afranius' *The Pretender*:

The course and end of your life of vice.

This chorusing of words intended for a single actor indicates that neither players nor spectators set great store by dramatic illusion. Afranius was still staged in the time of Nero, when actors in his play *Fire* were allowed to keep furniture they rescued from a burning house, perhaps realistically represented.

Another form of drama, which by the middle of the first century BC occupied an important place in the Roman theatre, was the mime. It had its origin in players or troops of players who earned their bread by presenting scenes from life or romance, spoken in prose; they included both men and women and acted in bare feet and without masks; there seems to have been a frequent element of impropriety in their productions. They became part of the officially sponsored entertainment at many festivals, and in Cicero's time had come to be used as tail-pieces (*exodia*) after tragedies, ousting the Atellan farces that had previously been used.

Their popularity led to successful attempts to raise their standard and give them literary form; authors began to write them scripts in the verse-metres familiar from comedy. A Roman knight, Decimus Laberius (106–43), won much favour with the crowd; he wrote in a highly alliterative manner, used the vocabulary and grammar of the lower classes, and generously met their appetite for obscenity. Julius Caesar, during his dictatorship, offered him a large sum if he would

appear on the stage as an actor in one of his own mimes. Had he refused, he might have been held to admit the unsuitability of his writing for a man of his station; if he accepted, he could be accused of being ready to do anything for money. He chose to interpret the offer as an irresistible command— 'what man could deny anything to a being to whom the gods had granted everything?'—but revenged his loss of dignity by two lines which he spoke in the mime:

> Then, Romans, we destroy our liberty

and

> Many must he fear, whom many fear.

Several of his works have names which had been used for comedies, e.g. *Aulularia*, *Gemelli*, *Piscator*, and they may have contained scenes suggested by such plays. *Aquae Calidae*, *Augur*, *Compitalia*, *Sorores*, *Virgo*, recall the same titles given to *fabulae togatae*. Some relation between these and the mime must be assumed, although nothing specific can be said about it.

Publilius, brought as a slave-boy from Syria, was freed and educated and then performed in his own mimes all over Italy; finally he defeated all comers at Rome in 46 BC. He was remarkable for the number of his well-turned sentiments, expressed in the Latin of educated men. This did not cause his works to be read, but they were pillaged for their nuggets of wisdom, which were formed into an anthology; this, enlarged by spurious material, had a wide circulation under the Empire. Learned men loved to quote his epigrams:

> O life, so long for the wretched, so short for the happy!

and

> Luxury lacks much, avarice everything

and

> The cure for injury is to forget.

The ancients expected their poets to be teachers. So when it took literary form, even this disreputable type of drama was made to serve the cause of moral improvement.

Plautus

PLAUTUS, the most original and vigorous writer of Roman comedy, came from Sarsina in Umbria, half-way between modern Florence and Rimini. It was an Italian town subjected to the Romans a dozen years before his birth. Whether Plautus was his real name or one humorously adopted for professional purposes,[1] and whether he had been an actor before he was a writer are questions which admit of fascinating discussion but no certain answer; fortunately they are of no importance to the historian of drama. Nothing shows that he acted in or produced his own plays, but he gives a strong impression that he understood the theatre for which he wrote. He would have an inexperienced audience, not very quick in the uptake, and so it was necessary to proceed more slowly than a Greek dramatist would, to say things twice, to introduce reminders about essential elements in the plot, and above all not to allow the spectators to become bored. They did not require complete coherence nor expect that characterisation should be consistent; these are merits demanded by a theatre-goer who can take a wide view; what was important for Plautus was the immediate effect.

All his twenty-one surviving plays are adaptations of Greek

---

[1] Plautus is a known family name, originally like so many a nickname referring to a physical peculiarity; it means 'flat-footed'. But *planipes*, which also means 'flat-footed', was a name for an actor in a mime, who wore no shoes. It is possible that the author adopted the name Plautus to suggest a connection with that simple form of drama. In one prologue he calls himself, or is called, Maccus and in another either Maccus or Maccius Titus. Here there is certainly some depreciatory joke. Maccus was a stock stupid character in Atellan plays, but Maccius is a name known from real life. Later generations believed the dramatist to have been named Titus Maccius Plautus; perhaps he was, but scepticism is not amiss.

comedies.[1] Three and probably a fourth are from Menander, two from Diphilus, two from Philemon, one apparently from Alexis, all authors of the great period of New Comedy. Of the other twelve one is from an otherwise unknown Demophilus, but all the rest have anonymous originals. There is nothing to show that any of them came from the Greek dramatists who were his contemporaries or belonged to the immediately preceding generation. On the contrary some of their original authors certainly lived about a hundred years earlier than he, and may even have been members of the great trio of that time.

Unfortunately it is impossible to say how Plautus got hold of these Greek plays. They may have formed part of the repertory of the Artists of Dionysus, but it is no more than a plausible guess that these visited the theatres of Greek cities in southern Italy, and there is no evidence that Plautus had any contact with them or with southern Italy at all. Perhaps the players for whom he wrote in some way obtained texts with which they provided him. It would be rash to suppose that he always admired the plays he adapted or thought them particularly suitable for his purposes; he may have had to use what he could get.

However that may be, the Greek authors provided him with stories of ingenious construction and scenes of dramatic tension. When these were embroidered and diversified, when their jests were multiplied and their comic possibilities exploited by a writer who possessed an unfailing vigour of expression and a rich abundance of language there resulted a new kind of popular drama which could entertain a wide range of tastes.

Variety is the obvious device to hold the attention of any audience. Metrical variety had become less and less used by the Greeks, and it is possible that in Menander's later plays it was entirely abandoned, in order to maintain a homogeneous medium; but the choral intermezzi were still there, to provide a change of metre and the charms of music. Deprived of a chorus, Plautus re-introduced these elements into the body of his plays. Whether the first to do it or not, he increased the

---

[1] The twenty-first, *Vidularia*, survives only in the sense that a single manuscript preserves about one hundred lines, many mutilated.

number of scenes written in the long trochaic or iambic lines, and on the Roman stage, whatever may have been done in Greece, these were delivered to an accompaniment by the piper. This makes likely a manner of speech not quite like that adopted by the actors for the unaccompanied iambic senarii (lines of six feet). Certainly differences can be detected in the language employed; often the vocabulary has a more elevated tone, the sentences use a greater wealth of words, and opportunities are seized for sound-effects; in particular the Roman delight in alliteration was catered for.

But this was not Plautus' only metrical means to variety. Far more striking and far more individual to him were scenes in various other metres, mainly cretics, bacchiacs and anapaests, which had in Greece been associated with song. They became more and more common as time went on, and in the late *Casina*, if the prologue is excluded from the count, nearer a half than a third of the play proper is of this kind. Sometimes several metres are used in conjunction; there may even be change from line to line, as occurs in the lyrics of Greek tragedy.

It is customary today to call these scenes *cantica*. The word was used by Cicero, but the late grammarians' attempts to define its meaning are confused and unhelpful. There is no certainty that it had the same denotation for him as for us; it may have covered everything apart from the iambic senarii. It is derived from the verb *canere*, which we translate 'sing', but there are many different ways of interpreting the word 'sing'; we even talk of a 'sing-song' voice. Perhaps the minimum sense of *canere* is 'to speak with attention to pitch and rhythm'. It is possible that there was no fundamental difference in delivery between the long iambic and trochaic lines and what we call *cantica*.

Certainly the latter were not sung in the style of arias in grand opera; the words were important and often indeed essential to the progress of the play; the vocalist must have concentrated more on getting the meaning across than on the musical qualities of his 'song'. There are even lines which an accumulation of consonants make it almost impossible to sing, in the usual modern sense of the word. Here at least emphasis must have been more on rhythm than on notes. Nevertheless

there are passages in ancient authors which suggest that these 'lyrics' made greater demands on the voice, and it may be that, particularly in the monologues, which are numerous, the actor was required to produce sounds that we should unhestitatingly call song.

Here may be mentioned an odd story in Livy; he says that Livius Andronicus, who acted in his own plays, found his voice giving way as a result of repeated encores and therefore obtained leave to employ a slave to sing the words while he put his unhampered energy into silent miming. This, Livy asserts, was the origin of the custom by which someone sang in time with the actors' gestures, the latter's voice being required for the spoken scenes only.[1] Even if he had no opportunities himself to see literary dramas performed, he must have known men old enough to have seen them. Yet if he believed it to have been the normal custom for one person to sing while another mimed, he must have been mistaken, since Cicero speaks of the singing of the famous actor Roscius.

There has been much argument about possible precedents for Plautus' use of *cantica*. At first sight an origin may be sought in imitation of the sung lyrics, mostly monodies, which became increasingly common in the tragedies of Euripides. Plautus often used the form for passages of elevated tone, whether meant to be pathetic or ridiculous, in which a character laments his or her situation, and the language is often singularly like that of serious laments to be found in the fragments of Ennius, the leading tragedian of the early second century. Both writers use much alliteration and assonance. But Plautus was the older of the two; chronology forbids any assumption that the initiative came from Ennius.

But whatever the origin of the *cantica*, they lend a peculiar flavour to Plautus' plays. They could be enjoyed not only by the mass of the audience, whom we can imagine to have been readier to listen to a 'musical' than to a straight play, but also by the more cultured hearer, who could appreciate the way in

[1] The first part of the story is credible. In London in November 1935 Mr Lupino Lane, having lost his voice, employed another person to speak his part while he himself acted it. The device caused such amusement that it was continued after Mr Lane's recovery.

which changes of rhythm coincided with changes of feeling or subject.

By variety of metre and the use of musical numbers Plautus introduced into his Latin versions of plays that had belonged to Greek New Comedy elements that had formed part of the attraction of Old Comedy for its diversified audience. There were also other ways of responding to the simpler tastes of his spectators which recall features to be seen in Aristophanes. Nothing shows that he knew that writer's work, but he may have come across isolated precedents in the authors of New Comedy; on the other hand he may have acted independently, knowing what would please in the theatre; certainly, if he found any hints in his originals, he developed them vastly.

First, there is the spicing of scenes with indecencies, mostly sexual, often homosexual, and largely depending on ambiguous words. These passages seem to occur more at random than they do in Aristophanes; they may be completely absent from long stretches of text. Some few of them suit their speakers, but for the most part they stand out as inappropriate interruptions to the course of events; the actor momentarily becomes an entertainer with a line of dirty jokes.

Another kind of entertainment was provided by playing upon words, a device even more prominent in Plautus than in Old Comedy. This can be done with wit; it can be suitable to the speaker; it can be pregnant with meaning. Nothing could be more effective than Hamlet's

A little more than kin and less than kind.

But whereas it is credible enough that an excluded lover should make a bitter play on words as he upbraids the *pessuli pessumi* (most wicked bolts) which keep him out, or that a parasite should repeat syllables as he gloats over his expected dinner, *quanta sumini apsumedo, quanta callo calamitas* (What consumption there'll be of cow's udder, what damage I'll do to the flesh!), yet often Plautus aims at nothing more than creating a sound-effect by capping one word with another that is similar. This is just a game irrelevant to plot or character. But there are also puns and sometimes the similarity of words is made the basis for repartee, as when one character says

nihil sentio, and the other replies *non enim es in senticeto; eo non sentis.* That might be represented by

> (A) I'm not aware of anything. (B) No, you're not in a warehouse; that's why you're not aware.

Jokes of this sort can be heard in popular entertainments today.

Words were a source of delight for Plautus. Not only did he use a rich vocabulary drawn from colloquial speech, but he loved to invent comical new compounds and derivatives. His inventiveness and fancy did not desert him in his treatment of personal proper names. Greek New Comedy, as we have seen, used many over and over again for different characters. Since Plautus' audiences were not familiar with the conventions that attached each name to a particular type of person, he adopted the natural practice, usual in the modern theatre, of providing each character with his own individual name. In all his twenty-one plays there are only three instances of duplication: two young slaves called Pinacium, or 'Little Picture', two young men called Charinus, and two old men called Callicles. These names may have been taken over from the Greek originals, a procedure he sometimes followed, as for example in *The Bacchis Sisters* the slave Lydus kept his name from Menander's *A Double Deceit.* But the other slave in that play became Chrysalus instead of Syros, while the young men Sostratos and Moschos exchanged those names for the less trite Mnesilochus and Pistoclerus. The former was common in real life, Pistoclerus is not recorded, although a quite possible compound. This illustrates Plautus' normal practice: many of his names are genuine; many may be his own inventions, but they are made on correct principles by analogy with forms he knew. Some of the latter kind are intended to have some point: Pistoclerus is a loyal (*pistos*) friend. A soldier, who is probably a parvenu, is called Therapontigonus, 'Son of a Servant', a theoretically possible but improbable and ridiculous name. A few are openly comic, although correct, formations: a parasite Artotrogus, 'Nibbleloaf', and a moneylender Misargyrides, 'Money Haterson'. A few others, Pyrgopolinices, 'Forte Grandstrife', and Polymachaeroplagides, 'Mickledagger McStrike', which improperly combine three

elements, have parallels in Aristophanes' Tisamenophainippos and Panourgipparchides and conceivably had precedents in New Comedy, but are probably the products of his own fertile invention, like the magnificent double-barrelled Bumbomachides Clutumistaridisarchides.

These names, which have more point for those who know Greek, are only a particular case of a problem presented by the occurrence in Plautus' text of fairly numerous words of Greek origin, which are sometimes given Latin terminations or even compounded with a Latin element, e.g. *thermopotasti*, 'you've had a hot drink'. Are these words which had been adopted in the popular language of Rome? Or were they introduced to mark the fact that the characters were Greeks? Would they be understood by the majority of the audience or only by a select few? One is tempted to compare modern plays in which a foreigner speaks a line or two in his own tongue, which only a part of the audience will understand, but then considerately uses English, even to his compatriots, with occasional lapses into supposed vernacular expletives like '*Donnerwetter*'. But there are only a few places where one of Plautus' characters utters a phrase in Greek with apparently no reason but that he is a Greek. On the other hand there are many passages where Greek words are used with the apparent expectation that they will be understood by many in the theatre. A spectator will not resent elements that are above his head, provided that they are not excessive and that his own tastes are adequately catered for. A dramatist does not have to write down to the lowest level in his audience. Many French words have today a meaning for Englishmen who could not follow a French sentence, and similarly English is invading French. It may be guessed that Greeks, both slaves and free men looking for employment or trade, were already common enough in Rome to have made a considerable contribution to vocabulary.

Consistently with this Plautus seems to have relied on an elementary knowledge of Greek mythology among many of his audience. That his references to it were automatically translated from the original Greek, without any care whether they would be understood, was a theory once propounded by scholars unable to imagine how a successful dramatist works. It is quite untenable because these references occur not only in

passages which may have a Greek origin but also in some which clearly are of his own composition. One need not suppose that every spectator had heard, for example, of Argus, but it was sufficient if many had done; and for those whose memories were hazy Plautus added a reminder: 'If Argus were their watcher, *he who was all eyes, whom Juno once attached as warder to Io*, he would never succeed in watching them.' Familiarity with Greek mythology will have come not only through contact with Greeks in person but also through its representation on works of art, which must have been explained and at least partially understood. Greek art and mythology had long been accepted by the Etruscans, the Romans' neighbours on the other side of the Tiber, from whom they received much cultural influence.

Another appeal to popular taste was provided by scenes in which characters exchange insults or threats. This seems to have been a standard form of entertainment in Italy. Horace recounts in the fifth satire of his first book how his travelling party, which included Maecenas and Virgil, were amused one night by the personalities exchanged by two 'parasites', a freed man and an Oscan (perhaps one should think of the Oscan plays from Atella) and the emperor Marcus Aurelius remembers another supper at which the company was diverted by the backchat between country-folk. Roman taste was also met by passages in which slaves are threatened with horrific and sometimes impossibly exaggerated physical maltreatment. The slaves themselves also anticipate or remember these punishments, frequently using comic language to refer to them.

Common to all this Plautine material is the characteristic of being designed for an immediate effect, to raise a laugh, without any regard for the progress of the action or appropriateness to the situation or to the character of the speaker, except in so far as scurrilities and foolish jokes are delivered mainly by slaves and men of low social standing. A standard motif developed for its own sake is the 'running slave', who often comes on in haste to deliver some piece of news, pretending to push aside invisible persons who crowd the street. Once Plautus doubles the absurdity by making such a slave, who carries information it is essential his master should have

without delay, withold it when he finds him until he has indulged in a long passage of backchat (*Mercator* 111–75).

As Plautus introduces jokes for their own sake, the actors lose connection with the character they are portraying; they cease to represent Greeks in Athens, and become entertainers on the Roman stage. 'Don't you know, woman, why the Greeks called Hecuba a bitch?' A slave, boasting of his success in cheating his master, which he represents by military metaphors such as were dear to Plautus, concludes 'I am not having a triumph; that has become such a common thing these days'; he is referring to the frequency of triumphs celebrated by Roman generals in the early second century, perhaps to the year 189, which saw no fewer than four (*Bacchides* 1072).

Unconcerned though Plautus is to maintain dramatic illusion and ready to forget the plot temporarily, he was by no means indifferent to the story, but carried it on clearly, making the progress of the intrigue plain. For its main lines he was indebted to the Greek original and, particularly in early plays, he took pains to see that the spectators followed it. Thus in *Poenulus* the trick to deceive the slave-dealer is explained three times (170–87, 547–65, 591–603). The interruptions to the plot by the miscellaneous jokes may even be seen as testimony to its importance. Close attention was necessary to follow Menander's dramas and his rivals probably wrote in the same manner. Plautus, with an audience on which such demands could not be made, caused the play to proceed by shorter steps than the integrated acts of his models. Then, after a passage of light relief, he would often return to the thread of the plot by repeating a phrase which had immediately preceded the insertion.

Important though the plot was, Plautus was sometimes ready to truncate it. To take an example, in Diphilus' *Klerumenoi* (*Drawers of Lots*) a girl of free birth had been exposed, rescued, and brought up in a household where both father and son fell in love with her. The father hoped to obtain her by marrying her to a complaisant slave; his wife, taking the part of the son, who had been sent abroad, wished the bridegroom to be another slave, who would be ready to make way for him on his return. All analogy shows that the girl's free birth would be established and she be united with the young

man in legal marriage. But, says the prologue to *Casina*,[1]
Plautus' adaptation,

> The youth will not come back to town today in this
> comedy. Don't expect it. Plautus was against it; he broke
> down a bridge on the young man's route.

The Latin poet was satisfied to concentrate on the earlier parts
of the play, the manoeuvres of the husband and the wife, and
the substitution, if that can be assigned to Diphilus, of a man
for the girl in the bed where the father expected to find her.

Another way in which he altered the proportions of his
originals appears in those plays where, as has been securely
established, he greatly expanded and elaborated the role of a
slave, making him much more prominent than he had been
in the Greek. Three of these have as their title the name of a
slave whose part was probably taken by the leading actor,
as that of Chrysalus must have been in *The Bacchis Sisters*.[2]

Plautine slaves are of two main types, the ingenious trickster
and the loyal servant. The former not only carries out the
intrigue invented by the Greek author but is given to boasting
elaborately of his cleverness; the supreme example is Chrysalus,
who in a long *canticum* compares himself to Ulysses and the
other characters to various figures who had parts, on either
side, in the Trojan War. These slaves are sometimes incredibly
insolent to their masters, in a manner which Plautus found it
amusing to ascribe to servants of Greeks, who had strange ideals
about freedom of speech. The honest retainers, on the other
hand, often moralise at length about duty to their masters,
uttering sentiments that would be highly approved by the
slave-owners in the audience. Plautus may have found hints
in his originals for what he so developed, but the prominence
he gave it was his own.

[1] The original title was *Sortientes*, a literal translation of Diphilus'
title; *Casina* seems to be that of a revival.

[2] At one point Chrysalus says 'It's not the act but the hatefulness
of the actor that cuts me to the quick; *Epidicus* is a play that I love
as I love myself, but there is none I watch with more distaste when
Pellio acts it.' For the moment he is no longer Chrysalus but the
actor who is Pellio's rival.

In 1968 publication of a papyrus containing parts of a section of Menander's *Dis Exapaton* which correspond to *Bacchides* 494–562 threw new light on the subject of Plautus' independence; it was found that he had made quite unsuspected changes. To explain the situation it will suffice to say that Mnesilochus had, while abroad in Ephesus to collect some money belonging to his father, fallen in love with a hetaira who was about to be taken to Athens. He wrote to his friend Pistoclerus there, asking him to find the girl, with whom he hoped to resume relations on his return. Pistoclerus succeeded, but fell under the spell of her twin sister, who used the same name, Bacchis. Mnesilochus, coming home, and hearing of this, is not unnaturally led to believe that the girl he loves has become the mistress of his friend. Before this he had intended to buy her release from a contract to a soldier, entered into before he had met her. His slave Chrysalus had made this possible for him by telling his father a false story explaining that they had been obliged to leave the money in Ephesus.

Plautus has changed the names of these three characters; in Menander Mnesilochus was Sostratos, Pistoclerus was Moschos, and Chrysalus was Syros. Sostratos, left alone after hearing of what he supposes to be his friend's disloyalty, reflects as follows:

> He's gone then . . .[1] She'll keep her hold on him. You made Sostratos your prey first.—She'll deny it, no doubt about that; she's brazen enough; every god in heaven will be brought into it. A curse on that wicked woman! (*Makes for the door of the house in which she is.*) Back, Sostratos! She may talk you over. I've been her slave (?) . . . but let her use her persuasion on me when my pockets are empty and I've got nothing. I'll give my father all the money. She'll stop making herself attractive when she finds herself telling her tale to a dead man, as the proverb has it. I must go to him at once.

At this moment the father returns from the market and Sostratos tells him that there was no truth in the story spun

[1] A few words are lost, indicated here by dots. Perhaps 'you'll keep your hold'.

by Syrus: 'forget it, and come with me to get the money.' The pair go off into the town, where it must have been left, and the act ends.

How did Plautus deal with this?

> Whether I should now believe my friend and companion or Bacchis to be my greater enemy, is a big problem. Did she prefer him? Let her have him! Excellent! I'll say she's done herself no good by that. Let no one ever take me for a prophet if I don't absolutely and completely—love her! I'll see to it that she can't say she got hold of a man she could laugh at; I'll go home—and steal something from my father to give her! I'll be revenged on her one way or another and make a beggar of—my father! But am I really in my right mind when I talk like this about what is still in the future? I love her, I think, if there's anything I can be sure of, but I'd rather outbeggar any beggar than let her get a featherweight of gold from my money. My God, she shan't have the laugh of me! I've decided to hand over all the gold to my father. So then she'll coax me when my pockets are empty and I've no resources, when it will mean as little to me as if she were telling tales to a dead man at his grave. It's quite decided that I give the gold back to my father.

Adding that he will prevail on his father not to be angry with Chrysalus, he goes in. Menander's scene between father and son has disappeared. Plautus had to make some cuts to compensate for his expansions, and this he thought he could dispense with. He must have observed that Nicobulus, as the father is called in his play, had earlier gone to the forum and had not yet come back, but perhaps he hoped that the spectators would not notice.

Menander allowed it to be understood from Sostratos' words that he still felt the girl's attraction—'she may talk you over'. Plautus makes it explicit in a sentence striking for its unexpected termination: 'if I don't absolutely and completely——' the context suggests 'ruin her', but surprisingly the conclusion is 'love her'. Pleased with this device, he repeats it twice, to produce jests that do not suit Mnesilochus' character but

drive home the point that he is still prepared to put the girl before his father. His infatuation is then confirmed, for the slowest hearer, 'I love her'. That is an avowal that Sostratos did not make; anger was uppermost in his mind. After declaring his love Mnesilochus expresses a determination not to let Bacchis get her hands on any of his money; this resolve is inadequately explained.

Plautus also modifies the purpose of the young man's action over the money. Sostratos thought of the effect on the girl: she would have no use for a poor man. Mnesilochus, whose whole speech is self-centred, thinks of himself; if he has nothing, he will be unable to respond to her wiles. Almost all that Sostratos said was concerned with how *she* would behave. The same preoccupation with her and her thoughts coloured a second soliloquy, which he delivered in the next act. He came back with his father, who left once again; then he broke out:

> Yes, I believe I should enjoy seeing this perfect lady, this love of mine now that my pockets are empty, making herself attractive and expecting—'rightaway' she says to herself—all the money I'm bringing her. 'O, yes, he's bringing it all right, generously by heaven—could anyone be more generous?—and don't I deserve it?' She has turned out well enough to be exactly what I once thought her—one can be thankful for that—and I pity that fool Moschos. In one way I'm angry, but on the other hand I don't reckon he's responsible for the wrong I've been done, but that woman, who's the most brazenfaced of the lot of them.

With that Moschos came impatiently out of the house where the two sisters were.

> *Moschos.* Then if he's heard I'm here, where on earth is he?—Oh, welcome, Sostratos.
> *Sostratos.* (*sulkily*) Welcome.
> *Moschos.* Why so downcast and gloomy? And the hint of a tear in your look? You've not found some unexpected trouble here?

Sostratos. Yes.

Moschos. Then aren't you going to tell me?

Sostratos. It's in the house, Moschos, you know.

Moschos. What do you mean?

Sostratos. [*A sentence is lost.*] That's the first wrong you've done me.

Moschos. I? Wronged you? Heaven forbid, Sostratos.

Sostratos. I didn't expect it, either.

Moschos. What are you talking about?

Here the papyrus ends, but it seems probable that the mis-understanding was rapidly cleared up.

Plautus, who had no chorus to cover a lapse of time, could not plausibly make Mnesilochus return instantly after going off to give his father the gold and to explain away the slave's story. Instead he advanced the entry of Pistoclerus. No sooner has Mnesilochus gone in than his friend comes out from the other house, into which he directs his opening words:

> Your instructions, Bacchis, shall take first place ahead of all else; I'm to look out for Mnesilochus and bring him back here to you in my company. Indeed, if my message has reached him, it's a puzzle what can be delaying him. I'll go and call here, in case he's at home.

Moschos did not babble like this nor did he need instructions from Bacchis; his single entrance line expresses his own eager-ness to meet his long-absent old friend. Pistoclerus' laboured explanations provide, even if it be inadequately, for a passage of time during which Mnesilochus may be supposed to have dealt with his father. So he can now emerge, and Plautus continues, summarising events since the end of Menander's act.

> *Mnesilochus.* I've returned my father all the gold. I'd like her to meet me now, now that my pockets are empty, she who despises me. But how reluctantly my father pardoned Chrysalus when I asked! But I did finally prevail on him not to harbour any anger.
>
> *Pistoclerus.* Is this my friend?
>
> *Mnesilochus.* Is this my enemy I see?

Pistoclerus. It is, to be sure.

Mnesilochus. It is he. I will go up and meet him face to face.

Pistoclerus. Welcome to you, Mnesilochus.

Mnesilochus. And to you.

Pistoclerus. Let us have a dinner to celebrate your safe return from foreign parts.

Mnesilochus. I've no liking for a dinner that will make me sick!

Pistoclerus. You don't say that you have been faced with something to upset you on your return?

Mnesilochus. Yes, and a very violent upset.

Pistoclerus. What caused it?

Mnesilochus. A man I previously thought my friend.

Pistoclerus. There are many men alive today who act in that manner and that fashion. When you count them as friends, they are found to be false in their falsity, busy with their tongues, but sluggish in service and light in loyalty. There is not a soul whose success they do not envy; but their inactivity makes it sure enough that no one envies them.

Mnesilochus. I'll swear that you've studied their ways well and have a good grip on them. But there is one thing more: their bad character brings them bad luck; they have no friends and make enemies all round. And in their folly they reckon they are cheating others, when they are really cheating themselves. That is how it is with the man I thought as good a friend to me as I am to myself. He took all the pains in his power to do me any harm he could and to get everything that belonged to me into his own hands.[1]

Pistoclerus. He must be a wicked man.

Mnesilochus. I think so.

---

[1] This speech and the previous one were omitted in some manuscripts of late antiquity and it is disputed whether they are by Plautus—if so, they may have been a second thought on his part, since their removal leaves no gap—or whether they were inserted by someone else for a revival of the play. Whatever the truth of this may be, the moralising lines were expected to win the approval of a second-century audience.

Pistoclerus. Speak out, I beg you, tell me who he is.

Mnesilochus. One who wishes you well. Otherwise I would pray you to do him any harm you could.

Pistoclerus. Just say who the man is. If I don't hurt him somehow, call me the worst of slackers.

Mnesilochus. The man's a rogue, but he's a friend of yours.

Pistoclerus. The more reason for telling me who he is. I don't care much for the friendship of a rogue.

Mnesilochus. I see that I can't do anything but tell you his name. Pistoclerus, you have utterly ruined me, your friend.

Menander made Moschos see at once that something was wrong, just as an intimate friend would, and Sostratos was quickly brought to explain his resentment. For Plautus this was missing an opportunity; he could use a motif that he may well have met in some other play. If Mnesilochus were to denounce the man he supposed to have injured him, but without giving his name, Pistoclerus with nothing on his conscience could be made to speak unwittingly in his own condemnation, and Mnesilochus could be made to lead him on. (More accurately, Pistoclerus condemns not himself, but the man whom his friend supposes him to be.) Plautus' scene is somewhat contrived, but it might be effective on the stage, as the audience enjoyed Pistoclerus' repeated failures to understand. One should not condemn it for not being Menander's; its explicit vigour will have made it more attractive to the Roman audience than his would have been. But it must be realised that Menander conceived the young men quite differently. His Moschos is sensitive and direct, immediately perceives the other's distress, and would not meet it with four pompous lines of generalisation about false friends; Sostratos, although not unresentful, does not see an enemy in Moschos, but puts the blame on the girl, not on his old companion. Plautus worked with stock motifs, Menander with lifelike figures of his own invention.

Now that it is possible to compare a passage of Menander with Plautus' version, there is proof that in his later works at least the Latin dramatist dealt very freely with his original. It was not just a matter of inserting extraneous jokes into a

more or less faithfully translated text. Scholars had realised that there must have been changes when a *canticum* (see p. 120) replaced a spoken scene, but not that a scene could remain spoken yet be given a new form. We now know that he could refashion both monologue and dialogue which were essential to the progress of the plot, making the new version do all that was necessary to carry the play forward, but substituting his own characterisation.

The result of this new evidence must be to show that greater difficulty than some have imagined must attend any effort to work back from Plautus to the Greek play he adapted. On the other hand since the failure to account for the movements of the father is proved to be due to him and not to Menander, there is support for those who think such imperfections reliable clues to Plautine workmanship. But although he is here convicted of carelessness, there is new proof of his independence; it seems he is to be credited with responsibility for a greater part of his plays than some scholars have supposed.

Terence

PUBLIUS Terentius Afer was believed by later Romans to have been born at Carthage, brought to Rome as a slave, and given a liberal education by his owner, Terentius Lucanus, who soon set him free. They may have had good reason for this belief, or the story may have grown from his name. Afer means a member of the dark native races of North Africa; an African would be a slave, and a manumitted slave took the middle name of his master. But the name Afer does not of necessity indicate a place of origin or a servile birth; it is attested as a Roman family name. If Terence did come from Africa, the excellence of his Latin is noteworthy but not unparalleled; Livius Andronicus, the father of Latin literature, was a Greek; Caecilius, the leading writer of comedy when Terence was young, is said to have been a slave from Gaul. Men who have won literary fame in languages not their own are not common in the modern world, but some can be named.

In his own lifetime Terence was charged with having received help in his dramatic work from friends who belonged to the best families. In the prologue to his last play, *Adelphoe* (*Brothers*), he wrote:

> Those ill-wishers say that men of famous families help him and constantly write along with him. They think this a violent aspersion, but he regards it as the height of praise if he is approved by men who have your unanimous approval, and that of the people too, men whose services everyone has on occasion used in war, in peace, in business.

This is typically elusive and evasive. Terence neither admits the charge nor denies it. If he had confessed it to be true, as it may well have been, it might have been thought that he had but a small share in the dramas which went under his name, that he was a mere front for some nobles; if it were false and

he had declared it so, the great men involved might not have welcomed their loss of literary glory, however undeserved.

Later it became widely believed that these men included the younger Scipio and Gaius Laelius, and ignorance of the fact that he was not their junior allowed the scandalous suggestion that their motive was pederasty. This charge may be dismissed, but a literary association need not attract the same disbelief. Terence's plays were produced in the years 166 to 160, when Scipio was about eighteen to twenty-four years of age. It is by no means unlikely that the young aristocrat, interested in Greek culture, should have dabbled in playwriting, although he would not have wished to be thought a professional dramatist, or that Terence, for anything we know not very much older, should have accepted his collaboration and patronage.

It must be emphasised, however, that very probably ancient guess-work invented the connection with Scipio and his friends; no reliable evidence seems to have survived, since one Santra, probably a contemporary of Cicero's, suggested a trio of older personages, arguing that if Terence had needed help, he would not have gone to men younger than himself. Nevertheless the accepted guess may have been sound, it may have been supported by oral tradition, and it may also be significant that *Adelphoe*, the prologue to which mentions these alleged collaborators, was performed at the funeral games of L. Aemilius Paullus, and Scipio organised those.

In any case the support of powerful men, whoever they were, with literary interests, would make it easier to understand the nature of Terence's plays, which make few concessions to popular taste. When he began to write, less than thirty years had passed since the death of Plautus, and it would not seem that the majority of the audience had greatly changed. The first two performances of *Hecyra* (*The Mother-in-Law*) were failures, and the prologue to the third, spoken by the leading actor, Turpio, explains why:

> Once again I am bringing you *The Mother-in-Law*, a play I have never been allowed to act in silence; disaster has swamped it. Your appreciation, if it can be allied to our efforts, will put an end to that disaster. On the first

occasion when I began to act it, the great renown of some boxers (expectation of a tight-rope walker was thrown in), friends getting together, a clatter of conversation, women's penetrating voices, made me leave the theatre all too soon . . . I brought it on again: the first act was liked, and then there came a rumour that gladiators were on the programme; the people came flocking in, rioting and shouting, fighting for places: when that happened, I could not keep *my* place.

Yet, unlike Plautus, Terence made almost no attempt to put in something for everybody in his audience. His plays give the impression of being what spectators ought to like rather than what they would enjoy. Although there are more long lines spoken to the music of the pipe than in Menander, the songs in varied metres, which had diversified the plays of Plautus and seem still to have been used by Caecilius, are no longer present. There are no indecencies, no puns, no slanging-matches, no gloatings over corporal punishments. Instead there is concentrated action, moving steadily forward, and dialogue that is often rapid and generally needs unremitting attention if the thread is not to be lost. Terence's plays resemble those of Menander rather than those of Plautus. In fact four of his six are adaptations of Menandrean originals and the other two are taken from Apollodorus of Carystus, a less-gifted follower of the great Athenian.

Anyone who wished to argue that Terence was not over-taxing the capability of his public might appeal to the fact that Caecilius had already shown a similar preference for plays by Menander. But so far as we can see, he was not true to Menander's spirit. Aulus Gellius, a writer of miscellanies in the second century AD, compares three pairs of passages by the two authors and exclaims at Caecilius' lack of taste. In one the Latin author introduces the old joke that the husband of a rich wife wishes her dead, and makes him imagine her boasting to her contemporaries and relatives that she has in her old age forced her husband to give up his young mistress, a thing *they* could not have done when they were still in their first youth; in another he causes the husband's friend to crack a coarse jest about her bad breath, wishing to raise a laugh, so

Gellius says, more than to provide words suitable for the character. Gellius accuses him of descending to the level of the mime. Caecilius' changes were not merely a matter of adding familiar motifs that would appeal to the more simple-minded. In these passages, at least, he dealt freely with the Greek, with which he kept no more than a minimal necessary relation. He seems to have felt no commitment to maintain a colloquial style: other fragments show that he often made great use of alliteration, a device which must have had a popular appeal, much as early drama in England used rhyme, still found in parts of our pantomimes.

Terence on the other hand attempted to transfer Menander to the Roman stage without changes and additions obviously inconsistent with the qualities of the Greek. In his prologues he speaks of 'literary art' and tells the spectators that they have a chance of 'bringing distinction to the dramatic festival'. But his admiration for Menander did not make him rest content with mere translation. Virgil was to be credited with the epigram that it was easier to steal his club from Hercules than a line from Homer; but it was his ambition not only to borrow from Homer but to improve on him wherever he could. Similarly Terence may have been aware that he could not hope to reproduce all Menander's merits, but he could try in some ways to better him.

The most obvious of his changes, and one which must have immediately struck anyone who knew the original plays, was to abandon the convention of the expository prologue. He retained a prologue, but used it for quite different purposes. Spoken by an actor, perhaps always by the principal actor, in his own person, not that of the character he was to represent, it gives the name of the play, as had been done in some of the Plautine prologues; twice Menander is mentioned as the original author, but once it is said that there is no need to name either the dramatist or the man he is translating, since the majority of the audience will already know. Presumably the minority, if it was a minority, did not care. But the greater part of the prologue is given over to a defence of Terence's use of his originals and to counter-attacks on a critic, an older writer of comedies; he is not named, but can be identified as one Luscius from Lanuvium.

An earlier move towards making the prologue a place for literary criticism has been seen in a fragment from some Greek author in which the god Dionysus complains of long-winded deities who set out all the facts, which the spectators fail to take in. He then proceeds to what promises to be a detailed exposition of the background to his play; the contrast between his theory and his practice is amusing. But it was Terence who took the decisive step of separating the prologue from the play and expressing in it seriously meant views on dramatic methods. This was to have long-lasting effects in the European theatre. One may compare the prologues to Ben Jonson's *Volpone* or *Every Man in His Humour*. Even when there is nothing more than mere *captatio benevolentiae*, as in Dekker's *Shoemaker's Holiday*, or witty trifling, as in Goldsmith's *She Stoops to Conquer*, a line of descent goes back to Terence, who established this form of independent introduction.

In the prologue to *Andria* (*A Woman from Andros*), which is based on Menander's play of the same title, he says that he had been attacked by his older rival for transferring to it matter from Menander's *Perinthia* (*A Woman from Perinthos*); his critics maintain that plays should not be 'spoiled' or 'adulterated'. He replies that he has the precedent of Naevius, Plautus and Ennius, whose 'negligence' he prefers to rival rather than the 'obscure carefulness' of the critics. It seems that he charges them with practising a fidelity to their models of which the public, who were not students of Greek drama, could not be aware, while they accuse him of spoiling plays by introducing foreign matter. He defends himself by declaring that his predecessors had also adulterated their plays.

A play may be 'adulterated' in various ways; he had done it in a particular manner, that of blending parts of two different comedies to make a new one.[1] So far as *Andria* is concerned, the fourth-century scholar Donatus was unable to identify much borrowing from *Perinthia*, but in two other plays also, *Eunuchus* and *Adelphoe*, Terence adopted this procedure of blending two originals, as their prologues explain. Its effects are clearly visible in both but they are easier to understand in the latter. In

---

[1] Some modern scholars use the word for adulteration, *con-taminatio*, in this restricted sense, as a technical term.

Menander's play the young hero had before it opened abducted a girl from a slave-trader on behalf of his brother, who loved her. Terence found in a play by Diphilus a lively scene of just such an abduction, which Plautus in his adaptation had for some reason omitted. He decided to enliven his play by using this scene, translated (so he unconvincingly alleges) word for word, to represent by stage-action what was only narrated in Menander.

This involved him in various difficulties. First, Diphilus' scene was enacted outside the slave-trader's house at the moment of the theft; his efforts to prevent it very naturally led to violence. In the play of Menander, and therefore in that of Terence, the slaver's lodging was not represented on the stage, so the scene had to be transferred to the street outside the house of the young man, whose raiding party he had followed. This necessitated some alterations of wording, but even so the exchanges remain more suitable to the earlier occasion. Secondly, Terence was obliged to introduce this scene after the opening monologue, which leads into a duologue where the young men's father indignantly reports that the theft has become the talk of the town. Clearly he cannot have learned this before the son had had time to bring the girl home; there is an absurdity in the time-sequence, which had to be ignored.

Thirdly, by causing the slaver to follow on the heels of the raiding party, Terence brings him to the young man's house before he is needed there by the plot of Menander's play, and he has to stand about, awkwardly forgotten, during scenes of explanation between the two brothers. There is perhaps a fourth point. The scene taken from Diphilus ends with an assertion by the young man that the girl is really a free woman and no slave. Nothing more is heard of this, and it is not clear whether Terence, unwilling to abandon a fine climax, left a loose end, or whether he believed it would be understood that the claim was a false one and no more than a move to embarrass her owner.

This will serve to illustrate the difficulties which may beset the transference of a scene from one play to another. Nevertheless at one time many scholars believed that it had been extensively practised by Plautus. He was even supposed to

have fused whole plays together, to make one Latin play out of two Greek. Today some hold that he cannot be proved ever to have resorted to either device. Certainly he 'adulterated' his originals by adding matter of his own invention; this kind of adulteration was not that for which Terence was reprehended, and Terence may be suspected of disingenuously sheltering behind him. Yet one need not deny that Plautus may well have found inspiration for some of his supplements in plays other than the one he was at the moment adapting, even if what he acquired was a suggestion rather than a model to be translated.

Terence's reasons for giving up the expository prologue are unknown, and no more can be done than speculate about them. Perhaps he found it unrealistic to make a character unashamedly explain the opening situation to the audience. But that is not altogether convincing, since in *Adelphoe*, his last play, much of the exposition is contained in a long opening monologue composed as an address to the audience, not as a piece of reflection; and he shows no objection to narrative monologues in the body of his plays. Perhaps he thought that more was to be gained by allowing the spectators to share the characters' surprise as facts were brought to light than by giving them a superior comprehensive view from the first. Either way of writing is defensible; each of the two forms of drama brings its own gains and losses. But it is to be noticed that the Terentian method of construction has predominated in the theatre ever since his day.

It is however one thing to write an original play in this manner, another to convert a drama written in the other way to the new fashion. In so far as an expository prologue contained information about the background necessary to make the characters' actions intelligible, this had to be conveyed, when the prologue was dropped, to the audience in some other way. On the whole Terence solved the problem not unskilfully; he succeeded in introducing explanations where they were needed.

Terence had a way with personal names that may be seen as significant of his relation to his models. Most are known from Greek New Comedy, and almost all are suitable for use over and over again. In fact Terence duplicated

even more than Menander had done; in his six plays there are three old men called Chremes, three hetairai called Bacchis, three married women called Sostrata. Yet he seems regularly to have replaced the name in the Greek original by a new one. Thus he at once declared his adherence to Greek dramatic methods and his own originality in handling his models.

A complete picture of the changes he made is impossible because so little detail is known of the Greek plays he adapted. A very little is given by Donatus and something can be deduced from study of his plays' structure and knowledge of Menander's methods of writing. But there are several cases where his object can be divined; it was to enrich the original material by additions that were Greek in spirit, sometimes taken from a Greek play, but likely to have a popular appeal. It has been seen how the *Adelphoe* gained a scene of lively action and some rough-and-tumble; let us consider the other two Menandrean dramas to which additions are certain.

Andria has a young man, Pamphilus, who is in love with a poor unprotected girl, Glycerium, but whom his father wishes to marry a neighbour's daughter, Philumena. He consents to this match, believing there to be an obstacle which will prevent it. Terence added a motif, perhaps of his own invention, perhaps taken from some other play, in the shape of a youth who is Pamphilus' friend and who loves Philumena. His jealousy is an easily understood emotion and the extra complication for Pamphilus provides the spectators with a further source of interest. This is a more likely way to explain the addition than Donatus' suggestion that it was done to avoid disappointment for Philumena (who never appears on the stage) when Glycerium turns out to be another daughter of the neighbour and so an eligible bride for Pamphilus.

The most pervasive additions are those made to *Eunuchus*, where there have been introduced the figures of Thraso and Gnatho, a soldier and his parasite, taken on Terence's own admission from *Kolax*, another play by Menander, which had a totally different plot. Thraso is made the rival of a rich young man, Phaedria, for a courtesan, Thais, and replaces some other rival, perhaps a less colourful soldier, perhaps a merchant, in Menander's *Eunuchos*. But Gnatho

makes an additional character, except inasmuch as at his first entrance he replaces a slave who brought the 'heroine' to Thais' house as a gift from the rival. His entrance monologue, describing his technique of flattery, is very amusing, but the entertainment is bought at the expense of letting his charge stand about in the street with nothing to do while he delivers it.

A second amusing scene is provided by the sixty lines with which Thraso makes his first entrance. More than half of this has no connection with the plot of *Eunuchus*, but exemplifies his tasteless boasting, to which he is egged on by the malicious Gnatho, whose irony he is too stupid to understand. This is certainly based on material taken from *Kolax*, although it cannot be determined how closely that play was followed. Although the latter part of the scene continues the same manner and characterisation, it is essential to the plot: Thraso boorishly invites Thais to dinner and Gnatho suggests to him a method of making her jealous which the audience will know to be certain to cause her great embarrassment; Gnatho is clever enough to guess that it will be very unwelcome to her. This must be Terence's composition, even if he was able to find some material for it in Menander's plays.

In the following passage Phaedria's slave brings Thais his master's gift of a slave-girl and a eunuch. Unknown to Phaedria, his younger brother has substituted himself disguised for the eunuch. Terence has made changes here, necessitated by the removal of the rival of Menander's *Eunuchos*, whose place is taken by Thraso and Gnatho. Their extent is not to be determined, but one exchange is undoubtedly based on *Kolax*: Gnatho suddenly bursts out laughing, and when asked why, replies that he had just thought of the soldier's quip at the expense of a man from Rhodes; this had been mentioned in the earlier part of the previous scene, and was an adaptation of a joke preserved in a fragment of that play.

Thraso and Gnatho next appear in the 'siege-scene', where an abortive move is made to storm Thais' house in order to recover the soldier's gift to her. This again is not only amusing, as the parasite's malice and the soldier's cowardice interact, but also has lively action on the stage, as the 'troops', who consist of four slaves, are disposed. Some of the material may

be taken from *Kolax*; that is no more than a guess, but it is certain that this scene is a lively replacement of some less noisy attempt at recovery in Menander's *Eunuchos*.

The two characters from *Kolax* are seen again at the end of the play. Gnatho arranges a pact between Phaedria and the soldier that they should share Thais' favours; it will be an effect of this that it will be the soldier who pays. Phaedria agrees moreover that Gnatho should transfer to his patronage. Although the matter is disputed, I have no doubt that those are right who see here a Terentian ending. In the earlier part of the play Phaedria has been portrayed as intensely jealous of Thraso, and Thais has promised to abandon the soldier so soon as she has secured the 'heroine', whom she hopes to restore to her parents. The pact is brutally inconsistent with this relation between them; moreover it utterly disregards the position of Thais. She is an independent and good-hearted courtesan, sincerely concerned to reunite the girl with her family, although not without self-interest, since she hopes that in their gratitude they will take her under their protection; this protection she has now attained. It is absurd that she should be disposed of behind her back, as if she were a slave, and condemned to the embraces of the ridiculous soldier, in order that Phaedria should enjoy her for nothing. It is a minor absurdity that he should saddle himself with the support of the dangerous Gnatho.

Very possibly this ending was taken from *Kolax*, where Thraso's rival in love was, unlike Phaedria, an impecunious young man, and the object of their attentions a slave, whose inclinations it may not have been necessary to consult. Terence's belief that the conclusion he gave to his *Eunuchus* would be welcomed by the Roman audience, who would enjoy its ingenuity, the soldier's foolish acceptance of a bad bargain, and the young man's combination of success with economy, is based on a difference between Greek and Roman society. In Terence's time at least the *meretrix* had an opprobrious name, and was despised and tolerated as a necessary evil; the Greek hetaira must not be sentimentalised, but by her name she was 'a companion' and she was accepted as a useful member of the community. The best kind of hetaira, of which Thais is one, could be a woman of some wealth, an

independent mind and self-respect. This was something not understood at Rome.

Another play the end of which some think Terence adapted in an attempt to meet Roman taste is *Adelphoe*; I believe them to be right. The theme is that of a contrast between two methods of bringing up a son, the one permissive, the other restrictive. Neither proves to be entirely successful but Micio, the father who practises the former method, is, until the last act, presented in a favourable light as generous, realistic and humane; when he has occasion to give his son an understanding reproof, the young man accepts it and reflects that their relation is more like that of brothers or friends than that usual between father and son, and determines to do nothing that would be against his wishes. The other father, his brother, who is harsh and without joy in life, finds himself in ridiculous situations and is at a loss when faced with a moral problem over which Micio has no hesitation: although it is not the match he would have chosen, he never doubts that his son should marry the poor girl whom he loves and who has borne him a child.

In the last act this martinet declares in a monologue that he sees that indulgence is the way to win popularity and that he will adopt that course for the brief spell of life that is left him. He proceeds in some amusing scenes to practise a new-found affability and generosity, not at his own expense but at that of his brother, whom he provides with a widow as a wife. In Terence's play the permissive parent feebly resists, but is so accustomed to letting people have their way that he has to accept this bride. Donatus remarks that in Menander he raised no objection to the marriage, and if he did not resist this, the heaviest of all the demands made on him, it is unlikely that he made any difficulties about any of the others, none of which are unreasonable. In Terence his ineffective objections are designed to show a lack of will.

Finally his brother says that the object of his apparent change of character was to show that the other's popularity did not depend on what was right and good and a true way of life, but on complaisance and indulgence. He offers himself as one with the knowledge to reprehend, correct, and where suitable support the young; thereupon the permissively

educated son declares that he will accept his guidance. Although Molière, Lessing and Goethe all felt that this ending was wrong, orthodoxy interprets it as supporting the view that the right form of education is a mean between the strict and the permissive. However much this may appeal to those who subscribe to that view, I do not believe that this was the play's intended message. The reason for the martinet's change of front must be given by the monologue; it was to win popularity. It is a dramatic necessity that the speaker of a monologue utters what he believes to be the truth. What he here says is quite inconsistent with putting on an act for a short time with the intention of exposing the weakness of his brother's way of life. It follows that Terence has altered the balance of the end of the play, to bring down the scales on the side of the man whose stern hard-working parsimonious austerity accorded more with Roman ideals than did his easy-going life-enjoying brother.

Other ways in which Terence enriched Menander were comparatively superficial. In *Eunuchus* the stage was made fuller by dividing a single part into two characters, Pythias and Dorias,[1] and in other plays a character is sometimes kept on after the point at which he must have left in the Greek. Breaking of the three-actor rule (see p. 78) together with the fact that he takes no substantial part in the second scene is the evidence for this change. Sometimes his continued presence allows him to overhear a monologue by someone else, a situation which Terence not infrequently contrives.

He also tried to reduce the number of non-speakers on the stage. Slaves, who in a Greek play would be given orders which they carried out in silence, are by him allowed a line or two. It is hard to say whether the motive was realism or simply a desire to make the scene more lively. He has been credited with realism, but on insufficient grounds. If, as Donatus seems to have believed but many modern scholars deny, he introduced Antipho into *Eunuchus* to provide a hearer for the young man's account of the rape he had perpetrated in his disguise as a eunuch, the reason was not a dislike on principle of monologues, which are of frequent occurrence. Perhaps he felt it to

---

[1] This is not universally accepted.

be unsuitable for the transgressor to confide directly to the audience what many of them must regard as a crime.

Nowhere can the words of Terence be compared with any extended passage of a Greek model; this prevents appreciation of the changes he made in the details of language. He seems to have broken speeches up, made the exchanges more rapid and multiplied interjections. What can be done is to observe how he differs from Plautus and even Caecilius.

Plautus exploited the natural genius of Latin for assonance, alliteration and full-blown, almost tautological, expression. Terence set to work with remarkable success to reproduce the merits of Menander's style, its simplicity, flexibility and concision, although Latin was an inadequate instrument for this purpose, having a limited vocabulary, if vulgar words were excluded, and a restricted ability to express nuances. Terence was praised by Julius Caesar as a 'lover of pure speech'. 'Pure speech' was that practised by the conventional educated upper classes, and may have been the nearest equivalent to Menander's standard in Greek. Terence used this kind of Latin with great skill, making next to no use of foreign words, and attaining speed by his brevity. Not only did he avoid repetitiousness, he often truncated sentences by leaving out a verb or a subject which could be understood, or could even reduce them to a single word.

The result is admirable and Caesar could compare him with Menander; but he called him a 'Menander halved', and regretted that he lacked 'power' or 'force' (*uis*), and spoke of his 'gentle' writings. What this means is perhaps that his writing is too equable, it lacks the ebb and flow which gives life to the Greek poet's writing and enables him to mirror every kind of emotion.

Epilogue

THE last recorded Roman revival of a play by Plautus, his *Pseudolus*, took place in the time of Cicero and, although it is dangerous to argue from silence, it is probable enough that in subsequent centuries he had more attention from grammarians than from actors. But Quintilian, writing about AD 90, mentions some comic actors as if their names were well known and implies that they appeared, wearing masks, in plays by Terence. It is possible that under the Empire Terence was more frequently revived than our very scanty sources reveal, although new comedies were by then written only occasionally and for the study rather than the stage. Some of his medieval manuscripts have illustrations of scenes performed by masked actors; these may be derived from an unknown artist of the fourth century, who may himself, however, never have seen a performance but have adapted earlier drawings. Donatus, if he can be believed, says that in his time (*c.* 350) female parts in Terence were played by actresses without masks.

But there can be no doubt that at Rome the predominant kind of play became that presented by actors of mime, which abandoned any claim to literary merit. Even in the days of Plautus and Terence a large part of the audience had simple unrefined tastes, which were not satisfied by their dramas. In the time of Augustus Horace alleges that the uneducated and stupid who form the majority will in the middle of a play demand a bear or boxers, for that is what the masses enjoy. Under the Empire their tastes seem to have been catered for. The performances of the mimic actors, who were never admitted to the guilds of the Artists of Dionysus, were despised by the cultivated writers who mention them, so that there is not much evidence. They seem to have been varied, ranging from turns and sketches to plays made of successive scenes, in which frequent elements were songs, dirty jokes, deceived husbands,

149

poisons, sleeping-draughts and trained animals, that certain recipe for theatrical success.

Yet if the mime was victorious on the stage, Terence was important in education. Boys were made to read him for his Latinity and his moral sentiments, while the impropriety of many actions done by his characters was conveniently overlooked. As Christianity spread, the less bigoted found themselves obliged to adopt the pagan system of education and to approve reading of the standard authors. We find Terence quoted by Saints Jerome and Augustine and other Fathers of the Church, although it may often be suspected that their knowledge of his lines came from anthologies rather than study of the plays.

The theatre itself, however, was widely condemned, both in the West and in the East. The denunciations show that what their authors had in mind was primarily the mime, but comedies were seen as tarred with the same brush. For Tertullian they were 'instigators of lust, licentious and prodigal; we should not accept when it is spoken what we abhor when it is done'. Presumably some Christians were caused to abstain from theatre-going, but many continued to attend. The disappearance of comedy from the stage was due to a lowering of educational standards rather than to the Church.

Terence continued to be copied and read during the Middle Ages. A dialogue composed perhaps in the seventh century and certainly not later than the ninth confronts him with a detractor, to whom he replies that he is loved by all. In the ninth century the nun Hrosvitha of Gandersheim was distressed that those who delighted in the sweetness of his language should be sullied by learning of wickedness; she offered a substitute in plays of her own composition, written in clear and vigorous prose, which celebrated 'the praiseworthy chastity of holy virgins' instead of 'the disgraceful lewdness of lascivious women'.

At the revival of learning Terence was printed, acted and translated. There were at least 446 complete editions between 1470 and 1600, mainly in Italy and France. Acting seems to have occurred principally in schools, where he was used in the teaching of Latin, even at first in Jesuit schools, although he was soon banned there. Performances took place in Italy as

early as 1476; Luther did not object to the practice in Germany, and in England the boys of St Paul's School recited *Phormio* before Cardinal Wolsey in 1528 and those of Westminster School acted plays of Terence before Queen Elizabeth in 1569. The performance of Terence in Latin became, and still is, a regular event at Westminster. The first complete translation into English was by a Puritan clergyman, R. Bernard (1598); Macchiavelli translated *Andria* into Italian and Ariosto *Andria, Eunuchus* and *Phormio*.

Plautus also became known, but a little later than Terence and less widely. Particularly in France he was unappreciated. Montaigne, who loved Terence, found him vulgar. He better suited the more robust taste of the English. Francis Meres declared in 1598 that Plautus was accounted 'the best for Comedy among the Latines' (*Palladis Tamia: Wits Treasury*, p. xv).

Far more important than revivals and translations were the new vernacular comedies which Plautus and Terence inspired. Although they at first made use of material from the Latin plays, their writers contributed much of their own invention. It is significant that whereas Plautus left his plays in their original Greek setting, they normally transferred them to their own country, and this new situation encouraged originality. Shakespeare, it is true, allowed his *Comedy of Errors*, based on Plautus' *Menaechmi*, to remain in a Greek city, but he enlarged the plot not only by material from the *Amphitruo*, which contributed the idea of indistinguishable servants of indistinguishable masters, but also in other ways, such as the development of the character of the wife Luciana and the introduction of the merchant Balthasar, both with non-Greek names. Perhaps the most important change was to imbed the story of the twin Menaechmi in the framework of that of Aegeon, in peril of his life when the play opens, freed and restored to his wife when it ends. This strikes a note of seriousness which can be heard from time to time in the comic centre of this play also.

But forty years earlier *Ralph Roister Doister* (*c.* 1553), by Nicholas Udall, the Headmaster of Westminster School, already adjusts figures borrowed from *Miles Gloriosus* and *Eunuchus* to suit their new place in English society, although the parasite's name, Merrygreek, reveals his origins, and by adding

other native figures makes something that genuinely reflects English life.

Although the vernacular writers had a fertile inventiveness which quickly carried them away from their classical ancestors, they learnt from them at least three lessons, without which modern drama would not have come into being. The first was to write in prose. Because the prosody of Plautus and Terence was not the familiar prosody of later poetry, but a better reflection of the phonetic facts of Latin speech, it was not recognised in the sixteenth century that they had written in verse. Freed by this misapprehension from the restraints of metre and of rhyme, the writer of comedy could develop a style which the flexible rhythms of prose made possible.

The second lesson was to treat the characters as individual human beings and not as the allegorical figures or exponents of abstract themes which they had been in medieval plays. The third lesson, as important as the second, was how to construct a plot, how to make scenes not merely succeed one another but grow one from another, and how to impose form upon a play by act-divisions which correspond to stages in the development of the story. This is what the ancient writers of comedy had to teach those who were setting that form of drama on a new course.

Appendix

Some Problems Concerning Old Comedy

1. *Was there any scene-painting?*

Aristotle believed that Sophocles (died 406/5) introduced *skenographia* (literally 'painting of the *skene*') *Poetics* 1449 a 18. Although this could mean no more than the painting of a permanent background, perhaps architectural, on the façade of the stage-building, that seems an improbable explanation, since such an innovation would have brought an equal benefit to his competitors, or at least to those whose plays were set before a palace or temple; it might have been resented by those who had imagined a setting in an army camp or on a solitary shore. Hence many have supposed that movable screens, on which a suitable background was painted, were placed against the *skene*.

Even if this was done in tragedy, it does not follow that such painted scenery was used in Aristophanes' comedies, or that it would have had any value there. Whereas tragedy usually observed the 'unity of place', Old Comedy is not so bound, but its action shifts location without apology and with the inconsequence of a dream. So *The Acharnians* opens in the Pnyx, then is outside Dikaiopolis' house in the country, then outside that of Euripides in the city, then in a private market-place, then outside the houses of Dikaiopolis and Lamachus. There is no opportunity for changing scenery to suit the different places, and no need for scenery; in fact things are better left to the spectators' imagination. Similar considerations will apply to most of Aristophanes' plays. A painted background showing houses would be in place throughout his last two surviving dramas, *Women at the Assembly* and *Plutus*, but is in no way necessary.

2. *Was the wearing of the phallus and padding universal?*

First a distinction must be drawn between actors and the chorus. Neither the text of the plays nor the very slight evidence of art gives any reason for supposing that the chorusmen were padded or equipped with phalli. In a majority of Aristophanes' plays, including the early *Clouds*, *Wasps* and *Birds*, such appendages were quite unsuitable. It is true that the choruses of the satyr-plays which followed tragedies wore coloured loin-cloths supporting an

erect phallus and a horse's tail; but that was a distinct form of drama.

The evidence of statuettes from the first half of the fourth century shows that many comic actors then, and perhaps all who played male slaves, wore a phallus. Aristophanes' text proves it for the old man Philokleon in *Wasps* and for Euripides' kinsman in *Women at the Thesmophoria*. The latter when detected in his disguise as a woman and stripped tries in a hilarious scene to hide the evidence of masculinity by pushing it backwards and forwards between his legs. The same actor might play more than one part in a play. If he had at some point to represent a woman, the phallus would be concealed by her long dress. Some male characters may have worn a long tunic that provided cover. The effeminate Agathon in *Women at the Thesmophoria* certainly had none that could be seen, and the absence of a penis may have been made visible to the spectators as well as remarked on by the kinsman of Euripides.

It has been argued that in *Clouds* Aristophanes attempted to get rid of this feature. In the parabasis the chorus says that the play has not come 'having sewn on a piece of dangling leather, red at the end, and thick, to make the children laugh'. That may mean no phalli (and if so, the characters' tunics cannot have been abbreviated); but it may be no more than a disclaimer of exaggerated caricature; it may also mean that the actors wore them tied up, a fashion to be seen in some artistic representations.

There are scenes where characters are beaten, notably one in *Frogs*, where Dionysus and his slave Xanthias are stripped to stage nakedness, that is to tights and phalli, and whipped to establish which is the god, for he will not feel pain. Padding would allow this to be done more realistically. But the starving Megarian of *The Acharnians*, although he might have a distended belly, could not be appropriately padded elsewhere. The fourth-century statuettes show that then at least not all actors were padded and it is plausible to suppose that Aristophanes' plays too had thin men as well as fat.

3. *Had the stage-building three doors or one?*

No tragedy suggests the use of more than central double-doors, and comedy was played in the same theatre. But when it was reconstructed by Lycurgus between 338 and 330 B C, three doorways were certainly provided, of which normally two and sometimes three were required by plays of that time. It is a matter of dispute whether more than one was already used by Aristophanes.

It would be possible to produce all his plays with only one door. The audience would accept it as a convention that the single stage-door was successively the entrance to different houses. Yet perhaps

imagination would be strained in that scene of *The Acharnians* (1097–1110, 1118–25) where the same door would have to serve over and over again in successive lines for that of Dikaiopolis and that of Lamachus. There are other plays where, if only one door was available, the dramatist seems to create unnecessary difficulties, notably a scene in *Clouds*. Pheidippides refuses to become a pupil in Socrates' school and retires into his own house. Strepsiades declares that he must do what his son will not do and join the school himself. He immediately knocks upon the door of the 'thinking-shop'. Is that the same door through which Pheidippides had gone only seven lines previously? He had to be removed from the stage, but if there was only one door, why did he not go off to the side, as if going to the town? Probability seems to me to be in favour of three doors. The stage-building was constructed for use in comedy as well as tragedy and there was no reason why tragedy should employ the side-doors that were needed for comedy.[1]

4. *Were there women in the audience?*

Some women certainly attended tragedies in the early fourth century. Were they also to be seen at comedies in the late fifth? One passage strongly suggests that they were, Aristophanes *Peace* 962–7:

> *Trygaios.* And throw some barley to the spectators.
> *Servant.* There! Done!
> *Trygaios.* You've given it them already?
> *Servant.* Yes, by Hermes. Of all the spectators here there's not one who hasn't got a barley-grain.
> *Trygaios.* The *women* didn't get any.
> *Servant.* No, but the men will give them some tonight.

The clue to these exchanges is that the word for barley (*krithe*) was also slang for penis. To build on a joke is dangerous, but this one loses point unless there were some women among the audience.

The passage has been interpreted to show that the women sat at the back, where grain scattered by the actor would not reach them. That is a humourless conclusion. The servant who cries 'There! Done!' so rapidly will not have made more than a single empty-handed gesture; so far as that goes, the women may have sat with their menfolk. Nevertheless it may be true that they did sit at the back. In any case it is not likely that they were very numerous. The festival may have been an occasion for leaving their

[1] Cf. K. J. Dover, The Skene in Aristophanes, *Proceedings of the Cambridge Philological Society*, 1966, pp. 2–17.

houses, but probably few husbands would encourage their wives to come to comedies or be willing to pay for their tickets. Many women would have no interest in the political allusions or knowledge of the persons attacked. It is hard to say whether they would have been bored or shocked by the numerous indecencies or whether they would have enjoyed them more if they sat together and apart. Aristophanes obviously wrote for a male audience; nothing is addressed to women. But that does not mean that women were excluded from the theatre. Nor can their absence from performances of New Comedy safely be deduced from the fact that Menander ended three plays by calling on men and boys for their applause; women may have been too few to earn a mention, or decorum may have required them to refrain from noisy approval. Slaves provide a problem of similar uncertainty. Presumably a ticket would get them in; but there would be few of them.

5. *Were any masks portrait-masks?*

The question arises with regard to Lamachus and Euripides in *The Acharnians*, to Socrates in *Clouds*, to others elsewhere. When living persons were introduced as characters in comedy was an attempt made to reproduce or caricature their features? Aristophanes explicitly says that the Paphlagonian in his *Knights*, who stands for Cleon, does not wear a mask that is like him. He gives as a reason that the real face was so frightful that the mask-maker could not stand trying to imitate it. It would be unwise to use a joke of this kind as a basis for generalising about the use of portrait-masks.

Clearly if a mask represented some living man's face, it must have been by way of caricature. The mask-maker would exaggerate features that were in any way striking, Pericles' high skull or Socrates' snub nose. It is by such exaggerations that the modern cartoonist at once distorts his subjects and also makes them recognisable. The difficulty of making a mask that would be, not a portrait, but a symbol of a real man can be overstressed. On the other hand it must not be underestimated. Some men's faces are so ordinary that they do not lend themselves to caricature. Perhaps Cleon's was such a one.

Glossary

anapaest: two short syllables followed by a long; see *metre.*

antepirrhema: a section of the parabasis (q.v.) symmetrically corresponding to the epirrhema (q.v.).

antode: a section of the parabasis (q.v.) symmetrically corresponding to the ode (q.v.).

bacchiac: a short syllable followed by two long; see *metre.*

choregos: lit. 'chorus-leader', not its leader and spokesman on the stage (koryphaios), but the man responsible for its costumes and training.

cretic: two long syllables enclosing one short; see *metre.*

deme: one of the administrative groups into which the Athenians were divided, for the most part territorially based but with hereditary membership. 2. The local centre of the group; in the country 'village'.

dimeter: a verse consisting of two metrical units; see *metre.*

dithyramb: a choral song of religious origin, but developed as a display of musical talent.

epirrhema: a section of the parabasis (q.v.), consisting of sixteen or twenty trochaic tetrameters.

hetaira: courtesan, lit. 'female companion'. The term covers a wide variety of women, slave and free; all that they have in common is that their relations with their 'lovers' are expected to be temporary.

iambus: a short syllable followed by a long; see *metre.*

liturgy: a public service required of the richer citizens in turn; at Athens the most onerous were the equipment, maintenance, and command of a naval vessel for a year and the dressing and training of a chorus to compete at a public festival.

metre: ancient metres were based on a division of syllables into long (or heavy) and short (or light). In Greek and in classical Latin prosody the former comprise all which contain a long vowel or a diphthong or which end with a consonant that precedes another in the same or the following word. They are indicated by a horizontal line (—) and the short syllables, all others, are indicated by ∪.

Some metres, including most of those used in comedy, are named after the feet which characterise them: *iambic* ($\cup$ —), *trochaic* (— $\cup$), *cretic* (— $\cup$ —), *bacchiac* ($\cup$ — —), and *anapaestic* ($\cup \cup$ —). But the unit was not the foot, but what is called the *metron*. The iambic metron was $\underset{\smile}{}$ — $\cup$ —, where $\underset{\smile}{}$ indicates that either a long or a short syllable is allowable; three of these metra constitute the iambic *trimeter*, always the metre of comedy's opening scenes. Subject to various restrictions, two short syllables may be substituted for a long. The trochaic metron was — $\cup$ — $\underset{\smile}{}$, usually grouped in fours, the final syllable of the last being suppressed; these make the trochaic *tetrameter*, which I have often called 'long trochaics'.

The Roman dramatists took over these metres, but with modifications: a syllable ending with a consonant was not necessarily long, and *spondees* (— —) often replace iambic or trochaic feet. The reason for these changes is disputed, but much of their scansion can be plausibly explained by the fact that Latin words, like those of English but unlike those of classical Greek, had a stress accent, which affected the length or weight of unaccented syllables. The dramatists scanned by ear, not by Greek rules.

ode: a choral song which was a standard element in the parabasis (q.v.).

orchestra: dancing-floor, circular in the Greek theatre, semicircular in the Roman, where it was used for seating.

parabasis: a section of fifth-century comedies in which the action was suspended and the chorus addressed the audience.

parasite: one who earned his meals by making himself agreeable, whether as a flatterer or a butt or a tool, to his patron.

parodoi: passages leading into the orchestra or to the stage past the ends of the semicircular or horseshoe-shaped auditorium.

phlyakes: comic actors of southern Italy.

satyr: mythological attendant of Dionysus, represented on the stage by a man naked except for a loin-cloth to which were attached an erect phallus and a horse's tail.

senarius: 'six-footer', the Latin equivalent of the Greek trimeter.

skene: stage-building, lit. 'tent'. A tent will have served as background and dressing room for early players.

tetrameter: a verse consisting of four metrical units; see *metre*.

trimeter: a verse consisting of three metrical units; see *metre*.

trochee: a long syllable followed by a short; see *metre*.

Select Bibliography

So far as modern scholarship is concerned, this list is very selective and confined to books in the English language.

1. ARISTOPHANES

(a) Surviving plays

The Acharnians 425 BC

Knights 424 BC

Clouds 423 BC

Wasps 422 BC

Peace 421 BC

Birds 414 BC

Lysistrata 411 BC

Thesmophoriazusae 411 BC
(*Women at the Thesmophoria*)

Frogs 405 BC

Ecclesiazusae 392 BC
(*Women at the Assembly*)

Plutus (*Wealth*) 388 BC

(b) Texts and translations

Best complete text, not always satisfactory: V. Coulon in Budé series (Paris, 1928–30) with French translation by H. van Daele. Only complete English commentary: B. B. Rogers (Bell, London, 1902–15); his text and neat decorous verse translation used in Loeb series. Several plays edited with commentary in a Clarendon Press series: *Clouds* (1965) by K. J. Dover, *Ecclesiazuase* (1973) by R. G. Ussher, *Peace* (1964) by M. Platnauer, *Wasps* (1970) by D. MacDowell; others are expected. Other useful editions: *The Acharnians* by W. J. M. Starkie (London, Macmillan, 1909); *Birds* by W. W. Merry (Oxford University Press, edn. 3, 1896), *Frogs* by W. B. Stanford (London, Macmillan, 1963), *Knights* by R. A. Neil (Cambridge University Press, 1901).

Some modern versions are far removed from the original text: being conceived as adaptations suitable for our stage. Readable and more reliable in detail are two Penguin volumes in prose, *Wasps, Thesmophoriazusae,* and *Frogs* by D. Barrett (1964) and *The Acharnians, Clouds* and *Lysistrata* by A. H. Sommerstein (1973).

(c) General

K. J. Dover, *Aristophanic Comedy* (London, Batsford, 1972): up-to-date, individual, wide-ranging; has a useful short bibliography.

C. W. Dearden, *The Stage of Aristophanes* (London, Athlone Press, 1976).

G. Murray, *Aristophanes* (Oxford, Clarendon Press, 1933) has enthusiasm which compensates for some untenable views. The most recent treatment of Aristophanes' political views is in G. E. M. de Ste Croix, *The Origin of the Peloponnesian War* (London, Duckworth, 1972), appendix xxix, pp. 355–76, where references will be found to earlier work.

2. MENANDER

(a) Plays of which more than 100 lines survive in a fair state of preservation

Aspis (*The Shield*)	*Misumenos* (*Hated*)
Georgos (*The Farmer*)	*Perikeiromene* (*Shorn Tresses*)
Dis Exapaton (*A Double Deceit*)	*Samia* (*A Woman from Samos*)
Dyskolos (*The Curmudgeon*)	*Sikyonios* or *Sikyonioi*
Epitrepontes (*The Arbitrants*)	(*The Man* [or *The Men*] *from*
Kolax (*The Flatterer*)	*Sikyon*)

Only *Dyskolos*, apparently the earliest, can be dated (317 BC); *Epitrepontes* and *Misumenos* seem to be late.

(b) Texts and translations

Text: F. H. Sandbach in Oxford Classical Texts (1972). Commentary: A. W. Gomme and F. H. Sandbach, *Menander* (Oxford, Clarendon Press, 1973); E. W. Handley, *The Dyskolos of Menander* (London, Methuen, 1965).

Menander still awaits his translator. E. G. Turner, *The Samian Woman* (London, Athlone Press, 1972) is a good version of that play. The most accessible translation of *Dyskolos* is by P. H. Vellacott (London, OUP, 1960), reprinted in Penguin Classics (1973) along with remains of seven other plays which are often unreliably presented. More faithful versions of *Epitrepontes* and *Perikeiromene* are to be found in L. A. Post, *Menander, Three Plays* (London, Routledge, and New York, Dutton, 1929).

(c) General

T. B. L. Webster, *An Introduction to Menander* (Manchester University Press, 1974).

3. OTHER GREEK COMEDY

(a) Texts and translations

T. Kock, *Comicorum Atticorum Fragmenta* (Leipzig, Teubner, 3 vols, 1880–8).

SELECT BIBLIOGRAPHY

G. Kaibel, *Comicorum Graecorum Fragmenta*, vol. I.1 (all published, Berlin, Weidmann, 1899): dramatists of Southern Italy and Sicily.

C. Austin, *Comicorum Graecorum Fragmenta in Papyris Reperta* (Berlin and New York, de Gruyter, 1973) purposely omits most of Menander.

J. M. Edmonds, *The Fragments of Attic Comedy* (Leiden, Brill, 3 vols, 1957–61) has an English verse translation of a very unreliable text.

(b) General

T. B. L. Webster, *Studies in Later Greek Comedy* (Manchester University Press, edn. 2, 1970).

O. E. Legrand, translated by J. Loeb, *The New Greek Comedy* (London, Heinemann, and New York, Putnam's Sons, 1917). The original French volume is entitled *Daos* (Paris, 1910).

G. Norwood, *Greek Comedy* (London, Methuen, 1931), useful for information on early authors other than Aristophanes.

4. PLAUTUS

(a) Surviving plays

In the first century B C the Roman scholar Varro listed twenty-one plays universally agreed to be by Plautus, and they can be presumed identical with the twenty-one we have. The following list gives the titles by which they now go and the author and title of the Greek original if known. A title not translated is a proper name.

Asinaria (*The Donkeys*) Demophilus, *Onagos*
Aulularia (*The Little Jar*) ? Menander
Amphitruo
Bacchides (*The Bacchis Sisters*) Menander, *Dis Exapaton*
Captivi (*The Prisoners*)
Casina Diphilus, *Klerumenoi*
Cistellaria (*A Little Box*) Menander, *Synaristosai*
Curculio
Epidicus
Menaechmi (*The Menaechmus Twins*)
Mercator (*The Merchant*) Philemon, *Emporos*
Miles Gloriosus (*The Boastful Soldier*)
Mostellaria (*The Ghost*) ? Philemon, *Phasma*
Persa (*The Persian*)
Poenulus (*The Little Carthaginian*) ? Alexis, *Karchedonios*
Pseudolus
Rudens (*The Rope*) Diphilus

Stichus Menander, *Adelphoe A*

Trinummus (*Three Pieces of Silver*) Philemon, *Thesauros*

Truculentus

Vidularia (*The Travelling Bag*), much mutilated.

Asinaria, *Cistellaria*, *Mercator*, and *Miles Gloriosus* are probably earlier than *Stichus* (200 BC). There is some reason for dating the rest between 194 and 184: *Pseudolus* belongs to 191 and *Casina* is later than 186.

(b) Texts and translations

Text: W. M. Lindsay in Oxford Classical Texts (2 vols, 1904–5); F. Leo (Berlin, Weidmann, 2 vols, 1895–6).

Translations: P. Nixon in the Loeb series; E. F. Watling in Penguin classics; G. E. Duckworth, *The Complete Roman Drama* (New York, Random House, 1942).

(c) General

E. Segal, *Roman Laughter* (Harvard University Press, 1968). See also below, under 'The Roman Theatre'.

5. TERENCE

(a) Plays

Andria (*A Woman from Andros*) 166 BC Menander

Hecyra (*The Mother-in-law*) 165 and 160 BC Apollodorus

Heautontimorumenos 163 BC Menander
(*The Man Who Punished Himself*)

Eunuchus (*The Eunuch*) 161 BC Menander

Phormio 161 BC Apollodorus, *Epidikazomenos*

Adelphoe (*The Brothers*) 160 BC Menander

These dates are probable rather than certain.

(b) Texts and translations

Text: R. Kauer and W. M. Lindsay in Oxford Classical Texts (1926). With commentary, G. P. Shipp, *Andria* (Melbourne, OUP, edn. 2, 1960); R. H. Martin, *Phormio* (London, Methuen, 1959) and *Adelphoe* (Cambridge University Press, 1976). Translations: J. Sargeaunt in the Loeb series; P. Borie, C. Carrier, and D. Parker, *The Complete Comedies of Terence* (New Brunswick, Rutgers University Press, 1974).

(c) General

G. Norwood, *The Art of Terence* (Oxford, Blackwell, 1923), may stimulate dissent and thought.

SELECT BIBLIOGRAPHY

6. GENERAL

(a) Festivals, Theatres, and Performance

H. C. Baldry, *The Greek Tragic Theatre* (London, Chatto and Windus, 1971) gives an excellent short account of the theatre in fifth-century Athens. Fuller and more specialised books include the following:

P. D. Arnott, *Greek Scenic Conventions in the Fifth Century BC* (Oxford University Press, 1962).

M. Bieber, *The History of the Greek and Roman Theatre* (Princeton University Press, edn. 2, 1961), lavishly illustrated, dogmatic text, good bibliography.

A. W. Pickard-Cambridge, *The Theatre of Dionysus in Athens* (Oxford, Clarendon Press, 1946), standard work on the buildings. A. W. Pickard-Cambridge, *The Dramatic Festivals of Athens* (Oxford, Clarendon Press, edn. 2 revised by J. Gould and D. M. Lewis, 1968), an outstanding work with extensive bibliography, but often needs a knowledge of Greek.

G. M. Sifakis, *Parabasis and Animal Choruses* (London, Athlone Press, 1971).

A. D. Trendall and T. B. L. Webster, *Illustrations of Greek Drama* (London, Phaidon Press, 1971).

T. B. L. Webster, *Greek Theatre Production* (London, Methuen, edn. 2, 1970).

(b) Origins of Comedy

A. W. Pickard-Cambridge, *Dithyramb, Tragedy and Comedy* (Oxford, Clarendon Press, edn. 2 revised by T. B. L. Webster, 1962).

(c) The Roman Theatre

W. Beare, *The Roman Stage* (London, Methuen, edn. 3 revised, 1969), wide-ranging and mostly convincing, but not on the 'Law of Five Acts'. Short bibliography.

M. Bieber, see above.

G. E. Duckworth, *The Nature of Roman Comedy* (Princeton University Press, 1952) thorough and sensible, has an informative chapter about influence on later literature down to twentieth century. Extensive bibliography.

(d) New Comedy

W. G. Arnott, *Menander, Plautus, Terence* (Oxford, Clarendon Press, 1975), an up-to-date survey with much bibliographical material.

INDEX

Acharnae, 71
actors, 15, 108, 127; costume, 18, 25, 55, 60; delivery, 80, 110, 120; in mimes, 116, 149; number of, 78–80, 111, 146; status, 109 f.; *see also* Artists of Dionysus *and* masks
acts, 80, 87, 113
actresses, 112, 116, 149
aediles, 109
Aelius Aristidēs, 74
(L.) Aemilius Paullus, 136
(M.) Aemilius Scaurus, 108
Aeschylus, *Choephoroe*, 67
(L.) Afrānius, 116
Agathōn, 13, 39
Agōn, 43
agōnothetēs, 69
Alexander the Great, 10, 11, 55, 67
Alexandria, library, 9
Alexis, 67, 119, 161
Apulia, 103, 105
amateur performers, 13, 104–5
(L.) Ambivius Turpio, 110, 136
Ameipsias, 46
anapaests, 22, 25, 43, 120
Anaxandridēs, 71, 73
Angelio, Nicolà, 113
Antiphanēs, 70, 84
Antipater of Macedon, 68
Apollodorus of Carystus, 73, 80, 137, 162
archōn epōnymos, 12
Ariosto, 151

Aristophanes, 9, 13, 15, 26–40, 41, 42, 44, 45, 55, 58, 59, 60, 61, 69, 71, 79, 101, 122, 159; attitude to war, 33 ff.; political opinions, 29 ff.; *Acharnians*, 18, 26, 43, 52, 58; *Aiolosikōn*, 57; *Babylonians*, 26; *Birds*, 27, 43, 56; *Clouds*, 27, 41, 42, 43, 57; *Ecclesiazusae*, 56; *Frogs*, 15, 46, 48, 57, 60; *Knights*, 41, 42, 43, 58; *Kōkalos*, 57; *Lysistrata*, 36–7, 58; *Peace*, 27, 46, 58; *Plutus*, 56, 57, 60; *Thesmophoriazusae*, 27, 57; *Wasps*, 53
Aristotle, 59, 79; on origins of comedy, 51–3
Artists of Dionysus, 75, 119, 149
Asia Minor, 60, 107
Aspasia, 21, 50
Atellan plays, 104–5, 111, 116, 125
Athenaeus, 9, 10, 53, 60
audience, composition, 18, 31, 36, 109; intelligence, 33, 35, 109, 118, 126, 136–7, 149; reactions, 30, 47, 111, 116, 127
Augustine, Saint, 150
Augustus, emperor, 75, 110, 149
Aulus Gellius, 137–8

Barrie, *The Admirable Crichton*, 84
Beaumarchais, *Figaro*, 84
Bernard, R., 151
Boeotians, 23, 35
books, format, 74

INDEX